The Great Church Year

Karl Rahner

THE GREAT CHURCH YEAR

*The Best of Karl Rahner's
Homilies, Sermons, and Meditations*

*Edited by Albert Raffelt
Translation edited by Harvey D. Egan, S.J.*

CROSSROAD • NEW YORK

1993

The Crossroad Publishing Company
370 Lexington Avenue, New York, NY 10017

Originally published as *Das Große Kirchenjahr: Geistliche Texte,* 4th edition
© Verlag Herder Freiburg im Breisgau 1987

English translation copyright © by The Crossroad Publishing Company

Printed in the United States of America

Library of Congress Cataloging-in-Publication Data

Rahner, Karl, 1904–1984
   [Grosse Kirchenjahr. English]
   The great church year : the best of Karl Rahner's homilies,
sermons, and meditations / Karl Rahner ; edited by Albert Raffelt ;
translation edited by Harvey D. Egan.
     p.   cm.
   ISBN 0-8245-1228-6
   1. Church year sermons.   2. Catholic Church—Sermons.   3. Sermons,
English.   I. Raffelt, Albert.   II. Egan, Harvey D.   III. Title.
BX1756.R25G7613   1993
252'.6–dc20
                                             93-3930
                                            CIP

Contents

YEARLY FEASTS

FEASTS OF THE LORD AND OF THE SAINTS

APPENDIX

INDEX OF BIBLICAL PASSAGES

Translation Editor's Preface

Karl Rahner's name is almost synonymous with abstruse, speculative theology. But it is often overlooked that, to Rahner, theology has no other task than to investigate the question of how the Gospel can be *preached* in a way that awakens and deepens Christian faith, hope, and love. To be sure, Rahner was convinced that "the strictest theology, that most passionately devoted to reality alone and ever on the alert for new questions, the most scientific theology, is itself in the long run the most kerygmatic."[1] Nonetheless, he insisted that all theology must bear witness to the Gospel of Jesus Christ in a credible and intelligible way.

It must also be emphasized that Rahner was a Jesuit priest for fifty-two years who did not enter the Jesuits to become a scholar or professor. He wished only to "minister to people," and viewed "the mission of the Society of Jesus [as] missionary and missions, the preaching of the Gospel at home and in actual missionary lands."[2]

This may explain why Rahner despised purely "academic" theology and distanced himself from theology as "scholarship." "I am no 'scholar,'" he protested. "In this work of theology, I only want to be a man, a Christian, and, as much as possible, a priest of the church. Perhaps a theologian cannot desire anything else. In any case the science of theology, as such, was never important to me."[3]

Rahner preached almost daily for much of his priestly life and preached numerous Ignatian retreats. He saw the priest not primarily as a theologian but as one who must preach and celebrate God's efficacious word. The church ordains the priest to proclaim the Gospel

---

1. *Theological Investigations*, trans. Cornelius Ernst, O.P. (Baltimore: Helicon Press, 1961), I:7.
2. *Karl Rahner — I Remember: An Autobiographical Interview with Meinold Krauss*, trans. Harvey D. Egan (New York: Crossroad Publishing Company, 1985), 21.
3. "Selbsporträit," *Forscher und Gelehrte*, ed. W. Ernst Böhm (Stuttgart: Battenberg, 1966), 21.

in her name. To Rahner, theology exists only because there is preaching, and not vice versa. Theology must be reflection on preaching and serve God's good news in Christ as given to the church. In fact, theology ceases to be theology if it no longer preaches and proclaims God's own word of love.

To Rahner, good theology exists for good preaching. He also maintained that he did as much theology in his homilies as he did in his meaty *Theological Investigations.* In fact, he preached as often as he could during the time he wrote the *Investigations.* His hand can be found in the impressive *Handbuch der Verkündigung* (Handbook of Preaching). Thus, Rahner the *priest* and *preacher* is present even in his most difficult works.

I have been reading Karl Rahner for almost thirty years and teaching his thought for over fifteen. I consider this anthology to be an excellent nontechnical point of entry into the life's work of this theological titan. The following one hundred and twenty sermons, homilies, and meditations on the liturgical year underscore why Rahner stands in the long line of Christian theologians who were likewise great preachers. Some of the Rahnerian themes in this volume are: the mysticism of daily life, the Ignatian mysticism of joy in the world, the Easter faith that loves the world, the experience of grace as the heart of human existence, a Christian pessimism that faces human mortality realistically, a Christian optimism that focuses on Christ's resurrection, an appreciation of the saints as belonging to the church's history of holiness, and the like.

Twenty-two selections make their first English appearance in this anthology. With a view to an English-speaking audience, I slightly emended some of the texts. Corrections, but not major retranslations, of already existing English translations were made. Footnotes were substituted for the awkward "list of sources" section of the German text.

I wish to give special thanks to Father Robert J. Braunreuther, S.J., of Boston College for his years of generous help to me in untangling Rahner's German.

These sermons, homilies, and meditations illustrate Rahner's view that to be a "Christian today means to adore God, to love him, to entrust oneself to God's incomprehensibility. It means assurance of eternal life, the immediacy of the vision of God. Jesus Christ enables and legitimates this relationship to God. In view of his cross and resurrection, in view of the unsurpassable unity between God and the human person, we can trust that our life's task of entering into immediate relationship with God will be blessed by God's victorious grace. It is really obvious that because of Jesus Christ people can trust God and build a community of faith, the church, a faith community with an historical and social structure that binds the individual.... That Christians and the church must, by the power of the Holy Spirit, engage themselves in the work of justice, love, and peace in a world that is God's creation is also self-evident."[4]

Harvey D. Egan, S.J.
Boston College

---

4. *Karl Rahner in Dialogue: Conversations and Interviews, 1965–1982*, ed. Paul Imhof, Hubert Biallowons, and Harvey D. Egan (New York: Crossroad Publishing Company, 1986), 330.

Editor's Preface

In the wide-ranging work of Karl Rahner (1904–84) texts devoted to spirituality assume an important place. Besides filling volumes 3, 7, 8, and 16 of Rahner's *Theological Investigations,* they have been published in several independent publications, in a wide variety of periodicals, journals, as well as other places. The fact that not just the lovers of his writings on systematic theology esteem so highly these works of the great theologian shows that they should not be consigned to oblivion or relegated to being dissected by historians of theology, even after Karl Rahner's death. Instead they should be made available for prayerful reading.

In the case of texts devoted to prayers, this could still happen according to Karl Rahner's wishes and with his cooperation.[1] The present collection tries to do this for the great quantity of sermons, homilies, reflections, meditations, and so forth, related to the church year. It goes back as well to an impulse from Karl Rahner himself, though it could no longer be carried out with him.

Reflections on the church year pervade Karl Rahner's lifework. Some of his earliest occasional publications are among them ("The Angels," "The Feast of St. Augustine," "The Transfiguration of the Lord"). He brought out *Kleines Kirchenjahr*[2] in 1954. Finally, sermons regularly delivered at Innsbruck, published as *Biblische Predigten*[3] in 1965, fill out the broad core of this collection. Besides these, others of the latest texts, such as an Advent meditation, "The Advent of the World and Our Advent," which Karl Rahner led four months before his death, came from the Karl Rahner Archives.

How is it that these writings from almost four decades have kept their vitality — even though the great distance in both language and content between the earliest occasional texts and the important works from *The Eternal Year* and from the later years is undeniable?

---

1. See Karl Rahner, *Prayers for a Lifetime,* ed. Albert Raffelt (New York: Crossroad Publishing Company, 1984).

2. ET: *The Eternal Year,* trans. John Shea, S.S. (Baltimore: Helicon Press, 1964).

3. ET: *Biblical Homilies,* trans. Desmond Forristal and Richard Strachan (New York: Herder and Herder, 1966).

To begin with, we are dealing with reflections nourished from the plenitude of great theology, both from the Christian tradition and from the systematic power of Rahner's thought penetrating this tradition. The texts are not tied down to their liturgical "occasions" but are integrally related to the world's and our history of salvation and perdition in its entirety. The two introductory Advent meditations — from the 1950s and the 1980s! — already make this altogether clear.

Second, we are dealing not just with theological reflections relevant for intellectual dialectic, as important as these indeed are. More recent literature on Karl Rahner's work — in the wake of Karl Lehmann's studies, has strongly emphasized how his theology is based on and in turn reflects spiritual experience. In this sense the meditation "Thomas Aquinas: Patron of Theological Studies" can be read also autobiographically. For Rahner the texts on spirituality are no less theological than the great essays in systematics. Rather, they often show more clearly the soil in which his theology is rooted, which is precisely not academic and elitist — something Herbert Vorgrimler has stressed many times. Right down to the style, which does not shy away from being almost banal ("The waiters scurry about, and the wine is good" — in Cana), this is clear. In general these reflections may allay anxieties about the "difficult" Rahner.

Third, his intensive prayerful reflection on biblical texts is striking. It shows how at home Rahner was in the church's tradition of biblical reading and interpretation, even before contemporary historical-critical exegesis made biblical study central. One certainly finds this newer technical method in Rahner's others works. In this way, he helped pave the way for ecclesiastical approval of "scientific" biblical interpretation. In his more theoretically oriented works this background is often not so evident, something that has at times given rise to deprecatory remarks. This shows how important it is always to sort out carefully the genre, the linguistic style, and the material background when it comes to the reception and interpretation of Rahnerian theology.

Considered in terms of their context, these works emerge from a "theology of the people," to use an expression coined on demand in the wake of the political theology of J. B. Metz, especially in relation to the Latin American theology of liberation: they are identified with authentic Christianity's potentiality as inherent in the popular church life of Middle European churches. They are, however, all the more remarkable in relation to their sometimes narrow focus, and they always openly integrate into their thoughts the real shifts in the secular situation out of which they arose.

The concreteness of these reflections is manifest as well in being related to situations such as Ash Wednesday for the artists, or the feast of the patron of the university, and so forth, which cannot be reduced simply to "writing just for the feast day." A good example of this is the meditation for the Ascension ("...Why Do You Stand Looking into Heaven?"), with its catalogue of upsetting questions prepared for an important occasion for German Catholicism, the Würzburg Synod. So these texts also demonstrate the different levels of pervasive pastoral activity alongside Karl Rahner's more scholarly work.

With this collection the reader is enabled to make a prayerful journey through the church year in the company of a great theologian. The volume arranges each meditation in accord with the course of the church year and the most recent order of liturgical readings. This was not possible to do with only two texts: "One Tiny Light in Endless Darkness" — on the disciples' lack of understanding — and "God Cheerfully Puts Up with Us." But in this way don't they make a good conclusion for the section on the saints of the church?

The editor needs to thank, first, all Karl Rahner's collaborators, who took the trouble earlier on with these works, especially Herbert Vorgrimler, as the editor of the *Biblical Homilies;* Johannes Beckmann, with his collection of *Meditationen zum Kirchenjahr* (Meditations for the Church Year); Karl Lehmann, who for example assembled many early texts for paperback books that have since gone out of print. Special thanks are due to Walter Kern, S.J., and Roman Siebenrock, who have selflessly supported this work and enlarged it with unpublished texts from the Karl Rahner Archives in Innsbruck.

Albert Raffelt

ADVENT

1 • Advent*

Today, on this Sunday, we begin the season of Advent. The term "advent" connotes not only an arrival, but also that which is yet to come. The very word itself expresses a strange interpenetration of the present and the future, of what now exists and what is yet to come, of possession and expectation. So too, in the liturgy of Advent, the present and the future of Christian salvation are mysteriously interwoven. The incarnation of the Word of God took place in the past and still continues in the present. Christ's return to judge all men and women and to complete his redeeming work is an event of the future, and yet he is constantly on the point of coming. The expectation of this return and the memorial of his entrance into the world are both celebrated in the liturgy.

At one and the same time the Advent liturgy's remembrance unites all of these within itself. It unites the past, that is, the Old Testament longing for the coming of the salvation that was still hidden in God alone; the present, that is, the salvation that is now taking place in the world but which is still hidden in Christ; and the future, that is, the salvation that will be unveiled with the transformation of the world at the end of time. The church must make memorial of and reexperience all three mysterious stages of salvation history. The inwardness of the salvation-less past must remain, because otherwise we would not be aware of what we are when we are left to ourselves alone, and because we would otherwise forget that if we are to possess God's grace, it must come to us from him alone. The inwardness of the salvation that is already taking place and being accomplished must remain, because it is ours only if we have grasped it in faith as that which belongs to us in the present. The inwardness of the future must remain, because the present is present only if we have seized it as the earnest that promises definitive redemption.

Through the work of God in Christ, time has become what it was supposed to be. Time is no longer the bleak, empty, fading succession of moments, one moment destroying the preceding one and causing it to become "past," only to die away itself, clearing the way for the future that presses — itself already mortally wounded. Time itself is redeemed. It possesses a center that can preserve the present and

---

*_The Eternal Year_, trans. John Shea, S.S. (Baltimore: Helicon Press, 1964), 13–18.

3

gather into itself the future, a nucleus that fills the present with a future that is already really effected, a focal point that coordinates the living present with the eternal future. The advent of the incarnate God, of the Christ who is the same yesterday and today and in eternity (Heb 13:8), from whom neither the things of the present nor of the future can separate those who believe in him and who are united with him in love (Rom 8:38–39) — this advent has penetrated into this time that is to be redeemed.

From this vantage point we shall once again, during this Advent, grasp more deeply what Advent faith is, and thus make our hearts ready for it. Our conception of the Christian faith is often too one-sided. We conceive it only as a set list of determined facts that must be held as true. These facts stand by themselves on this list, and we just think about them. These facts, however, are fundamentally an event that still endures. We are situated right in the midst of this event, and we are, precisely through faith, drawn into it, so that we are caught up in it.

In the present time of faith, we do not merely take notice of an event, an eternal reality, that happened only once, some time ago. We do not only notice that "later" (in a future that now is entirely unreal) something shall once again happen in salvation history. The believer does not only have certain thoughts and opinions about something, thoughts which remain separate from the event thought about. Her "outlook on life" does not merely look upon something that remains external to her and that should be represented in her only by her thoughts about it. In faith the believer "thinks" not only her "thoughts." Faith is more than this: in and through us and our freedom, faith is God's grace working to assimilate the very reality of the event thought about.

By means of faith the salvation of the believer really takes place in the believer himself. Salvation itself comes out from the past into his present, into him, and it becomes present in his time. Christ lives in him. The believer becomes subject to the inner law of each event that is believed. In a mysterious way he becomes a contemporary of the incarnate Son of God. He dies and lives with him. The reason is that through faith Christ lives, in the Holy Spirit, in the believer. Furthermore, in all truth and all reality, this Spirit is gradually shaping the life of the believer into the image of the life and destiny of the incarnate Word of the Father.

Moreover, by this very fact, Christ is in a mysterious way already present in the believer as her future. This future has already come into the believer in a hidden way; she is already, in a hidden way, what she will be when all that is now hidden is unveiled. What will one day be our complete perfection has already begun. And this reality begins precisely because we believe. It is by faith that we are the people of God and children of eternal life, in whom the strength of eternity has already become an operative reality. This one event that is "now" taking place in the world began with the incarnation of God's Son (which was the real, not merely conceptual, reconciliation of God and the world).

This event will be completed with Christ's "second coming," which is not so much a second arrival as a bringing to perfect completion God's own life already established in the world by the Christ event. This event permeates the believer to the extent that she believes and loves. The believer already possesses his future because his future *is* Christ, and Christ is in the believer. The believer hopes for and awaits her future not as something yet to come which is still unreal, but rather, because she believes, as an event that is happening right now and is developing into her own perfect completion that is to be unveiled.

During this Advent season, let us be more earnest people of faith. Such a season, coming between autumn and winter, can invite us to a livelier awareness of faith, if there is at least a grain of faith already in us. As the autumn season fades and winter begins, the world becomes still. Everything around us turns pale and drab. It chills us. We are least inclined toward lively, hectic activities. More than in other seasons of the year, we prefer to stay home and be alone. It is as if the world had become subdued and had lost the courage to assert its self-satisfaction, the courage to be proud of its power and of its life. Its progressive growth in the swelling fullness of the spring and summer has failed, for the fullness has again vanished.

And the fact that the next spring will once again bring a new growth only more strikingly draws our attention to the endless coming and going of the seasons, in which nothing seems to be really permanent, if indeed the approaching winter has as much real significance for us as spring and summer. In this season, time itself bears eloquent witness to its own poverty. It disappoints us. It cannot maintain itself. What it seems to extract from the future and draw into its present is constantly slipping away from it into the past.

Here is the moment to conquer the melancholy of time, here is the moment to say softly and sincerely what we know by faith. This is the season for the word of faith to be spoken in faith: "I believe in the eternity of God who has entered into our time, my time. Beneath the wearisome coming and going of time, life that no longer knows death is already secretly growing. It is already there, it is already in me, precisely because I believe. For the cycle of birth and death to stand still in the true reality all I have to do is believe in the coming of God into our time, really believe. In the act of believing, I patiently bear with time, with its hard and bitter demand that brings death in its wake.

And I dwell no longer on the thought that time has the last word to say, which is a denial.

"Listen, my heart, God has already begun to celebrate in the world and in you his Advent. He has taken the world and its time to his heart, softly and gently, so softly that we can miss it. He has even planted his own incomprehensible life in this time (we call it his eternity and we mean thereby that which is nameless, which is wholly other from the time that makes us so hopelessly sad). And this is precisely what happens in you yourself, my heart. It is called the grace of faith, the grace of the gradual falling away of fear of time, of the fear that fades away because he who is more powerful than time (which he made to be redeemed into eternity) has done great things to it. A now of eternity is in you, a now that no longer has any denial before it or behind it. And this now has already begun to gather together your earthly moments into itself.

"No brighter joy could be expected by you, poor heart, in a season of Advent that lasts for a lifetime (since *your* advent will end only when you hear the words, 'enter into the joy of your Lord'). No brighter joy, for now you still feel too keenly the harsh press of the shackles of time, even though they have already begun to fall away from your hands and feet. The only thing that must live in you is a humble, calm joy of faithful expectancy which does not imagine that the tangible things of the present time are everything. Only humble joy, like the joy of a prisoner, who will stand up even while he is still imprisoned, because, lo and behold, the bolt has already been torn off the door of his dungeon, and so freedom is already guaranteed.

"Is this joy, this Advent joy so difficult? Is resignation and hidden despair really easier? Childish, stubborn defiance and willed malice: that is what despair and resignation amount to. You rightly recognize these, my heart, only when you run away from them, only when you do not dawdle and dispute with them. Only the heart that really does not want to enjoy them, but instinctively recoils and runs from them under the impulse of that eternal life that we call grace — only such a heart can recognize them. But perhaps you don't quite know whether you have chosen Advent joy or the despair of winter that leads to cold death? Just to ask such a question is a mistake, because we can never be neutral about this when we ask it. And to give the second answer would be death, the death that the human being cannot free himself from.

"Ask not, doubt not. You have, my heart, already chosen the joy of Advent. As a force against your own uncertainty, bravely tell yourself, 'It is the Advent of the great God.' Say this with faith and love, and then both the past of your life, which has become holy, and your life's eternal, boundless future will draw together in the now of this world. For then into the heart comes the one who is himself advent, the boundless future who is already in the process of coming, the Lord himself, who has already come into the time of the flesh to redeem it."

2 • The Advent of the World and Our Advent*

We would like to try a brief meditation on the Advent in which the world as a whole lives, and in which every single individual lives for himself or herself. In this kind of meditation, anything spoken in human words is but a sort of external spur toward or modest hint at what actually ought to take place in such a meditation: a turning away from the multiplicity and noise of everyday, a silent turning inward to oneself, a listening to what God may want to say softly in the human conscience, a courage for the kind of stillness in which even the manifold dimensions of our lives are capable of uttering their authentic truth. In such meditative prayer the inner word of grace and our inmost being, and the outer word of the gospel and the church are supposed to meet each other and unite. We are supposed to let the word of grace come to us and to let the word of the gospel be grasped not just by our ears and our minds, but also at that place within ourselves where we stand before God with our freedom and love.

We live in Advent. This means that during these days we live along with the part of the church year called Advent. But also and more precisely it means: *the world as a whole lives in a history* which, whether one knows and realizes it or not, moves toward a second coming, that is, toward God's definitive victory in history as judgment and eternal salvation. But Advent also means that every person and every Christian is and should be an Advent person — not just in this part of the church year, but also in his or her entire life. This means being a person who cooperatively enacts the one and final movement of the world and history toward God's arrival in it in freedom, in faith, hope, and love.

The liturgy of Advent also reminds us, to begin with, of an immense, long section of the history of human salvation and loss down to that great pause in salvation history that occurred in the Word of God's

---

*"An Advent Meditation," given in Nürnberg on 13 December 1983. Previously unpublished. From the Karl-Rahner-Arkiv, Innsbruck. Trans. Frederick G. Lawrence, Boston College.

becoming human in Jesus of Nazareth. In that segment of perhaps millions of years to this break, which was correctly perceived in the New Testament as being the end and goal of history, history was the history of open questions, of the creature's impatient waiting for an undisclosed future, of the experimentation of a thousandfold attempts in which humankind tried, even under a mysterious providence of grace, to say in all the many religions what humanity is up to, and toward what remote future it is moving. The drama of human history, looked at in itself, was open to victory and defeat, to eternal salvation and to everlasting doom.

It was not clear in this drama itself (prescinding from God's hidden, eternal plan finally revealed in scripture) whether it ultimately will end as the blessedly cheerful play of God's love, whose wisdom enjoys being with human beings, or as the distressing tragedy of a world, wishing to be God itself, and losing itself eternally in its own nothingness. Even in this Advent-like great period of humankind from the start of human history until Christ, God himself was mysteriously at work already in his uncreated grace as the innermost finality of the world. But this was hidden, and God had not yet definitively established himself in the world with his self-communication to the world. To this extent, this entire, unimaginably long period of the history of humankind and of salvation was simply Advent, headed toward a still outstanding future that remained unknown — a question about the future without any already clear answer in history itself.

Even so, the Advent hope already was living secretly out of God's grace in this time; and so it expected salvation and did not despair. Because in Jesus of Nazareth the eternal Word of God assumed a piece of human history, which has an indissoluble unity, as his own reality and history, a radical break enters into the history of humankind and of salvation: no longer can God allow the world as a whole to fall out of his love and grace. The lasting freedom of human beings is so caught up and surpassed by God's greater free love that the freedom of humankind as a whole yields itself and surrenders itself in an infallibly free way to the God of love, and really accepts the proffered love which is God himself.

By believing in God's becoming man as God's irrevocable decision for the world, and by professing the resurrection of Jesus as the already achieved assumption of a portion of the world that stays in the world, we Christians live in a period of salvation fundamentally different from people before Christ. We could say: against all expectations, and maybe against our own short-lived impressions, the drama of world history as a whole is already decided. Indeed the decision is for the eternal salvation of the world which is fulfilled not in virtue of any finite giving on God's part, but by *the* gift which God himself in his inmost reality is. Once this outcome of salvation history has been enacted, life is only a matter (but only with relentless seriousness) of the individual person's existing in solidarity with this foundational decision of the drama of the world.

Our Advent is thus an Advent "after the birth, death, and resurrection of Christ." And this "after" gives our Advent a character not there for people before Christ. Our Advent has to it an inexorable seriousness, because in it there has to occur the acceptance of God's gift, which is God himself, and God's offer already has been revealed in this world. Our Advent has a blessed joy about it because it has already been assured that humankind as a whole has been swept up by the powerful love of God despite its gruesome history; and now it is only a matter of each individual's not rejecting the event which is already given, the victory of God's love for the world.

And yet because the revelation of this love's victory still has to be revealed even after Christ; because the brief moment of the transfiguration of the dark world into God's eternal light still goes on and seems to be unendingly long to us, in spite of its inexorable seriousness and its integrally blessed joy, it still seems as if we remain caught in the provisional character of the world.

Thus Advent demands that we look to the *future;* we are people of expectation and hope. Too quickly and too easily do we get immersed in what we call the present, although it is basically only the transition from a past which derails us, and to a future we do not yet possess. We are all too easily ones who forbid themselves dreams and distant hopes, and who are proud that they "soberly" (as they say) throw themselves "with both feet" into the immediately urgent tasks alone.

But if we do not look toward the future, we basically do not know at all what the meaning and purpose of the present task is. Advent summons us to look to the future and to plan something for the day after tomorrow, trusting in the conviction that if our plan for the near future should collapse, we have still survived the near future with courage against shortsighted resignation and we have demonstrated that we have faith in the eternal future of God. In Advent we should really ask ourselves in complete intimacy and concreteness if the spirit and heart in us still have a little room for novelty and future beyond the present.

Advent is the time of the *secret experience of the apparently inexperienceable.* This statement may sound like cheap paradox for the sake of making an impression. But this statement basically is still true — the truth of the good news. Does not the Spirit of God, as Paul says, already pray in us now with inexpressible sighs? Haven't we, according to Paul, received the Spirit as the down payment for eternal life? Doesn't it hold true for us (Jn 5:45) that we are pupils of God himself? That the Spirit's anointing we have received from God is already within us, so that no one else has to teach us anymore (1 Jn 2:27)? That we are already born of God right now? So the period of Advent is actually not simply just the time before something that has not occurred yet. But just as well it can be understood as the period for the quiet growth of a life already given; and it works just like the time when, like the seed long-since sown in springtime, God's inward arrival comes through unobtrusively and slowly, but with terrific force and becomes manifest in all the seeming banality of our lives.

As Christians see and experience it, the present already bears the future within itself. And the eternal future of God is already the force and the power in the midst of the present. We shouldn't forget this in the Advent of our own lives. We shouldn't simply be charmed by the blossoms and leaves on the trees of our lives, which temporarily still hide the fruit of eternity ripening on this tree.

Of course only one who can be still and pray; only one who is patient and does not drown out the frightening silence in which God dwells, and which often comes over us, with the racket of everyday life and the shouts coming from the amusement park of the world, can already hear with ease and already discretely appreciate something of the eternal life that is already inwardly given to us in this fragmenting time as the indwelling of God in us. Whoever can wake up and be quiet and wait can already experience right now how Advent mysteriously lets the inexperienceable God be experienced. We need only just to have learned in a way that is fitting for Advent that stillness can say something more sublime and blessed than the tumult in the marketplace of life; that if one has the ears of faith, the emptiness of disappointment, of failure, and of abandonment is filled up by the eternal address of God, in which he announces not this or that thing which is pleasing to us, but instead, superabounding all things at once, he announces himself, the eternal, holy, loving, and forgiving God.

3 • Advent as Antidote to Utopia*

Christianity is faith in the future — in a blessed, infinite future, which is the unveiled presence of the infinite God as our eternal life. Of course there are people for whom this future is too distant and therefore faith

---

*Opportunities for Faith, trans. Edward Quinn (New York: Seabury Press, 1974), 21–24.

in it appears to be too illusory. Nevertheless the true Christian looks toward the future and is a genuine Christian only if she loves the future more than the present, if she does not misuse God and his eternal life in order to glorify and defend a present situation. For her the present is the provisional, something to be conquered, the transitory, not her lasting home. She lives on this infinite future in her criticism of the present.

If then the Christian's basic attitude is given a formal expression, it cannot be described as conservative. For he cannot regard heaven as a reward for conserving the present and at the same time consider the restlessness of time, the continual decay of every present moment, and calculated dissociation from earthly things as signs that the world and he himself are still really on the way, making these things the criterion as to whether he really wants to be on the way and whether he accepts the constant alternation of interior and exterior life as material for faith in the future still to come.

If, however, the Christian is a person of the future, by contrast with other people of the future, she is not a utopian. Of course Christians and, perhaps, the church too in the concrete have often been reactionary in recent centuries. Old ideas, old social orders, cultural forms, old positions in scholarship were defended as if Christianity stood or fell with them. People therefore fought against phases of the future which came nevertheless, had to come or at least could come, and which anyway were no worse than the times to which they had been accustomed and which they then defended as something that could not be abandoned. None of this can easily be excused.

This reactionary-conservative stance did, however, imply something more: the rejection of an intramundane utopianism. The Christian is awaiting the real future, the future that is the consummation of God's deed, of the coming of his kingdom, of his grace, not the mere fruit of intramundane history which the human being herself makes and controls. And therefore she cannot be a fanatic in pursuit of her own objectives in the world.

Once again, however, since the Christian was recruited too frequently from certain classes which sociologically are inevitably conservative, he was often lazy and easygoing, conservatively attached to the existing order, because he knew as a Christian that tomorrow (as also today) sin, suffering, and death, futility and decay will rule. Formerly he certainly assumed too quickly that he knew the limits of what was possible to human beings in this world and that the programs planned by others were the expression of impious pride; when he appealed to the unchangeable natural law, he too often confused its perpetual character with the time-conditioned form to which he was accustomed.

Even so, the Christian is less of a public danger than the non-Christian seeking an intramundane utopia. For the latter wants to experience the consummation of the redeeming future while she is still in this world: she must therefore force it to come, she must hate people who prevent this future; she is necessarily impatient, she cannot enjoy the present since for her it is nothing more than the raw material of the future; she is a fanatic for plans and programs and must sacrifice the present and its human beings to these.

The present has meaning for her only insofar as it contains creative possibilities for the future. A person who thinks and feels like this, who simply cannot find in a "contemplative" way what is permanent and meaningful in the present, who can value recreation only as a means of gathering strength for work and work itself merely as drudgery for the future, such a one is a utopian. The Christian as an individual of the divinely effected advent of the eternal future cannot support her in this, although both — Christian and utopian — are persons of the future.

Now this is odd. Faith in Advent is a better presupposition even for an intramundane future than the antifaith of the utopian who wants to produce the definitive future herself. There are many reasons for this. The human being of Advent really has an absolutely infinite future before her, which already exists, although it has not finally reached her: she calls it God. The person of Advent believes that no one escapes *this* future, even if she lived in the Stone Age or will not herself experience the end-stage of history, the absolutely classless society of communism.

The person of the Advent of God is already aware of the future within the present: he calls it grace, love, and God's Holy Spirit. He has no need therefore to sacrifice the present to the future, but for the same reason he does not need to explain the present as the permanent, as the consummation never to be surpassed. He will see intramundane recessions as signs that we have no lasting home here and will welcome all the immense advances of the intramundane future — which certainly exist — as promise and test of the eternal future of God, which they will never overtake.

Someone who must not make the present or the early future into an absolute does not get attached to the present, since she does not feel that she is banished from paradise when she has to leave it; nor does she think that we necessarily have to solve economic problems with blood and tears in order to bring about that future already saturating everything here, of which no one any longer says what it really involves and why this involvement is supposed to be so blessed, although it still takes place in space and time, between birth and death.

The person of the Advent of God then can meet the future with composure: he worships neither the gods of the present nor those of the future. He proceeds toward his future perhaps more slowly than the person of utopia. And why not? He cannot and will not spare his descendants the task also of becoming aware of the finiteness and the transitoriness of this earthly life and nevertheless bearing it and plucking from the tree of this present time the fruits of eternity, which is no longer time and is offered only to those who are willing to die.

It is not true then that Advent-expectation of God's eternity is bound to make us lazy and rigidly conservative. In fact, only a person who believes in this Advent of God can voluntarily leave this present behind; and she alone resolutely practices during her life the total renunciation of death. Someone who does not act in this way may call herself a Christian, but she is not really one. But why should someone who is so disposed, who is resigned to leaving all things, why should she find more pleasure in the present than in the future? Why should she stubbornly defend what she wants to forsake anyway, at the latest in voluntarily accepted death?

Only the person of the Advent of God is down to earth. He knows that all the answers which human beings produce only raise new questions and that every new order carries within it the area of its own death, if only because it is finite and therefore has possibilities alongside it which it does not itself realize.

There are two churches in the world (their frontiers do not necessarily coincide with the frontiers of religion and those of the iron curtain): the church of God's Advent and the church of humanity's utopia. Some, of course, who possess the membership card of the one party belong in their innermost attitude to the other. For in the church of the utopians there are people who love the person of today and not only of tomorrow and acknowledge in him or her an absolute significance; and in the Advent church there are people who see the church mainly as the preacher of a "better world" here below.

4 • With Jesus to Jerusalem*

Advent, Mt 21:1–11

The Gospel for the first Sunday of Advent in this church deals with Jesus' entrance into Jerusalem. For the most part in the four evange-

---

*Sermon given on 11 November 1980. Previously unpublished. From the Karl-Rahner-Arkiv, Innsbruck. Trans. Frederick G. Lawrence, Boston College.

lists we have harmonizing reports about this event, which introduces Jesus' passion. Even if we assume the most obvious fact that these four reports, each in its own style and intention, stylizes this occurrence in the light of its own basic themes, no reasonable doubt as to whether this event took place makes any sense. Jesus moves toward his destiny, he enters the stronghold of his enemies, he lets go of the protection of his followers — though these intentions on his part would have to be interpreted more exactly. He takes a stand against his enemies not in his home territory of Galilee, but in *the* city of his Father and his people.

Too, whatever we may think about a possible development in Jesus' understanding of himself and his mission, and however much more clearly Jesus interpreted what stood before him toward the end of his life, there is no reasonable doubt but that at this time, when he dared to enter Jerusalem, he must have and did figure on a violent death at the hands of his enemies. Thus he could not have avoided at all at least the question as to how he was to understand this death he had to count on in relation to his knowledge about his Father and about his mission. How he actually did this is documented at least in the interpretative hints at the Last Supper and the evocation there of the servant of Yahweh in Deutero-Isaiah, where the servant of Yahweh is established as the one chosen by Yahweh to be the covenant of the people and the light to the gentiles, sent as a prophet, entrusted with tasks for Israel and the nations, saved after suffering mortal need, and finally glorified.

Now it is a sacred truth for Christians that the life of Jesus is a creative model for each of our lives. Not in the sense that we are supposed to imitate and copy him, but in the sense that the innermost formative power of a genuinely human life lived from God and oriented toward him has achieved its purest expression in Jesus; and so we can discern in that life how this innermost force, that we reject all too often, actually desires to shape our lives also. We can affirm more exact and profounder things about Jesus as a creative model of our lives. We can say that his life in its irreducible concreteness, and not universal and abstract laws, is the true law of our Christian lives, because he has given his Holy Spirit into our hearts. But at the moment it may suffice for us to say one can discern in his life what has a sacred validity for our lives as well.

Thus with regard to Jesus' entry into Jerusalem.

Our lives are not only a march down a path with endless turns; this path has a goal and an end, whether we know it or not. We don't just march through this and that, by thousands of things, in order, after all that has gone by, to end at nothing; while we are ever passing particular things afresh, we are heading through all things toward one thing alone, toward the totality we are accustomed to call God, usually thinking little about this mysterious word. Most people seem to know of this unspeakable, infinite end of our paths, embracing all in one, only by means of a secret presentiment that cannot be articulated. But we Christians ought to acknowledge this end of the path which is our perfection, and so travel our path that it is also clearly discernible what its goal is. In biblical language we could say we are pilgrims along the way to the heavenly Jerusalem; we want to get there, to arrive at the heavenly city where there is no more night, because God himself is its light.

Such a path to God who is all in all is only traveled if we are impelled by the courage that is ready to go further, and to let go of what deceptively presents itself as happiness, luring us to stop. One only pushes further along if a person has what it takes for maintaining an ultimate distance in relation to everything transitory; if a person weeps as one not weeping, rejoices as one not rejoicing; gains as one who has nothing of one's own, as the apostle says; if one is converted to advance further, takes a hold in the readiness to let go. One has to be on-the-way, so that even the religious dimension also falls under the law of this onward movement that lets go. One has to be on-the-way so that possession and loss, joy and sadness, winning and losing, are bound together mysteriously into unity again by God's unfathomability, to which one surrenders, dumb struck, without oneself being able to control this surrender.

For our journey too heads primarily toward that Jerusalem where we have to die with Jesus; we will suffer the death that takes everything away, even the control over this letting-go. Everything that has just been said about this journey into God's incomprehensibility as a dying with Jesus does not mean, or it does not necessarily mean right now, the muffling of our lives into a mystical silence. That we can calmly leave to the last moment of our life. Every moment of our very lives this letting-go is being exercised in union with the act of attainment that advances our life movement. One must allow oneself to surrender without reservations to living and to weeping in order to be able to realize that mysterious possibility characteristic of explicit or anonymous Christians, namely: to let laughter *and* weeping, poverty *and* possessions enter equally into that unfathomable, all-encompassing plenitude (not disposed of by us, but disposing beyond us) called God. Only Jesus gives us the courage for letting ourselves in for God in this way, and so we justly call him the God of our Lord Jesus Christ.

This mysterious journey of our lives, heading to the Jerusalem of the unfathomable God, and which for this reason seems like an endless journey into emptiness, should therefore exhibit itself in a very everyday and taken-for-granted manner: ordinary days with bitter weeks and happy holidays, with work in the days and guests in the evenings, and the duties of normal human life. Because such living proceeds along relentlessly, as if by itself, even when this movement seems so easy and obvious, sweeping everything along with it, so that it almost appears to us like a standstill, without any motion. We have only, full of trust, to surrender ourselves to the serene wisdom of this movement; to let come what may come, let go what may go, to accept with patience everyday occurrences; to regard the great events of life yet again with the Christian's serene detachment proper to eternity. Then the journey to Jerusalem goes forward by itself. Be patient, we are getting there, because the innermost force of this movement is God himself.

One might think that what was just said about the detached onward march toward the silent infinity of God is just a universal humanistic moral maxim, which one could also represent without thereby being Christian; or one could even cast into doubt its general validity as a mere stoicism. Yet if what was affirmed is oriented to the death of every person, a matter that surely no one ought to philosophize away, and which, empirically speaking, takes us all, then the objection to what was said as a stoic interpretation of life with only a particular validity is certainly not justified. This is especially so since *within* this interpretative framework very many different lifestyles, among which Christians too may choose, have both space and validity.

But the decisive thing is this: that this relentless journey without a stop at any assignable place under our control is not lost in a vacuum of ultimate meaninglessness; that God's judgment standing over all such routes does not condemn us, but acquits us. With ultimate confidence we know all this only in our believing view of Jesus and his entry into the Jerusalem of his death and the heavenly Jerusalem of his risen life with God. And in this faith we grasp that our journey is only possible in the power of that Spirit of God who has prevailed victoriously and irrevocably in the world in historical tangibility in Jesus' death and resurrection. Consequently, Jesus' entry into his eternal Jerusalem is not just a moral and ultimately unnecessary model for our life's journey, but the really creative original image and the source of the divine power that moves our lives' course toward God and lets them really arrive at being with him. We really march with Jesus to Jerusalem.

5 • The Judgment of the Son of Man*

First Sunday of Advent (C), Lk 21:25–33

It is strange that the Gospel read at the beginning of the time of preparation for Christmas is that of the end of the whole history of the world. Yet that is not really surprising. For what is afoot in a small beginning is best recognized by the magnitude of its end. What was really meant and actually happened by the coming, the advent, of the redeemer is best gathered from that completion of his coming which we rather misleadingly call the second coming. For in reality it is the fulfillment of his *one* coming which is still in progress at the present time.

For that reason, however, our church Advent is not a mere looking back to something past but is the human being's entrance by faith, hope, and love into the process which began when God himself entered the history of his world and made it his own. As a result, that history is inexorably moving toward the day which today's Gospel places prophetically before our eyes. From the picture of the fulfillment we are to gather what in reality is already happening in the depth of our life and our reality, though unobtrusively and quietly and therefore in a way which in our sinful blindness we may overlook. God has started on his way. He is already there, hidden, and the revelation of his being is at hand.

Now when it is manifest that he has come, we shall see him as the Son of man. As one of us. As one who has lived our life among us, just as it is, short, bitter, mysterious. It is as the Son of man that God will then question us about our life. In that judgment we shall not be able to say that he, the eternal in his infinite harmony, cannot after all enter into our life with sympathetic understanding of its fragility and unsolved enigmas. He not merely entered into it by sympathetic understanding, he literally lived it. He himself became flesh. Not the remote God but the Son of man will be the judgment or the justification of our lives. The man who is God will be our judgment. Because he is human, he knows just how it is with human beings. Yet he, the eternal, remote God, is as closely concerned about us as only one can be who loves what is human and hates inhumanity in human beings from his own experience.

---

*Everyday Faith, trans. W. J. O'Hara (New York: Herder and Herder, 1968), 11–13.

Is it more blessed or more dangerous to be judged by a man and not solely by a God who was not himself involved in the history he is judging? Who can say? At all events the Gospel tells us the fact. The Son of man is to judge. If, however, the man who is God is to be our judgment, and if in his coming he traveled as we do from the womb of his mother to the bosom of the earth, then the face of the Son of man, in which we shall one day read our judgment, already mysteriously gazes at us from every human face, because all are his brothers and sisters: the pure face of the child, the careworn faces of the poor, the tear-stained faces of sinners, even the embittered faces of our so-called opponents and enemies. One day we shall have to "raise our heads" and look into the face of him who comes as the Son of man, for he is after all the God of eternity. And from his countenance all will look at us: all those around us to whom we were good or guilty. A voice will come from that mouth: what you did — or did not — do to the least of my brethren. That voice from that face will not die away and will fill our eternity from end to end. Shall we be able to raise our heads with the confidence of the forgiven and the living toward that face of the Son of man?

6 • The Last Days and the Lord's Coming*

First Sunday of Advent (C), Lk 21:25–28, 34–36

You will probably have noticed that in its liturgy the church uses disturbing texts which are difficult to explain and whose meaning isn't clear to us at first sight. That seems to be the case with this Advent reading. Of course we can easily divide it into three parts: the signs of the end of the world; the coming of the Son of man, which arouses courage and hope; a warning to beware of the cares of everyday life.

Advent really means future. The inward readiness required in Advent is contemplation of the start of God's coming into our world (the "first" coming of the Word of God made flesh into our world). It is also contemplation of the fulfillment of that very same coming (the "second" coming of the Son of man).

---

*Meditations on Hope and Love, trans. V. Green (New York: Seabury Press, 1977), 9–13.

In the first two verses of the text Jesus speaks of the signs that announce the end of the world and its history. He uses words that we don't understand when we hear them the first time. That doesn't mean that we can't today conceive of an end to the world. That kind of end of human history as such is a more rational prediction for us than for past generations. But a question remains: What has such a utopian or rationally conceivable end of the world to do with us here and now and with our religious life?

It is very hard to accept that when the end of humankind does come, the sun will really grow dark, the moon cease to give light, the stars fall from the sky, and "the powers in the heavens" be shaken, as the parallel text in Mark 13:25 puts it. But we do have to understand these prophecies of a cosmic catastrophe as referring to the end of human history. They ask to be interpreted quite radically if any sense at all is to be got out of them. But what are we to make of the first two verses of the text?

First we have to realize that Jesus is not a reporter back from a mission to a future end of the world which he has to all intents and purposes already experienced, and is trying to describe as it really is. This is withheld even from Jesus' human consciousness. Jesus isn't looking back to us from that future. Instead he is with us. He is looking together with us, forward to an inconceivable future. In the ultimate depths of his existence before God he knows of the end of everything and accepts that the reality of the world and of history will come to an end.

That inward knowledge of the transience of all things takes on a kind of outward, objective pictorial life. It emerges in terms of the images available to Jesus in the mental and linguistic world of his time.

What Jesus wants to describe is the tendency to end which is inherent in all human and earthly reality. He is citing the way in which all reality has a religiously absolute significance which is accepted by a person of faith who wants to live in accordance with the will of God. Because he looks forward to the end of the world (and not back from it), because he looks from the innermost experience of finiteness and the death-destined nature of his own human existence as a life approved by God, Jesus sees his own death and the collapse of the religious and political society to which he belongs. He sees the end of the world in the very same perspective, although that does not mean that he is interested in knowing how long the intervals of time between those events are. Therefore he speaks out of a profound experience of that finiteness which is also our own, if only we do not suppress it but are ready to accept it.

All that Jesus has to say of the outward events leading up to the end of the world recalls our actual internal and external memories of disappointments, illness, pain, growing old, failures and people dying; experiences we live through and suppress; experiences which always have an inward and an outward aspect; experiences which are our own and those of the world at the same time.

We celebrate Advent by perceiving and accepting those indications of the end of the world in our life. We should accept them realistically, and in a hope which is final and supreme and authenticated in itself and not from without.

Our hope is then that that absolute end will be a blessed resolution of all things. Signs of such a culmination meet Christians everywhere in their life. When they die, that end which is completion has arrived for them.

That end, which is both individual and the end of the world, is, so the second part of the text (verses 27–28) says, identical with the coming of the Son of man. Here we presuppose that Jesus identifies himself with that Son of man; that the coming in a cloud accords with an image used in Daniel 7:13 (an expression for the status which God gives the Son of man). We acknowledge what is said in the text when we say the Apostles' Creed and pray: Thence he will come to judge both the living and the dead. Of course we have no reason to think of this coming of the Lord as something local, as a process we can see with our eyes. If we look at it more closely, we can see how wrong that would be.

The process which by the grace of God moves the world and its history toward fulfillment, and which entered into a triumphant and irreversible phase in the death and resurrection of Jesus, is the coming of Christ. At least, it will be the coming of Christ when that process reaches its end: its completion or fulfillment. Everyone then will be with Christ. When Christian hope summons us to await the coming of Christ, that means that we take our place in faith, hope, and love in the process propelling the world toward everlasting fulfillment of the universe and of history in God by virtue of its participation in Jesus' death and resurrection. That means that as free Christian men and women we are liberated from all powers and all compulsion in our existence and that no thing or event can have the last word in our lives. We expect and await that last word of forgiveness, grace, freedom, and fulfillment from that which we know as God, who has already promised it to us in Jesus and in his life and death. It means too that he will grant us that last word (which — ultimately — he himself is), when in death and in the end all our own answers are transformed into a question: a single question that we ourselves are no longer able to answer. If this word of God's is spoken, and the end which is fulfillment comes about, then the Son of man will have come, for the word of God begins in him, and begins there definitively and triumphantly.

7 • He Is the One Who Started It*

Second Sunday in Advent (C), Phil 1:6–11

Our text comprises the introduction to this letter, apart from the address and the salutation. The church at Philippi had sent a representative to visit Paul in prison and bring him a contribution for his own support and for his work. Paul refers to this matter of his support, about which he will have more to say later. We shall glance at these verses and those immediately preceding, which are omitted in today's lesson, so as to round off our passage.

Paul is thinking of his community. It is his favorite, a flourishing community in the midst of its pagan environment, clinging to the word of faith and the gospel hope, looking forward in love to the day they all await, whether it come in death or in the end of the world's history: the day of Christ. When the apostle thinks of this community he can say: "I thank my God in all my remembrance of you." This gratitude for the vigor of the gospel, for the good estate of the church, for the faith and love of the Philippians quite naturally becomes a prayer; for Christians have not yet reached the end of the road, they must still fight and grow and increase so that they may be really perfected on Christ's day. So he continues: "Always in every prayer of mine for you all making my prayer with joy."

Can we say the same of our own prayer? Then he tells the reason why he so joyfully gives thanks and prays for this church. It is not simply their Christian life, their faith, their conversion, but also the way they have associated themselves with St. Paul's missionary intentions, the way they not only receive from him but also give, the way these new converts feel they have a responsibility and a mission, along with the apostle, to this pagan world. That is why they have prayed for him and supported him as well with their material gifts. So Paul goes on: "Thankful for your partnership in the gospel from the first day until now." He puts it very discreetly, almost in veiled language, in very general terms; but he is not talking about some abstract interest, he is

---

Biblical Homilies, trans. Desmond Forristal and Richard Strachan (New York: Herder and Herder, 1966), 133–36.

talking about partnership in prayer and about material support. Here is the reason for the apostle's gratitude and joyful prayer. What Paul sees in this small alms — pleasing but in itself insignificant — is a token, a tangible proof, an embodiment of their whole attitude. And so his mind's eye is led from this little offering to their whole Christian life, still growing, still in route, still to be perfected, and he says: I am sure that he who began the good work will bring it to completion at the day of Jesus Christ.

We are all the work that God the Father has begun in his grace through Christ Jesus in the Holy Spirit. *He* has begun the good work in us, we have not. But he has begun it through our freedom, and it is always questionable, as it were — it is always the one great all-embracing question, comprehending time and eternity — whether the work that has been begun will be brought to completion.

And when the apostle asks this question, when he asks whether what he has begun with words and tears, with penance, anguish, and all the power of his apostolic work and suffering will really be brought to completion or whether it will run down and atrophy — when he asks whether these men and women who have now made a start will one day enter the glory of divine light as children of the light, asks with fear and trembling because no one is certain of his salvation — then he lifts up his eyes to God, his heart is filled with confidence, and he says: I am sure that God, who has begun this work, will bring it to completion.

And we too may say this, frail and helpless as we are, we whose Christianity is always running down and atrophying, we whom the stream of daily life is always threatening to swallow up, extinguishing whatever light and power, life and glory have begun to emerge in our Christianity. Instead of studying ourselves we ought to say: he who has begun this work — and it is not we who have begun it, not we in our weakness, even in our freedom — God, in the glorious power of his grace, will bring it to completion. And that is our bold assurance, our splendid sovereign confidence. He says: it is right for me to feel thus about you all, because, he says — and here something entirely personal and genuinely human comes into the power and grandeur of God's work — because I hold you in my heart, for you are all partakers with me of grace, both in my imprisonment and in the defense and confirmation of the gospel.

Ah, if every priest could say that to his congregation! If God would grant the clergy everywhere the grace of such a relationship, both divine and human, with their people, so that each could say: You are all partakers with me in my work, in the defense and confirmation of the gospel. And then he tells them again how he loves them and how close to them he feels: God is my witness. What Paul says here is not a pious cliché, not just the conventional language of the priest, preacher, and apostle. No: God is my witness, how I yearn for you all — and we may quite legitimately translate the rest so: with the deepest love of Jesus' heart. Then he returns to what he has said at the beginning, that he prays for them with gratitude and joy.

And this is what he prays for: And it is my prayer that your love may abound more and more, with knowledge and all discernment. How strange, yet how splendid and how profound! I think it was Leonardo da Vinci who once said that love is the mother of all important knowledge, love and nothing else. May your love abound more and more with knowledge and all discernment. Only where love grows does true gnosis, true knowledge, grow; and God's grace gives one light to understand what a person is before God only in proportion as one loves from the heart.

And then Paul says that this knowledge that comes from love is given them, so that they may choose what is right. How difficult it often is for us to know what to do. Only the knowledge which is born of great love will really show us. And what will it all lead to, once love abounds more and more and the fair light, the joyous blessed light to see our life as God does, abounds in us and we keep choosing the right way at all the crossroads of our existence? That you may be pure and blameless for the day of Christ, when he appears at your death or at his second coming, filled with the fruits of righteousness which come not from ourselves but through Jesus Christ, to the glory and praise of God.

We need add nothing more. This short passage, this little introduction to an affectionate letter of St. Paul to his favorite community, says enough.

8 • The Stumbling Block of Salvation History*

Second Sunday in Advent (C), Lk 3:1–6

The scandalous thing about Christianity, Christ himself, and his church will always be that they are historical. Precisely in the fifteenth year of the emperor Tiberius, people think, precisely in Judaea and

---

*Everyday Faith, 20–22.

Galilee, precisely under the petty princes of those days, under a certain Pilate and under Annas and Caiaphas! Why did the salvation of all human beings not begin at the very beginning of all? Why not everywhere and always? Is the God of eternity, to whom all the world belongs, not equidistant from every place and time?

And yet it was then and there that the word of the Lord went forth to John and the decisive phase of the sacred history of redemption began. And so things have remained. People have to be baptized precisely with water, and nothing else will do. They have to have the word of forgiveness of sins spoken to them by a human mouth precisely on a Saturday afternoon in a wooden box — called a confessional — and not merely want to hear God's quiet voice in the voice of their own hearts. And the beauty of God's nature is not in fact the church in which people find the body which once suffered on the cross for us under Pontius Pilate. The words in the catechism and not the ideas in the empyrean of metaphysics are the truths by which people can live and die.

God himself can find human beings everywhere, where the person inculpably and with a clear conscience cannot advance. And God in his mercy will do so liberally, without our having to arrange for it. But that does not prove that we can prescribe to him where we will be pleased to allow ourselves to be found by him. He can follow all ways; we, his creatures, only those which he has prescribed for us.

Now he *has* marked out certain definite ways of salvation for us. It is not the case that all our ways lead to God. He has marked out definite paths for us so that we may know and acknowledge that salvation is *his* grace, his free, gratuitous grace and not a right of our own, something he owes us. So that we may realize and acknowledge that he is not at our disposal but that we have to stand at his, that he is God and we his creatures.

He has marked out definite ways of salvation for us because he himself — grace beyond all measure! — willed to walk them, because he himself willed to become human, caught like us in space and time and history from which in truth no human mind can extricate itself in this world. He himself was born under the emperor Augustus, precisely in Nazareth from which no good can come, suffered under Pontius Pilate, imprisoned in the here and now, in the not-then and not-there of a real human being. Dear grace of a God who loves humanity. We do not need to seek God in his kingdom of infinity where after all we would hopelessly lose our way as though in a trackless void.

In fact Christianity is so human and so historical that it is too human for many people, who think that the true religion must be inhuman, that is, not of the senses, nonhistorical. But the Word was made flesh. The word of the Lord went forth to John in the fifteenth year of the emperor Tiberius. And so it has remained. Christianity is an historical and a very concrete and sturdy religion, a stumbling block to the proud, who really — at least in religious matters — do not wish to be human beings, but it is grace and truth for those who with humble hearts are willing to be human beings in space and time even when they are adoring the God of eternity and infinity.

9 • Making Ready the Way*

Second Sunday in Advent (C), Lk 3:1–6

With this Gospel text for the second Sunday in Advent, Luke begins his version of the public life of Jesus. In the first two chapters, of course, he has told the story of Jesus' infancy. Because Luke, so to speak, begins all over again with this third chapter of his Gospel, and since he is now recounting the events which make Jesus' infancy (as Luke sees it) significant and credible for us, the "second beginning" has a chronological reference to the year 28/29 of our era, to the time of the emperor Tiberius, Augustus's stepson, in whose reign Jesus was born.

This formal opening and the reference to a specific time and political situation fit Luke's special theological intentions and ideas. New Testament theologians specializing in biblical salvation and redemption history think of Luke as the theologian among the evangelists of the *church in time,* for he sees the church as entering into its own era (one, that is, with its own specific significance and importance) between the history of Jesus and the last days.

I should like to ask at this point a certain latitude in treating the text in a somewhat old-fashioned though no less relevant way.

The text speaks of John the Baptist as the forerunner of Jesus. Of course this function of the Baptist in regard to Jesus and his mission is a very special one; it isn't a function of our own lives. If however we try to discover a kind of "forerunning" in our own lives, or to make it an important characteristic, then we have to remember the special problems and dangers of that kind of use of a particular biblical image. Nevertheless, this kind of application of the Baptist story is justifiable in the sense that we receive strength to bear life's burdens when we learn that the history of salvation already features a situation which, in spite of its uniqueness, is rather like our own.

Meditations on Hope and Love, 15–20.

I am not concerned here with the substance of the Baptist's message, nor with the fact that a word is used of him and his activity that we already find in Isaiah 40:3–5. I am interested in the fact that Luke, like the other three evangelists, puts the figure of the Baptist at the beginning of the gospel of Jesus, and therefore portrays him from the start as a forerunner of Jesus.

That is not so obvious as it might at first seem.

About twenty-five years after the Baptist's death, so the Acts of the Apostles tell us (19:1–7; 18:25), in Ephesus, and therefore a long way from Palestine, there were disciples of John who knew nothing of Jesus and his church. The argument of the first chapter of John's Gospel is directed against them too (1:6–8; 15:29–34). Therefore we can be sure that John the Baptist did not seem from the start to be no more than the messiah's forerunner, the predecessor of one whom the Baptist from the start picked out and directly identified as Jesus. According to the Gospels (Mt 11:2–6; Lk 7:18–23), even at the end of his life (when he was in prison), the Baptist still wasn't wholly clear about Jesus' messiahship. Therefore we are justified in seeing the clarity and lack of ambiguity with which the Gospels present the relation between John the Baptist and Jesus, and quite straightforwardly and emphatically subordinate the Baptist to Jesus, partly as the result of theological reflection among the first Christians.

The first Christians had, in their understanding of Jesus, to come to terms with the astonishing fact that Jesus let himself be baptized as if he were a sinner. Therefore they could not ignore the relation between John and Jesus, as they did other religious movements and trends of the time, which are more or less uniformly passed over by the Gospels. It is in that perspective that we have to see the special nature of John's activity.

John is indeed a forerunner. He precedes without sure and certain knowledge of whom or what he is serving. He may not himself share the immediate experience of the salvation that has become present in Jesus; he longingly foretells it. What he awaits and expects overtakes him without really catching up with him in the sense of his seeing clearly what he was aiming at.

His preaching of the coming of God as judgment is overtaken by Jesus' proclamation of the coming of God as liberation and forgiveness. John is the forerunner. He is that and no more, because he was that and did not wish to be anything more than that; because he was ready to humble himself; to diminish himself so that he who was to come could grow in stature; because he resigned himself to the task of the moment; for all those reasons he belongs to the history of Jesus and of ultimate salvation, and is blessed with the fullness of the future which he was able in his own time to greet longingly but only from afar.

Surely we are all forerunners? We are all pilgrims on the wearisome roads of our life. There is always something ahead of us that we have not yet overtaken. When we do catch up with something, it immediately becomes an injunction to leave it behind us and to go onward. Every end becomes a beginning. There is no resting place or abiding city. Every answer is a new question. Every good fortune is a new longing. Every victory is only the beginning of a defeat.

Surely we are forerunners? As parents we are the forerunners of our children. As old people, the forerunners of the young. As the scientists and scholars of today, the forerunners of those of tomorrow. As the politicians of today, the forerunners of those to come, who will scatter and suppress those of today.

We so quickly change the goals, words, and obvious characteristics of our projects, of politics, of the sciences, and of art. Every human being seems to march into her present moment with the feeling that now the real thing is coming, the truly valid thing that is once and for all, only then — very soon, alas! — to perceive that her present is turning into past; that she is old-fashioned and out-of-date; that she no longer understands and is no longer understood.

Aren't we always dispatching messengers from the dungeon of our compulsions and disappointments? We send them to find the real thing, that which is ultimately valid, even though we do not really know where to direct these messengers of our unassuaged longing?

Isn't death, which swallows us all, the only thing that we are sure to catch up with on our way? In our strange confusion we try to hold back the fleeting moment and to get to the next moment ahead more quickly than ever it could get to us. We who on all human pathways are always forerunners of the transient are always tempted to elevate our plans and projects to the level of something that is to come, an ultimate that will remain forever. It seems that something of the idiocy which makes people see everything and everyone else as transitory and themselves as ultimate, and refuse to be mere forerunners of an incalculable future, is an almost inevitable feature of the world on its way.

Everywhere, always, we are no more than predecessors. The goal of our journeying seems always to remain far ahead of us, to stay beyond our power and always to fade into new perspectives of distance, even when we think we are approaching it.

We should remember the Advent spirit which John the Baptist, as Jesus' forerunner, experienced before us: a willing acceptance of the small, seemingly mundane task which this particular moment puts before us; a humble readiness to do the one small thing even when we see the greater thing that is denied us; unenvying preparedness to acknowledge a greater excellence in others, even when we cannot bask in the reflected glory; hope that the unutterable will come to us too in our restriction and imprisonment, from which we can no longer break out; the assurance that all finite things, even death, can be inwardly fulfilled by the eternal God of love and light, if only they are accepted in hope, and that every setback in life can be a resurgence; the certainty rising from all the graves of disappointments that even the cry in the wilderness will be heard by someone, and that all that sowing of our tears will bring forth a harvest of joy, even if only in the storehouses of eternal life; readiness to undertake a further journey even when we had thought that at last we were home forever.

It is an Advent journey when we continue on our way and see coming toward us what we could never catch up with in our walking: God himself who secretly allowed us to go where we thought we were going — toward our own goals — and who gives us himself when tangible things are taken from us. After all, we ourselves are forerunners and everything tangible is transitory. Those who innocently take and innocently leave as the moment asks, are in Advent; from them nothing will really be taken away, for everything that they have to leave behind is only a sign that they have to go a longer way before they truly come to the everlasting light — light and life eternal.

Life is a unique Advent. The question is: Are we ready to accept and celebrate it in that sense?

10 • The Advent of Faith*

Third Sunday of Advent (A), Mt 11:2–10

The Baptist stands in the Advent period. He fits into *our* Advent season. For isn't our life still Advent: faith, expectation, patience, and longing for what is not yet visible? Do not we Christians have to build on what is "merely" hoped for and believed in? If we really want to be Christians, do we not, with God's folly, have to sacrifice the bird in the hand here on earth for the sake of the two in the heavenly bush — monetary advantage, pleasures of the body, harsh insistence on our

*Everyday Faith, 14–16.

rights, for the sake of the kingdom of heaven, that kingdom of heaven, alas, which no eye has seen?

The Baptist of today's Gospel belongs to such an Advent of waiting for what is still to come. He *is* in reality what we ought to be in our lifelong season of Advent. He was in prison. He had been stupid enough to speak the truth even to the master of the state. How could anyone be as politically unrealistic as that? He sits there. It serves him right. No one gets him out. His friends do not start a revolt. They are much too insignificant for that, only interested in theology and quite ineffectual in real life, or so it seems at any rate.

And God, too, leaves his preacher of penance where he is. He too seems to be on the side of the big battalions. And yet he was working miracles in his Son. But — is it tragedy or comedy — those miracles cured a few poor wretches of apparently no great importance for the kingdom of God. Those miracles did not free the holy prophet, the blood relation and quite official precursor of the man who was working the miracles. He remained imprisoned until he was "liquidated."

It is not easy for a prophet to sit in prison waiting for certain death, written off, and at the same time to take an interest in miracles which are of no help to himself.

But the Baptist is not a reed shaken by the wind. He believes despite everything. He is the messenger preparing the way for God, in his own life and heart first of all, preparing the way for the God who takes such an inhumanly long time to come and does not even hurry when his prophet is perishing, the God who always seems to arrive only when it is too late. The Baptist knows that God always makes his point, that he wins by losing, that he is living and gives life by being put to death himself, that he is the future which seems to have no future.

In a word, the Baptist believes. It was not easy for him. His heart was bitter and the sky overcast. The question in his heart has a rather agonized ring: Are you he who is to come? But that question was nevertheless addressed to the right person, to God who is man. In *prayer* we may show even a frightened heart to God, a heart that can practically do no more and no longer knows how long its strength will hold out. In a heart that prays there still remains faith and this receives a sufficient answer: "Go and tell John what you see . . . and blessed is he who takes no offence at me" even if he sits abandoned in prison.

We are in Advent all through our lives, for we Christians await one who is still to come. Only then shall we be proved right. Until then, however, the world seems to be right. The world will laugh, you will weep, our Lord said. We too are sitting in a dungeon, in the prison of death, of unanswered questions, of our own weakness, our own meanness, of the hardship and tragedy of life. We shall not get out alive.

But everyday we shall send the messengers of our faith and prayer to him who will come thence to judge the living and the dead. These advent messengers will come back each time with the answer: I am coming; blessed is he who takes no offence at me.

11 • A Voice in the Wilderness*

Third Sunday of Advent (B), Jn 1:19–28

After the prologue, the general introduction, and the summing up, St. John opens his Gospel with a portrait of St. John the Baptist. Plainly, he is thought of as an Advent figure, the representative human being midway between the past and the coming of the Lord. No wonder, then, that the church conjures up the figure of the Baptist in two of her Advent Gospels, in order to tell us what Advent is. For the Lord has come and yet he is still coming.

He is already here, but is in our midst, still, as the hidden God; and so we are still those who have no lasting city here, pilgrims between time and eternity, people who must still await God's coming, people who keep Advent even at Christmas time and must remember that we are still at the beginnings, still on pilgrimage; that we must still make our way through time, amid sorrow and distress, but with a heart full of faith, toward the eternal light that still awaits us. What this means for us is that eternity is not yet here. But it does not mean that we must not cherish the light that is already lit, and it does not mean that we ought to turn our backs upon this world. It means that we must not neglect the other light. We should look to the precursor.

He is in the wilderness. Obviously because he finds these surroundings appropriate to his life — the parched solitude, the endless spaces, where no one can feel at home. Inevitably we keep discovering that we too are in the wilderness, the wilderness of a great city, the wilderness of isolation, a wilderness that seems to have no center, a wilderness we cannot feel at home in. And we are also men and women who would live in a wilderness if we had to give our outward environment the shape of that which is within us.

Then scripture says that the emissaries of the Pharisees ask John who he is, indeed half suggest that he has only to seize his opportunity and his whole life will come to fruition. Why not? The Lord himself has

---

*Biblical Homilies, 65–67.

said that among those born of women none is greater than John. But John says: "No, I am not." Do we not experience something similar in our own lives? Have we not constantly to take a firm stand and say: no, I am not — I am not strong, I am not blessed, I am not one who has a happy life ahead. Time and again a person is put to the test, to see whether he or she will hold his or her ground and say no; for the real meaning of my life consists in admitting my pettiness and sinfulness, so as to clear a space and allow meaning to enter my life. Somehow or other we too must be people who renounce self-assertion and our towering pride, to say: I am not. All I am, says the precursor, is the voice of one crying in the wilderness.

How strange! This is a quotation from Isaiah, and here is the voice from the wilderness where everything is swallowed up by the wind, where nothing has any settled shape, where the cry is lost upon the air. Dies away, that is, but is not lost. For though it reaches nothing else, it does reach the one to whom it is addressed. And so it always means something other than itself.

We too should be the voice of one crying in the wilderness, should cry to God continually although our cry seems to be swallowed up by endless silence and solitude, and even when there seems to be no answer to our call. We shall hear the answer. It is not just an echo, not simply consolation in the faith; it is the eternal word of God himself, filling this emptiness — the wilderness of my heart that is so often left waiting without hope and without faith, in the desolation of this life — filling it with eternal light, eternal truth, the eternal reality that is the only reality.

But we must not say these three things and leave it at that. There is a fourth thing to be said: among you stands one who is to come, the unknown one and the long awaited, as we best know him. And because the invisible is something we cannot do without — for it is the ultimate bond between alpha and omega — it is true that he is already in our midst: in all our wildernesses, in every feeble self-denial, in every whispered cry to him, he is already here.

Yet it is always Advent in this Christmastide. What a harsh Gospel! We shall only find consolation in it if God gives us the grace to do so. All the same shall we not hold out a little while in the wilderness of our life? Even if we must always be saying no. Even if we must keep taking leave of ourselves, keep tasting the bitterness of our desolate world. Even then shall we not say to the unshakable center of our lives: You are here. You are the Lord of my faith, you are my strength and my delight. You are the Christmas in the Advent of my existence?

12 • Patience with the Provisional*

Third Sunday of Advent (B), Jn 1:19–28

Once again the Baptist stands before us in our Advent longing and expectation. The question is put to him: What are you really doing, if you are not the real, expected messiah? That is a language we can understand only too well. The people of Advent, of waiting for God, of burning longing for the eternal, can be overcome by the most terrible and dangerous impatience that there is, a religious radicalism which has the appearance of being glorious and sublime but in reality is the contrary of the truly Advent attitude.

Humanity thirsts for God, hopes in him, hopes that he will soon establish his kingdom. He wills the unconditional, the radiant truth whose splendor at once burns every doubt from the mind, the radical goodness which would destroy all fear that goodness itself is only a form of self-seeking. But only precursors ever come; only beginnings are made; messengers come but always with God's truth still in merely human words which obscure it. Those messengers of God are only human beings with human traits and sometimes inhuman ones. All that ever happens are God's saving deeds (called sacraments) in human ceremonies. All these provisional things simply continue to proclaim that they themselves are not the reality. The reality is merely hidden there in all the figurativeness of words, of human beings, and of signs.

Then the persons, who even in their purest religious feeling are sinners, may lose patience. What are you doing in religion, you human beings, words, signs, if you are after all not the reality, not the unveiled God immediately present? Then the impatient think that this God may perhaps be found outside the human beings, the words, and the signs of the church: in nature, in the infinity of their own heart, in political projects to establish forever by force, here and now, the kingdom of God. Or somewhere else.

But in the end these impatient people realize, very often too late, that they have wandered into the wilderness of their own empty hearts where the devils dwell, not God; into the loveless desert of a blind and cruel nature which is only benevolent on Sunday afternoons; into the arid wasteland of the world where the waters of ideals ooze away the farther one advances; into the desolate wilderness of a politics which

---

*Everyday Faith, 17–19.

brings about not the kingdom of God but simply the tyranny of naked force.

No, we are not spared it. We have to hear the voice of one crying in the wilderness, even if it confesses: it is not I. We must have the patience of men and women of Advent. The church is only the voice of one crying in the wilderness, announcing that the final radiant kingdom of God is still coming and that when God wills, not when it suits us. We cannot try to ignore that voice simply because it comes from the mouths of human beings; we cannot disregard the messengers of the church because they too are not worthy to loosen the sandals of the Lord whose forerunners they are, or because they cannot call down fire from heaven like Elijah.

For it is still Advent. The church itself is still an advent church; for we are still waiting for him who is to come in the unveiled radiance of unconditional Godhead with the eternal kingdom. And that church rightly tells the impatient who want to see God directly here and now: Prepare for this God the true way, the way of faith, of love, of humility, and the way of patience with its unimpressive provisional messengers and their poor words and small signs. For then God will certainly come. He only comes to those who in patience love his forerunners and the provisional. The Pharisees of the Gospel, however, who rejected the forerunner of the messiah because he was not the definitive reality, did not recognize him who was the definitive reality either.

13 • We Should Not Fear His Nearness*

Third Sunday of Advent (C), Phil 4:4–7

The church at Philippi was the first Christian community in Europe. It was founded by St. Paul on his second missionary journey, during a brief sojourn which had to be suddenly broken off. This flourishing community, where a truly Christian life was led, was St. Paul's favorite church. Of course its members were human as well; there were small irritations and difficulties, but all things considered, it could fairly be described, in St. Paul's phrase, as the crown of his apostolate. He writes

---

*Biblical Homilies, 137–41.

to them from captivity, as his letter says, out of gratitude for the offering which a representative of the community has brought him.

We do not know for certain where Paul was imprisoned. Perhaps this was the first captivity at Rome, but it may well have been an earlier one at Ephesus about which little is known. So Paul may be writing from Ephesus to his church in Europe. At all events it is a personal letter, an intimate letter. In it Paul does not deal with weighty matters of abstract theology, but heart speaks to heart. So the various parts of the letter are loosely connected.

In one place Paul says something about himself, how he is, what he is doing, what his hopes are; he interpolates prayers; then he speaks of his expectations for the community, his gratitude to it; then he mentions various individuals among the Philippian Christians.

Thus today's text from Philippians is a short passage which is complete in itself. Let us just glance at it together. Paul says: "Rejoice in the Lord always." Yet another exhortation to us Christians to rejoice, to rejoice in the Lord, in the consciousness that we are united with Christ, live in him, act through his grace, and so rejoice through his grace. We are reminded to rejoice, admonished to rejoice; so to rejoice is a Christian virtue. There is no need to be reminded of, and admonished about, things over which we have no control. So if we must be reminded and admonished to rejoice, it is probably because we do not rejoice as we can and ought to do.

Today, then, let us hearken to the apostle as he urges us once more to rejoice in the Lord always. You see, he knows that this is easier said than done but at the same time it is important, and so he adds: "Again I will say, Rejoice." And now quite a different admonition follows: "Let your gentleness be known to everyone," he says. Not everything the Christian cherishes, thinks, believes, practices, suffers, and hopes for is known to others and intelligible to them. For as Paul says in another passage: "The gifts of the Spirit of God are spiritually discerned. The spiritual person judges all things, but is himself judged by no one."

But, Paul says here, others should always observe your goodness, your kindness, your inner peace and equanimity. They may not realize that these are especially Christian qualities, but that is neither here nor there. They must notice that you are considerate, helpful, benign, tranquil, self-possessed, candid, and loving. That is something anyone can see. The ultimate roots of it may not be apparent, but at least the prints of your Christianity must be seen. "Let your forbearance be known to everyone," says St. Paul. And who knows, they may have an inkling that our life is drawn from a deeper source than theirs. "Let your kindliness be manifest to everyone," says Paul.

Strange, in the midst of these admonitions Paul interjects something that is not an admonition at all: "The Lord is at hand." How strange: when he is preaching about morals he thinks of Christ; when he is thinking about the Christians and when he is thinking about all the rest of humankind, he thinks of the Lord. He thinks of the Lord as of someone nearby, someone who once lived among us and has simply gone away and is in heaven; he thinks of the Lord as of one abiding with us in his Spirit, in his word, in his brother and in his sister, as of one who is coming, who would penetrate ever further into our lives, who would absorb our lives ever more completely in himself, who with his Spirit and his power, with his own history which is still going on, is engaged in one tremendous advent. And he is close to us as well, in the destiny that leads our lives toward a single goal, to death and judgment, which may be nearer than we think. The Lord is near. He is close to all of us. Are we close to him?

We ought not to fear this nearness. We should feel that it is a blessed, protective nearness, the nearness of our salvation, of our strength, the nearness of promise and fulfillment, the nearness of authentic reality, the nearness of that to which our entire being, history, and destiny is directed. If we felt the nearness of the Lord in this way and if we were close to him in this way by faith, hope, and love, then his nearness would be joy and peace to us.

That is why Paul continues: "Have no anxiety about anything." He means that torturing, consuming, destroying anxiety that degrades a person and breaks him, that does not let him rise above his fate. He means the anxiety that pagans experience. This, he says, we are to have no part of. We should repudiate it. Are we lighthearted and untroubled people? Can we cheerfully face the day? Paul does not think so. He knows we have our worries; he knows that the pressure, the narrowness, the distress of life tell on us. All the same he thinks and says: "But in everything" — everything that worries, harasses, cramps, distresses or pains us — "let your requests be made known to God — with thanksgiving."

All prayer should tell God our distress and so be candid and open, unconstrained and tranquil, calm and unanxious. In all prayer and supplication — with thanksgiving. Astonishing. When Paul is speaking of prayer, supplication, prayer that arises from the troubles of life, he thinks of thanksgiving, of "eucharist" — the word used here.

When we pray, are we only little beggars before God, wrapped up in our own worries? Is our heart ever enlarged in thanksgiving, as it were a great preface in the eucharist of which our life is the celebration — thanksgiving that we Christians are created, called, sanctified, redeemed, pardoned, preserved, rescued in God's providence, that we are God's beloved children, that God's Spirit is given to us, that eternal life awaits us, that the Lord is near, that he is kind and clement and that his mercy is unbounded?

Do we ever give thanks that our thanksgiving and our petitions reach the ears of God, and that we ask God to perfect the good work which he has begun in us — and for which we are just thanking him — on the day of Christ that is not far off? "And the peace of God, which passes all understanding, will keep your hearts and your minds in Christ Jesus." So this peace is in Christ Jesus, to whom we belong, whom we love, whose body we receive. Ultimate, all-embracing peace we have in him. It surpasses all our thought, even all our desire. And accordingly we often hardly realize that we already possess it.

Yet it is there, and Paul says of it: let this blessed tranquility which is God's peace stand guard, as it were, before your hearts to defend them, almost — the Greek word can bear such a sense — place our hearts under arrest and keep them in custody. The peace of God, after all, is not of our doing or making; it is God's doing within us, the doing of the power of his grace. And so we wish, pray, and supplicate that this mighty peace may, as it were, attack all our hearts in all its native force, guard the gate of the city of each heart, keep watch there lest any discontent, any animosity, any discord, any schism should creep in, any murmur of distrust of God, of our own life, or of our fellow men and women, whereby we might lose this perfect peace. May the peace of God, which passes all understanding, keep your hearts — for if it keeps your hearts, then it will keep your minds, your projects, your decisions, and your desires — in Christ Jesus.

There is today's epistle. Let us turn it into a prayer so that our prayer and supplication may reach the ears of God, so that peace and joy in Christ Jesus may dwell evermore in our hearts, so that we may bless the eternal Father for calling us into the kingdom of the Son of his love, so that we may be at one and enjoy peace, and so that our Christian attitude in Christ Jesus may be plain to everyone through our forbearance and benignity, so that they too — whether or not they explicitly discover the Lord and his grace — may to some extent meet Christ in us, at least in that consideration and kindness which, human though they seem, are ultimately a fruit of God's grace. May that grace keep our hearts now and evermore.

14 • What Shall We Do?*

Third Sunday of Advent (C), Lk 3:10–18

Today's Gospel from the third Sunday in Advent — by omitting three verses which relate a part of the Baptist's denunciations — links itself to the Gospel of the second Sunday of Advent. Luke tells us again of John the Baptist, the forerunner of Jesus, and of his preaching.

The text is divided into two parts. In the first part, John answers his audience's question about the consequences for their lives of his basic message: the news of the imminent judgment and the demand that they should radically change their lives. In the second part, John rejects the claim that he is the messiah, and that he can act as the mediator of the Spirit of the kingdom that is to come.

The first section (with which I am mainly concerned here) is not so surprising. There is always the temptation to shrug off these moral injunctions as obvious, even as banal. But if we look at them closely, they are most compelling.

John is said to be the one whom Isaiah previously proclaimed as the voice in the wilderness, the one who was to announce God's coming salvation, the prophet of a final, imminent divine judgment, a last chance for radical conversion, the impossibility of satisfying God by anything other than a definitive conversion which fundamentally transforms all one's life from what it has been hitherto. And now people ask this preacher of a radical religious change and new start, what they actually have to do if they really want to obey that uncompromising message. The answer appears to be just a string of moralistic clichés, which you can find elsewhere, and which don't have to be preceded by any apocalyptic rant to make them comprehensible. Tax collectors mustn't make unjust demands; soldiers should be honorable men who don't terrorize the neighborhood and are to be satisfied with their wages. John doesn't question, of course, the calling or work of the tax collectors and soldiers in the pay of the occupation authorities — work which for pious people then was very dubious and even contemptible.

Even when he goes on to say that they must share their food and clothing (if they have enough of them) with poor neighbors, John does not go beyond what seem to be the obvious dictates of common human morality. If we make a further list of advice in the same style for other professions and situations, the apparent contrast would remain

---

*Meditations on Hope and Love, 21–26.

between a radical command to change one's life and those everyday maxims which the Baptist's audience must certainly have been aware of, and followed or ignored, before they heard his sermon; and, goodwill apart, certainly didn't fulfill much more effectively once they had heard him in the vein of our text.

What does this mean? This Gospel gives no direct answer. All we know is that these apparently contradictory things somehow go together and make sense.

We have all certainly had the experience that the demands of a seemingly ordinary, everyday morality are not so easy after all — as long, that is, as we do not fall into the error of counting as moral principles only what suits us and happens to be easy for us. Everyday life as it is already asks a lot of human persons as they are. To keep on through dull, tedious, everyday existence can often be more difficult than a unique deed whose heroism makes us run the danger of pride and self-satisfaction.

If we remember that the religious and moral value of life is more than the mere collective significance of individual moments; that it forms a whole with its own character as that very whole, even when it is realized through the sum of individual actions, then a life spent in duties, in the constantly renewed will to be just and good to others, a life in which human beings do not allow themselves to sink into tired resignation on account of the meaninglessness of their day, a life of good spirits which is a divine gift and virtue, and so forth — a life like that no longer stands in striking contrast to John's call to conversion. Such a life of apparently humdrum moral ordinariness in fact posits that conversion not as happening at a specific moment in time, but as a hidden principle permeating the apparently everyday nature of life as a whole.

But that is not all. What we make of the apparent contradiction does not depend on that. There is something else, imperceptible perhaps, here and there at least, in our performance of obvious everyday duties, some of which may even be of advantage to us.

In ordinary circumstances, life constantly maneuvers us into situations in which the obvious aspect of humdrum chores disappears or seems absurd. Suddenly common morality just isn't worth it. Its banal meaning vanishes or has to change to something quite different. The meaningful utility of an action dies or moves into the realm of the holy. The duty remains unrewarded; indeed, doing it seems instead to be punished.

A respectable citizen is no longer the honorable individual to whom people look up but a fool who just doesn't know how to get along in life. All of a sudden, people take incredible advantage of selflessness;

they no longer respect honesty but even use it as a weapon against an honest person.

There are a thousand ways in which everyday morality can become a mysteriously awful thing, in all its obviousness and quite apart from any special heroic situations. It isn't worth it any longer; it no longer yields the measurable return which the doer himself got out of it. A reasonable and honorable egoism (which can also be a collective matter) becomes something quite different, or it's given up as unprofitable. It just doesn't pay — either in itself or us.

But what happens to that everyday virtuousness when it doesn't pay any longer, even in a sublime sort of way, and yet isn't given up as meaningless? It becomes a kind of "forerunning" of the God of salvation and freedom. When we say that, the word "God" must not be thought of as referring to anything else that we might connect with it. It means what it says. It means that what we mean by God is experienced precisely in this quiet but extraordinary transformation, just as it occurs in fulfilling our everyday morality.

God is the one whom we meet, even though perhaps without naming him, and unconsciously, when we dare to be foolish, when we avoid conflicts and power struggles that we had a chance of winning; when we love without the initial certainty of being loved in return; when we remain true to our convictions even to our disadvantage, and that disadvantage is not merely an episode in a battle we are sure to win in the end; when, to put it in a nutshell, we are true to our conscience and no longer confuse its demands with the claims of that obvious material utility and significance primarily (and quite justifiably) announced by everyday morality.

When such a demand of conscience transforms everyday morality behind its facade, if we refuse that challenge (perhaps quite unobtrusively), God is judging us. But it can be God coming as ultimate freedom, as saving freedom, if we obey the sudden call. That can happen quite quietly in the usual fulfillment of everyday duties. We seem to be moving along the well-worn paths of normal human conduct, rationally and respectably, behaving (even if with advantage to ourselves) with respect to others. Then, suddenly, in the twinkling of an eye, we are in the wilderness — God's saving wilderness.

If we recommend everyday morality and do not tacitly cancel the recommendation when it doesn't pay, we are in fact calling for a radical change of heart, even though we can't fix it at a specific point in time and life. Then we call on and praise the grace of God, which fills those depths to which the paths of our modest everyday life do in fact lead, right up to the point where we let ourselves fall fearlessly into that profundity.

What shall we do? Somewhat intimidated, people asked that question after John the Baptist's frightening sermon about sin and the inevitable judgment, about all-transforming conversion. John answered them; and suddenly his answer holds us just where we are, living quite ordinarily; where we are, carrying on patiently. His answer means that it is here precisely that we can experience the coming of the Kingdom of God, if only we want to, and if only we can surrender in hope to the hidden meaning and innermost power of this everyday life of ours.

15 • God Is with Us*

Fourth Sunday of Advent (A), Mt 1:18–24

This text provokes many questions. For example, we might ask why Matthew, in contrast to Luke, portrays Joseph and not Mary as the one who receives God's news about the birth of the savior of the people of Israel. We might ask what Joseph's motives are (for they are not clear from the text) for wanting to divorce his wife. We could once again pose the question (very popular recently) of the historical formulation used here to describe the virgin birth, and its significance for our faith. We might consider the meaning of giving a name and the significance of the name Jesus — "the Lord saves." We might ask what the prophet originally intended by the quotation from Isaiah 7:14, whose meaning here is highly controversial. But those are questions outside the scope of this short meditation.

Here we are concerned with the name "Emmanuel," the announcement that "God is with us" through this Jesus.

One connotation of "God is with us," that is not superficial or erroneous, is worth noting. When we say that the human person as a created being is certainly concerned with God, that God is the Lord and goal of humankind, that without him there is no meaning to our life, that he is our helper and savior, on whose gracious providence we are dependent, that he of his mercy will forgive us our guilt, that we shall have to plead our responsibility before his court of judgment, that for those who believe in, hope in, and love him, he prepares an eternal life of happiness, then we have interpreted "God is with us" in the right way and in a number of its aspects. It would be a wonderful blessing if

---

*Meditations on Hope and Love, 27–32.

all human beings were to realize that interpretation of "God is with us" in their lives. All those explanations are ultimately directed in hope to the one deeper mystery of "God is with us."

But none of them reaches the absolute Christian understanding of "God with us." If we said that God was close to us only in his finite gifts, in placing us as creative beings in our own reality, and guiding that reality to its immanent fulfillment through the forgiveness of our guilt and the final validation of our own mature existence; if we said that God himself was close to us only insofar as all these created human realities came from him and referred to him and prompted us to refer to him in acknowledgment and thankful, prayerful love; then we should misunderstand the radical nature of the Christian understanding of "God with us."

God himself is with us. God himself is with us through himself and not merely through the mediation of finite gifts to a finite creation. Scripture and tradition testify to the highly nuanced nature of the ultimate mystery of our existence: namely, that God communicates himself to us in his own infinite and incomprehensible reality. He gives us his own Spirit, who sounds the profundity of the Godhead, God's own inward life. Thus the Father and Son come to reside in us, just as the Son is one with the Father from eternity. We share in the divine nature; we are no longer mere servants but truly God's children born of God. We shall see and love God not in the mirror and likeness of creaturely mediation but directly, face to face. Traditional theology speaks therefore — lest the radical nature of this biblical teaching be diminished subsequently — of uncreated grace, of the fact that direct perception of God is not mediated by a created reality, from which God would then have to be recognized. Classical theology speaks of the direct indwelling of the threefold God in the human person, of the self-communication of God.

At first all that may sound rather abstract. But it is the ultimate truth about humankind, whether we have already reached it and realized it in the banality of our everyday existence or not. Because we are finite beings, when we live from ourselves alone we succumb to an almost irresistible inclination to think quite finitely of ourselves and of our fulfillment. We tend to be falsely unassuming, to be satisfied with the visible and tangible. If it were a matter of our own perspective alone, we would be quite right to be content with a finite happiness. Every sin in the world, because it posits a finite good as absolute, testifies to that false contentment to which we may not resign ourselves.

We are forbidden to do so not only by a law of external origin, one that remains alien to us, but by the fact that God in his very boundlessness, in the sovereignty of his mercy and loving kindness, has already made himself the innermost law of our nature, before we become conscious of ourselves and fear to let ourselves fall into that incomprehensible infinity which already fulfills us from the innermost core of our being, and we take shelter in the finite margins of our existence and try to find happiness there. The statement that God is with us (as Christians understand it absolutely) says that we cannot be immoderate enough in that thirst that God himself has given us; in our craving for freedom, happiness, the closeness of love, knowledge, peace, and ultimate fulfillment. Any guilty immoderacy in our lives, if we consider it closely, is only that lack of control which posits a finite reality as absolutely necessary for our own happiness. A person like that is guilty because he does not dare to make the believing, hoping, loving leap into the incomprehensibility and unrestrictedness of his true happiness, which consists only of the incomprehensibility of God.

The abstract interpretation which I have offered of the "God with us" of the text in question is not so distant as it at first seems. It seems so because we are distant from our own "supernature," which is God himself. Whenever we hear in ourselves the infinite claim and summons of existence (which is already inwardly blessed) accepting no more conditions and limitations apart from the fact that we are the beginning but not the fulfilled infinity; whenever there is a will to unconditional love which opens out to others in a way that must incur the danger of mortal self-denial; wherever in the fall toward the mortal darkness of death we still believe that that experience is finite and that the hope of everlasting life is infinite; in those and many other basic events of human existence, we experience the hope and belief that God himself — and no finite thing — is the fulfillment of all finite human being.

That is the meaning of "uncreated grace." It is a grace mediated by Jesus Christ, yet it is at work in all world history and human history as its innermost realization of what it is potentially. Therefore it is the innermost core of all human existence.

But the doctrine of "uncreated grace" indicates more than an unutterable bliss as the future of humankind. With it we reach the ultimate gravity of the Christian notion of the human being. This God who is "God with us" in that way is not only the illimitable mystery that remains absolute mystery even in direct apprehension of God, and thus can be borne by human perception only if that perception is itself fulfilled in the love which alone makes it possible for God who is love to be perceived as greater than one's own heart (with its craving for enlightenment).

This "God with us" is not only the God of absolute freedom (of decisions which can no longer be negated, and arrangements which can only be endured and accepted in the unconditional surrender of love which loves this divine freedom as such). It is rather the incredible closeness of God which gives Christian "morality" its ultimate radicality. Many thousands of reversals occur in human history and in an individual's life which are wrong by the yardstick of the very nature of the human being and his finite world; they are, therefore, objectively refused by human morality, but do not really cancel the ultimate affirmative relationship to this God who gives himself and is so incomprehensibly close to us. (There are many "objective sins" which imply no "subjective guilt" and therefore do not stand in the way of salvation — that is how scholastic theology would put it.)

Repeatedly, however, human freedom (acting on the material of worldly morality) offers a no to that God of absolute closeness, without, however, specifically formulating it like that. Then we have sin ("grave sin") in the Christian sense. Sin is not only saying no to the objective structure of the human person and the world, and therefore to the commandments of the God who wills those structures (but only with the will that accords with the conditional and finite nature of those structures); it is saying no to God himself in his absolute closeness to us. It is the no of human freedom denying itself the absolute venture of the love of God and its own love.

It is both terrible and comforting to dwell in the incomprehensible nearness of God, and so to be loved by God himself that the first and last gift is infinity and incomprehensibility itself. But we have no choice. God is with us.

THE CHRISTMAS SEASON

16 • Christmas: "Ever Since I Became Your Brother…"*

The celebration of Christmas is such a pious custom! The Christmas tree, the pretty presents, the excitement of the children and a little Christmas music are always beautiful and touching. A religious mood intensifying the atmosphere makes it especially lovely and touching. To be sure, we are all secretly a little self-indulgent — who will blame us? — and so we readily let ourselves fall into a mood that is peaceful and comforting, just as we pat a crying child on the head and say, "It isn't so bad, everything will surely turn out all right."

Is this *all* there is to Christmas? Is this the main point? Or are the beauty and coziness, the stillness and intimacy of Christmas only the fine, gentle echo of an event that is today's real celebration, an event that takes place somewhere else altogether, much higher in heaven, much deeper in the abysses, and much more inwardly in the soul? Are the joy and peace of Christmas only the expression of a mood, in which one dreamily takes refuge? Or are they the outward expression marking the sacred celebration of an actual event? Even if we should not want it to be true, even if we grasp no more from it than a little childlike romanticism and homey comfort, Christmas is by all means truth and reality. In the face of it we bravely open our hearts so that it may also happen to us and through us.

Christmas is more than a bit of cheerful mood. The child — he is the one who counts today. The important figure in this holy night is the child, the one child, the Son of God, and his birth. Everything else about this feast is based on and quickened by this, or else it dies and turns to illusion. Christmas means that he has come. He has made the night bright. He has turned the night of our darkness, our incomprehensible night, into Christmas. The terrible night of our anxiety and helplessness is now a holy night. This is what Christmas tells us. Through this feast, the moment when this event took place once and for all should also become a reality in our hearts and should remain there to form our entire outlook on life, our *Christian* outlook.

If we mortals are completely immersed in the average experiences of our blind, routine, monotonous daily life, then we will have to come

---

*The Eternal Year, 19–26.

to the frightening and discouraging view that — in small things and great — nothing of importance really happens in the world. To be sure, we might think that there is an eternal rise and fall of world events, of the destiny of nations, even of personal experiences, sometimes good and joyful, usually bad and gloomy. Ultimately, however, all this circles in upon itself, aimlessly and without direction. It wastes away blindly and without meaning. People hide the senseless purposelessness of events only by anxiously taking care not to think beyond the next day. Seen only from our point of view, we are an enigma, an eternally frightening and mortal enigma.

If we should examine the birth of the child of today's feast merely from our point of view, then we could say of him and of us, too, only what is written in the dismal, bitter text of Job 14:1–2: "Man that is born of a woman is of few days, and full of trouble. He comes forth like a flower, and withers; he flees like a shadow, and continues not." From our point of view, we could be no more than a tiny point of light in the unlimited dark, a point of light that can only make the darkness even more frightening. We would be no more than a sum that didn't come out right. We seem cast off into time, which makes everything disappear, forced into existence without being asked, laden with wearisome toil and disappointment. Through our own fault we burden ourselves with pain and punishment. We begin to suffer death in the moment when we are born. We are insecure and driven to be childish about all that is illusory, all that is called the sunny side of life — which in reality should be only the refining means of ensuring that the martyrdom and torture of life do not end too quickly.

But if in faith we say, "It is Christmas" — in faith that is determined, sober, and above all else courageous — then we mean that an event came bursting into the world and into our life, an event that has changed all that we call the world and our life. This event alone has provided a goal and a purpose for everything. It has not only put an end to the saying of Ecclesiastes that there is nothing new under the sun, but also to the eternal return of modern philosophers; it is an event through which our night — the fearful, cold, bleak night where body and soul await death from exposure — has become Christmas, the holy night. For the Lord is there, the Lord of creatures and of my life. He no longer merely looks down from the endless "all in one and once for all" of his eternity upon my constantly changing life that glides by far below him. The eternal has become time, the Son has become man, the eternal purpose of the world, the all-embracing meaningfulness of all reality has become flesh.

Through this fact, that God has become man, time and human life are changed. Not to the extent that he has ceased to be himself, the eternal Word of God himself, with all his splendor and unimaginable bliss. But he has really become human. And now this world and its very destiny concern him. Now it is not only his work, but a part of his very self. Now he no longer watches its course as a spectator; he himself is now within it. What is expected of us is now expected of him; our lot now falls upon him, our earthly joy as well as the wretchedness that is proper to us. Now we no longer need to seek him in the endlessness of heaven, where our spirit and our heart get lost. Now he himself is on our very earth, where he is no better off than we and where he receives no special privilege, but our every fate: hunger, weariness, enmity, mortal terror and a wretched death. That the infinity of God should take upon itself human narrowness, that bliss should accept the mortal sorrow of the earth, that life should take on death — this is the most unlikely truth. But only this — the obscure light of faith — makes our nights bright, only this makes them holy.

God has come. He is there in the world. And therefore everything is different from what we imagine it to be. Time is transformed from its eternal onward flow into an event that with silent, clear resoluteness leads to a definitely determined goal wherein we and the world shall stand before the unveiled face of God. When we say, "It is Christmas," we mean that God has spoken into the world his last, his deepest, his most beautiful word in the incarnate Word, a word that can no longer be revoked because it is God's definitive deed, because it is God himself in the world. And this word means: I love you, you, the world and human beings. This is a wholly unexpected word, a quite unlikely word. For how can this word be spoken when both the human person and the world are recognized as dreadful, empty abysses? But God knows them better than we. And yet he has spoken this word by being himself born as a creature. The very existence of this incarnate Word of love demands that it shall provide, eye to eye and heart to heart, an almost unbelievable fellowship, an astonishing communion between the eternal God and us. Indeed, it says that this communion is already there. This is the word that God has spoken in the birth of his Son.

And now there is stillness in the world only for a little while. The busyness that is proudly called universal history, or one's own life, is only the stratagem of an eternal love that wills to enable the individual to give a free answer to its final word. And in this prolonged short moment of God's silence that is called history after the birth of Christ, the person is supposed to have a chance to speak. In the trembling of his heart that quivers because of God's love, he should tell God, who as man stands beside him in silent expectation, "I" — no, rather he should say nothing to him, but silently give himself to the love of God that is there because the Son is born.

Christmas means that God has come to us, come to us in such a way that from now on, even in his own awesome, glorious splendor, he can only be "at home" with the world and with us. Through the birth of this child everything is already transformed. With the inexorability of love, everything is already pushing out from that inmost center of reality which is the incarnate Word. It is pushing out toward the countenance of God, and now we need not fear that before God's countenance the world will have to be burned to nothing by his consuming fire of holiness and righteousness.

All time is already embraced by the eternity that has itself become time. All tears are dried up at their source, because God himself has wept with them, and has already wiped them from his eyes. All hope is already real possession, because God is already possessed by the world. The night of the world has become bright. God does not allow our stubborn defiance and weakness to be greater than our hearts, and so will not have it be as small as a tiny child who is born and who lies in a crib. Our heart does not want to admit that midnight is already past and that a day without evening already penetrates the night. All bitterness is only the reminder that it is not yet clearly known that the one world-Christmas has dawned; and all the happiness of this earth is only the mysterious confirmation, which most people do not understand, that Christmas is already present.

The feast of Christmas is therefore not poetry and childish romanticism, but the avowal and the faith, which alone justifies a human being, that God has risen up and has already spoken his final word in the drama of history, no matter how much clamor the world keeps up. The celebration of Christmas can only be the echo of that word in the depth of our being by which we speak a believing amen to God's word that has come from his vast eternity into the narrowness of this world, and yet has not ceased to be the word of God's truth and the word of his own blissful love. When not only the glimmer of candles, the joy of children, and the fragrance of the Christmas tree but the heart itself answers God's childlike word of love with a gracious yes, then Christmas really takes place, not only in mood, but in the most unalloyed reality. For this word of the heart is then truly produced by God's holy grace; God's word is then born in our heart, too. God himself then moves into our heart, just as he moved into the world in Bethlehem, just as truly and really, and yet even more intimately. When the heart itself answers, we really open its gates high and wide, and God comes and takes possession of our hearts, just as in the first Christmas he came and took possession of the world.

And now he says to us what he has already said to the world as a whole through his grace-filled birth: "I am there. I am with you. I am your life. I am your time. I am the gloom of your daily routine. Why will you not bear it? I weep your tears — pour yours out to me, my child. I am your joy. Do not be afraid to be happy, for ever since I wept, joy is the standard of living that is really more suitable than the anxiety and grief of those who think they have no hope. I am the blind alleys of all your paths, for when you no longer know how to go any further, then you have reached me, foolish child, though you are not aware of it. I am in your anxiety, for I have shared it by suffering it. And in doing so, I wasn't even heroic according to the wisdom of the world. I am in the prison of your finiteness, for my love has made me your prisoner. When the totals of your plans and of your life's experiences do not balance out evenly, I am the unsolved remainder. And I know that this remainder, which makes you so frantic, is in reality my love, that you do not yet understand. I am present in your needs. I have suffered them and they are now transformed, but not obliterated from my heart. I am in your lowest fall, for today I began to descend into hell. I am in your death, for today I began to die with you, because I was born, and I have not let myself be spared any real part of this death.

"Do not be sorry, as Job was, for those who are born; for all who accept my salvation are born in this holy night because my Christmas embraces all your days and all your nights. I myself — my whole being and my whole personality — are truly engaged in the terrifying adventure that begins with your birth. I tell you, mine was no easier and no less dangerous than yours. I assure you, though, it had a happy ending. Ever since I became your brother, you are as near to me as I am to myself. If, therefore, I, as a creature, want to prove in me and in you, my brothers and sisters, that I, as creator, have not made a hopeless experiment with the human race, who then shall tear my hand away from you? I accepted you when I took my human life to myself. As one of your kind, as a fresh start, I conquered in my failure.

"If you judge the future only according to yourselves, you cannot be pessimistic enough. But do not forget that your real future is my present, the present that began today and shall never again become transitoriness. And so you are certainly planning in a realistic way if you rely on my optimism, which is not utopia but the reality of God. This reality — incomprehensible wonder of my almighty love — I have sheltered, safely and completely, in the cold stable of your world. I am there. I no longer go away from this world, even if you do not see me now. When you, poor mortals, celebrate Christmas, then say to everything that is there and to everything that you are, one thing only — say to me: 'You are here. You have come. You have come into everything. Even into my soul. Even behind the stubbornness of my wickedness, which doesn't want to let itself be pardoned.' Say only one thing, and then it is Christmas for you, too; say only: 'You are here.' No, don't say anything. I am there. And ever since then my love is unconquerable. I am there. It is Christmas. Light the candles. They have more right to exist than all the darkness. It is Christmas, Christmas that lasts forever."

17 • Christmas: The Feast of History*

This brief reflection is not intended to deal directly with the mystery Christians believe and acknowledge and celebrate at Christmas. Instead our reflection concerns the unremarkable fact at first sight that we celebrate Christmas *yearly* and assign the remembrance of the Christmas mystery a definite place in the astronomical, seasonal, and civil calendar. Were we to say something like this is truly obvious, since such celebrations recurring each year belong to the basic condition of human life and religions, then we aren't answering our question, but only making the inquiry more general. One can certainly assume that many of our familiar, yearly secular holidays and celebrations arose in imitation of the church year with its yearly recurring series of Christian feasts — a series of religious feast days with their creative model, in their turn, in the unfolding of festivals in ancient Israel before Jesus.

But if we consider the ancient Jewish and the Christian calendar of feasts more closely, it occurs to us that these yearly feasts celebrate either cyclical events as ever new or unique events that determine in their historical singularity the existence of those who come after. If we celebrate the beginning of spring or the summer solstice; if we celebrate thanksgiving for a harvest; if there is a mother's day, a national day, but also a feast for guardian angels and similar festivals of a lasting religious truth, then the reality being celebrated is itself there as something actually present and is celebrated as such. Something ever valid and so also occurring right now is being celebrated. It is unquestionably understandable that we celebrate something this way, that is, it can be taken into the dimension of human and social expressiveness because it is present now.

As was already the case with some ancient Jewish festivals, however, with properly Christian feasts something entirely different is going on. These feasts do not celebrate the validity of an always permanent

---

Herausforderung des Christen. Meditationen und Reflexionen (Freiburg i. Br.: Herder, 1975), 33–35. Trans. Frederick G. Lawrence, Boston College.

nature, even if moving in a cycle of ever new repetitions; but they celebrate the uniqueness of history: the birth of Jesus under Augustus, his death under Pontius Pilate, and so forth. In these feasts, the celebrants do not remain in their present moment; and they do not make what is always valid in their existence explicit in religious or profane celebrations.

But they turn their gaze back to the historical past; they celebrate the remembrance of an always unique historical event. They do not celebrate the present; they do not proclaim the immediate future; rather, they take up a stance toward an apparently past, always unique event, and they are making room for its meaning and power for their own present and future. They share in the eternal validity of an ever unique historical reality. Neither do they transform this historical reality into an always valid idea for which this historical reality would ultimately be just an instance besides which there are (or there are at least conceivable) also other equally legitimate realizations of the idea; nor do they let this unique historical reality collapse back into an already finished past, in which there is no significance left for now or for the future.

Of its very nature as an ever renewed return of the same, a year's rhythm is primarily only adequate for the first-mentioned kind of human celebration: the celebrative encounter with ever present reality, of something that of itself always enters anew as the same in the phases of our natural living. From the very start, Christianity has resolved upon the celebration of the unique death of its Lord, and upon marking the ever unique events of salvation history within the cyclical rhythms of nature. Moreover, this may seem obvious to us because we are accustomed to this sort of thing already from archaic times, for example, by the yearly celebration of the start of a regime, of a national victory, and so forth. But even if we prescind from the question whether such *profane* celebrations of historical occurrences have their origin in the religious celebration of history experienced as a history of salvation, this specific type of celebration is altogether less than obvious.

To understand this profane kind of celebration here we cannot just consider the nature of human beings that ceases to be such the moment they would stop caring about their historical origins and know themselves as responsible only for the present and the future, but not for the past. Here we can only say: Christians are so very conscious of the lasting validity of unique historical events that, for example, they also realize the past prior to Jesus as codetermined and sustained by the cross and resurrection.

For Christians, history in its uniqueness, and not properly the abstract idea, is the true reality and what is eternal. And so they can celebrate historical events, that is, freely give them power over their own existence. It means at first only human beings' tribute to the natural presuppositions of their historical existence that they celebrate this festive remembrance of history, the events of which are always unique and irrevocable and possess their own rank with the cyclical rhythms of nature, of the year's seasons, and on certain days of the astronomical year. But besides this it can be a confession of hope that totally impersonal, tough, indeed grotesque nature, with its pressures and perishings, is still disposed of in such a way as to enter, once it has been illumined, into the definitiveness of the history of truth and love.

Perhaps as children we have sung, "Every Year the Christ Child Comes." In this song the celebration of Christmas is conceived quite naturally. In truth, on Christmas we celebrate the reality and faith proper to an historical event: that in Jesus, the crucified and risen one, God himself has irreversibly directed history toward the arrival of God in a world definitively completed by truth and love.

18 • Christmas: Grace in the Human Abyss*

It is no easy matter to write a commentary or something like a leading article for Christmas. The hearer or reader will have the same feeling. Every year it is the same thing: a certain amount of "Christmas spirit," a few pious and humanitarian phrases, a few expensive presents and the trouble of having to say thank you for them afterward. And then everything goes on as before.

If one is a Christian, one very definitely has the duty of not being under any illusions about this magical Christmas spirit. For a Christian cannot be a person who hides the pitiful reality of human life under pious phrases. By God, she cannot. For doesn't the Christian hang up on the walls which enclose her life, as a sign of her faith, a cross, a gibbet on which a man is nailed and dying? For her, then, Christmas can only mean the beginning of the life which in this world ends on this cross — or in death or the empty bitterness of total disappointment — it all amounts to the same thing.

After Christmas — this must be said at Christmas — everything goes on as before. We carry on as before. We go forward wonderfully well — to the moon or even farther. And finally to death, but for

*Everyday Faith, 37–42.

a respectable person of East or West it is best not to talk about that, because it isn't done, unless of course one is making an existentialist commotion about it, for there is money in that.

Is one angrily to escape somewhere during these days, then, or calmly to take part in "Christmas" because it is still best, still the most respectable thing, not to show one's innermost feelings? It would be possible, of course, instead of either of these, to do something else. One could in fact consider what Christmas actually means if it is understood in a Christian sense. An answer to that question might be of interest to the non-Christian as well. One might even ask oneself whether after all in one's heart of hearts, officially Christian or not, the unlikely courage to believe in Christmas, the real Christmas is in fact present after all. And this quite apart from whether one admits it or thinks oneself unable to believe.

God made Christmas without consulting us. It follows that it is in fact possible that we believe more than we admit, more than we know in our theoretical opinions about ourselves and our life. How is this? We human beings are of such a kind that we are always beyond and above ourselves. It is our burden and our dignity. We are free and responsible for ourselves; we are those who hope. We are always already beyond and above what can be mentioned, designated, and specified. We live the tangible on the basis of the intangible. We are grounded in the abyss of what cannot be named or expressed.

We can certainly, of course, shut ourselves off and say we can make nothing of it. We can try to stick to what is commonplace and within range, to inspect what light falls on and refuse to turn to the unfathomable light which alone makes visible for us what it shines on. Yet even so mystery permeates our human existence and compels us again and again to turn our eyes toward it: in the joy which has no longer an object, in the anguish which ends the obvious matter-of-factness of our existence, in the love which knows itself unconditional and eternally binding, in the question which takes fright at its own unconditionality and unlimited scope.

In this way we are always finding ourselves facing a mystery which is, which is without limit, which grounds without itself having a ground, which is always there and always withdraws, intangible. We call it God. We point to mystery as such when we say God. When we do not overlook thought because of what is thought of, joy because of what gives joy, responsibility because of what we take responsibility for, unending future because of the present, immeasurable hope because of the object of striving here and now, we are already concerned with God, whether we give to this namelessness this or that name or no name at all.

And if in the depth of our being we have accepted this thinking, loving, hoping human reality despite all the overhasty, impatient hurts and protests on the surface of our existence, then we have by that very fact entered into relations with God, given ourselves over to him. Many will do this even if they think that they do not know God (he must of course always be known as incomprehensible, otherwise something else has been mistaken for him), even if in their mute reverence they do not venture to name him.

In such acceptance of human existence, obediently entrusting itself to mystery, it is possible for what in Christian terminology is called grace to occur: God is mystery, and remains so. But he is the abyss in which the existence of the human being is accepted, he is presence and not simply remoteness, forgiveness and not simply judgment. He fills the unending question of thinking, the immeasurable scope of hope and the infinite demand of love with himself, silent still and in that ground of our being which only opens out to us if we obediently allow ourselves to be encompassed by this mystery, without seeking to master it. If this happens, however, Christmas is already within us, that coming of God which Christianity acknowledges always to occur by the grace of God in every human being who does not refuse it by that guilt which is both terror of God and proud self-sufficiency.

But we are men and women of history, of the tangible here and now. And this coming of God, his action in us, was intended to be tangible and irrevocable, irrevocably and tangibly historical both as God's self-giving and as God's coming definitively accepted by the human person. Consequently, humankind has experienced in human history this coming of God as definitive, unsurpassable and irrevocable. In Jesus of Nazareth. In him surrender to the infinite mystery as such is present as humankind's action. And this itself, like everything that involves freedom and decision, is grace. In him, God as ineffable mystery (and remaining so) has expressed himself as Word wholly and irrevocably. In him that Word is "there" as spoken to all of us, as the God of inexpressibly close presence and forgiveness.

Here question and answer, unmixed and inseparable, have become one. The one person is there in whom God and man are one, without detriment to one or the other.

Even when someone who is still far from any explicit and verbally formulated revelation accepts his human reality in silent patience, or rather in faith, hope, and love (however these may be named), as a mystery which loses itself in the mystery of eternal love and bears life in the very midst of death, that person says yes to Jesus Christ even if he does not realize it. For if someone lets go and jumps, she falls into the depth which is actually there, not merely the depth she has measured.

Anyone who accepts her human reality — that is indescribably difficult and it remains uncertain whether we really do so — has accepted the Son of man, because in him God accepted humanity.

We read in scripture that those who love their neighbor have fulfilled the law. This is the ultimate truth because God himself has become that neighbor, and so in every neighbor it is always he, one who is nearest and most distant, who is accepted and loved. If we accept the silent mystery which encompasses our existence and surrounds us as what is remote and yet overwhelmingly close, if we accept it as saving presence and tender love given without reserve, if we have the courage to understand ourselves in this way, which can only be done in grace and faith, if we recognize the ground of this presence and its absolute promise and advent in him whom we call the Godman, then we have made the Christmas experience of grace in faith.

If in this way some have courage explicitly to believe in the truth of Christmas, if the others silently accept the unfathomable depth of their human reality which is namelessly filled with joyful hope and are themselves accepted by the first as "anonymous" Christians, then all can celebrate Christmas together. The apparently superficial and conventional business of Christmas then acquires truth and depth after all. The apparent falsehood of the whole business is then not the ultimate truth about it. Behind it stands the holy and silent truth that God has in fact come and celebrates Christmas with us.

So we are more honest, more profoundly true, if we go beyond an initial, only too justified skepticism in regard to ordinary conventional Christmas, and celebrate it candidly without taking our own skepticism seriously, as the sign that God's advent among us long ago outstripped all our plans and all our disappointments. Then if after Christmas things go on as before, it nevertheless remains true that God has accepted us. And the abysses within us are filled with his grace.

19 • Holy Night*

Why do we call the feast we are keeping today a "sacred night"? Historically speaking, of course, we do not know for certain that Jesus was born at night. The account of the shepherds who were keeping the night watches over their flocks and heard the heavenly message of

---

*Everyday Faith, 31–36.

the savior's birth is not of course in itself a conclusive proof that Jesus himself was born at night. And yet Christendom has always thought of this blessed birth of the redeemer as taking place at night. The German language has even incorporated this conviction into the name it gives the feast: *Weih-nacht*, "sacred night." Why?

Night for the human person has two aspects. Like almost all the factors in human existence, it has a double meaning, is ambiguous. Night can be something uncanny and somber, the time when no one can work, as Jesus says in scripture; it is felt as akin to death; it is the time of what is undefined, uncertain and dangerous, of what is obscure and impalpable. Consequently, in the religious domain night can have this symbolic meaning. In scripture "night" stands for the time of unbelief and sin, the time of judgment and divine visitation. Therefore Christians must be children of the day, they must shine like stars in the night so that they are not taken by surprise by the judge who comes like a thief in the night. Consequently, we must watch, we may not sleep, we must rise from sleep and walk as though in the daytime.

But for human sensibility, even as this finds expression in scripture, night has yet another aspect. It is the time of silence and concentrated strength, self-contained, ready to wait and allow things to mature. It is in the middle of the night that the cry is heard that the bridegroom is coming. Night in scripture is the time of heavenly dreams. Because night is the time of liberation from the enslaving impressions and ties of superficial everyday routine, it is a time of prayer, and so Jesus spends whole nights in converse with God. The night can be affectionately regarded as God's creature, so that the psalmist (74:16) can pray: "Yours is the day, yours also is the night." And Daniel (3:71) summons the night to praise God, just as of course, according to the psalmist, every night hands on to the next the message of the glory of God, for already in the psalm (19:3), the heavens by their silent grandeur and immeasurable vastness speak to the pious mind of God's greatness.

Why can we feel about the night in such different ways? We experience it as a beginning, as something still indefinite, which has still to be followed by what is really meant and decisive: the light of day. Beginning and possibility, however, are ambiguous; a good promise which is not yet fulfilled, a vast, free possibility which has not yet found its realization, the plan which is splendid but has not yet been carried out. All that is necessarily ambiguous: promising and threatened and threatening at one and the same time, something provisional which may still set off for distant goals but which is still uncertain of arriving.

Now if there is a moment in history, the history of the individual and of humankind, which resembles an absolutely first beginning, full of incalculable possibilities and promise, a beginning which conceals everything mysteriously within it, and if this starting point of an ineffable, infinite beginning even bears within it the certainty of its own realization, is already sure of its triumph, is already as much fulfillment as promise, then that moment would deserve to be called the holy night. Night, because a beginning, holy night because a blessed and unconquerable beginning; of such a beginning we would have to say: holy night, sacred night.

And so we sing: "Silent night, holy night." Everywhere in the world these words are sung for this feast. And it was not by chance that in the fourth century this feast was placed at the season when in nature too the sun, as it were, begins its course anew. At that time they fixed the beginning of the "sun of justice" as the prophet calls our savior, on the day of the pagan *natalis solis invicti*, the festival of the birth of the "unconquered sun-god."

With a sacred right. For this hour *is* the holy and sacred night. Faith tells the Christians: that was the beginning. There God himself came gently forth from the terrifying radiance in which he dwells as God and Lord, and came to us; he quietly entered the poor dwelling of our earthly existence and was found as a man; he began where we begin, quite poor, vulnerable, quite childlike and gentle, quite helpless. He who is the infinite, distant future which of ourselves we never reach because it seems to retreat farther and farther away as we hurry toward it on the hard roads of life, he himself has approached us, arrived among us, because otherwise we should never have found our way to him.

He has accompanied us on our way to him so that this may find a blessed end, because the very end itself has become our beginning. God is near; his eternal word of mercy is where we are; it is a pilgrim on our paths, experiences our joy and our distress, lives our life and dies our death. He has brought his eternal life quietly and gently into this world and its death. He has redeemed us, for he shared our lot. He made our beginning his own, followed the path of our destiny and so opened it up into the infinite expanses of God. And because he accepted us irrevocably, because God's Word will never cease to be man, this beginning which is ours and his is a beginning of indestructible promises, and his silent beginning by night is a holy and sacred night.

This also shows how we must celebrate Christmas. As the mystery of the holy night. Our heart must be quiet, recollected and gentle, unreservedly open like the heart of a child which does not yet shut itself to any of the possibilities of its existence but is unsuspectingly ready for them all. What is in the background of our being, its breadth and range beyond our control, must silently prevail in us, just as the night — by causing what is manageable and measurable to fade — brings the far distance close, without narrowing it.

We must dare to admit this nocturnal silence into our interior selves, by abandoning that flight into business, chatter, and fuss by which we try to run away from ourselves and the mystery above us because, unaccustomed to it, we are frightened even by the great mystery of infinite love. We ought not to profane the sacred night on which our life too was hallowed, by festivities which are too facile. The familiar, childlike character of this feast which is of course quite appropriate to such a day, ought nevertheless to remain transparent to the ineffable mystery which alone makes human beings profoundly familiar with one another and gives them the promise of eternal youth.

Christmas is celebrated, as it must be, if it is not to degenerate into a purely secular festival, only by those who allow to recede — in the silence of the sacred night of quiet detachment and submissive devotion — in their own hearts that multiplicity of things, persons, and endeavors which at other times cloud the view of infinity. Sometimes, at least for a little while, they extinguish the earthly lights which usually hide the stars of heaven, and allow themselves to be addressed by the unutterable, wordless presence of God which speaks by its own silence, if we have ears for it. We should feel as we do on a clear winter's night when we go out under the starry sky; the light of human presence and of the safety of home still follows us, but above us is the sky and we are conscious of the silence of the night, which at other times may appear to us sinister and terrifying, as the quiet presence of the infinite mystery of our existence, which is both saving love and immeasurable grandeur.

It is the holy night of Christmas! The eternal future has entered our time. Its radiance still dazzles us, so that we think it is night. But at all events it is a blessed night, a night in which there is already warmth and light, which is beautiful, welcoming, and secure by reason of the eternal day which it bears hidden within it. It is a silent, holy night for us, however, only if we admit the holy silence of this night into our inner selves, only if our heart too keeps watch in solitude.

It can do so easily. For such solitude and quiet are not hard. The only difficulty about it is that of all lofty things which are simple and great. For of course we *are* solitary. There exists in our heart an interior land where we are alone, to which no one finds his way but God. This innermost, unfrequented chamber of our heart is really there — the only question is whether we ourselves avoid it foolishly out of guilty fear, because no one and no familiar things of this earth can accompany us if we enter it. Let us enter it quietly and shut the door behind us. Let us listen to the unutterable melody which sounds in the silence of that night.

The silent and solitary soul sings here to the God of the heart its quietest and most ardent song. And it can have confidence that he hears it. For this song no longer has to seek a beloved God beyond the stars in that inaccessible light in which he dwells and which makes him invisible to all. Because of Christmas, because the Word was made flesh, God is near and the quietest word in the stillest room of the heart, the word of love, comes to his ear and his heart. And those who have entered into themselves even when it is night, hear in this nocturnal quiet in the depth of the heart God's gentle word of love. One must be calm, not afraid of the night, hold one's peace. Otherwise we hear nothing. For the ultimate is only spoken in the silence of the night, now that in our night of life, through the gracious coming of the Word, there has come to be Christmas, holy night, silent night.

20 • Christmas: The Great Joy*

Let us keep Christmas, a festival of faith and of love for the Word who became flesh, a festival also of love for one another because human beings can love others since God himself became man. Let us worship God because he loved human persons and his poor flesh so much that he placed it imperishably for all eternity in the very midst of the blazing flame of his Godhead. Incomprehensible God, adventurer of love! We had thought that the human being, pitiable as he is, could only be a primitive, unsuccessful trial model for the superman who has still to come; it is hard for us to bear with ourselves — and especially with others — just as we are. Not unreasonably, for the human being is difficult to endure, for she is a continual failure and falls from one extreme to another.

And yet, as the church sings in its noblest hymn, he did not disdain the Virgin's womb. He himself came into his creation, into humanity. If it were not for this fact of facts, would we have the courage to believe that God was successful with his work? He himself has entered into all the narrow limits of human beings which it would seem could only exist at an infinite distance from him: his mother's body, a small defeated native country under foreign occupation, a desperate state of the age, a narrow-minded milieu, unsuccessful politics, a body marked out for

---

*Everyday Faith, 28–30.

death, the prison of incomprehension, the monotony of the working day, of complete failure, the dark night of abandonment by God and of death. He spared himself nothing.

The narrow confines, however, into which God himself has entered, must have an issue. It must be worthwhile being a human being, if God was not satisfied to be in himself but also willed in addition to be one of these human beings, and if that was not too dangerous or too trivial for him. Humankind is not a herd, but a sacred family, if God himself is a member of it as a brother. The tragedy of its history must after all have a blessed outcome, if God does not just observe this hardly divine comedy unmoved from the throne of his infinity but takes part in it himself, as seriously as all the rest of us, who have to do so whether we want to or not.

The so-called genuine reality both of the embittered and disillusioned and of the superficial bon vivant is reduced to a mere semblance which only unbelieving fools take in deadly earnest or with greedy seriousness, now that God himself has become the true reality behind and in the midst of this appearance. Eternity is already in the heart of time, life is at the center of death, truth is stronger than lies, love more powerful than hatred, the wickedness of human beings already irrevocably conquered by God's grace.

Christianity is indeed an optimism about human beings such as only God could conceive. It is not surprising that it seems so unlikely to us. There is no need for the superman if God himself became man. Mere humanism is long since obsolete if in the Son of the Father and of the Virgin humanity is to become God, as the fathers say, if the human being is infinitely more than human. Human beings can be exacting; in fact, properly understood, they can never be demanding enough in regard to God; there is only one thing which they may not do: will to be less than brothers and sisters of the eternal Word of the Father who became flesh.

Up, then, and let us be kind at least on this day and this holy night. Perhaps we shall then see that it is not really so difficult, and then we shall also contrive to be so in the new year too. Let us be kind! We have no right to demand a better world if we do not begin the improvement ourselves in our own heart. Let us be kind today! After all we do not have to be malicious and bitter and defend ourselves greedily and anxiously against others.

God has come. No one can take him from us and he is everything. He is our brother. So it is right to bear in our own heart our brother's love of humanity and his kindness, to be gentle and forgiving, hopeful, serene and cheerful, unsuspicious and loyal. God himself has tried this and has told us that it works. His experience is more decisive and credible than ours: we can be better than we think. More can be made of us than we suspect. If Christ is formed in us, we can never form too high a conception of ourselves. We are more than we can imagine.

So let us sing with the gaiety of a heart which is set free for God's eternal youth. The darkness has become bright. God himself has prepared a festival for himself which did not exist before in his heaven: he has become man. Heaven and earth ring out in God's silent, holy night which is lighter than the gloomy day of men and women: glory to God, peace to those in whom God was so well-pleased. Let us fall on our knees and joyfully read the Gospel: At that time a decree went forth from the emperor Augustus....

21 • Christmas: The Answer of Silence*

Letter to a Friend

Christmas? One says the word almost with despair, for can one really explain to anyone nowadays what it means to celebrate Christmas? It is obvious that the feast is not merely the Christmas tree, presents, family gatherings, and other emotionally appealing customs which are themselves only kept up with a certain skepticism. But what more is it? Let me attempt to give you something like a recipe.

The great experiences of life are of course one's destiny, a gift of God and of his grace, but they nevertheless mostly only fall to the lot of those who are prepared to receive them. Otherwise the star rises above their lives but they are blind to it. For the sublime hours of wisdom, art, and love, we must prepare ourselves wholly with soul and body. So it is with the great days on which we celebrate our redemption. Do not leave them to chance; do not drift into them listlessly in an everyday frame of mind. Prepare yourself; determine to prepare yourself — that is the first thing.

Another thing. Have the courage to be alone. Only when you have really achieved that, when you have done it in a Christian way, can you hope to present a Christmas heart, that is, a gentle, patient, courageous, delicately affectionate heart, to those whom you are striving to love. That gift is the real Christmas tree gift, otherwise all other presents are

---

*Everyday Faith, 23–27.

merely futile expense which can be indulged in at any time. First of all, then, persevere for a while on your own. Perhaps you can find a room where you can be on your own. Or you may know a quiet path or a lonely church.

Then do not talk to yourself the way you do with others, the people we argue and quarrel with even when they are not there. Wait, listen, without expecting any unusual experience. Do not pour yourself out in accusation, do not indulge yourself. Allow yourself to meet yourself in silence. Perhaps then you will have a terrible feeling. Perhaps you will realize how remote all the people are whom you are dealing with every day and to whom you are supposed to be bound by ties of love. Perhaps you will perceive nothing but a sinister feeling of emptiness and deadness.

Bear with yourself. You will discover how everything that emerges in such silence is surrounded by an indefinable distance, permeated as it were by something that resembles a void. Do not yet call it God! It is only what points to God and, by its namelessness and limitlessness, intimates to us that God is something other than one more thing added to those we usually have to deal with. It makes us aware of God's presence, if we are still and do not flee in terror from the mystery which is present and prevails in the silence — do not flee even to the Christmas tree or to the more tangible religious concepts which can kill religion.

But that is only the beginning, only the preparation of a Christmas celebration for you. If you persevere in this way and, by keeping silence, allow God to speak, this silence which cries out is strangely ambiguous. It is both fear of death and the promise of the infinity which is close to you in benediction. And these are too close together and too similar for us to be able of ourselves to interpret this infinity which is remote and yet close. But precisely in this strangeness and mystery we learn to understand ourselves rightly and to accept the dear familiarity of this strange mystery. And that is precisely the message of Christmas: that in reality God is close to you, just where you are, if you are open to this infinity. For then God's remoteness is at the same time his unfathomable presence, pervading all things.

He is there with tender affection. He says: Do not be afraid. He is within, in the prison. Trust to this close presence, it is not emptiness. Cast off, and you will find. Relinquish and you are rich. For in your interior experience you are no longer dependent on what is tangible and solid, what by affirming itself isolates itself, what can be held fast. You have not merely things of that kind, for infinity has become presence. *That* is how you must interpret your interior experience and in that way know it as the high festival of the divine descent of eternity into time, of infinity into the finite, of God's marriage with his creature. Such a festival takes place in you — the theologians aridly call it "grace"; it takes place in you when you are still and wait and — believing, hoping, and loving — interpret correctly, that is, in the light of Christmas, what it is you experience.

It is only this experience of the heart which brings proper understanding of the message of the Christmas faith: God has become man. Of course we repeat that so easily. We think of the incarnation as though it were a sort of disguising of God, so that fundamentally God remains purely and simply God and we do not rightly know whether he is really here where we are. God is human — that does not mean he has ceased to be God in the measureless plenitude of his glory. Nor does it mean that what is human about him is something which does not really concern him and is only something assumed accessorily which says nothing really about him but only something about us. "God is man" really says something about God.

God's human nature must not be equated with God's divinity in total identity of kind nor yet simply be juxtaposed with God as a reality which perpetually relapses into its own mere identity. We must not link it with him merely verbally by an empty "and." If God shows this human nature of his, it always comes to us in such a way that *he himself* is there. Because we only juxtapose divinity and humanity in the incarnate Word of the Father, instead of understanding that they both spring from the one selfsame ground, we are constantly in danger of missing each time the point where the blessed mystery of Christmas finds the place in our self-transcending human reality at which it fits into our life and our history as our salvation.

Do not forget that, as faith testifies, Jesus is true man, that is, one like you and me, a finite, free person obediently accepting the unfathomable mystery of his or her being; one who must answer and does answer, who is questioned and hears the question, the question which is infinite and to which answer is only given in that ultimate act of the heart which surrenders itself lovingly and obediently to the infinite mystery, in an act in which acceptance takes place in virtue of the very reality which is accepted. That was the case also for him whose beginning you are going to celebrate. Because he accepted as a human being, you too can dare to do what he did: quietly and with faith to say "Father" to incomprehensibility, to accept it, not as deadly remoteness and consuming judgment on our wretchedness, but as measureless, merciful presence. For he is both God and man: giver, gift, and reception, call and answer in one.

It would be good, then, if we were to call on the experience of our heart in order to form some faint conception of what is meant by the incarnation of the eternal God. It would be well if this were to be done in that silence in which alone we are present to ourselves in self-awareness. Such silence, correctly understood in faith in the Christmas message, is an experience of what is infinite in human reality, an experience of the person's being which tells us something which is only so because God himself became human. We would experience ourselves differently if God had not been born a man.

If we accept the silent tremendous reality which surrounds us like remote distance, yet close and overwhelming, if we accept it as saving presence and a tender unreserved love; if we have the courage to understand ourselves in a way which can only be done in grace and faith — whether this is realized or not — then we have had the Christmas experience of grace in faith. It is very simple but it is the peace which is promised in their goodwill to those of God's good pleasure.

22 • St. Sylvester: The Year's Spiritual Balance Sheet*

31 December

This is the last day of a year, so it is appropriate for us to take leave of the year in a Christian way. Each in the depth of her heart must take her leave of herself for herself. For each person is different from the next. Every year that someone has lived through is therefore different from that of any other. God leads each by her own path. And in his infinity, in the incalculable plenitude of the possibilities which he contains within him and which as the creator and Lord of our life he can distribute, he is not a God who is compelled to treat two people precisely alike, even once, as though, so to speak, he could not think of anything different.

And yet the year of each human being in another sense is precisely the same as that of his neighbor and of everyone else. For it is past. That at least is common to them all. We are taking leave of the past year. We are doing it together in our churches in the community of the one body of grace. We are leaving a year behind us with its many days, its work, its cares, its disappointments, its bitternesses, with the plans we have had and which have perhaps come entirely to nothing or have only partly been realized. We are leaving it behind with our

*Everyday Faith, 47–51.

guilt, our failure, in fact with everything that our niggardly heart has made of the year.

To whom are we to give this year of which we are taking leave, which we are leaving behind? Is it still possible for us to give it to anyone? Is it not simply gone, nonexistent? Is it not obliterated, departed, by the mere fact that we are taking leave of it and that it is no longer within the range of our possibilities of decision in the way it once was, when it was lived through, day by day and hour by hour?

On the contrary, if we see it in a Christian way, if we take God into account, if we recognize ourselves for what we are, spiritual beings of eternity, we must in fact say that the past year is the year which has been gained, retained, the irrevocable, enduring year. The years which we have lived through are our years. Whether the coming years will also be our years, God knows, we do not. The past is ours, as Christians we can calmly say this, and we can hope and wish that God will give us a long future in this life, this finite life, and that this too will become our own by enduring even while it appears to pass away.

Who preserves the past, enduring, irrevocable year for us? God. He has entered it in what scripture calls the "book of life." He knows it, and in his sight it remains present. What we ourselves *are,* we in our spiritual reality, in our historical-spiritual physiognomy, what we have indelibly stamped into our spiritual reality in our life and during this past year — this God has inscribed in the book of life. Because in this way this year is still there, in an hour of farewell such as this, we can still make of it what it ought to be.

Let us bid farewell to the old year thankfully so that it may become what it ought to be, the gift of the grace of God. For God has given us all the days of this year. And if we have truly accepted them as gifts of his love — and it is always within our power to do this — they have been blessed days, days of grace and salvation.

We must never think of ourselves so sullenly, wearily, skeptically, or morosely that this brooding actually becomes a mistrustful way of thinking about God himself. If we were only to say that we have been poor, failures, burdened, weary, afraid, that we have been adequate neither to our life nor to God's call, then we would perhaps have said something true. But if as Christians we were to say no more than this about ourselves and our past year, we should be unjust to God.

Has he not preserved us in his grace? Has he not repeatedly given us the blessed body of his Son? Isn't his Holy Spirit in our hearts? Have we not after all borne God's burden through the year, though perhaps only with difficulty and groaning under it? Has God's grace not done good to others even through us? For that matter we cannot say that the good that we did not find difficult to do was no true goodness in the eyes of God; and it is not even necessarily true that we have often or mostly omitted the good which we found difficult, except when it was forced from us by God through the hardships of life.

Have we not resigned ourselves even after some grumbling and protest to much that we found hard, and accepted it? And that means, even if we do not very explicitly realize it, that we have accepted God, because it is only possible calmly to accept what is deadly by reaching out to true unlimited life. If we had not done that, we should not now, on the last evening of the year, have come before the face of God at all, and in that case we should certainly not be able to look back on this year, and could not bless it.

But because by God's grace it was what it was as we lived through it, because despite everything it was more God's gracious deed in us than our failure, we can bless it, we must and may do so. We can take leave of this year gratefully and entrust it to the grace and love of God, the love of the God who is eternity and who preserves for us for our eternity what we are taking our leave of today and tomorrow. What we give in gratitude, God receives in grace, and what is so accepted by him is redeemed and made holy, blessed and set free. And so it remains for eternity: a year of ours which is saved and acquired forever.

And then we go on and we take with us from this past year our old selves with the old tasks, the old cares, the old burdens and anxieties, the old fear which stands somewhere in our souls too, with the feeling of being poor and of having to ask every day for bread and for strength to endure at least for a day.

But even if now as we are taking our leave of the old year, we are not yet looking forward into the new, we can nevertheless take ourselves heartened into the new year. Even just as we are, for simply like that we are the creatures of God the eternal Father, the work of his hands. He made us. He takes responsibility for what he has made. He answers for world history and the life of each one of us. He has encompassed us with his goodness, his love, and fidelity. If we take with us into the new year the burden of our past, ourselves with all our cares, with all our weakness and weariness, God, faithful and good, goes with us. And the burden which we go on carrying into the new year is not greater than we can bear. Even if it were to crush us, God would receive us into his own blessed happiness. And what seemed the ultimate pain and the ultimate torment, in reality would simply be relief from all burdens and entry into God's incomprehensible life.

We do not bear more than we are able to bear. If we have the impression that what was light and joyous in the old year remains behind and its burden comes with us, let us say as we take leave of the old year: "My God, you are coming with me and so I will gladly take with me from the old year everything which I cannot simply leave behind as yours, for you to preserve for me as my eternal life."

So let us bid farewell to the past year. It was a year of the Lord, a year of his grace, even a year of growth in the interior life, even if we did not perceive this, because it is in our weakness that God's strength must triumph. And so at the end of the year we can all truly praise God and thank and glorify him, for he is good and his mercy endures forever.

23 • New Year's Day*

Today, dear Christians, we celebrate New Year's Day. Even though the liturgy celebrates the Solemnity of Mary, Mother of God and the Giving of the Name Jesus, let us not hesitate to use the secular marking of a new year to stimulate us to solidly Christian thoughts. After all, whatever is human is also Christian. Since we, too, are human, this is New Year's Day for us, too. As far as we are concerned, the year begins on 1 January rather than on the first Sunday of Advent. (Historians of the liturgy are not yet sure whether the church year begins with Advent or not.)

In the business world, the first few days of the new year are given over to the closing and balancing of the books. If in an agraphon† the Lord says that we are supposed to be good money changers, then on New Year's we may be permitted to try to take something like a "balance" of our whole life. We can attempt it, for in our time — on New Year's Eve — we old people are quite alone; that night the young people are somewhere else. We can, then, calmly look back over the many years that we have already lived; the present day warns us of their fleetingness, and of their significance.

In festive seasons such as this one, we are inclined to let past and present become glazed over by a cheerful glitter of holiday ideals. But this is dangerous, because it easily turns into a sham. When we once pass the peak of life, nobody asks us about our ideals; but rather they ask about our accomplishments: not about what we would like to do, but about what we do. And, at our age, we are no longer readily given the chance still to become what we are not yet.

So there is really nothing left for us to do except to draw up a kind of "balance" of our life, sensibly and seriously. We do this with the ex-

---

*The Eternal Year, 27–39.

†See, Joachim Jeremias, Unknown Sayings of Jesus (London: S.P.C.K., 1964), 76–78. —Trans. ed.

pectation that during the coming year many addresses may be crossed off the mailing list. We do this with the uneasy feeling — is it hope or fear? — that everything can still change, because we certainly have not carefully looked into and around all the nooks of our journey through life. Moreover, in spite of the experience we have had of ourselves, we still do not really know who we now actually are. Dear Lord! what surprises can life still hold, what surprises can we still try to get ready for? We draw up this balance with the probability (which almost borders on certainty) that in death we shall be what we now already are, with the certainty, then, that we are old. Yes, my friends, this magnificent insight, that we are old, shall be all that I as the "examiner of the books" shall be able to add to our "balance." But it seems to me that this fact is important, and obscure enough, to permit me a few minutes of your time.

We are already rather old. Now, certainly, it is hardly deniable that this is so in the externals, in business and professional life. Death is always close to us, but not everyone lives as if he were close to death. We have already moved perceptibly closer to death. We are getting old. We no longer agree so readily with the opinions that we formed just yesterday. We are beginning to cherish rest, peace, and calm, and we are annoyed when anything happens that we aren't used to. "Enthusiastic" words inspire us less than they used to, and "profound" thoughts often seem to tax our strength beyond endurance. When we declare that something is disgraceful or shocking, our very declaration often amounts to an endorsement. The charming wonderment of a young mind, which used to be in us, has been transformed into a vague feeling of unfamiliarity toward everything. Everything is familiar to us, and we have already experienced everything; yet somehow it is hopeless, and terribly repelling. It is as if all things are still under control, yet they provoke us to irritation. We have been asked too many questions, and are now beginning to turn in upon ourselves as if threatened.

We have become unfeeling toward reality; it seems to be waiting gradually for us to bid it farewell. Our mind still works on: we read, we listen, we talk, and we try to keep on studying. These demands are tedious, but somehow we don't like to admit it. Indeed, we even have the impression that we could keep on living, and we would like to keep on living. We think that the trees we planted are perhaps just now beginning to bear good fruit, and so it would not be so easy for us to depart this life right now. But even if we were permitted to stay awhile, all this would still continue on in the same way. So it remains true: we are slowly getting old and tired. We feel as if we "still" have vigorous strength on hand, just as the afternoon is beautiful, because it is not yet evening, even though the afternoon secretly bears the evening within itself. Nothing is to be said against all this. We have neither to complain about this old age nor apologize for it. For its burden is obvious, and we are familiar with its blessing, too.

But (and this is the really alarming question of our old age) have we not also become old and tired in that "inner" person that Paul speaks of? "Though our outer nature is wasting away, our inner nature is being renewed every day" (2 Cor 4:16). Isn't our life's experience just the opposite (and this is our secret worry)? Though the outer nature is still quite well preserved, the inner nature is decaying more and more day by day. Hasn't our inner nature, too, become old and tired? Doesn't our spiritual "nature" disappoint us more and more?

At some time or another in the past, when we consciously set about becoming human beings and Christians, did we not fancy that the coming life would be more beautiful, more adventurous, more fruitful?

Perhaps we once wished to become "holy"; perhaps not. In any case, even if we can now no longer bring ourselves to use this word in so carefree a manner as before, and even if a certain embarrassment creeps over us when a preacher tosses this word off so calmly, in younger days we did not think this way. The only thing that we can say is what we might have done and should have done, and what we still should do and — yes, this is just the point (may I say it softly?) — still should *will* to do. Dare I still, right now, say that we *will* it, when we were really supposed to have become it? In bygone days, we wanted to become holy. Once we desired to wear ourselves out completely for God's honor and for the kingdom of heaven, we wanted to burn our life in the ardent flame of love. And we did not become holy.

We have certainly become more holy in the years of our life that we review in memory. We have worked. And because we worked — *mirabile dictu* — we even really forgot ourselves once in a while and loved God, and worked for his glory through what happened to us. God has so often met us in his sacraments. Why should we think that the selfishness of our heart in its secret pride is so powerful that it could plug all the cracks against the pressure of his grace? We have experienced the ups and downs of life. We have tasted its bitterness. Why should the scorching, pitiless summer have brought only aridity and not even a little fruit? Finally, hasn't God-given contrition kept the harvest of our work quite unsoiled even if the abyss of guilt once swallowed it up? No, once more we want to be simple and modest in the trials that confront us. We want to shun the secret fancies (the human being's ultimate pride) that our evil stubbornness could be victorious over God's gloriously strong love, which, when it will, dissolves even the obstinate insolence of the heart. We also want to let him be greater in our life than our barren heart and admit that he can reap a harvest even out of the stony field of our soul, a harvest that praises the power of his grace. We have become holier.

But we haven't become holy. Not because we haven't worked any miracles or converted any nations or directed the inexorable stream of universal history into another bed. But rather because we haven't loved God as we really should, with our whole heart and with all our strength. We cannot yet forego this duty. We cannot be satisfied with ourselves yet. Our heart doesn't love without measure and without bound as it could love and must love. It loves a little, yes; but a little in this matter is almost worse than nothing. For the heart that completely denies itself still hasn't found its master. One thing is still left; the heart must surrender itself entirely and without division.

But who will gather up this divided, disunited heart and make it sincere, so that it can surrender itself to God, all at once, without division? Alas! our poor dilapidated heart! It is so strange: it yearns a little for stronger love, and conceals a wicked annoyance at the boundless demands of love; and both of these together are covered over by a feeling of weakness and feebleness. The heart of someone who is growing old, and who did not become holy, feels like this. The heart is well disposed, but it feels too keenly its weakness. The real opportunities for unconditional, boundless love (can we want to love any other way), the inevitable opportunities that are sent to the human person — not chosen by him — no longer present themselves. Did we really waste the best hours of our life, the precious opportunities for loving God? Perhaps we have not even noticed when and where they moved through our life. Are they irretrievably lost, so that we are left only with sadness? Perhaps resignation to what we are is now the best thing for us, a resignation that silently adores God, prostrate at his feet. What we could have been and have not become will then simply disappear into his fathomless will. *Plorenus coram Domini qui fecit nos* — we shall weep in the presence of the Lord who made us. Is this the answer?

But suppose we should now admit that we have refused opportunities; suppose we confess that we have neglected them; suppose we admit that we have been dull, easygoing servants? All this is fine. But if we admit this simply because it is the right thing to do, without knowing whether we are really contrite or just cowards, then we would be no better off. For even while we were admitting this we would be saddened by the knowledge that even our repentance does not truly purify the inner nature, because it is only a part of what we have become over the year — old and tired and somewhat bitter in the "inner nature." In this case, even our repentance would be ourselves all over again; it would be the repentance of the subdued that leaves one unchanged.

Yes, that is the way it is; even life in the Holy Spirit seems to have fallen into the clutches of the mortal law of decay and of death. And if we answer, "It's not a law, but guilt," then this harshest of judgments would only help us if we could somehow get rid of this guilt. But this seems to be not only our guilt but also our punishment, and we do not quite know how to get rid of it without thereby denying the guilt.

Is there no consolation in this balance? If we only knew whether we should really seek consolation after all! Perhaps it would be better to weep quietly and without hope, not letting ourselves be consoled until the day of the Lord comes. For on that day we wretched, woebegone beggars, with our empty hands and our lazy hearts, we who do not even know whether we are worthy of pity or contempt, will find the mercy of the Lord, because his merciful love pardons boundlessly and beyond all expectations.

Is our consolation to be precisely this: plainly and honestly to admit that our wretchedness in all its bitterness is the end result of our life? We will perhaps express it thus: "Father, receive me only as one of your meanest servants, me, the lazy and stubborn servant. In your kingdom give me only the crumbs from the table. Your servant should have earned your kingdom through the sheer dazzling workings of your grace. But now my last deed, all that's left to me, is to bow down mutely before you in my darkness, the darkness of one who has squandered grace. Whatever deeds and works I could have offered you from the vessel of my heart, as my meritorious earning of your kingdom, would always have been your grace, because you alone, through the Holy Spirit, bring such works to realization. But now my heart remains almost empty; I have wasted all that you gave me. This chasm of my being praises your loftiness, and even my tears for myself give witness to the splendor of the love you wanted to send me, that I have squandered. But your servant must confess to you that there is too much yearning for you in his heart for him not to want to welcome you, with tears of joy, as your gift. Merely because he has to welcome it as a boundless gift from you is no reason for him not to want it. It is your gift, you who are love, the love that exists only in you, the love that crowns the wretched person, and — wonder of wonders — that gratefully accepts a heart just so long as it is only there, and willing to let itself be accepted, because you are the one accepting it."

Is such a confession our consolation, our sole consolation over the meager balance of our lives? Is this perhaps even *the* consolation, the genuine good fortune, the only genuine faith in the mercy of the Lord? For in each case a human being must once and for all leap away from herself, she must will to rely upon herself no longer, she must set herself free. Even when she boasts about the grace that actually elevated her, even this boasting is a praise of grace. And we can only do this if we have taken hold of grace in order to set it free, received it in order to pour it out as a sacrifice of praise before God, and thus to become poor. But doesn't this happen more readily, indeed doesn't it happen — for us sinners who can be poor in spirit only if we really possess nothing — only if grace is to be had in weeping because we have refused to cooperate, and in grieving because we have frivolously wasted grace? Is the spirit allotted to us except in the bitterness of being flesh, is life allotted except in the darkness of death? Isn't the balance of despondency therefore the best profit for sinners — and when weren't we sinners?

But, dear Lord, isn't this consolation too subtle, too crafty? Isn't it really the ultimate devilishness of our heart — of our heart that really believes that it sees through the bitter experience of our wretchedness and emptiness, and understands that it is just a pious game of God's love? In regard to this consolation, do we not think in the deepest abyss of our heart that God frightens us only so that his consolation may afterward seem more blessed to us? Do we not fancy that he makes us poor only that we may afterward find the kingdom of his grace more glorious; do we not imagine that he lets us fall into sin and the refusal of his grace only so that he may be able to try out the generosity of his love? Do we not think this way? Indeed, doesn't this consolation ultimately mean that we have secretly told ourselves: "Be reasonable, give in, repent and admit your wretchedness in order to please God, so that he may have the joy of being generous and merciful"? With this subtle, wily rhetoric of ours, haven't we lied about God's judgment and about our refusal of his grace, about our refusal that did not have to be, but that did happen, that is irremediable and is not the way to obtain God's grace?

God, have mercy on us! How mad our thinking is! How is God's grace supposed to be recognized as grace without doing violence to grace in the process? How is guilt to be acknowledged in the act of repentance, without making guilt and repentance into a secret trap, which ensnares and clutches God's grace all the more surely, the more absolutely it seems to surrender a person to the "righteous judgment of God"? Accordingly human beings, who are certainly all sinners, cannot decide whether they have figured out this trap, this trick that spins back and forth on the kaleidoscope of the world and of the soul, until black again becomes white.

This consolation therefore turns out to be very unconsoling. It is dangerous, and in reality it is no consolation at all. Even in the spiritual life — indeed, especially in the spiritual life — there is something like an indeterminate entry. We want to supervise and exactly determine an action in process so that we may know for sure what our manner of doing something is. We want to observe a process; and through the very act of observing the process we necessarily change it, because the observing itself is a part of the observed event. We can find no neutral viewpoint outside of the thing for our supervision. The test is itself already a deed. And we ourselves cannot determine with the certainty of a mathematical balance how it turns out. Yet it is itself an entry in the balance, and, God knows, it is the most obscure entry, because it wants to clarify everything and bring everything into order.

And this is most dangerous. Whoever desires to take hold of his consolation *and* of God's grace, spoils it. The observing of an event has a fatal influence upon the thing observed. Whoever enjoys the pleasure of his love, perverts it. Whoever consoles himself with his remorse, lets the spring of honest tears dry up. Whoever draws up a balance in order to establish with a sigh of relief that now it is clear that he has taken hold of God's grace — at least through his complete surrender before the God of grace — this individual has already falsified the balance in the very process of drawing it up. Ultimately, even the heart must remain there in the body, always hidden, continually beating, but never shut off and dismantled as an airplane engine for a checkup.

We wanted to take hold of ourselves to make sure of what we possessed now, since there probably will not be much more added to what we already have. But it didn't succeed too well. What, then, is left for us? Nothing, except to add further entries to life's credit sheet, to the figures that God shall total up! This is the only way that real, unconditional surrender before God's grace is possible for us. Only this way, indirectly. There is nothing left to us but to sow, not to reap; to gather, not to count up what we have gathered — even the final definitive statement of the deficit would still be such a reckoning! Nothing is left for us except to let the heart keep on doing its work: "good works." For these are the work of the heart, because in them alone the heart really possesses itself, because it forgets itself in its deeds, because it "goes out" of itself, it spends itself, and truly possesses itself only by losing itself.

So we have to pray, and not muse over how we are doing. We do not have to know exactly how well we are doing; but we do have to love. We have to perform love's deeds and offer love's sacrifices. But we dare not seek love's feelings, precisely because in this matter we never quite know what intention these feelings spring from, and for this reason they are no safeguard for us. In God's eyes it is our heart that counts; but what counts for us, what we have to depend on, is our stalwart deeds. In the performance of our deeds in bygone days we were always feeding with frightful delight upon our own dispositions and sentiments; we have wasted and soured them. That is why today, under different circumstances, we can perform our good deeds with sentiments that are not one bit purer than they were before.

The ancients, too, certainly put their dispositions into their deeds; they did not need to stand in fear of them. If we would only learn to fear our profound thoughts and our lofty sentiments! If we would only faithlessly and skeptically once again practice a little more the "ethics" of results instead of the "ethics" of feelings. If we would give a little where it hurts, and let ourselves take advantage of it. If we really forgave from the heart, and prayed at length, and even fasted once in a while. If we would hope in good works before the judgment seat of God and expect more from the rosary, even if recited merely from duty, and from the cup of cold water given to one of the least of his brethren, than from our confounded mystical sublimities or unnerving "existential anxieties" — philosophical or theological — then we would be much better off.

Are we capable of doing this? Can we maintain that this is beyond our power? Can we say that we are too old for this? If this is what God wants of us, is it not enough, and more than enough, and not, as we tend to think, too trivial? We cannot become holy, so far as I can see: but in God's name, we can become patient and pure, and unafraid before people (in spite of our inner timidity). We can become more poor in spirit, and we can kneel for a longer time in church: that we can do, if we will to do it. Our body can do that, even if the heart might not be able to. "If we will to do it" — this is no invitation to test skeptically whether we are able to will to do it. Rather it is the challenge to do it, even though it might seem that we can't; and when the good deed is done, to notice that we were, after all, quite able to do it. We are not to think back over this willing and ability with a shudder, but we should begin again today. Enthusiasm is not necessary for that. To begin today for today; that is all that is necessary. *Sufficit dies malitia sua* (Sufficient for the day is the evil thereof). Tomorrow will take care of itself. Then let the flash of God's judgment come into our life when it will. It will only be the dawn of eternal life.

And the angel of judgment shall all the more surely raise us up to the heights of heaven because of the cup of cold water, than because of our lofty reflections.

How is our balance doing now, at the end? There is the most reliable entry, the only one that puts the balance in order, the entry that makes us forget to ask about the result of the balance: carry on with the hard, customary, routine duties of the Christian life of good works. Carry on! Today and tomorrow. As long as it pleases God to let you carry on. Be on the lookout a little lest you allow those rare opportunities for greater good works slip by. And as long as our good works always give us a little pain and are bitter to the heart, as long as we do the net good work, in order to forget that the first was good, then we also know that this work is not yet degenerating into external routine, and that we have not grown pharisaically hard in the doing of good, in spite of our years.

Thus the balance becomes a dropping of the balance — I forget what lies behind me. The balance becomes a running after the prize of eternal life in the bittersweet difficulties of Christian daily life.

When we run the course in this way, then we are allowed everything. In this course, we may even be permitted to draw up a balance, thankfully or contritely. When we run the course in this way, then some day even that awareness of having been chosen out for heaven, an awareness that steals softly and furtively, like a shadow, only through the heart's most secret chamber, may come over us. Delightful grace: already the tree of life is bending lower and lower, already it is beginning to sink down into God's land. Already freedom is gradually being transformed into the blessed impossibility of escaping from God's love. Already the heart senses that the battle against God's tenacious love is already lost. He is too near, and right now his love is so near that it takes away from us the fear that we, at the end, could still love something else besides just this love. When we run the course in this way, then we cannot find words glorious enough to praise the goal toward which we are hastening. For even our most clever illusions are punier than his reality, in which we will share. When we run the course in this way, then even the expectation of having spread out before us, on our last day, our whole life and all its possibilities, even the ones we neglected and refused, will not do us any harm. For in God's land there is no resignation. God will kiss all the tears from our cheeks; even the blessed tears of repentance will then not be too bitter for him. But how shall tears dry up and resignation change into laughter, if the neglected possibilities of life do not also become reality?

Let us therefore run forward, singing: it is good. *Felix culpa* (Oh, happy fault!)! Everything is good! And for her who runs to meet God nothing is past and lost forever. God has already bestirred himself and is quite near in the impatience of that love that makes all things new. He is near! *Hodie, si vocem eius audieritis,* "Today, if you hearken to his voice...." Our past fickleness is the starting point of the eternal God. Glad tidings! We are running toward God — and *he* is already near!

24 • New Year Meditation*

A new year is coming. What will it bring? I do not mean for the world, for politics and the church. I mean, for me. Precisely for me. This

---

Everyday Faith, 54–70.

question and this concern are justified. For one day I shall depart, I shall no longer be here. And it is my faith, not my egoistic imagination which tells me that then I shall really exist, that I am what I have become here and now, that the yield of this time here is gathered in what we call eternity, mine and yours, unique, inexchangeable, untransferable.

And so I have a right to ask what the new year will bring me. And all other history is ultimately only important (though it is so to a degree which superficial people are far from realizing) for what it brings for this and that person, for you and me in that eternity. For all else passes and is not very important because it is soon over. It is possible, of course, to say that this transitory reality, rightly understood, is itself eternity in process of becoming; the eternal being the temporal brought to perfect fulfillment, not something coming afterward in a temporal sense, for otherwise this would pass away in its turn.

And so I am interested in what the new year will bring. I am interested in it with the whole seriousness of eternity. For what is coming will not depart. It is coming to stay. It occurs in order to be, not to pass away. It plunges into the void of time in order to fill it. It is the mystery of eternity in time. It is impossible for me to take what the new year brings as seriously as it needs to be. For as long as I am passing with my human reality through time as it flows away, I always think it contains nothing but itself. I have perpetually to rouse myself. What is eternal is happening in me now, once and for all, now when I think that what is passing and passing away is not very important.

Not all my moments are equally full of this happening which abides. When would a moment of my time be "fulfilled," as we speak of the "fullness" of time which came for the world as a whole with the incarnate Word of God? Evidently it would occur if a moment came in which, with complete awareness, courage, and determination, I had concentrated myself completely and, having collected myself entirely and comprised myself in my freedom, I gave myself wholly to God, quite unselfishly, in that indescribable way which we call love of God, of God whom we only really know if we achieve that indescribable thing. And this would not be with sentimental, unctuous familiarity, but with stern severity and silent fidelity, for God is incomprehensible. I should then possess myself only in such a way that my self-possession would be an act of perfect self-giving and dispossession.

And all that is meant, of course, as a Christian act. For whether one realizes this or not, the occurrence of such an act, in the present order of things, is faith and grace. The God in question can only be reached because he himself, while remaining infinite, has come close to us (whether this is known or not) in Christ Jesus. He is the word of love which God has spoken into our world in such a way that it can be heard where otherwise we would hear nothing but the silence of God, and we do not know whether that is a blessed word of love or implies eternal damnation. But when does such an act take place in me? When do I concentrate myself wholly and in entire freedom give myself to God?

It is of course right, praiseworthy, and good to say (but it ought not to set us too much at ease) that we think of God, we mean well, keep his commandments, and therefore (so we think) nothing can really happen to us; he must be gracious to us; he must reward us (as we Catholics say), at least he must pardon us (as many others say).

All that may of course be true. Indeed it is true, but not the whole truth which I am concerned with here. After all we have to love God with our whole heart, with all our strength, with our whole soul. And yet that has to be done while we are still on pilgrimage far from the Lord, while we still do not see him face to face. For the promised blessedness is only to be the final, abiding perfect completion of time, of love in time.

We must therefore have given ourselves totally to him in the freedom of this time, in order totally to attain him. It cannot be done for less. No quarter is given. And all grace consists in his bestowing on us the gift of doing this. It does not consist of his giving beatitude without our doing it ourselves (in time as eternity). Even the poor crucified thief was heard in such a way that in his last hour he began to believe and to love with his whole heart, with all his strength and with his whole soul.

But when does this happen with me? Where is God's grace totally victorious in the total freedom in which the cowardly and frightened creature, who elsewhere will not abandon self, finds the courage to take the plunge, really to forget self completely for the sake of God? Where and when shall I achieve that? I must already have contrived to, I may tell myself encouragingly. For, of course, I trust that I am living in God's grace, that I have found his mercy and his Holy Spirit which is poured out in our hearts as love of God. And so (it may be said) the situation is not so dangerous and terrifyingly improbable in regard to that total love of God, without attaining which no one can definitively find his God.

Can we say, it may be asked (in order to have to ask less anxiously), that one must somewhere and somehow love God in the center of the person, really genuinely and honestly, but one does not need to have yet comprised one's whole life in this total love of God "now," at the moment when we are anxiously framing the question? For by asking it, we show that we are still journeying, still in the historical course of human existence. And for that very reason we do not yet have to be finished, because as an historical being one cannot yet be finished. The course has to be run, it may be said. It is not permitted deliberately to stand still, benumbed; we have to will to go on, to grow in this love.

And if one does this, the argument runs, then even now everything is as it should be, even now when we do not yet find a totally all-transforming love in ourselves, covetous and selfish as we are, though believing and of goodwill; we have charity and it will grow, if we do not deliberately waste the opportunities offered by life and the grace of God.

Once again, all that may be correct. In fact it is correct, and that is a consolation. But it is not complete consolation, for, even so, some-where or other in my life the moment of the fullness of time must nevertheless occur. That one, comprehensive, great and holy event must occur, the moment, still and silent like a Christmas night, in which a person's heart gives him so wholly into the hands of the incompre-hensible (into which it is a terrible thing to fall), that the gift is not secretly taken back again, as mostly happens.

Can one dare to hope that one's own heart will one day succeed in doing this? Do we already hope because we have perhaps already be-gun to hope, and because we think we love to some degree or desire such a love? Is it a sufficient earnest of such audacious and yet mortally necessary hope that one day we shall really love totally? It may seem that the older the heart becomes the less it succeeds in doing so. It be-comes tired and dull, cold and apathetic. One scarcely knows whether one is going on because one cannot do anything else, stiff and numbed as one is by the daily drill of the past, or whether one can no longer do anything else because this inability is the blessed reward of genuine freedom? Has virtue degenerated into routine, momentum into futile agitation, fidelity into custom?

Where is there the fullness of time in my life, where is the decisive hour which comprises the whole of my human reality? It must exist. For, of course, a human being does not really put his life together piecemeal out of individual good deeds. Each, rather, is potentially the whole, the possibility of giving the whole life to God. If this were not so, a single action could not decide a whole life. But this is what every action in the full sense does — "grave" sin and also a "grave" good deed, which must also exist and which must be just as essentially different from a slight good deed as the grave sin is from the venial sin. But when have I performed important actions of that kind, which weigh as heavy as I do, because they place a whole human being on God's scales?

People often speak of the greatest hours, the finest and holiest mo-ments of human life, and mean by them — according to what is being celebrated — first communion, wedding day, the reception of the body of Christ, ordination, and so on. Are these events the turning points of life which we are seeking? Are they the fullness of eternity entering into a moment of time? We might think so. For what could be greater and more decisive, for example, than the moment when one actually enjoys the bread of eternity which is the body of the Lord who has given himself to death for us?

And yet everyone knows that it is not only possible to receive unworthily this bread which is the fullness of time and so eat life to one's condemnation; everyone also knows that with the fullness of the sacrament one does not always receive the fullness of what that sacrament signifies and of itself contains, the fullness of grace. This is so even if it is not received unworthily. Not every reception of the fullness of time is a reception of the fullness of my time. One can live in the moment of Christ and yet one's own life may pass dead and empty, or at least very unfulfilled, through its own time. It would indeed be wonderful if in such sacramental form the fullness of one's own time were found, if the fullness of time were present here and now in my life. Then everything would be there. The eternal plenitude of God would be present, and this inner presence would be tangibly present in its own manifestation, which could not be plainer, at once personal and ecclesial, vitally concrete and liturgical. The plenitude would be present fulfilled in the sign, in the symbol of the banquet of eternity, of the banquet of perfect accomplishment. One would empty the chalice of one's own life completely and it would be perceptibly one with the chalice of Christ.

It can be so, and so it perhaps ought to be. But we cannot in fact say whether God has intended for everyone that the decisive hour of her life is to occur precisely when the sacramental sign of the fulfillment of the world and of the individual is set up, in blessing and forgiveness, in the individual's life. It may be, after all, that only a small part of this grace is received, and only a part of the grace for which there would in fact be room in the heart, if it were not more cowardly and niggardly than it need be.

It is therefore possible that the greater hour, the time of greater plenitude, may occur where the sign (in the wider sense) is poorer and more ambiguous and not an *opus operatum*. It may be that one person will drain the chalice of his life with his life and his death in an hour which is not that of the eucharistic meal, although even so he lives this hour of his in dependence on the hour of Christ. For Christ acquired everyone's own hour in his, that hour which becomes present in the sacrifice and meal of the mass.

It is possible that someone may suddenly break through all the barriers which previously had fenced around her anxious egoism and emerge into the vastness of God, in a silent, unnoticed resignation, in an apparently small sacrifice. Perhaps she herself does not notice much about it, nothing that she would think worth entering in her diary. It is only that she has suddenly become so open. There is suddenly something nameless and mysterious present, colorless as it were and indescribable.

But everything is different. This reality that is present cannot be set side by side with the other things which fill out the domain of life like a lumber room. It cannot be compared with them and classified with them in agreement or contrast. The person has renounced, has set out, relinquished. And now he is suddenly everywhere and possesses all, thinking perhaps it is "nothing" because it is everything. He needs no ground to support him anymore because he himself has become something like a poised totality, supporting himself (in God's totality) without falling because there is nothing onto which in his solitude and renunciation he could fall.

It is possible that someone may be frightened of this silent infinity which has opened out to her, not in abstract thoughts, but in the experience of the accepted capacity of her being, which is spirit. She has fled back as if in terror to what is familiar in her life, to tangible human beings, to limited duties, to explicitly formulated precepts. And then she does not properly realize that while all these things are certainly necessary (if reason and not fanaticism is to prevail), they are not needed in order to flee from the other.

They are there as the way of accomplishing genuine acceptance of the infinity which is really to be found in them and which is not merely set before us as a reward for our finite good works. In these good works, if they have the weighty character of which we have spoken, there is, of course, grace. Now this grace is, ultimately, God himself, the "uncreated grace," the eternal Spirit of love. That is the God who is himself present in those works. He is not only promised to good works, it is he in his own reality who gives these works only so that they may be what they should and must be (if they are to be something of value at all, that is, "saving acts"): gates open into the free infinity of God.

Naturally moral good works and sentiments (if and where they exist purely as such) would be events which, closed in themselves, would be rewarded with something which was God's gift, but not God himself. The "good works" of the professed or anonymous Christian contain the infinity of God himself as the condition of their possibility (and this is therefore called grace) and as their reward (called eternal life). And since God has willed no other world but one into which he has given himself and not merely his created effects, it is the case that all that is finite is only meaningful as an outlet into immeasurable, silent, and incomprehensible infinity.

Consequently, it is possible that an onion or two thrown over the garden fence to a poor person may be a decisive turning point — a little kindness which really forgets to look for gratitude, forgiveness which does not notice at all that it is forgiving, a drop of blood flowing from the heart and falling somewhere, impossible really to say where, but without bitterness; silent endurance of mortal pain almost without knowing why, or whether one will be able to. Or someone is entirely alone and does not flee from the solitude or mirror himself in it. Or someone is decent in a quite commonplace way and as a result is simply regarded as a fool, yet is not up in arms about the madness of a world that regards the just person as a fool.

He does not bestow on himself (as a substitute for the praise of others) the consolation of honor and recognition for his decency. He does not secretly store this up, in order to bring it up again later and collect the praise of the world, or at least of his friend or his spouse when he complains of the injury done to him. He is simply decent, and that is that. That is the wonder of quite unself-conscious decency, a decency that has become quite naive once more and which is the pure love of God in the everyday world. Or someone does her duty; she does not commit adultery, in deed or in thought, although this obligation of fidelity seems like death to her, and she feels as if she were obliterating her very self. Or someone prays. And suddenly she has forgotten that she is praying, she has forgotten that she wants something (and is therefore trying to get what she wants), she has forgotten she is speaking.

There is only one there: God himself, silent, mute, but there, nameless, inexpressible and incomprehensible, incomparable and unutterable, but there. He is there almost because we are no longer there, grasped because we abandon self and depart from ourselves. He is there because we are finally no longer at home in ourselves, but — but it is no longer possible to express this further; for if one tried to say it in the very moment of leaving self behind, one would already have turned back into the definable limits of one's own statement and one's own reality. If one states it (which one sometimes has to), one does not by making the statement perform the action which the statement is about.

Such decisive hours do in fact exist. They can exist. But one does not have them merely by talking about them. For able people can talk about them because they have heard about them from others or because they have detected the inevitable remnant of them which as the mark of spirit and grace is found even in the most unspiritual and graceless deeds and experiences of the human person. For we would cease to be spirit (which we are even if we are whetting the knife to kill like wild beasts), we would cease to be constantly "tempted" by grace (which we always are), if we had experienced nothing at all of what is actually accomplished only in such decisive hours. But not every experience is an experience accepted and grasped with the utmost strength of the heart. We have not the fullness of time and eternity contained in our heart simply because we have enjoyed a slight taste of it and are philosophizing grandly about this small sample.

And so the question remains: Has such a decisive hour of the fullness of my time occurred? A foolish question. One cannot really ask it in that way. For, of course, it would be of no use to me if I could make such a statement about an earlier moment of my life. Perhaps I can make it. Perhaps I can conjecture that it was when as a child at my first communion I invited the Lord to come into the young heart that loved him.

But if I raise the question, I am obviously asking because I think that what happened then matters to me now. And that is in fact false. For all that matters is the fullness of my time which has not elapsed. It really only matters to me if now or tomorrow such an hour of eternity occurs. For as long as one is a pilgrim, as long as time is still time, each moment is like a relay runner with a torch, who has not only to keep the burning light for himself but has also to hand it on to the next individual. Only when the latter grasps it and carries it on has the former's run any value and validity.

Life is not really composed of parts, when it is spirit and not physics that is in question; but the whole runs as an indivisible unity through time, in a process of becoming through everything. I therefore have nothing simply because I acquired it earlier, but I have what I became earlier because in this enduring process I become it anew. The earlier is always only the summons to bring about what has already been, and the promise that what has already succeeded will also succeed now. It is therefore only out of very incidental theoretical curiosity or in the sorrow of contrition aiming at transforming past into future that one can turn back to one's past, in order to seek out what lofty hours of eternity occurred in it.

Instead of asking, therefore, whether such a decisive hour has already occurred in our life, poor and empty as it is, full of illusion even in the so-called good which we have done, it would be better to ask where is such an hour coming from to me out of what is still to come? I have to find it in what is coming toward me. And that is also where I must seek the past hours. For only if they are there will the hours which God in his grace may have bestowed on me in the past remain for me. The treasure of the past is the freedom of the future.

For we have, of course, acted in order to be able to act, loved in order to begin to learn love. Out of the future with God's grace, which is without repentance, there really comes to me once again my whole past, for it to be preserved or redeemed. For what can be lost by someone who finds God, and what opportunity is missed if we still have the good fortune of having a heart and the ability to love God with our whole heart?

God's just anger, however, falls on those who do not believe with their whole heart the blessed message of that grace of his which is without repentance, which is our whole opportunity for life. The kind of realism which simply knows what is in oneself and in human beings generally forgets what is most real of all, God, the eternal future and the person's glorious grace of making such a future his own. The fulfillment of this total possibility need not always and everywhere take place to the accompaniment of emotion and tears of joy as we should no doubt like it to do.

It is to the tired and worn heart, burnt to dry ash by the invisible flame of suffering and disappointment, that this blessed opportunity has been chiefly, not least, promised: blessed are those who mourn, blessed those who thirst.

And so the new year is coming. A year like all the rest. A year of trouble and disappointment with myself and others. When God is building the house of our eternity, he puts up fine scaffolding in order to carry out the work. So fine, that we should prefer to live in it. The only fault we have to find with it is that it is taken down again. Then we call this dismantling the painful fragility of our life. We lament and become melancholy if in the prospect of a new year we think we can see nothing but the demolition of the house of our life, which in reality is being quietly built up for eternity behind this scaffolding that is put up and taken down again.

No, the coming year is not a year of disappointments or a year of pleasing illusions. It is God's year. The year in which decisive hours are approaching me quietly and unobtrusively, and the fullness of my time is coming to enter my life. Shall I notice those hours? Or will they remain empty? Because to me they will seem too small, too humble and commonplace?

Outwardly, of course, they will not look any different from anyone's everyday moments of good works and proper omissions. Consequently, I may overlook them: the slight patience which makes life slightly more tolerable for those around me; the omission of an excuse; taking the risk of building on the good faith of someone whom I would be inclined to mistrust because I think I have had unfortunate experiences with them before; genuine acceptance of there being good grounds for someone else's criticism of me (how hard this is when something is at stake which involves my self-esteem); to allow an injury done to me to die away in myself, without prolonging it by complaints, rancor, bitterness, and revenge; fidelity in prayer which is not rewarded with "consolations" or "religious experience"; the attempt to love those who get on my nerves (through their fault, of course), and not merely to put up with them by swallowing one's rage out of calculated egoism; the attempt to see in someone else's "stupidity" a different kind of intelligence which is not mine but need not necessarily be stupid on that account; the tolerance which does not pay back another's intolerance in kind; the endeavor not to trade on one's virtues as a charter for one's faults; a prompt will to improve oneself when we see sins in others and would dearly like to reform them; the firm conviction, firmly maintained against oneself, that we very willingly and very easily delude ourselves and leave a number of faults and pettinesses undisclosed which would strike us as patently obvious in anyone else; the suppressed complaint and the self-praise omitted, and many other things which would only be really good if one practiced them constantly, though it is true that it is better to do something than not to do anything at all, for one cannot manage everything at once.

We only need seriously to try to do such commonplace everyday things. Then they become terrible. They are almost deadly if they are not taken in careful homeopathic doses. For in all these cases we are the one who gets the worse of the deal; one has the impression of paying out more than one gets back. It brings in no returns, neither in the world, nor by a good conscience or inner recognition for so much self-made virtue; for even that loses its attraction.

And then in all these trifles that go with a decent attitude (which fundamentally is very Christian, at least without realizing it), the point comes where morality actually becomes really moral and religious, the point where it becomes the gate to the infinite and eternal. Where one is rewarded by nothing more, that is, by nothing specific, whether outside or within, then in truth God is present as that "nothing," and finite loss is infinite gain. And appreciation of the latter is exercised by that loss. One pays for it in life with oneself. God is not to be had for less.

We ought to learn this mysticism of everyday life. Only then does fulfillment of the law out of respect for the prescriptions of the supreme government of the universe (which can never be fully achieved and which simply irritates and makes one resentful like an overworked laborer) become voluntary striving in the spirit of the children of God. Such mysticism of everyday life is grace. Wholly and entirely grace. But that of course does not mean that there is nothing to do but impiously to wait until God's grace compels one against one's will. It "compels" in fact by bestowing the goodwill, and the goodwill thus given by God, viewed from below, is the great and honest endeavor of the human being himself. And this has to be carried out properly, by learning to form a taste for eternity in time by practice in the mysticism of daily life.

If this is practiced, people will be found ready to see the more sublime possibilities of life, the hours of heroic sacrifices (if they are offered to them), the mortal trials, holy extravagance, and follies and finally that death in which we die our own death, which is then a death in the death of Christ. How can we be equipped if we have not previously been on the watch for and, as far as possible, trained ourselves for such sublime hours, which we cannot give ourselves, but which arrive by their own inscrutable law?

Anyone who has not discovered the taste of eternity in time flees in alarm from such hours; she is afraid, feels herself overtaxed. It does not even occur to her that the great grace of life is in fact confronting her. She takes it for granted that "this" cannot be expected of her. And certainly it cannot be expected of her inner lack of courage which is the ground of her own judgment of herself.

The mysticism of everyday life should be practiced. It is the contrary of that "fidelity to duty" of the pedant who, hardened in "virtue," would prefer best of all to continue forever the existence of a minor official of the good God, provided he always received his salary punctually here below (law and order and the "victory" of "right-thinking people" on earth). It is certain that everyday routine exists and we cannot escape most of it. Even the saints yawn sometimes, and have to shave. It is not so sure that hours will be given us which even from our point of view will be great and important. There must therefore be an eternity in everyday life. For we know that every human being we see, walking about to all appearance appallingly commonplace, is valuable enough to become an eternity, and to do this here on earth where all he seems to do is to earn a living none too easily, marry, and abuse the politicians if he is not actually watching a football match or treating us to his opinion of Picasso.

Perhaps for this very reason the decisive hours only come to us in the garb of everyday life. Many everyday situations will not be decisive turning points at all. One cannot of course put forward one's full powers at simply every moment. And for the greatest freedom, most has to be given, because the innermost reality is founded on the profoundest capacity and this is a gift bestowed on us. To be able to put forward one's full powers in complete freedom is the greatest gift. It is not bestowed on us at every moment. Yet precisely this can be given to us in a trivial everyday situation. Who can say when this hour comes? We always act into an incalculable future, with the risk and opportunity that the incalculable implies. Suddenly, where we only faintly perceived it as we accepted the incalculable, the high fulfillment is given us.

And yet it is ours because we have accepted it (though unknown) in faith.

The year of such possibilities is coming. We ought to celebrate New Year with more faith than we do, listless, fainthearted, and unbelieving as we are. The future is coming. Foolish people think it comes seeking the past like a morbid and deadly obsession. In reality it comes because it wills to become eternity. The future does not become smaller but only really attains its identity when it becomes the past, the past which, in the human being who possesses God, is limitless present. The future which abides is coming. In the fullness of my time, through the decisive hours of believing, hoping, and loving freedom.

What will the new year bring to me? God in the fullness of my time. Who knows? It could even be that the last fleeting moment will no longer extend the torch of eternal life to another moment, but rather that now this torch itself will shine as everlasting light. Who knows? I run, the apostle says. I do not look back. I do not think I have already laid hold, but I run in order that I may lay hold. One can also address a maranatha† to the new year. For the Lord is coming. In the new year of my life too. What is the new year bringing me? Jesus Christ the crucified and risen, the mystery of his death and life in my life and death, his clear light in the toil of my faith, his promise in the labor of my hope, his love for me in the ever new attempt to find him by love through sharing his lot. The year of the Lord is coming.

25 • In the Name of Jesus*

1 January, Lk 2:21

We are beginning a new year in secular life, not a new church year. But the earthly year, everyday life, the life of work and worry, is of course the field in which our salvation has to be worked out in God's sight. And so we have every reason to begin this year too in God's name. Let us in God's name then begin once more, go on once more, honestly and unwearied. Time presses. One can fall into despair or melancholy when one realizes on New Year's Eve that yet another part of one's earthly life is irrevocably past. But time presses on toward God and eternity, not toward the past and destruction. And so — in God's name!

---

†The early Church's Aramaic prayer, "Come, O Lord" (Rv 22:20). —Trans. ed.
Everyday Faith, 52–53.

There is a pious custom of writing C + M + B [Caspar, Melchior, and Balthasar: the names given to the Magi by tradition] above the doors at Epiphany. Let us inscribe above the gate of the new year the name of God, the name of the God in whom is our help, the name of Jesus. Jesus means: Yahweh helps. Yahweh was the proper name of the God of the Old Testament nation of the covenant. That we can give God a name, God the nameless and incomprehensible, whom the human person of himself ultimately knows only as remote and obscure and incomprehensible, is due to the fact that he made himself known in the history of his own action and speech.

We can perceive from the way in which he acts how he really wills to be in our regard. All the experiences which people have had with the living God in his action in us are summed up in the "name" of their God. Only a proper name, never a merely abstract general concept, comprises the full, indivisible, and irreducible totality of what can be experienced of a living person through lasting relations with them.

And Jesus as a proper name tells us how Yahweh willed to be in our regard: close, loving, helpful, faithful to the end. In Jesus and by him we know what we have in God. Otherwise we do not. He is the Word of the Father, in whom as the word of mercy God expresses himself to the world. Consequently if we wish to say who our God is, we must say "Jesus." If we were to forget this Word, God would disappear for us into the dark inaccessibility of an incomprehensible "ground of the world."

But we Christians know the definitive name of God: Jesus. For that is the name which that child received who is God and the eternal youth of the world, who is a man and as such the eternal countenance of God. Let us give this name to the coming year. Let us sign the cross of this Jesus on brow, mind, and heart. Let us say with relief: our help is in the name of the Lord! And then stoutheartedly let us cross the threshold of the new year. If his name shines above it, even its darkest hour will be an hour of the year of the Lord and of his salvation.

26 • The Holy Family*

Lk 2:42–52

It is a dark Gospel the Church has us read on this day of the Holy Family and of all families redeemed by Christ. A father, a mother, a

---

*Der Volksbote (Innsbruck) 50, no. 1 (5 January 1950): 12. Trans. Frederick G. Lawrence, Boston College.

child, parental love, parental care, a mother's pain, a child's obedience, growth in age and wisdom before God and humankind are the topics of this Gospel. But isn't it almost a mistake to select this Gospel? This child goes his own way. Weeping, the parents look for a "lost" son. And even when everything is "all right" an unfathomability stands between mother and son as both dividing them and binding them together.

God, who reigns as the real Father of this family, seems to work more as a threat to this family than as its bond and its eternal transfiguration. Even if the "problems" of this family were supposed to be joined together in this family portrait, the questions posed here seem not to be the right ones or relevant to our lives. These days where do threats to the family arise from the heavenly calling of a child? For us threats come from the quest for satisfaction that mixes up wide-ranging drives with the true love of the heart; from embittering poverty; from the triviality or dullness of the heart; from enticements; from the flight from the sorrow which is the price of true love; from the defiance and disobedience that signal the fact that the child has not gained self-control.

But even if it sounds exaggerated and extreme, it remains true: every unhappiness and all the problems of the family stem ultimately from a falsely understood heavenly calling of each person who makes up the family. Because all the tragedy and all the guilt of people are only possible (of course guiltily and responsibly possible) because the human being thirsts for the infinite, and an infinite calling, and so is the eternally unsatisfied one here below.

Because God is thus always sought, even where he is sought in perverse or earthly places, therefore the "crisis" of the Holy Family narrated in today's Gospel is indeed a heavenly tableau of the earthly threat to the family. But at the same time this portrait shows the healing power that can overcome these earthly threats. Again, what threatens the family? The quest for self. What is this self-quest most profoundly? Nothing but the desperate anxiety that one cannot be happy if one takes sacrifice, suffering, and self-denial upon oneself. This anxiety would only be too justified, it would only legitimate this quest for self all too much, were there only the world and its narrowness, were this narrowness the only space where happiness could reside, and into which one would have to force one's way with violence.

Only one who (knowingly or as concealed from oneself) goes into the house of the Father, into God's comprehensiveness, and who believes that earthly fulfillment is not ultimate, can be saved from this anxiety, and so freed from this quest for self. One who is involved in what is God's can deny self and sacrifice, can give without counting the cost, can love without waiting to see if the love will be reciprocated sufficiently, can let others have the last word, can keep from turning service into a sophisticated method of control. That person can do it. Because he or she knows that in this way happiness lost is preserved in the eternity of God (which people can already share in now). And so the family has to come together in what is the Father's in order to be a holy family. And only this kind of family is happy.

27 • Forgiving Each Other*

Feast of the Holy Family, Col 3:12–17

Our text is taken from St. Paul's letter to the Colossians. He writes from prison to a church in Asia Minor with which he is not personally acquainted, to warn them against entangling themselves in a misguided angel worship, part Jewish and part gnostic, which seemed to threaten their faith in Christ the sovereign Lord and his redemption.

Paul says: "Put on then, as God's chosen ones, holy and beloved, compassion, kindness, lowliness, meekness, and patience." We are God's chosen ones because he knows us, he has called us, he has conceived and planned our life, he leads us, he has given us a special vocation and even the grace to respond to it. And so we are holy, for we are consecrated and anointed by the Holy Spirit of God which is poured forth in our hearts. That is why we are truly God's beloved, loved with the unutterable love of God, the holy, the almighty, the everlasting.

That is why Paul says that we must "put on" the inmost spirit of the virtues he enumerates. It is a startling image the apostle uses here: "putting on." Exegetes have long been puzzled by this image. Elsewhere too St. Paul speaks of putting on Christ. Possibly he had in mind some cultic gesture familiar to the pagan religions round about, whereby a person donned the robes and symbols of a god and mimed him so as to feel that he was in some sort transformed into the object of his worship.

However that may be, we have indeed put on the Lord. We have been transmuted by his Spirit into his image and likeness. We must live him, recreate his image in us. Not, of course, by mere outward imitation, an outward mime. We put him on in such a way that we are actually drawn into him, we reflect his being and his life and so prolong his life within history until he comes again.

---

*Everyday Faith, 52–53.

And so we are to imitate his virtues. The virtues St. Paul enumerates here are social virtues, the virtues of life lived in community as human beings and as Christians. "Put on the inmost spirit of compassion, kindness, lowliness, meekness, and patience." We need not enlarge upon these individual virtues. We all know how necessary they are in our life with one another. We all know how difficult they often are to practice, and so we can only acquire these virtues — this patience, this kindness, this humble deference, this forbearance, this longanimity, this generosity of heart as it were — if we put on Christ the Lord.

"Forbearing one another and, if one has a complaint against another, forgiving each other." Every person is a burden to her neighbor and perhaps for that very reason — alas, how slow we are to grasp the fact — a grace. She may wrong us, our neighbor. She may really be a burden to us, and perhaps she should not be. And yet, even such burdens should be an extra weight of grace for a Christian. So we should bear them, and forgive our neighbor any extra weight there may be through her fault.

The Greek term Paul uses to convey this forgiveness includes the word charis, "pardon." Accordingly he continues: "As the Lord has forgiven you, so you also must forgive." We must forgive one another, as the Lord has forgiven us. Or did he not have to forgive us? Did we not need his pardon, poor sinners that we were, whose sins, whose monstrous sins, our Lord God had to forgive us in Jesus Christ? Why then can we not do the same?

Paul moves on, but still he thinks in the context of this putting on of Christ: "And above all these" — he does not repeat the words — "put on love, which binds everything together in perfect harmony" in the holy garment that the Christian must put on to follow Christ. We must put on love, which is the bond of perfection. It embraces everything else, and without it nothing is of any use. It binds everything together. We might say that it binds everything together so stoutly that with it we are properly girded and equipped to travel down the road of life into the everlasting light.

Paul continues, and when he speaks of *agape*, love, he also thinks of peace. So he says: "Let the peace of Christ rule in your hearts" like an umpire, like someone who rules and governs, reducing everything to order, keeping our spiritual life running smoothly as one might say. This deep, wholly interior peace must live and rule in our hearts, rule over everything dark and bitter in our lives, for those things too can be engulfed in Christ's peace.

"And," says Paul, "be thankful." We clutch avidly at God's gifts, forgetting him himself in our desire for them. Be thankful. "Let the word of Christ dwell in you richly, as you teach and admonish one another in all wisdom — keep each other right," Paul really means. Sing psalms and hymns and spiritual songs in grace, sing God the secret song of your heart, at least in your heart, the song of your soul, the song that should be heard in your heart above any merely rational thought, the song that knows only the heart and God — this is the song you must sing in your heart by God's grace — the unutterable melodies that the Spirit of God can sing in your heart. It may sound to us like stammering and, as Paul says, groaning, and yet it is the sweet song we sing to God in thankfulness, the beginning of the endless praise of eternity.

"And whatever you do," Paul concludes before going on to speak of the duties of people in particular states of life, "whatever you do, in word or deed, do everything in the name of the Lord Jesus, giving thanks to God the Father through him." Everything that is right can be done in him and his name. And if it is said and done in him, then it will be right, and it will be the thanks, the eucharist — as we might say — that we owe God the Father, who has called us into the kingdom of the Son of his love so that everything in us and in our lives may praise and glorify him.

28 • If the Heart Is Alive
It Thinks of God*

Feast of the Holy Family, Col 3:12–17

In verse 17 of this chapter in Colossians Paul says, "Whatever you do, in word or deed, do everything in the name of the Lord Jesus Christ." We must do everything, he tells us, in the name of Jesus Christ. This is what is meant when we say in the language of spirituality that we must have a good intention in whatever we do. A good intention, something good in view. Paul says: we must do everything in the name of Jesus. In the Bible the name is equivalent to the person. To speak of someone's name is to speak of someone's person; it conjures up the presence of the person. So when something is done in a person's name, it is done by that person's power and by his commission.

Thus acting in a person's name is acting by his or her commission. If we are speaking of God, this means acting in the power of his grace, in a frame of mind that is worthy of him, inspired by him; it means

---

*Biblical Homilies, 151–53.

acting in vital union with God, with God in view, to his glory. So in everything we do or suffer, say or think, we should consider that we are commissioned by Jesus Christ our Lord: if we do or say or think a thing, it must be done in union with him and by his grace, for him, to his glory.

We must remember that we belong to the sovereign Lord, that we live and die to him. Paul says in Romans 11:36 that everything is from God, exists by him and for him, and therefore concludes: to him be glory forever. That sums up the content of our verse: because everything derives from him, is sustained by him, strives toward him with its inmost being, the individual must assent to this reality, must accept everything from God, do everything with and through him, everything for him. And so all is done to his glory, done in the name of our Lord Jesus Christ.

If we interpret what Paul says in this way, then of course we must add that it is not enough to add that intention to what we do and say. It is an excellent thing, praiseworthy, Christian, and sanctifying, to renew our good intention frequently; for instance, saying in the morning, "let everything be done to God's glory," and raising our hearts and minds to God in the course of the day's work to offer and consecrate to God whatever we are doing. But this attitude of heart, this explicit good intention, must really penetrate and fill what we do — or rather, grow out of it.

If we saw things as they are and experienced human life as it is in reality, then these things, the whole of life, would tell us, as it were, that it is all from God, through God and for God. Then we would perceive the incompleteness of all that is not God, catch the deeper meaning behind things, without which they remain tentative and even pointless — much ado about nothing.

Only God in things gives them their fullness, their significance, their orientation. And if we would allow outward things and our own experiences to speak of this glory of God, then our good intention would grow out of them automatically. If the bitterness of life spoke to us of beatitude; if the truth we think about spoke to us of God's eternal truth; if the mysteries and riddles of this life reminded us that God is the solution and the primal answer to all mysteries and riddles; if all trouble spoke to us of everlasting peace, all beauty of God's surpassing beauty that cannot fade; if all the love that we are given and give had God in it to keep it new and strong, then our good intention would grow out of our lives of its own accord.

So we must learn to listen more attentively, and pray for a heart of flesh to perceive the mystery of God in all we do and say and think, in all we undergo, in all our loving; a heart that will say yes, will perfect, affirm, consolidate the inner movement of our life toward God, making it pure and complete, so that our daily life will be steeped in a good intention.

Of course we must agree that all this will not happen without cooperation on our part. It must be cultivated, ever and again dug up from among the rubble in which our daily life buries it, and looked after. That is why an explicit good intention is a useful and wholesome thing; stopping a moment to pray and renew our purpose of serving God. Not as though the explicit good intention were the only one. One can live to the glory of God implicitly, silently, in a general, diffuse intention that nevertheless impregnates everything.

It is not just our head, our little thoughts, that must think of God but our activities, our life, all our being. And where the heart is alive, experiencing the griefs and the joys of life as they really are, where the heart has not culpably shut itself away from this authentic existence, there the heart does think of God though without so much as one explicit word. But if this is to be the case, a Christian mentality must be cultivated; we need explicit prayer, explicit recollection, we must say short prayers during the day, think consciously of God sometimes, direct our intention to our Lord Jesus Christ. And so we must often hearken to the words of St. Paul: "Whatever you do, in word or deed, do everything in the name of the Lord Jesus."

Then our whole life and everything that was in it can one day be described in that line of Paul's to the Romans: Everything was from God, everything was through God, everything was for God, and so now his glory, which is our blessedness, is forever.

29 • The New Style in Remorselessness*

Feast of the Holy Family, Col 3:12–17

During his captivity at Rome St. Paul receives news from a Christian community in Asia Minor which he did not found himself. It was founded by a disciple. Paul's reply is this letter to the Colossians. In the first part of the letter he goes into certain misinterpretations, partly of

---

*Biblical Homilies, 142–46.

Jewish and partly of gnostic origin, which were a danger to the community. He represents to them the surpassing dignity of Christ, which is not to be compared with any angelic principalities or powers that there may be in the world. These Colossians were tempted to reverence such angels and so to imagine that Christ was only one among the cosmic powers. In the second section, from chapter 3 onward, Paul then discusses the moral life of the Christian, as he is fond of doing after the dogmatic part of a letter.

In chapter 3, verses 1 to 18, Paul considers the conduct of the individual; then toward the end of the chapters he considers the duties involved in the various states of life. Today's text occurs in the first part of chapter 3. It is full of beauty and meaning. It speaks to us as God's chosen ones, holy and beloved, and calls upon us to practice many virtues: compassion, kindness, lowliness, meekness, patience, love; to pursue peace, to pray, to sing spiritual songs — in a word, whatever we do in word or deed, to do everything in the name of the Lord Jesus.

Now we may be struck by something in the list of virtues which the apostle commends to his community: he admonishes them to practice lowliness and then forgiveness: "Forbearing one another and, if one has a complaint against another, forgiving each other; as the Lord has forgiven you, so you also must forgive." So it is clear that when he inculcates peace it is not simply the peace of the individual heart within itself that is meant but peace among Christians.

Does not Paul justify this admonition to peace by saying: "You were called in the one body"? Now it is extraordinary that in so short a letter, where there is so much to be said, Paul should urge mutual forbearance and forgiveness upon his readers. Let us picture this community for a moment: they are zealous souls; they are all Christians, recent converts full of the enthusiasm of the recent convert, who knows that he or she must shine like a star amid the darkness of the world; a community whose every member has become a Christian out of sheer conviction, in defiance of his whole environment.

So this church takes its Christianity in deadly earnest; the members who have found their way to it know they share with all other members the profoundest experience of their life — the tremendous decision for Christ and Christ's redemption. And yet Paul admonishes them to bear with one another and forgive one another.

Not only that; he has the admonition on the tip of his tongue, as it were. It is not an admonition given in view of the peculiar circumstances of this one church; for he says practically the same thing in the letter to the Ephesians, chapter 4, verses 31 and 32. So it must obviously be an admonition appropriate and important to every Christian.

If we turn to the sermon on the mount, we find Jesus himself admonishing us to forgive one another and be reconciled. We find a kind of sequel to the doctrine of Jesus Ben Sirach, chapter 28, in the Old Testament, which reminds and admonishes us that we can only beg God's forgiveness if we in our turn are prepared to forgive our fellow men and women. The Lord even includes this petition, and this assurance to God that we forgive others, in the Our Father. He tells us the parable of the unmerciful servant (Mt 18) to warn us that if we are unforgiving, God too will be so. In Matthew 18 the Lord tells Peter that we must forgive each other seventy times seven, which in plain English means till the cows come home. And in Luke he says: "Forgive, and you will be forgiven." Small wonder, then, if St. Paul takes up Jesus' admonition to write it on the hearts of the Colossians. Is it an admonition that we too are ever and again in need of and must take to heart?

When all is said and done, we are the same sort of people as the people of that age, whom Jesus and Paul admonished. But if we are really to grasp what it means to be forgiving in our own day-to-day lives, it is important to realize that nowadays we have a different way of being irreconcilable: the style has changed. Where people live cribbed, cabined, and confined, on top of each-other, as we say, or where people are very spontaneously vital and down to earth — and there is probably less of either thing today than there used to be — anger, hatred, rancor are very straightforward, concrete, and active.

There you have the vendetta; implacable enmity is handed down from generation to generation; clan or tribal warfare is endemic; one stands behind one's father, one's mother and brother, and an enemy of one's kin is one's own enemy; there you have wholehearted enmity to the death, or whole-hearted friendship and fidelity to the death. Among ourselves these things are no longer "done"; they are replaced, or at least discreetly veiled, by pale convention. We do not fall upon each other knife in hand; we do not take special precautions to ensure our status as guests so that we cannot be attacked; it is easier to withdraw from people and live aloof; we can more readily avoid each other.

And so, I suppose, we hardly notice that this evangelical admonition speaks to our condition and that we by no means automatically comply with it. We may well say: What enemies, pray, have I? Whom do I refuse to forgive? It may be true that there are some things one cannot be expected to put up with. It may be a duty for me to stand up for my rights. It may simply be impossible to live in perfect peace with my neighbor. Even saints have sometimes gone to law in defense of their rights; sometimes they had no choice. And to draw the line at certain impositions may be an act of virtue that contributes to the Christian education of another.

But precisely because there are such cases and because there is now a different way of being unforgiving and remorseless — a different style — we may overlook the fact that we do not automatically comply with this admonition. For when today's text tells us that we are to forgive others as God has forgiven us, then obviously it places us in a delicate position. How has God forgiven us? Not by saying, as people do, we had better forget all about it. Not by saying, as it were, oh, never mind.

He does not forget that way. He forgives us by seeking us out, by loving us, by loving us with all his heart, by giving us everything — that is, himself. He forgives us by making something else out of our evil deed, our sin, the ill will of our hearts, the injury we have done him, giving us another chance, a new start in life, forgiving without reserve and with all his heart, thinking of nothing now but mercy, compassion, love, and faithfulness unto the end, so that all that is left of the past is the goodness of it.

Do we forgive this way? Candidly and lovingly? Or do we avoid people if they are uncongenial, if they get on our nerves, if they have hurt our feelings at some time or other? Do we tolerate them on these terms, rather pleased with ourselves for not assaulting them or even saying anything injurious? And what of the state of our hearts? What judgments do we pass there? What of those secret thoughts? What is our real attitude toward people, there within our hearts? Do we accuse no one there? Do we really try to understand others? Have we ever tried to stand coolly aside from our anger, resentment, and pride and really study others; tried to understand them in the light of their ideas, their cast of mind, their dispositions, the kind of life they have led, their temperament, their upbringing and education, their experiences? Or do we think that our instructive reactions, as they say, are the best guide to judgment where people are concerned?

It is difficult to forgive and really bear with others. Let us not say "tolerate," which implies that the other person is a burden that really ought not to be thrust upon us. If we translate properly: "Bear with one another as Christ bears with you," as a patient, loving mother does with her child, then we shall perceive how difficult a thing is required of us. And yet to forgive in this way, not merely forgive the injuries done us but give ourselves to others and bear with them as God gives himself to us and bears with us, is the only way to comply with the admonition of the gospel. It is hard. Only by God's grace can we be so selfless, only when God himself is our partner and God's freedom has become our own.

30 • Why Are We Hated?*

5 January, 1 Jn 3:13–18

The third chapter of St. John's first letter, especially the first part, is devoted to brotherly love. Today's text is drawn from that chapter. Let us simply consider verse 13 for a moment. There we read: "Do not wonder, brethren, that the world hates you." If we look at the context within which this verse is to be seen, we find the following: we should love one another, and not be like Cain who was of the evil one and murdered his brother. We must not be people who hate others because we cannot endure goodness.

And then, in this connection, he says without any apparent need: "Do not wonder that the world hates you." According to John, love, kindness, holiness, and justice arouse hatred; and because this is so, because astonishingly the apostle takes the fact for granted, he says: "Do not wonder that the world hates you." He assumes that Christians are people who do good works, like Abel. So John thinks that goodness and justice provoke the antagonism, anger, and hatred of unjust persons, because they cannot endure the contrast with themselves; they want to see their actions endorsed by the actions of others, and are forced to blame themselves and disavow themselves if they encounter others whose deeds are just and good, so good that they even love their evil fellow man or woman.

So goodness stirs up malice, love stirs up hatred, and justice injustice. Injustice comes to light and is exposed because it cannot bear goodness. Now John says that this must happen to us; he admonishes us not to be surprised when it does happen to us. Of course the warning shows that we need to be rallied and encouraged to face this strange experience of good stirring up evil in this world which is divided and on trial, this world where everyone is asked to choose between good and evil, loving and hating, justice and injustice.

But it seems to me that we have an altogether different reason for being surprised at this verse of scripture. Does our heart need to be strengthened against the hatred which St. John says the world bears us? Let us be perfectly frank. Can we say that the world hates us? Are we persecuted for being Christians? Do we suffer violence and impoverishment for conscience' sake? Can we say that we do not belong to this world and therefore feel the lash of its hatred?

---

*Biblical Homilies, 184–87.

Or must we say: no, to be honest we are no better off than many other countries, we have our difficulties and perhaps our tragedies, but we cannot really pretend that the world hates us because we are just, because we love those who hate us.

Now if such is the case, are we what we really should be, people that St. John can assume will be hated by the world and who must be admonished not to wonder at that hatred? When we read this passage we ought to wonder, indeed be alarmed, that we are getting on so well in this country. We must ask whether we are the Christians we should be. By this standard of real Christianity we may well find ourselves wanting before God and our conscience. Were we strictly faithful to what we know is right, were we wholeheartedly on the side of the gospel, had we not taken this world of hatred and injustice into ourselves and given it room there, perhaps we should be less popular, perhaps we should realize more keenly that we are different from the children of this world.

Of course we are in danger of misapplying this criterion which shows our Christianity in such an unflattering light. There are Christians who think that to stand against the world would simply be old-fashioned and reactionary. There are Christians who come into conflict with non-Christians and rightly so, because the latter do not object to real Christianity but to the unchristian ways of us Christians, because we are a stumbling block to non-Christians instead of being the people we should be, so that others confuse us with our religion and conclude — alas — that they must reject our religion because they are rightly dissatisfied with ourselves.

In such cases we dare not say: we must not wonder that the world hates us. No. We should indeed wonder, not at others but at ourselves. All the same, this gives us no right to condemn everything about the church, Catholic practice, and Christianity as inadequate, out-of-date, reactionary, or even false, simply because it does not meet with the approval of the world. For here we are told: "Do not wonder that the world hates you." Do not wonder either if this hatred, this bitter hostility toward everything Christian, holy, divine, and Catholic, masquerades under the pretext that only what is old-fashioned, reactionary, musty, and primitive is being attacked. We ought not to wonder at the hatred of the world, even this concealed hatred, which can be a real hatred and must only confirm us in our faith.

So this world really places us in a strange position. We must not wonder at the hostility of the world, but wonder that there is so little hostility toward us. We must not provoke it with anything that is not the pure and genuine Christianity of love, truth, and fidelity to conscience. In other words, in ourselves and in the world we must constantly discern the Christian spirit from the unchristian spirit. That is difficult. We need the light of God, a fidelity and a purity of conscience that is able to criticize ourselves and criticize the world.

A staggering task. We must keep asking ourselves whether we are not too much like humankind in general, whether we are not — in St. Paul's phrase — too much conformed to this world. We must keep asking whether we do not misrepresent Christianity and give scandal to those who are not Christians but quite possibly are in search of true Christianity, because we pretend to be Christians and are nothing of the kind. May God give us the grace to bear the real hatred of the world with courage and equanimity, steadfast in our own genuine Christianity; and may God give the church of today and her hierarchy, and each one of us in his own life, the grace not to make Christianity seem to the world unworthy of credence through our own fault.

31 • Epiphany: The Blessed Journey of the God-seeking Person*

Most likely we have all taken part in the festivities of these last few days of the holy Christmas season. We are merry and joyful, or perhaps, since it is not always easy to be in a festive mood, we were only quiet and thoughtful; perhaps we were even a little melancholy. But still, it was a break from the routine monotony, and it did us all some good. For, in these days devoted to children and to *the* child, our hearts have been a little lighter and a little more responsive to the things that lie behind mere routine.

The feast of the Epiphany, the manifestation of the Lord, closes this festive season. It is, properly speaking, still the feast of Christmas, that Christmas which came to the West from the eastern part of the church in the fourth century A.D., and was fixed here near the Christmas feast that was already celebrated on 25 December. It is the feast of the proclamation and manifestation of the savior and redeemer to people beyond his own nation, to the "gentiles," that is, to all nations and all persons collectively. The message of this feast is that the grace of our God and savior Jesus Christ and his love for us has appeared.

In effect, this feast speaks to us and says: Behold, God is present, still quiet and gentle, just as the spring remains in the tiny seed, quiet

---

*The Eternal Year, 41–48.

and certain of victory, hidden under the wintry earth, yet already more powerful than all the darkness and all the cold. Epiphany is the feast that announces: God is here. God has become a man. He has entered into the poverty and the narrow confines of our life. God has so loved us that he has become one of us.

As a result, it is no longer doubtful how this drama that humankind plays upon the stage of its history will turn out. It is now certain that this tragedy that seemed to be so aimlessly improvised, full of blood and tears, is nevertheless a divine comedy, full of heavenly purpose-fulness. Now God no longer merely gazes down upon the drama, but he himself has a role to play and he himself speaks the decisive word, the key word. Epiphany — feast of the Lord's manifestation, which is still the celebration of the holy night that is brighter than our gloomy day, because it is the night that welcomed the eternal light into our darkness.

However, there is yet a *new* movement in this second Christmas feast, one that did not stand out so much in the first. Not only has God come to *us*, but in the power of this divine action the human being has come into the movement; people themselves go to him who has come to them. Indeed, one of the names we give to this feast, to this "supreme day" (as the Middle Ages called it), is the feast of the Three Kings.

Untheological and unhistorical this cherished name for the feast may be, because the wise men at the crib neither constitute the subject matter of the feast, nor were they kings, nor were there, for sure, even three of them; yet the name Three Kings points out to us a significant aspect of the feast's mystery: that the first men searched thoroughly for the child who was their redeemer, roving like pilgrims, journeying from afar and through every sort of danger. So this day is the feast of the blessed journey of the person who seeks God on his life's pilgrimage, the journey of the one who finds God because he seeks him.

When we read of the magi in the first twelve verses of the second chapter of Matthew, we are really reading our *own* history, the history of our own pilgrimage. Led by the star, three magi from far off Persia struggled through deserts and successfully asked their way through indifference and politics until they found the child and could worship him as the savior-king.

It is our history that we read there. Or better: it *should* be our history. Do we not all have to admit that we are pilgrims on a journey, people who have no fixed abodes, even though we must never forget our native country? How time flies, how the days dwindle down, how we are eternally in change, how we move from place to place. Somewhere, and at some time or other, we come into existence, and already we have set out on the journey that goes on and on, and never again returns to the same place.

And the journey's path moves through childhood, through youthful strength and through the maturity of age, through a few festive days and many routine weekdays. It moves through heights and through misery, through purity and through sin, through love and through disillusion. On and on it goes, irresistibly on from the morning of life to the evening of death. So irresistibly, so inexorably does it move on that we often fail to notice that we fancy ourselves to be standing still, because we are always on the move and because everything else also seems to be going along with us, everything else that we have somehow managed to include in the course of our life.

But where does the journey lead? Did we find ourselves — when we awoke to our existence — placed in a procession that goes on and on without our knowing where it is leading, so that we have only to settle down and get accustomed to this motion, learn to tolerate it, and conduct ourselves in an orderly and peaceful fashion, and not dare to consult God's will to find out where this procession is really going?

Or do we actually look to find a goal on this journey, because our secret heart knows that there is such a goal, however difficult and long the road might be? Is the human being merely a point in the world, in whom the world's nothingness is personified?

Does our spirit glow, only to realize painfully that it emerged from the darkness of nothingness to sink back into it again, just as a shooting star glows for a moment when it travels through our atmosphere on its dark journey to the empty universe? Do we run the course only to lose the way in the end? And does not the heart and the mind dare inquire beforehand about the law of the road, without growing stiff in terror over the speechless, helpless shaking of the head which is the only answer? Or cannot such a question be asked? But who could forbid the heart such a question?

No, we know very well that *God* is the goal of our pilgrimage. He dwells in the remote distance. The way to him seems to us all too far and all too hard. And what we ourselves mean when we say God is incomprehensible: ground of all reality; sea to which all the brooks of our yearning make their way; nameless "beyond" behind all that is familiar to us; infinite enigma that conceals all other enigmas in itself and forbids us to seek their definitive solution in what we know or in what can be experienced here on earth; boundless immensity in purest simplicity, in actuality, truth, light and life and love.

To him flows the huge stream of all creatures through all time, through every change and every succession. Does not our poor heart also have to set out to seek him? The free spirit finds only what it looks for. And God has promised in his word that he lets himself be found by those who seek him. In grace he wills to be not merely the one who is always a little farther beyond every place that the creature on pilgrimage has reached, but rather to be that one who really can be found, eye to eye, heart to heart, by that small creature with the eternal heart whom we call the human being.

Behold, the wise men have set out. For their heart was on pilgrimage toward *God* when their feet pointed toward Bethlehem. They sought him, but he was already leading them because they sought him. They are the type of those who yearn for salvation, yearn in hunger and thirst for righteousness. That is why they did not think that the human person could dare omit his one step just because God has to take a thousand in order for both to meet. They were looking for him, for salvation, in the heavens and in their heart. They sought him in seclusion and among people, even in the holy writings of the Jews. They see a strange star rise in the heavens. And God in his blessed kindness even allows their astrology, foolish though it may be, to succeed this once, because their pure hearts did not know any better.

Their hearts must have trembled a little when the theory drawn from their obscure knowledge of the Jewish expectation of salvation and from their astrology should now suddenly become applied in practice in a very concrete journey. Their bold hearts must have been a little frightened. They would almost have preferred that their hearts not take quite so seriously the noble principles of the theoretical reason, principles so foreign to reality and so unpractical. But the heart is strong and courageous. They obeyed their hearts, and they set out.

And suddenly, just as they leave their native land behind them, at the moment when they dared to take the leap into a hazardous venture, their hearts become light, like the heart of one who has ventured all and is more courageous than is really possible — according to everyday proverbs. They travel over tortuous paths, but in God's eyes their path led straight to him because they sought him in sincerity. It frightened them to be so far from their familiar native country, but they knew that in journeying everything has to be transformed, and they marched on and on in order to find the native land that will be more than a tent by the wayside. They knew from their own deeds (life is more than the mind's theories) that to live means that we are always changing, and that perfection means passing through many levels of change.

So they journeyed. The way was long and their feet were often tired, their hearts often heavy and vexed. And it was a strange, painful feeling for their poor hearts to have to be so entirely different from the hearts of others who, engrossed in their everyday affairs with such perfect stupidity, looked with pity at these travelers walking past on a journey that was so uselessly squandering their hearts. But their hearts carry on to the end. They do not even know where the courage and strength keep coming from. It is not from themselves, and it just suffices; but it never fails as long as one does not ask and does not peer inquisitively into the empty reaches of the heart to see if something is inside, but bravely keeps on spending the mysterious contents of the heart. Their hearts cannot be intimidated. They do not look arrogantly upon the men whom they pass. But they do move past them, and think, He shall also call these men, when it pleases him to do so. But we dare not be disloyal to the light, just because it does not yet seem to shine for them.

From the scribes in Jerusalem they got sullen information; and a cunning commission from a king. But from these sources their ears heard only a heavenly message, because their hearts were good and were full of yearning. And when they came and knelt down, they only did what they had in reality always been doing, what they were already doing during their search and journey: they brought before the face of the invisible God now made visible the gold of their love, the incense of their reverence, and the myrrh of their suffering. Then their path led out from the land of salvation history. They disappear from our horizon as quietly as they came (like those who die). But whoever has once poured out his whole heart for the star, to the very last drop, has already encountered the adventure of his life in that single instant.

These men, who have disappeared from our horizon, had royal hearts. If their real journey continued on to the invisible, eternal light — indeed, if it really began only when they returned to their own country — then such royal hearts found their definitive home. And that is why we want to call them by that joyous name of days gone by: the holy kings from the East.

Let us also step forth on the adventurous journey of the heart to God! Let us run! Let us forget what lies behind us. The whole future lies open to us. Every possibility of life is still open, because we can still find God, still find more. Nothingness is over and done with for him who runs to meet God, the God whose smallest reality is greater than our boldest illusion, the God who is eternal youth and in whose country there dwells no resignation. We roam through the wilderness.

Heart, despair not over the sight of the pilgrimage of humankind, the pilgrimage of human beings who, stooped over with the burden of their suppressed terror, march on and on, everyone, so it seems, with the same aimlessness. Do not despair. The star is there and it shines. The holy books tell where the redeemer is to be found. Ardent restlessness urges us on. Speak to yourself! Does not the star stand still in the firmament of your heart? Is it small? Is it far away? But it is there! It is small only because you still have so far to go! It is far away only because your generosity is thought capable of an infinite journey. But the star is there! Even the *yearning* of the inner person for freedom, for goodness, for bliss, even the *regret* that we are weak, sinful people — these, too, are stars. Why do you yourself push clouds in front of the star — the clouds of bad temper, of disappointment, of bitterness, of refusal, clouds of sneering or of giving up — because your dreams and expectations have not been realized?

Throw down your defenses! The star is shining! Whether or not you make it the lodestar of your journey, it stands in your sky, and even your defiance and your weakness do not extinguish it. Why shouldn't we, then, believe and go on the journey? Why shouldn't we look to the star in the firmament of our hearts? Why not follow the light? Because there are people like the scribes in Jerusalem, who know the way to Bethlehem and do not go there? Because there are kings like Herod, for whom such news of the messiah only means inconvenience for their political plans, kings who even today make an attempt on the child's life? Because most people remain sitting at home with the sullen worldly wisdom of their narrow hearts, and consider such adventurous journeys of the heart as nonsense? Let us leave them and follow the star of the heart!

How shall I set out? The *heart* must bestir itself! The praying, yearning, shy but honest heart, the heart well-versed in good works sets out, and journeys toward God. The heart that believes and does not become soured, the heart that considers the folly of goodness to be more sensible than the cunning of egoism, the heart that believes in God's goodness, the heart that will lovingly let its guilt be forgiven by God (this is harder to do than you may think), and that lets itself be convinced by God of its secret unbeliefs — that is not surprised at this, but gives glory to God and confesses — such a heart has set out toward God on the adventurous journey of a royal heart.

A new year has begun. During this year, too, all the paths from east to west, from morning until evening, lead on and on as far as the eye can see, through the deserts of life, with all its changes. But these paths can be turned into the blessed pilgrimage to the absolute, the journey to God. Set out, my heart, take up the journey! The star shines. You can't take much with you on the journey. And you will lose much on the way. Let it go. Gold of love, incense of yearning, myrrh of suffering — these you certainly have with you. He shall accept them. And we shall find him.

LENT

32 • Mardi Gras Tuesday: Christian Laughter and Crying*

Can the subject of our reflection for Mardi Gras Tuesday be anything but laughter?

We do not mean the sublime heavenly joy that is the fruit of the Holy Spirit, nor the joy that "spiritual persons" like to talk about in soft, gentle terms (a joy that can easily produce a somewhat insipid and sour effect, like the euphoria of a harmless, balanced, but essentially stunted person). No, we mean real laughter, resounding laughter, the kind that makes people double over and slap their thigh, the kind that brings tears to the eyes; the laughter that accompanies spicy jokes, the laughter that reflects the fact that a human being is no doubt somewhat childlike and childish. We mean the laughter that is not very pensive, the laughter that ceremonious people (passionately keen on their dignity) righteously take amiss in themselves and in others. This is the laughter we mean. Is it possible for us to reflect on this laughter? Yes, indeed, very much so. Even laughable matters are very serious. Their seriousness, however, dawns only on the one who takes them for what they are: laughable.

Is laughter such as we mean proper even to a spiritual person? Naturally, if it doesn't suit us, we should not toil over it. Such laughter must come from the heart — yes, from that heart that not even the saint is complete master of. In order to be a spiritual person, then, one does not need to force this laughter when it doesn't come of itself. We do not doubt the spiritual worth of someone who doesn't laugh in this way. By no means. The question is only this: whether or not the spiritual person must rightly call this laughter into question, whether or not she has to attack it as incompatible with the dignity of a spiritual person. No! Not at all! Let us explain and justify this laughter. When we do so, laughter shall smilingly tell us very serious things.

In the most pessimistic book of the Bible we read: "There is a time to weep and a time to laugh; a time to mourn and a time to dance" (Eccl 3:4). This is what laughter tells us first of all: there is a time for everything. The human being has no fixed dwelling place on this earth, not even in the inner life of the heart and mind. Life means change.

---

*The Eternal Year, 49–55.

Laughter tells us that if as people of the earth we wanted to be always in the same fixed state of mind and heart, if we wanted always to brew a uniform mixture out of every virtue and disposition of the soul (a mixture that would always and everywhere be just right), laughter tells us that fundamentally this would be a denial of the fact that we are created beings. To want to escape from the atmospheric conditions of the soul — the human soul that can soar as high as the heavens in joy and be depressed down to death in grief — to want to escape by running under the never-changing sky of imperturbability and insensitivity: this would be inhuman. It would be stoical, but it would not be Christian. This is what laughter tells us first of all.

It speaks to us and says, "You are a human being, you change, and you are changed, changed without being consulted and at a moment's notice. Your status is the inconstancy of transformation. Your lot is to stop and rest at no one status. You are that manifold, incalculable being that never factors out without a remainder. The being that can be broken down into no common denominator other than that which is called God — which you are not, and never will be. Woe to you if, while immersed in time, you should want to be the never-changing, the eternal; you would be nothing but death, a dried up, withered person.

"Laugh with me," says laughter. "But not all the time! Always and everywhere I want to be quite little, like God's great and noble creatures. Only the laughter of hellish despair should be continual on this earth. Only the devils should laugh like this, not you. But laugh sometimes, and laugh with ease. Do not be afraid of laughing a little stupidly and a little superficially. In the right spot this superficiality is deeper than your toiling thoughtfulness, which was suggested only by a spiritual pride, a pride that does not want to endure being a mere human being. There really is a time for laughter; there has to be, because this time, too, is created by God. I, laughter, this little childish simpleton who turns somersaults and laughs tears, I am created by God.

"You cannot encircle and capture me. You cannot put me down on your spiritual budget in so many precisely figured columns, like nickels, dimes, and pennies. It is hard to prove that, according to God's will and according to the principles of ascetical and mystical theology, I am supposed to crop up, to turn my somersaults just where I please. But for all that, I am one of God's creatures. Let me into your life, then. Don't worry, you won't lose anything by letting me in. The fact that you shall still weep and be sad takes good care of that worry."

Laugh. For this laughter is an acknowledgment that you are a human being, an acknowledgment that is itself the beginning of an acknowledgment of God. For how else is a person to acknowledge God except through admitting in her life and by means of her life that she herself is not God but a creature that has her times — a time to weep and a time to laugh, and the one is not the other. A praising of God is what laughter is, because it lets a human being be human.

But it is more, this harmless laughter. True, there is a laughter of fools and of sinners, as the wise Sirach instructs us (21:20; 27:13), a laughter which the Lord cursed in his woes (Lk 6:25). Naturally, we do not mean this laughter: the evil, unhappy, desolate laughter which seeks to help us escape the incomprehensibility of history by trying to comprehend this drama of history as a cruel, silly trick, instead of revering it as a divine comedy, serene and confident that its meaning will one day be clear to us.

We are thinking here of that redeeming laughter that springs from a childlike and serene heart. It can exist only in one who is not a "heathen," but who like Christ (Heb 4:15; cf. 1 Pt 3:8) has thorough love for all and each, the free, detached "sympathy" that can accept and see everything as it is: the great greatly, the small smally, the serious seriously, the laughable with a laugh. Because all these exist, because there are great and small, high and low, sublime and ridiculous, serious and comical, because God wills these to exist — that is why this should be recognized, that is why everything should not be taken as being the same, that is why the comical and the ridiculous should be laughed at. But the only one who can do this is the person who does not adapt everything to himself, the one who is free from self, and who like Christ can "sympathize" with everything; the one who possesses that mysterious sympathy with each and every thing, and before whom each can get a chance to have its say.

But only the person who loves has this sympathy. And so, laughter is a sign of love. Unsympathetic people (people who cannot actively "sympathize" and who thus become passively unsympathetic as well) cannot really laugh. They cannot admit that not everything is momentous and significant. They always like to be important and they occupy themselves only with what is momentous. They are anxious about their dignity, they worry about it; they do not love, and that is why they do not even laugh. But we want to laugh and we are not ashamed to laugh. For it is a manifestation of the love of all things in God. Laughter is a praise of God, because it lets a human being be a loving person.

But it is more, this harmless, innocent laughter of the children of God. All that is fleeting is an image, even the pleasant and rather casual laughter of everyday life. And in this case we do not even need to discover the likeness. The word of God himself has declared the real analogies. Scripture accepts this laughter that almost always borders on the trivial. Laughter, not merely a smile. Laughter, not merely joy and confidence. And scripture makes this small creature (which, of course, will have to grow dumb and dissolve into nothingness when it treads the halls of eternity) into a picture and likeness of God's own sentiments. So much so that we would almost be afraid to attribute to God the harsh, bitter, scornful laughter of pride. The thrones in heaven laugh (Ps 2:4). The almighty laughs at the wicked man, for he sees his day already approaching (37:13). Wisdom, speaking of the ungodly, tells us that the Lord shall laugh them to scorn (4:18).

God laughs. He laughs the laughter of the carefree, the confident, the unthreatened. He laughs the laughter of divine superiority over all the horrible confusion of universal history that is full of blood and torture and insanity and baseness. God laughs. *Our* God laughs; he laughs deliberately; one might almost say that he laughs gloatingly over misfortunes and is aloof from it all. He laughs sympathetically and knowingly, almost as if he were enjoying the tearful drama of this earth (he can do this, for he himself wept with the earth, and he, crushed even to death and abandoned by God, felt the shock of terror). He laughs, says scripture, and thus it tells us that an image and a reflection of the triumphant, glorious God of history and of eternity still shines in the final laugh that somewhere springs out from a good heart, bright as silver and pure, over some stupidity of this world. Laughter is praise of God because it is a gentle echo of God's laughter, of the laughter that pronounces judgment on all history.

But it is still more, this harmless laughter of the loving heart. In the beatitudes according to Luke (6:21), this is what we find: "Blessed are you who weep now, you shall laugh!" Of course this laughter is promised to those who weep, who carry the cross, those who are hated and persecuted for the sake of the Son of man. But it is *laughter* that is promised to them as a blessed reward, and we now have to direct our attention to that point.

Laughter is promised, not merely a gentle blessedness; an exultation or a joy that wrings from the heart tears of a surprising happiness. All this, too. But also laughter. Not only will our tears be dried up; not only will the great joy of our poor heart, which can hardly believe in eternal joy, overflow even to intoxication; no, not only this — we shall laugh! Laugh almost like the thrones; laugh, as was predicted of the righteous (Ps 51:8).

It is a most awful mystery, this laughter of finality, this laughter which will accompany those who have found mercy and are the saved as they depart this drama of universal history, this laughter that in the heavens will be the last laugh (just as in hell that last laugh will be incessant weeping), when the stage and auditorium of universal history have become empty forever.

But you shall laugh. Thus it is written. And because God's Word also had recourse to human words in order to express what shall one day be when all shall have been — that is why a mystery of eternity also lies deeply hidden, but real, in everyday life; that is why the laughter of daily life announces and shows that one is on good terms with reality, even in advance of that all-powerful and eternal consent in which the saved will one day say their amen to everything that he has done and allowed to happen. Laughter is praise of God because it foretells the eternal praise of God at the end of time, when those who must weep here on earth shall laugh.

The seventeenth, eighteenth, and twenty-first chapters of Genesis tell a strange story, the story of Abraham and his wife: how he became the father of all believers in receiving the promise of a son, because he believed, against all hope, in God who makes the dead live and calls into being that which does not exist (Rom 4). In the telling of this promise and its fulfillment, it is also said that the father of all believers and his wife — she who in her hopeless old age bore him his son, from whom Christ is descended — laughed (Gn 17:17; 18:12–15; 21:6). Abraham threw himself on his face and laughed. Sarah laughed to herself. "God has made me a laughingstock," she says, when she had borne the son of promise. The laughter of unbelief, of despair, and of scorn, and the laughter of believing happiness are here uncannily juxtaposed, so that before the fulfillment of the promise, one hardly knows whether belief or unbelief is laughing.

Fools laugh, and so do the wise; despairing nonbelievers laugh, and so do believers. But we want to laugh in these days. And *our* laughter should praise God. It should praise him because it acknowledges that we are human. It should praise him because it acknowledges that we are people who love. It should praise him because it is a reflection and image of the laughter of God himself. It should praise him because it is the promise of laughter that is promised to us as victory in the judgment. God gave us laughter; we should admit this and — laugh.

33 • Lent: "My Night Knows No Darkness"*

Does it not seem strange that even today the church dedicates a special season to penance? We can easily understand that people of

---

*The Eternal Year, 65–72.

earlier centuries may have required such a season for the housekeeping of their spiritual and religious life: they were joyful, content, and carefree people, whose heartfelt laughter rang out as they celebrated Mardi Gras in the streets. That is why they could experience — so we like to think — a short season of composure, of reflective seriousness, and of ascetical checking of their zest for living, and feel this only as a pleasant change in the tides of their life and of their soul.

But for us? Don't we feel that the church's proclamation of the season of seriousness, of contemplation, and of fasting is strangely at cross-purposes with reality? Doesn't a season of fasting seem to us almost like a ceremony from the good old days, a ceremony that comes to us with a light covering of dust? What meaning, what purpose does such a season have today for men and women who are suffering want, who are past all earthly hopes and are bitter at heart — people who would gladly fast, if they weren't already starving?

No, for us the season of fasting begins long before Ash Wednesday, and it will also continue far beyond the forty days until Easter. It is so real that we need not utilize this Lenten season — now permanently fixed in the liturgical year — like a conveniently available stage prop for our feelings.

The nonliturgical season of fasting of our present-day life seems to us even harder and more bitter than some of the painful times of a past race. For we suffer not only from lacking the contentment and the carefree security of life, not only from sitting in darkness and in the shadow of death, but above all — dare we be bold to say how it really is? — we suffer because *God* seems to be far from us.

God is far from us. This is not a statement that applies to everyone. It is not a statement that should alarm the God-filled heart. But it is also not a statement in which the person to whom it applies dare take pride, thinking that at least the bitterness of her heart is infinite. This is not a statement that trumpets forth a characteristic that the person should ignore, a characteristic that would seem to prohibit God from bestowing his nearness and the certainty of his blessed love, as if despair makes a person's heart greater than good fortune does. To make the distance of God into the proud nobility of the human being (as do many forms of that interpretation of life called existential philosophy) is sin, at once stupid and perverse. In many people, God's distance is simply a fact that is there and that demands an explanation. It is a pain, the deepest pain of the fasting season of life, the season that lasts as long as we travel as pilgrims, far from the Lord.

God's "distance" here does not mean that a person denies the existence of God or that she ignores God's existence in her own life. This may often — but by no means always — be a false reaction to the situation that we mean. Here God's distance means something that can be found just as well — indeed, even above all — in believers, in human beings who yearn for God, in persons who gaze out toward his light and the gladness that his nearness brings. Even these persons (yes, especially these) can and must often experience what we mean: to them God seems most unreal — he is mute and silent in refusal, as if he embraces our existence only as an empty, distant horizon would embrace it; our thoughts and the demands of our heart go astray in this pathless infinity and wander around, never to find their way out.

God's distance means that our spirit has become humble in the face of an insoluble puzzle. It means that our heart is despondent over unanswered prayers, and is tempted to look on "God" only as one of those grand and ultimately unbelieved-in words under cover of which people hide their despair, because this despair no longer has the power to accept even itself as real. God seems to us to be only that unreal, inaccessible infinity which, to our torment, makes our tiny bit of reality seem still more finite and questionable. This infinity makes us seem homeless even in *our* world, because it leads us to the extravagance of a yearning that we can never fulfill, and that even he does not seem to fulfill.

Yes, it appears that contemporary Western humankind, more than the people of earlier times, must mature expiatingly in the purgatory of this distance from God. If in the destiny of individuals it happens that besides the blessed day of the near God, there is the night of the senses and of the spirit, in which the infinity of the living God comes nearer to human beings by seeming to be more distant and not at all near, why should such times not also be experienced in the destiny of nations and continents? Why shouldn't this, in some way and in some measure, be the holy lot of all? (That the blame for such a condition belongs, perhaps, to one particular era, is no proof against the fact that this condition can be a "blessed fall" [*felix culpa*].)

Seen from this point of view, the declared atheism of many people, theoretical as well as practical, would then be only the false reaction to such an event — false, because impatient and mistaken. It would be reactionary in the proper sense: it clung to the childish experience of the near God as claim and condition of worshiping acknowledgment. When that childish experience is gone, then a person can no longer start with God, and there is nothing for her. The atheism of our day, then, would be the stubborn blocking off of the self against calling out in the dark purgatory of a choked-up heart for the God who is always greater than the God thought of and loved the day before.

Enough. There is a distance of God that permeates the pious and the impious, that perplexes the mind and unspeakably terrifies the heart. The pious do not like to admit it, because they suppose that such a thing should not happen to them (although their Lord himself cried out, "My God, my God, why have you forsaken me"); and the others, the impious, draw false consequences from the admitted facts.

If this God-distance of choked-up hearts is the ultimate bitterness of the fasting season of *our* life, then it is fitting to ask how we are to deal with it, and (for us it is the very same question) how we can today celebrate the fasting season of the *church*. For when the bitter God-distance becomes a divine service, the fasting season of the world changes into the fasting season of the church.

The first thing we have to do is this: stand up and face this God-distance of a choked-up heart. We have to resist the desire to run away from it either in pious or in worldly business. We have to endure it without the narcotic of the world, without the narcotic of sin or of obstinate despair. What God is really far away from you in this emptiness of the heart? Not the true and living God; for he is precisely the intangible God, the nameless God; and that is why he can really be the God of your measureless heart. Distant from you is only a God who does not exist: a tangible God, a God of a human being's small thoughts and his cheap, timid feelings, a God of earthly security, a God whose concern is that the children don't cry and that philanthropy doesn't fall into disillusion, a very venerable — idol! That is what has become distant.

Should one not endure such a God-distance as this? Indeed, we can truly say: in this experience of the heart, let yourself seemingly accept with calm every despair. Let despair fill your heart so that there no longer seems to remain an exit to life, to fulfillment, to space and to God. In despair, despair not. Let yourself accept everything; in reality it is only an acceptance of the finite and the futile. And no matter how wonderful and great it may have been, let it be really you; your own self, you with your ideals, you with the preliminary estimate of your life (which was sketched out and planned with such shrewd precision), you with your image of God, that satisfies you instead of the incomprehensible one himself.

Make *yourself* block up every exit; only the exits to the finite, the paths that lead to what is really trackless, will be dammed up. Do not be frightened over the loneliness and abandonment of your interior dungeon, which seems to be so dead — like a grave. For if you stand firm, if you do not run from despair, if in despair over the idols which up to now you called God you do not despair in the true God, if you thus stand firm — this is already a wonder of grace — then you will suddenly perceive that your grave-dungeon only blocks the futile finiteness; you will become aware that your deadly void is only the breadth of God's intimacy, that the silence is filled up by a word without words, by the one who is above every name and is all in all. That silence is God's silence. It tells you that he is there.

That is the *second* thing you should do in your despair: notice that God is there. Know with faith that he is with you. Perceive that for a long time now he has been waiting for you in the deepest dungeon of your blocked-up heart, and that for a long time he has been quietly listening to you, even though you, after all the busy noise that we call our life, do not even let him get a word in edgewise, and his words to the person-you-were-until-now seem only deadly silence. You shall see that you by no means make a mistake if you give up your anxiety over yourself and your life, that you by no means make a mistake if you relax your hold on self, that you are by no means crushed with despair if once and for all you despair of yourself, of your wisdom and strength, and of the false image of God that is snatched away from you.

As if by a miracle, which must be renewed every day, you will perceive that you are with him. You will suddenly experience that your God-distance is in truth only the disappearance of the world before the dawning of God in your soul, and that the darkness is nothing but God's brightness, that throws no shadow, and your *lack of outlets* is only God's incomprehensibility, to whom no road is needed, because he is already there. You shall see that you should not try to run away from your empty heart, because he is already there, and so there can be no reason for you to flee from this blessed despair into consolation that would be no consolation, into a consolation that does not exist. He is there. Do not seek to hold him fast. He does not run away. Do not seek to make sure of yourself and to touch him with the hands of your greedy heart. You would only be clutching at a straw, not because he is distant and unreal, but because he is the infinite who cannot be touched. He is there, right in the midst of your choked-up heart, he alone. But he is all, and so it appears as if he were nothing.

If we do this, then peace comes all by itself. Peace is the most genuine activity: the silence that is filled with God's word, the trust that is no longer afraid, the sureness that no longer needs to be assured, and the strength that is powerful in weakness — it is, then, the life that rises through death. There is nothing more in us then but God; God and the almost imperceptible and yet all-filling faith that he is there, and that we are.

But one thing more must still be said: this God-distance would not be the rising of God in mortal, choked-up hearts if the Son of man, who is the Son of the Father, had not suffered and done just this with us and for us and on our behalf in his own heart. But he has suffered and done all this. It happened in the garden, from whose fruit human beings wanted to press out the oil of joy, the garden that was in truth the garden of the lost paradise. He lay on his face; death crept into his living heart, into the heart of the world. Heaven was locked up and the world was like a monstrous grave; and he alone in that grave, choked up by the guilt and helplessness of the world.

As refreshment, the angel who looked like death passed him the cup of bitterness, that he might sink into agony. The earth wickedly and greedily gulped down the drops of blood of his mortal terror. God blanketed everything as with a night that no longer promised day. One can no longer separate him from death. In this vast death-silence — men slept, dulled by grief — in this death-silence the small voice of the Son floated somewhere, the only sign from God that was still left. Each moment it seemed to be stifled. But a great miracle took place: the voice remained. The Son spoke to the awful God with this tiny voice that was like a dead man's, "Father" — he spoke to his own abandonment — "Your will be done." And in ineffable courage he commended his abandoned soul into the hands of this Father.

Ever since that moment, our poor soul, too, is laid in the hands of this God, this Father, whose former decree of death has now become love. Ever since that time, our despair is redeemed, the emptiness of our heart has become fulfillment, and God-distance has become our homeland. *If* we pray with the Son, and, in the weary darkness of our heart, repeat his prayer in the garden. In pure faith. No storm of rapture will spring up, when his words mysteriously rise up somewhere in the depths of our hearts as our own words. But their strength will suffice. For each day it will be just enough. So long as it pleases God. And this is enough. He knows when and where our heart will be sufficiently purified — only here on earth can it be purified — to endure also the dazzling dawn of his blessedness. Our poor heart, that now in faith in Jesus Christ shares with him the night, which to the believer is nothing other than the darkness of God's boundless light, the darkness that dazzles our eyes, the heavenly night, when God is really born in our hearts.

All of this cannot be simply a religious poem for Sunday thoughts. It must be practiced in the burden and bitterness of daily life. If you begin to practice it, to stand firm and willingly drink the cup that contains poverty and want and God-distance, a blessed fasting season begins for you. Will you try it? Speak to the nearby God of your heart and say, "Give me your grace that I may do it."

34 • A Theology of Lent*

The idea of preparing for the annual feast of Easter with forty days of fasting (a number held sacred since scriptural times) instead of a week (the usual practice up to the third century) prevailed in the East toward the end of the fourth century. Rome did not accept the idea of a forty-day fast before Easter until the seventh century. Since then this *Quadragesima* has remained in both East and West, though with modified significance.

What meaning can we give to the idea today? Has Lent any significance at a time when a modern industrial society takes no notice of it (and hardly can)? It cannot properly be the time for baptism candidates and public penitents any more. And what does "preparation" for Easter mean: days of silence? preparation of the heart for the renewal of the baptismal vows on Easter night? The yearly retreat for religious communities? All these motivations behind Lent are justified and meaningful, and they can certainly be elaborated and developed.

However, could we not apply the sort of "Copernican revolution" in modern piety, which is justified and based on the unequivocal dogma of the church, to the significance, the "theology," of Lent too? To explain what I mean, I must begin further back.

Catholic doctrine has always known that not only are the explicit devotional exercises (prayer, reception of the sacraments, works of penance, and so on) "meritorious," that is, events of growth in grace, of maturity in Christian-moral personhood, of one's movement to one's ultimate end in the beatific vision of God, but that the same may be said of all works which one performs daily "in a state of grace" if they are freely posited and not sins.

For the earlier devotional life of the average Christian, however, this teaching was not really a conviction determining one's actual life. Properly religious life, in which the human being has something to do with God and God with the human being, did not begin until he had proceeded beyond the profane world and secular life to the point at which one began to pray and grow in grace through receiving the sacraments, at which one turned to God in a reflexive way through petitionary prayer, almsgiving, and (partly meaningful, partly superstitious) religious customs, "religious folklore."

A sublimer spiritual teaching knew something, certainly, of "good intentions" which enabled a person to sanctify the deeds and sufferings of one's daily life, but for the average Christian that was no more than a distant theory, and even in this teaching "good intentions"

Christian at the Crossroads, trans. V. Green (New York: Seabury Press, 1975), 81–83.

seemed mostly to be little more than an external addition by which a wholly profane work, which remained wholly profane, could still become "meritorious." There were two worlds: the earthly, profane world in which normal persons spent most of their time willy-nilly, and a religious world — appended as a heterogeneous element, fostered mainly by priests and nuns ("religious people") — which people "in the world" could only with difficulty and in small doses bring to bear on their secular existences.

Today Christianity is slowly learning that it can and must live and understand everything in profane life as a process of salvation (or damnation) if it is not to incur a false secularism such as appears to be in vogue today. Everything that is not sin but is freely and responsibly posited is, for the Christian in a state of grace, an event of this grace, a piece of salvation history borne up by the Spirit of God, an acceptance of his eternity. What we usually call "the religious life" and anachronistically regard as an addition (even if a necessary one) to profane life, is in fact the reflexive, individual, and social coming-to-itself of *the* life of grace which evolves at the heart of "profane" life and is only the obverse of profane life (provided, of course, that it is not a sinful no to God); it is an explicit and reflexive acceptance of the personal salvation history which unfolds in the daily life of the individual.

When, in prayer, we expressly "awaken" the "theological virtues" of faith, hope, and charity to God and our neighbor, we are not supplementing our profane life with the virtues, but making *this* faith, *this* hope, and *this* charity, which permeate our life if it is truly Christian, clear to ourselves in an explicitly formulated way. When we celebrate the Lord's death in the eucharist, we are celebrating the passion of Jesus in which we share "anonymously" in the passion and death of our own lives. When we perform an "act of hope" by "supernatural" grace, it is a "ratification" of that "perseverance" and "not despairing" which animate the daily round and possess an unconditionedness *in* that daily round which longs for an infinite satisfaction. And so on.

Is it now clear what is meant by the "Copernican revolution" in modern piety? It consists in the experience that the real depth of the apparently superficial and "worldly" everydayness of life is filled and can be filled with God and his grace, and that because of this ultimate meaning of apparently secular life, the expressly religious becomes intelligible and practicable for the men and women of our time. Conversely, of course, it cannot be denied that if the expressly religious is genuinely practiced, it in its turn illuminates this anonymous Christianity of the secular daily round.

The same may be said of Lent. Lent is the religious explicitness of that period of "fast" and "passion" which extends over our whole lives.

Today's welfare and consumer state has accommodated itself to a permanent lie: the impression is universally given that serene happiness is everywhere the rule, or if that is not strictly true in every case, it soon will be with goodwill and the irresistible progress of humankind.

Evidently no one would wish to quarrel with the ideals of more health, wealth, freedom, and so on by which modern persons set such store. The fact is that many things remain: pain, old age, sickness, disappointment in marriage, in one's children, in one's job, and at the end of it all death, which no one escapes and which is already a controlling, permeating factor of life. The question can consequently be only *how* one is to cope with this reality of suffering and death.

Cynicism and stoicism do not go very far. In faith, hope, and love a Christian understands this aspect of her life as a sharing in the Lord's passion. The acceptance in belief and hope of one's own passion is exercised by what in Christian asceticism is called "voluntary renunciation." In Lent, however, that which one must necessarily suffer in life in sober realism and can live in hope as a *Christian* passion becomes publicly known, in ecclesial, liturgical, and sacramental explicitness, as a freely loving participation in the passion of Christ.

35 • Ash Wednesday*

Mardi Gras Tuesday is over. There is a time to laugh and a time to weep (Eccl 3:4). Now we hear the words, "Remember, man, that you are dust, and unto dust you shall return." With the dust of the earth the priest traces on our foreheads the sign of the cross, the sign of the Son of man, so that what we are in reality may be made perceptible in sign: persons of death and persons of redemption.

Dust is a good subject for reflection on Ash Wednesday, for dust, the symbol of nothingness, can tell us a great deal.

The prayer that accompanies the distribution of ashes comes from Genesis (3:19), where the divine judgment is pronounced over all human beings, who had become sinners in their first parents. The divine judgment falls dark and hopeless over all: "For out of the earth you were taken; you are dust and to dust you shall return."

We dare not introduce into this text our platonic outlook on life, and think, Oh fine, the human body is clearly declared to be mortal. But what of it, for the soul is certainly immortal, and it can find no fault

---

The Eternal Year, 57–63.

with this death, which in the long run isn't so bad. On the contrary, this text, this judgment, is directed to the whole person: "You are dust."

Dust is an image of the whole human being. We may subsequently modify this image by distinguishing a twofold meaning: one meaning for the human body and one for the soul. Even in this distinction, however — which is certainly justified in itself — we stick to the one compact statement of scripture only when we do not forget that the assertion made in Genesis is concerned first of all with the whole person; and that this one assertion contains everything that pertains to the person, body and soul, even if it does so in different ways. *The human person,* therefore, and not just a part of his essence, is dust.

Understood in this way, dust is naturally an image, a graphic symbol. But it is an image that is fuller and deeper than our metaphysical ideas, which are often so remote and diluted. What, then, does this image tell us about the human person?

The symbol of dust was used as a declaration of the human person's essence not only in Genesis. "For he [God] knows our frame; he remembers that we are dust" (Ps 103:14). In Ecclesiastes 3:20 we read, "All are from the dust and all turn to dust again." Pessimistic? Yes, but this must be endured so that the joyous message of the new covenant can be grasped. Even pessimism can be inspired by God.

In the book of Job (4:19), the despondent Eliphaz complains in these words, "Even in his [God's] servants he puts no trust...how much more those who dwell in houses of clay, whose foundation is in the dust, who are crushed before the moth." "I am merely dust and ashes," says Abraham to God, in order to move him to pity for a sinful race (Gn 18:27). And if a person's death is to be described, Qoheleth again has recourse to the image: "before the silver cord is snapped, or the pitcher is broken at the fountain, or the wheel broken at the cistern, and dust returns to the earth as it was...vanity of vanities, says the Preacher; all is vanity" (Eccl 12:6–8).

Dust — truly a splendid symbol. Dust, this is the image of the commonplace. There is always more than enough of it. One fleck is as good as the next. Dust is the image of anonymity: one fleck is like the next, and all are nameless.

It is the symbol of indifference: What does it matter whether it is this dust or that dust? It is all the same. Dust is the symbol of nothingness: because it lies around so loosely, it is easily stirred up, it blows around blindly, is stepped upon and crushed — and nobody notices. It is a nothing that is just enough to be — a nothing. Dust is the symbol of coming to nothing: it has no content, no form, no shape; it blows away, the empty, indifferent, colorless, aimless, unstable booty of senseless change, to be found everywhere, and nowhere at home.

But God speaks to us: "You are dust." You — the whole of you — are dust. He does not say that human beings are only dust. It is an existential expression, not a complete formula of our essence. It can be spoken, though, even by itself, because the truth that it expresses must be experienced and endured to the full, so that whatever further is to be said about us (and there is a lot more, indeed everything, left to be said), this first assertion is not denied, watered down, nor essentially restricted.

For it lies in a completely different dimension. We are not a little dust and also, at the same time and in the same dimension, still a lot more, so that to be a creature of dust would not be so bad. Rather, we are *all* dust, and are more than dust only when we really admit this dust-existence, accept it, and "endure through it" with body and soul.

And because it is a question of an existential formula in this sense, then scripture can address this formula to human beings plainly, in all its harshness. Scripture need not add the comforting thought that we are more than dust, because this added notion, spoken in the wrong place, would be no comfort at all. Rather it would be the temptation not to take this dust-existence seriously, but to deceive ourselves about it.

Truly, then, scripture is right. We are dust. We are always in the process of dying. We are the beings who set our course for death, when we set out on life's journey, and steer for death, clearly and inexorably. We are the only beings who know about this tendency to death. We are dust!

To be sure, we are spirit, too. But left to its own resources, what is spiritual existence except the knowledge of things incomprehensible, the knowledge of guilt, and the knowledge that there is no way out of all this. We have enough spirit in us to know God. But what does this mean except that we know we stand before an unfathomable being whose ways are unsearchable and whose judgments are incomprehensible? What does this mean except that we stand before the holy one as lost sinners? What does this mean except that with our minds we grasp the meaning of what we are in reality: dust and ashes?

Perhaps this dust might want to boast that it is immortal spirit. If so, what would this boast mean except that this dust is, by its very nature, subject to the judgment, that as a sinner this dust has already been judged? What else would it proclaim by this boasting of its eternity except that it is dust, nothing but the commonplace, nothing but the abnormality of guilty indebtedness, nothing but anonymous insignificance, nothing but nothingness? Taken by itself, what is the spirit except the possibility of measuring the finite with an infinite norm, only to perceive with horror that the eternal cannot be reached.

And so through practical experience we come to realize that we are dust. Scripture tells us that we are like the grass of the field, an empty puff of air. We are creatures of pain and sin and of drifting perplexity, who are constantly and continually losing our way in blind alleys. We torture ourselves and others, because we do not know whether guilt comes from pain or pain from guilt. Despair is always threatening us, and all our optimism is only a means of numbing our hopeless, bleak anxiety. Dust, that is what we are.

It is not easy for the person to avoid hating himself (as Bernanos tells us). Actually, if dust really belongs to us, is really a part of us, then we shouldn't hate it. That is why oriental people, keenly aware of their origins, had such a remarkable relationship with dust, our proper image. He strews dust on his head, weeping and lamenting (Jos 7:6; 1 Sam 4:12; 2 Sam 1:2; Job 2:12; Lam 2:10). In tears he throws himself down and sits in the dust for which he was made (Is 47:1).

Because proud hatred and triumphing over one's enemies in white-hot intensity basically only enkindles despair about oneself (one hates *oneself* in the other and cannot stand the other because one despairs of one's own self as it is seen in others), for that reason we cast our enemies into the dust and make them eat dust (Is 25:12; 26:5; Jos 10:24; Ps 110:1; Mich 7:10; Ps 72:9; Is 49:23).

Dust doubtlessly has an inner relationship, if not an essential identity, with another concept of both Old and New Testaments: the concept of "flesh." "Flesh" certainly designates, in both testaments, the *whole* human being. It designates the whole person precisely in her basic otherness to God, in her frailty, in her intellectual and moral weakness, in her separation from God, which is manifested in sin and death. The two assertions, "we are dust" and "we are flesh," are, then, more or less essentially similar assertions.

From this conclusion, however, we must now go on to understand the change that the sentence "the human person is dust" undergoes in the Christian economy of salvation. The good news of salvation rings out: "The Word became flesh." St. Paul said that God sent his own Son in the likeness of human, sinful flesh (Rom 8:3). We can add to this and say that God himself has strewn his own head with the dust of the earth, that he fell on his face upon the earth, which with evil greed drank up his tears and his blood. Even more, we can say to him exactly what is said to us, yes, we can tell the eternal God: "Remember, man, that you are dust, and in death you shall return to dust." We can tell him what he told us in paradise, because he has become what we are after paradise. He has become flesh, flesh that suffers even unto death, transitory, fleeting, unstable dust.

But ever since then, as Tertullian says, this *caro* has become the *cardo salutis.* Flesh has become the hinge, the pivot of salvation. Since then, flesh designates not only the pivot and hinge of the movement into nothingness and death, but also the pivot and hinge of a movement that passes through dust's nothingness and forlornness into life, into eternity, into God.

Ever since that moment, the sentence of terrifying judgment, "dust you are," is changed for the person of faith and love. This is not the one who despairs at the downward movement of returning into the dust, and who "puts on the brakes" because he wants to stop this movement short of anxiety and terror. Rather, the individual of faith and love is the one who causes the movement to swing further, right into the midst of the dust and through it. This judgment still has a mysterious and shocking sense. The old sense is not abolished. The old sense must be endured and experienced in tears, in the experience of nothingness and of death, in evil and in dying, in the bitterness of internal and external limitations.

But even this existential sense of the pronouncement that we are dust contains another depth. The downward motion of the believer, the descent with Christ into the dust of the earth, has become an upward motion, an ascent above the highest heaven. Christianity does not set free from the flesh and dust, nor does it bypass flesh and dust; it goes right through flesh and dust. And that is why the expression "dust you are" is still applicable to us; rightly understood, it is a complete expression of our life.

When on Ash Wednesday we hear the words, "Remember, you are dust," we are also told then that we are brothers and sisters of the incarnate Lord. In these words we are told everything that we are: nothingness that is filled with eternity; death that teems with life; futility that redeems; dust that is God's life forever.

To say this is easy. To endure it is hard. But we have to endure it. In the boredom of everyday routine, in the disappointments that we experience in everything — in ourselves, in our neighbors, in the church — in the anxiety of time, in the futility of our labor, in the brutal harshness of universal history. Again and again we shall lie in the dust of our weakness, humiliated and weeping (grant, God, that this image shall never be realized in all its reality: in these days, a grave of atomic dust is all too possible). We shall experience again and again that we are dust. We shall not only be told this in a ceremony, but we shall experience it in life, and throughout life.

Just as the dying in baptism is only the beginning of a lifelong dying into the death of Christ, so too, the cross of ashes is only the renewed beginning of the return movement into the dust. Just as the sacrament of baptism is an image and symbol of the approaching humble reality of routine everyday life and of the splendor and glory hidden therein, so too, the sacramental ashes are an image and a symbol of the approaching humble reality of everyday life, and of the splendor and glory hidden therein.

36 • Ash Wednesday: "Remember, Man, That You Are Dust"*

It seems to me that *contemporary* artists and writers are more interested in truth than in beauty, if the latter is understood in the traditional sense. They speak more than heretofore about the unredeemed misery of our existence; they say that we are dust and ashes and return to dust, tired wanderers on dusty roads. Going where? We do not know. All amusements seem almost to be only a facade hiding anything but a natural *joie de vivre*. Is it then still necessary that we should gather here to be signed with a cross of ashes and to be told: "Remember, man, that you are dust and will return to dust"? Is it still necessary to commemorate the death of the Lord, which is only too present to us in our own life and in every mortal person, in whom we encounter Christ according to his own words?

Yes, indeed, "It is right and fitting," as we say in the preface of the mass. But there is a difference whether we proclaim our own misery or whether we let Christ tell us about it in the words of the church. For if we say it ourselves it is almost inevitable that we should either protest against it or indulge in self-pity; at best we shall be at a loss, not knowing what to do about it all.

It makes a difference whether we mourn for ourselves or whether another is mourning for us. The latter comes very near to being a genuine comfort: true our misery is not taken from us, on the contrary, the other says, with almost cruel directness that we are ourselves dust and ashes. But he who mourns with us has taken them into his very heart.

This mourning of Christ and the church on our behalf means, first of all, that we are allowed to mourn, for our sorrow has not yet been overcome, neither by our own strength nor by the comforting of another. It means further that we are allowed to weep, we need not pretend that we can get over everything keeping a stiff upper lip, we may well be completely bewildered, unable to produce a harmony out of all the

---

Grace in Freedom, trans. Hilda Graef (New York: Herder and Herder, 1969), 113–16.

contradictions and dissonances of our life. For God alone can do this, and we ought not to pretend that we, too, could do the same. But if we entrust ourselves completely to the ineffable mystery of our God, we shall not, indeed, be freed from our bewilderment. On the contrary, this will fall into the holy darkness in which it will become almost more cruelly painful than before. Nevertheless, there is no other way to dissolve it; it is still falling and has not yet been dissolved; therefore we are allowed to mourn.

The sorrow of Christ joins our sorrow and says: Your mourning is mine. In the darkness of death I cried out: My God, my God, why have you forsaken me? But before that I had said — an incomprehensible mystery — Father, into your hands I commend my spirit. Do not say that it was easier for me to mourn, because I was also God. I was and I am a man like you. True, I was the man in whom the Word of God had made humanity his own; but because of this absolute nearness I was also more exposed than anyone else, I could experience more poignantly what it means to be human, who is not God.

And how can you know what happens when God's omnipotent love takes the misery of his creature to his own heart and lets it penetrate even into the center of this heart? How do you know what happens when his omnipotent love compels the ever-blessed God to suffer the misery of the creature as his own? Your sorrow is my own sorrow, thus says the voice of Christ in the words of the church today.

But in thus mourning with us Christ and the church are also asking us if we hear and accept the accusation underlying this mourning. Not all, but much of what we call our pain ought to be called our guilt. We cannot separate our guiltless torment from the torturing guilt in which we have involved ourselves. We are always experiencing the one pain in which our own guilt also calls to us, the guilt of unredeemed lust and rebellious despair. Hence, while sorrowing we also always accuse ourselves. And if Christ sorrows with us, he does not relieve us of the accusation which we should level against ourselves, if we would only understand our sorrow correctly.

The words said to us on Ash Wednesday as our truth, our comfort, and our indictment are written in scripture at the beginning of the history of humankind; they are a statement and a judgment of what the human being is from the beginning. These words concern a beginning, but they are said by God. They sound like a statement about our future, about the abyss of death into which we shall fall. But our future is not what is said to us in these words, so that we should know whence we come and what we must endure; our future is he who says these words; their deepest sense is that *God* is addressing us.

He speaks to us because he wants to be involved with us. He has not yet finished speaking, he will have done so only at the end, when he will have fully communicated himself. In hard words he reveals to us the abyss of our origin, in order to promise us himself as the abyss of our future. He is ours, this is our expectation and our hope against all hope. The future is different from the past, else it would not be future. But there is future because there is hope.

What has just been said about the meaning of the Ash Wednesday words could not have been said otherwise; yet all this will remain empty talk unless everyone applies it to himself, changing the general into the particular, for only thus can these words be realized in an individual life. Thus death will perhaps mean only the quiet patience with which we endure the boring daily round, a request for pardon and its granting; perhaps it means the patience with which we listen to, and bear with another, or the unrequited faithfulness of love. Such death may also mean that we overcome our irritation with someone we find uncongenial, or that we have the courage of our convictions without being accorded the esteem that often goes with it; it may mean being faithful to one's own vocation even though this may not be popular at the moment.

Nevertheless, all this is only a "meaning" — the words still remain general and carry no obligation. They can be made binding only by the action of one's own heart, for this alone creates reality, eternity in time. For all these ordinary daily actions of a decent person really involve a death, namely the silent, unsung relinquishing of oneself and of the blind desire for felt happiness which is so unrewarded that we only experience it as just part of the daily round and cannot even savor it as an action that is its own reward. We die throughout our life. What matters is if we do it willingly, if the passion of Christ is also our own deed through which we receive grace.

37 • He Came on the Side of the Weak*

First Sunday in Lent (A), Mt 4:1–11

The Gospel tells us what came as the result of Jesus' fast in the desert — his temptation by the devil. Its place in our Lord's life is at

---

*Biblical Homilies, 13–16.

the beginning of his messianic activity. Before he begins to announce the kingdom of God that has come in his person, before he begins to preach, he prays. Before he appears in public, he goes into the wilderness. Before he mingles with the multitude, he enters the solitude. Before he seeks out men and women, he first seeks the face of his Father in heaven. And he fasts.

Jesus is truly a man and, because he is truly an historical man, everything he does or suffers must reveal and make concrete all that flows from his union with the eternal Word of God in his human nature. Although he is always in that which is his Father's, although his soul in its depths is always united in prayer with the eternal God, there are times in the life of Jesus when this hidden union with God is realized in what might be called an express and deliberately willed prayer.

Therefore Jesus goes into the desert, therefore he fasts; therefore he leaves behind everything else that a man needs even for bare existence, so that for this once not just in the depths of his heart but in the whole range of his being he can do and say what is the first and last duty of humankind — to find God, to seek God, to belong to God to the exclusion of everything else that makes up human life. And therefore he fasts. Therefore through this cruelly hard act, this denial of all comfort, this refusal of food and drink, through the solitude and abandonment of the desert, through everything else that involves a rejection, a self-denial of the world and all earthly company, through all these he proclaims this fact: one thing only is necessary, that I be with God, that I find God, and everything else, no matter how great or beautiful, is secondary and subordinate and must be sacrificed, if needs be, to this ultimate movement of heart and spirit.

In this desert of solitary prayer, Jesus is tempted. If we look more closely at these three temptations of our Lord, we see that in all three the devil seized on the apparent discrepancy between what Jesus knew about himself and what he was so immediately experiencing. Jesus knew that he was the Son of God. On this the devil — however we are to conceive him — fastened. If you are the Son of God, he says, then you should not be hungry, you should not be unheeded, you should not be powerless.

And in truth, if a man knows that he is the blessed Son of God, if he knows that he is not merely surrounded by God's loving grace but is so caught up in the whole of his human reality, so gripped in the depths of his being, that everything felt or known or experienced there is truly the reality of the eternal Word of God — is it possible that he should suffer hunger or thirst, that he should find himself in misery in the midst of a terrifying solitude and abandonment, where there is no one to care about him, where he is so pitifully poor and lonely and abandoned, where no one notices him, while elsewhere the world makes its din and convinces itself of its own importance and goes about its business without any reference to him?

Can he be reduced to such poverty and powerlessness that he has not even a piece of bread, that he can command nothing, that he has no one to minister to him? Is it possible that the kingdoms of the world with all their power and splendor should recede so far into the distance as to leave him all alone, insignificant, poor, hungry, and weak?

So the devil plays on this discrepancy between what Jesus knows himself to be in his true inmost reality and what he is experiencing in his hunger, in his neglect, in his weakness, and says to him: Take firm hold of your inmost reality and make your protest from there; say that there must be bread, that attention must be paid to you, that the kingdoms and the power of the world must belong to you.

And what does Jesus do? He once again abandons, so to speak, his awareness of his divinity and takes his place on the side of the poor, the abandoned, and the weak. He does not answer the temptation by saying: I am the Son of God indeed, but it is fitting that he should be alone and hungry and weak. He says only what anyone could say: though he is hungry, he wishes to live on the bread of God, that one must not tempt God, that one must serve God. That one must do what all of us must do: resign ourselves to the reality that falls to our lot, even to poverty, even to loneliness, even to weakness.

In this way the Son, reminded of his divine sonship by the powers of hell, embraces the common lot of us all — poverty, loneliness, the demands of God's service. He begins his messianic mission, in which not just in the depths of his being but in the action of his heart he strides across the infinite gulf that separates God from the creature, and finds himself where we are, the poor and weak, and lonely and abandoned, he to whom the devil had said: If you are the Son of God.

Since we are human beings and not the devil, we must say: If you are the Son of God, then you must be a son of man like ourselves, for our burden of toil and suffering can only be lifted if you act with us and desire nothing other than to share in our lot.

If we learn from this believing, hoping, loving stride across every-thing merely of this world that we are children of God, if we accept all the more willingly what falls to our lot, whether it be poverty or loneliness or the inability to change the world around us, then we are truly following Christ, then we are surrounded by God's grace and love, then God speaks to us with that power which can never leave us lonely and abandoned, and says: You are my son, I have loved you with an everlasting love.

38 • We Never Know When Lightning Will Strike Us*

Third Sunday of Lent (C), 1 Cor 9:24–27; 10:1–5

Today's text is taken from St. Paul's first letter to the Corinthians. Whereas other writings of St. Paul are either very personal letters of his to a church or an individual, or else deal with one particular subject, the first letter to the Corinthians — and to some extent the second also — takes up a series of unrelated questions and difficulties that had happened to arise in this metropolitan Christian community.

In chapters 8 to 10 of this letter Paul discusses the question of food that has been offered to idols. May a Christian eat meat that has been sacrificed to the gods during an act of pagan worship? To this eminently practical question, which fairly bristles with difficulties, St. Paul devotes three chapters, and today's text is drawn from those chapters.

On the one hand Paul was magnanimous in this matter. He was not a timid soul. He was not the man to maintain that the narrowest, harshest, most inexorable principle must be the right one. In practical matters he allowed the utmost possible freedom; he did not imagine that heroism must be demanded of Christians at every turn. He was considerate and level-headed.

Yet the apostle knows that Christianity does call for heroism, not because there is an ultimate point where a person must halt in God's name, but because Christianity is a categorical decision for God and his will. And Paul knows that there comes a time when there is nothing for it but to decide whether one wants to be a Christian or not. This is the context in which he is speaking now.

Perhaps we could put the marrow of today's text in the following way: Paul tells us something here about the gravity of the absolute decision which has to be made sooner or later in every human life. And because he understands that gravity, the apostle, like the church in every age, is not surprised that the Christian keeps encountering situations which seem vexatious, which he would gladly avoid, which involve this radical, inexorable decision — and that over what seem to be trifles, or over obscure moral questions that could apparently be debated forever, so that if an individual did not care to make his decision he could keep finding new grounds for putting it off or taking the easy way out.

---

*Biblical Homilies, 117–20.

No, says Paul. And he gives us illustrations, first from the sport that was popular in the great cities of that age, and then from the Old Testament. No, says Paul. There are moments of decision when all that is left to one is either to remain inflexibly faithful to God and his will, so that one simply cannot do a given thing, or to attempt a compromise at the price of one's salvation.

The example which Paul cites from the world of sport does not really seem to go to the heart of the matter. There is a race in the stadium. Naturally there will be one winner, the one who finishes first. The others also run; they will be second and third and will receive honorable mention; after all they are great athletes.

Now our life is not quite like this. The example is not particularly apt, for in human life everybody is running her own race. A human being is not compared with others; she either arrives and is the victor or does not and loses everything. That is really the point Paul has in mind. In Christian life everybody can be a winner and be crowned with the laurel of eternal life. But one can also lose the day and be utterly defeated, not coming in second or third but forfeiting absolutely everything. And this is the lesson of our lame comparison. Everything in this life is so mixed up.

There are no utter geniuses and utter dolts. Nobody is so poor that he could not be poorer, nobody so rich that he would not like to be richer. Nobody loves God so much that he could not love him more. In this world there is nobody totally destitute of goodness, whose heart is no longer capable of any spark of longing for God.

And so it is difficult for us to understand that our life centers more and more exclusively and radically upon one great question, even though we remain quite unaware of the fact, though we seem to go on and on in a world where there is no such thing as black and white, only various shades of gray. And yet all the while we are approaching a situation (even if it is met with in all its starkness, as it were, in purgatory) where we shall either have loved God with all our heart and all our strength or be lost.

We need not be anxious. We too are wandering in the wilderness, as Paul reflects in the second part of today's text, for we are the people of God. And though God, the maker of things visible as well as things invisible, has built us a house on this earth that we love and feel is our home, we still remain pilgrims here, in search of our true country. On and on we go through the wilderness.

Paul says: During their years in the wilderness — which were only a foreshadowing and parable of ours in the desert of this life — most of them were not pleasing to God. I say: We too are on a journey, on pilgrimage between time and eternity, earth and heaven; we have much to do; at God's word we must keep dividing our heart; not only may we keep compromising, we must — dividing our heart, our time, our mind, and our strength, so that we finally perceive that we have no lasting city here and are still in search of the truly perfect one which God, and he alone, can give us.

And yet in the midst of our lives, of our freedom and our struggles, we have to make a radical, absolute decision. And we never know when lightning will strike us out of the blue. It may be when we least expect to be asked whether we have the absolute faith and trust to say yes; when we must turn our backs on many things in order to cleave to God and his word in Jesus Christ.

Let us keep praying: God, give us the inner strength and steadfastness to keep our hearts awake, ready to say yes without reserve when the time comes to say it, despite all our worldly wisdom, all our contrivances, all our compromises; so that by your grace our poor divided lives may receive that perfection which can be ours for eternity.

39 • Conversion or Ruin*

Third Sunday of Lent (C), Lk 13:1–5

In this Gospel I read a passage that shocks me. One could render it freely as follows: "Don't think you are better than those political groups that have collapsed. If you keep on this way you will all be destroyed." It doesn't shock me that the savior, as we call him, made a gloss on a political event. Today we can probably already understand it, although the preaching in the churches is still too pious and has little to do with real life.

First, I am shocked that Jesus threatens *everyone* with ruin, if they keep on as they have been up till now. For at first sight it seems to me too easy to threaten everyone, and everyone at the same time. Because if one threatens everyone with perdition, one must have set aside the objection that surely not everyone is lost; because the world goes on, one must have been exaggerating. One has to grant that it is too easy to criticize everyone, because, if this world is really to progress at all, a position of radical and total universal skepticism is a contradiction in terms and in fact.

---

*Herausforderung des Christen, 53–54. Trans. Frederick G. Lawrence, Boston College.

Isn't this just what happens to preachers today when they repeat this saying of Jesus in our own time? They will say that no one can flee their lone decision — this will be clear at death at the latest — and that therefore everyone, and not just those with bad luck, will be destroyed if they do not turn their lives around. Preachers on this saying of Jesus will say that all need to be converted anew. Everyone! Everyone has to say: I! And as long as they do not say this in the practice of their living (and not just in some ideology erected for and against others!), so long do they belong to the "everyone" who are headed for destruction.

Look to yourselves and to your circumstances alertly and critically. We all tend to figure that others are lost, thinking that clearly this does not hold true for us, so long as we go along somewhat justly in the world; because we are surely all right. Or where we concede that is not the case in every respect, it has to do with a matter of no real importance. Or we say that a person can't disrupt her or his life every day. It is unrealistic to demand this or to do this, and it leads to hypocrisy. For at any point we could challenge ourselves, disavow ourselves, change ourselves, be converted — however one may wish to put it. We could do this today. Perhaps in some small way. It may indeed be a petty matter, but it can transform a life — and so save us.

40 • The Christian, the Devil, and Culture*

Thursday of the Third Week of Lent, Lk 11:14–18

In today's Gospel, Jesus drives out a devil and heals a dumb man. Jesus regards this healing of a malady which had been caused by diabolical influence as a sign that the kingdom of God has come, a kingdom that cannot be divided, a kingdom that stands in diametrical opposition to everything that is of the devil, to everything diabolical and infernal. On the one hand, Jesus regards things which are of purely earthly significance, things like bodily health which concern purely earthly welfare, as subject to diabolical influence; on the other, he regards what is right and good in this earthly dimension as a sign that the

*Biblical Homilies, 45–49.

kingdom of God, the kingdom of eternity, has come. All this is clearly relevant to our theme.

We can state it quite simply. Even in this Gospel, which has no intention of expounding cultural-political principles, it clearly emerges that every human being and every Christian has a cultural mission. Culture is taken here in the widest sense: everything in this earthly life that is worthy of human dignity, everything toward which a person feels herself drawn or fitted in her history or in her concrete situation, through her spirit or through the forces of nature.

Wherever the person makes something richer and more meaningful of his life, wherever he creates works of intellect, of science, of art, of literature, wherever he stamps the imprint of his spirit on the things of earth and expands his own being, there we find culture; and the human being is called to this by God not only for the reason, suggested in passing by today's Gospel, that he has powers given to him by God to be developed, but also quite clearly by virtue of the fact that he is a Christian.

The Christian is the person of eternity, the man or woman of God-given truth, the one who hears the word of the living God from beyond this world; the Christian is not just someone who prays: "Thy kingdom come" or "Let this world pass." The Christian is not just an individual who is waiting for eternity and who looks on all earthly things as temporary; as a Christian she is a person sent into the world to carry out the earthly mission of her creator and Lord, the creator of heaven and earth.

And why? So that everything that is good and wholesome, meaningful and upright, luminous and beautiful, and complete and splendid on this earth is given to know, through this healing which routs the powers of darkness, that the kingdom of God has come.

This earthly culture is not of course itself the kingdom of God, but is somehow a sign, a promise, a kind of sacramental sign that God loves this world, that he does not let it sink into the chaos of the diabolical, that he loves it, despite its sinfulness, in that same earthly structure which he gave it, that he guards it and cherishes it and enfolds it in the love of his creative will, and therefore that it is through his will that this particular world should exist, this culture, this spiritual universe of human beings.

God himself with his eternal kingdom is coming into the darkness, so that it may become light, for faith tells us that there is something fundamentally sound, pure, true, and mature, some real culture, some genuine humanity that comes only from the grace of Christ, from the pierced heart of the savior, and, in consequence, that wherever this culture truly corresponds to the divine will and plan of creation, something more is present, and it shows forth God's grace in the sound humanity of this earth. That is why the Christian as such has always a cultural mission.

The second lesson which we can draw from this incidental meaning of today's Gospel is that this world is a divided world. It is not merely a creation of God that has perhaps failed to achieve its fully earthly perfection. This world in which culture, humanity, and the creative design of God are to be realized is also a world in which there is evil and darkness and hell.

That is why the human being in all her creative activities, in all her earthly achievements and potentialities, in her literature and art and science and philosophy, is always liable to be seduced into falsity by the spirit of darkness, is always under the temptation to create a culture that is basically diabolical. That is why such a culture, such an earthly creation of the human person, must be exorcised and freed from all diabolical taint.

This is not entirely self-evident, as we know. We are in great danger of deceiving ourselves on this point. We tend to see the hand of the devil, the dark seductions of the abyss, only when we sin against the precepts of the book, against the express prohibitions of the ten commandments of God. And when we do not offend against these, then we think everything is in order, and we may easily find ourselves drifting with the tide, accepting as self-evident a "culture" that has been basically made diabolical by the forces of debasement, by sheer luxury, by wild, senseless, formless, and unhallowed sexuality, by the demons of covetousness and pride and self-imprisonment in things of earth — all this can easily happen.

We can let ourselves think that because a thing is obvious, because it is widespread, because everybody does it, it must be right and proper. We can let ourselves think that because this debased culture is widespread it must be acceptable, because it is widespread it must be right and even becoming for us. And if we fight against it, we can let ourselves think that we are fighting in the name of what we call the old values, and thus be merely preserving what was evil yesterday against what is evil and earthly and thoroughly worldly today.

It is not as easy as all that for us Christians; we cannot fulfill our cultural mission by just saying yes and amen to every current trend, nor can we content ourselves with an appeal to the past, for that too must be subject to a judgment, to a discernment of spirits. So it is not as easy as all that for the Christian in his task, in his mission to this world, and to present-day life. He must be a discerner of spirits. He must have the courage to say yes or no to both new and old alike; he must have the courage to develop by himself a Christian culture, a culture which belongs both to the present time and to God, a culture which is therefore a Christian, purified, and exorcised culture. This mission he can fulfill only with the help of courage and light and strength from above.

Even so it will happen that this Christian leaven, when mixed with the dough of this world, is fated never to become entirely pure, entirely radiant, entirely aflame. We are still the laborers who must bear the heat and the burden of the day, who will never fully achieve the mission on which we are sent: for the fact remains that this culture, toward which we have a mission and a duty, which we are to perfect in a Christian manner, which we are continually to purify from the power of darkness and of evil, will only reach its fulfillment in the kingdom of God.

Before that comes about, we can with the finger of God show signs here and there that the kingdom of God has come into this world in the form of something bright and wholesome, something sound and true. More than this we cannot do. But even this is a noble mission set before us as men and women, and as Christians, a mission against the darkness, to enkindle the faith that the kingdom of God has come.

41 • Law and Grace*

Fifth Sunday of Lent (C), Jn 8:3–11

We are all familiar with this Gospel. The "cream" of wholesome society accuses the adulteress. Jesus does not condemn her. The accusers have to slip away as the ones really accused, after they wanted in vain to compel Jesus to be unjust either to human beings or to the law.

We, too, are no better than these Pharisees who desired to entrap Jesus and the adulteress. For instance, we complain about the political parties; nevertheless, they are as they are because they have to respect our own egoism. We lament the younger generation; but it is the way it is because it grew up under their elders, under us. We accuse the church as a poor sinner; but we have helped add to its guilt — we, who indeed are this church. We usually feel ourselves beset by the guilt of others, instead of recognizing ourselves in others. When we admit our faults, that again is mostly only a particularly good trick of self-defense. Because our admitted mistakes are supposed to be removed by this

---

*Herausforderung des Christen, 51–52. Trans. Frederick G. Lawrence, Boston College.

admission from the criticism of others. Who really succeeds in being more horrified by their own egoism than by that of others? This miracle of grace seems to be more than rare.

What is disturbing and incomprehensible at the end of the story of the adulteress seems to me to be this: Jesus pronounces his "Neither do I condemn you" before he knows that this woman will sin no more. Once translated into our situation, have we ourselves already experienced or even done something like this? I doubt it. One must have already accepted the mystery of *God* to be able to understand and do anything like this. Otherwise people or also the law that protects people are always done an injustice. But mediating between people as they are and the law that states what people ought to be are only God and his grace. To them we ought to submit ourselves the moment we stand there at once the accusers and accused.

42 • Taken Up in the Eternal Day of the Son*

Thursday of the Fifth Week of Lent, Jn 8:46–59

Today's Gospel contains part of the controversies that Jesus carried on in the temple during his sojourn in Jerusalem for the feast of Tabernacles. We might consider it under two headings: What does Jesus say about himself? And what conception of himself, according to St. John, does Jesus reveal here?

The first thing that Jesus says is that he comes from God. He exists from all eternity. "Truly, truly," he says, "before Abraham was, I am." He is speaking with his human words, and therefore what he says he is thinking with his human thoughts, with his human soul, with his created mind which did not always exist, which came into being when he was conceived by the doing of God in the womb of the Blessed Virgin.

Yet he knows that he is the one who dwells with the Father from all eternity, who appears and speaks and acts with this created reality which is his human nature. If one may put it that way, he feels it in his bones: I who stand here, I who speak, I who appear, I am the one who is with the Father from all eternity. Here speaks an I — that is,

---

Biblical Homilies, 72–75.

a person — who is God himself. And so this day that he speaks of includes all the days which make up the history of finitude, and at heart everybody must rejoice to see the dawning of Christ's day, the one day of eternity, which shall have no evening.

In the second place, Jesus says that he tells the truth. He says, "If I did not speak as I do, I should be a liar like you." By this he does not mean that human beings often tell untruths. If he calls poor human creatures liars, he means something more. He is thinking of all that is brittle, fragmentary, obscure, discordant, and opaque in our souls; and then he perceives that he is different from others, that he is at one with himself, knows what he is and what he wants, perfectly understands himself, is not darkness as we are, we who creep painfully from one shattering experience of ourselves to the next, experiences that at once belie and unmask us, laying bare all the fatal flaws, all the black abysses there within. This Son of man who comes from God knows he is not like that, he behind whose human nature stretches the seamless eternity of God; he knows that he is not like other humans. He tells the truth, he is truth.

And in the third place, as Jesus says, he does not seek his own glory; he obediently serves the Father and does his will. Though Jesus is nothing less than the revelation of God in this world, though he is the existence and the presence of God on earth, though he is the self-disclosure of the eternal God among us, he does not seek his own glory but the will of him who sent him, the will of him from whom he proceeds as the Son, the Word, from all eternity; and he would save us, he would rescue us, he would bring us God's mercy.

And so he who is before Abraham was, is also selflessness, defenselessness, service, devotion, self-effacement, sheer mercy incarnate. He is the one who can only think of himself in terms of something quite other — the Father, or his own being-in-us. He is the true middle, which only exists because it proceeds from one thing and connects it with another, the mediator in all his fullness and human reality. He is the Word which the Father utters for us as well as for himself, the salvation which is only where it wants to be, if it has reached us and taken root in our hearts as that self-revealing Word of the Father.

In the fourth place, therefore, Jesus knows that he is the sinless one. "Which of you convicts me of sin?" he asks. He asks this question in the infinite humility of his human heart, without self-assertion, without boasting; he cannot help seeing himself for what he is, experiencing himself just as he is made in his created humanity, just as he is begotten in his eternal generation by the Father — the unalloyed expression of the eternal, holy Father.

And so: Who can accuse me of sin? He knows that he is pure service, pure devotion, pure obedience, pure love, God's sheer prodigality to the world; and he knows that all this is the diametrical opposite of all that we must call sin — self-isolation, self-assertion, refusal to serve, refusal to devote oneself, trying to keep oneself for oneself, refusal to listen, indocility to God: all that is sin, and all that is the utter opposite of what Jesus knows, experiences, and declares himself to be in this text.

And we shall have to say that we are also the opposite of what he is. But no: we may, and must, say something different. We are sons and daughters in the Son, God's beloved children, because he is the one who speaks to us today. So we may and must say: We are the ones God has thought of from all eternity, we are truly caught up in the Son's eternal day. In that day we are thought of, in that day we are loved, in that day we are foreseen, in that day we are preserved, by the faithfulness of the everlasting God. We are the ones, too, who come from God and his love. And so we must not seek our own glory but God's service.

We are the ones who daily experience God's word anew: Your sins are forgiven, you are sanctified, justified, loved; God's Holy Spirit has been given to you to be the center of your life and your love. Shaken by God's forgiving grace in his Son, you, a child of God, may say with St. Paul to the darkness of this world: He has delivered me from the dominion of darkness and transferred me to the kingdom of his beloved Son. So by God's grace we have a self-awareness that constantly asserts itself, by God's grace, against that other, native one we have as stiffnecked sinners, as lying human beings. In the ultimacy of that light we simply believe and flee to the Son who speaks to us like this today as to our salvation and redeemer, our grace and justification.

And when we do so, we can say something more about ourselves than our mere human, earthly experience of ourselves would have us say. If we are children of the Father, sons and daughters in the Son, then the glory that the Son tells us today is his, is destined for us as well, now and forever.

43 • Monday of Holy Week*

We are at the beginning of Holy Week. If we want truly to be Christians, this week ought to be a time when we share in a special way in the passion of Christ. We do this not so much by indulging in pious feel-

*Grace in Freedom, 117–18.

ings, but by bearing the burdens of our life with simple fortitude and without ostentation. For we share by faith in the passion of our Lord precisely by realizing that our life is a participation in his destiny. We find this difficult, because so often we fail to understand that the bitterness and burden of our own life do — or should — give us a mysterious share in the destiny of all human beings.

Internal and external distress carries the deadly danger of egoism, because it tempts a person to think only of herself, to be only concerned with her own affairs and thus to increase her distress by her self-centered loneliness in a vicious circle. But it should, and it can be different. We can freely accept our own distress as our contribution to the destiny of all persons, whose burdens are thus mysteriously lightened. This can be verified in everyday life.

Persons who suffer selfishly, who rebel and complain, actually seek to transfer their own burden to others, instead of bearing it silently so that it may be easier for them. But this is only the commonplace appearance of a more profound, all-pervading law: we always bear also the burden of others, and we should know that they, too, bear our burden in a thousand different ways which we do not know at all, beyond the restrictions of time and space to the very limits of human history.

Or have we never been terrified because the whole sorrow and torment of humankind seemed to confront us in a seemingly insignificant experience, in a tormented child, in a beggar or a dying person? And did not this sorrow seem to invite us to recognize it as our own and to help to bear it, and to accept our own sorrow in such a way that all humankind's sufferings would be made more bearable and be redeemed? If we were aware of this, we would also better understand that we can share in the passion of the Son of man during this Holy Week; we would understand that his passion is the unique acceptance of the passion of humankind, in which it is accepted, suffered, redeemed, and freed into the mystery of God.

44 • Tuesday of Holy Week*

In Holy Week we often speak of the passion, the cross and the death of Jesus. But this passion confronts us even, indeed first of all, in our practical life, not only in our pious thoughts. This can be ob-

---

Grace in Freedom, 118–19.

scured both by the mysterious horror of the cross itself and by the fact that we have become too familiar with the language in which it is expressed. Today we still speak of the cross only in the explicit language of the church and religion; perhaps some pious old Christians may still use the expression for the experience of their own life. This linguistic change makes it more difficult to relate our own life to the passion of the Lord.

But what do we mean when we speak of the cross, the passion, of death in relation to Jesus? In him these words had certainly a very deep and mysterious meaning. Nevertheless, the Son of man, too, experienced them as we do, only today we use different expressions. What is meant by them does not only take place in those moments when the incomprehensibility of life can no longer be shirked, for example, when our dearest die, when a lifelong love is forever destroyed by unfaithfulness, when the doctor tells us that death is imminent and inevitable.

What is meant is always present, especially if we do not want to admit it, if we suppress it and cover it over. It is always there: in the mute presence of death throughout our life, in the loneliness which is there even when we are quite near to our beloved, in the colorless daily round, in the thankless performance of our duty selfishly exploited by others, in the fatigue and deterioration of our life, which was once so marvelously colorful and exuberant. This passion and death are present when the inner voice through which a person had expressed himself has ceased to make itself heard and when all our life and all our hopes have ended in inevitable disappointment.

We ought to allow our living experience once more to fill the empty verbal shells of an all-too-familiar religious language, so that the word of the cross and of the imitation of the crucified Lord might suddenly receive an intelligible content and a power that force us to make a decision. Then we would know that we must truly act out our faith when we are asked: Do you accept the cross of your life, do you know that it means sharing in the passion of the Lord? Then we would meet not only in the liturgy of the church but in our very life the words: Hail, cross, our only hope in this passiontide, the passion that is also ever present and is always suffered even in the most commonplace life.

45 • Wednesday of Holy Week*

The car in which we ride through life may seem to us a fine, comfortable caravan which takes us on a holiday trip though beautiful scenery. But it is also the prison van of our finite being, in which we are shut up with our disappointments and the misery of our boring daily life, in which we ride on to our final end, which is death.

We all are cross-bearers in the sober sense which we have discussed above. No one can rid himself of this cross of existence. But precisely for this reason it is difficult to know whether we accept this cross in faith, hope, and love to our salvation, or whether we only bear it protesting secretly, because we cannot free ourselves from it but are nailed to it like the robber on the left of Jesus, who cursed his fate and blasphemed the crucified Lord by his side.

It is almost impossible to distinguish and decide between these two attitudes. And yet all depends on this distinction. Everything — that is the meaning which we give to our life or rather which we allow God to give it, and thus our salvation. The one question is whether we accept it or not. When do we accept it?

Certainly not if we talk much about it and imagine ourselves very brave. Certainly not by exaggerating the little sorrows of our daily life and whining and whimpering about them. Certainly not if we imagine that the will to bear the cross prevents us from defending ourselves and from leading a free, healthy, and sound life as long as is at all possible. Nor does the word of the cross allow us to be indifferent to the cross of another and only interested in our own comfort. But to accept the cross does not mean either that we should take a perverse pleasure in pain or be so dulled that we no longer feel it.

But in what, then, does this acceptance consist? It is difficult to say, because it can take so many forms that a common factor is scarcely noticeable. It may appear as a brave will to fight on, as sober patience, a heroic love of the cross, uncomplaining sharing in the fate of others, self-forgetfulness in the sorrows of one's neighbor, and in many other forms.

It seems to me that the crucified Lord has fathomed all these forms when he cried out on the cross: My God, my God, why have you forsaken me? and when he prayed: Father, into your hands I commend my life. In the first quotation the cross remains incomprehensible and is not explained away, while in the second it is accepted as this remaining mystery. Both together constitute the truth of the acceptance. The whole may be present even if we only utter the first cry while the

---

*Grace in Freedom, 120–21.

second is there, though it remains unspoken. Whether or not we become wholly dumb when death takes away our voice, that is perhaps the last mystery of our life.

46 • Holy Thursday*

On Holy Thursday Christendom commemorates the institution of the eucharist by our Lord. It happened on the night he was betrayed. Ever since then Christians have celebrated this meal despite all their divisions, though in sorrow that they cannot all celebrate it together.

Nevertheless, it is a consolation that all who call themselves Christians do celebrate it, even though their interpretation of what happens at it is not everywhere quite the same. The meaning of the sacred meal is immensely wide and diversified. We gather round a table, the altar, confessing by this very fact that we are to be united in love like a family. We know by faith that the Lord has promised to be present in such a congregation and is mysteriously there among those who share the meal. His death is proclaimed until he comes again, the death which brings us forgiveness and life, but which also takes us, who die throughout our life, into its incomprehensible mystery and melancholy.

But the meal that is celebrated is already filled with the blessed joy of eternal life which we hope for and expect. Christ unites us in the church, the community of those who believe and love, which is his body, by giving himself to us in the elements of bread and wine, the perfect signs of his body and blood. In this meal the word God speaks to us, the word of eternal love, becomes radiantly present in our darkness. In this sacrifice Christ, who has given himself for us once and for all, is presented as the church's gift to the eternal God.

Now it is true that, from God's point of view, the liturgical celebration of this sacred meal contains what it signifies and gives what it says. Nevertheless, as far as we are concerned, it receives its ultimate truth and fulfillment only when it is celebrated as that "communion" which takes place in the daily round of our earthly life. Even in the eucharist Christ becomes our salvation rather than our judgment only if we also recognize him in the least of our brothers and sisters whom we meet in ordinary life.

We announce the death of the Lord in the mass to our salvation only if in serene faith and hope we also encounter it in its everyday form of

---

*Grace in Freedom, 121–22.

sorrow and disappointment. This is how we must live if the eucharist is to be our salvation and not our judgment. But this awesome truth contains also a blessed mystery: many may perhaps meet the Lord in their daily life by faithfully obeying the transforming voice of their conscience even though they have not yet found the holy table of the church where he celebrates his sacred meal with us.

47 • Jesus' Last Supper and Our Eucharistic Community*

This evening we celebrate a memory wherein this our celebration also has another celebration as its object: the founding eucharistic meal by Jesus that we celebrate daily. On this occasion we are asked to reflect more exactly about *what* the historical link was between the church's eucharistic meal and the Last Supper; about *what* Jesus actually celebrated with his disciples before his death; about *how* and *why* the cross and resurrection of Jesus are equally constitutive for this our eucharistic meal as its link back to Jesus' last meal with his disciples prior to his death.

In it there becomes sacramentally, tangibly present in our midst the death and resurrection of Jesus, which in sacred signs intend to integrate us into their reality; so do we intend to open ourselves to this one saving event, and indeed again by its power and not our own. In this meal the church actualizes its own nature as the community of those who believe in God's mighty and irreversible coming. In it we encounter in sacramental sign our own future, the nameless and unbounded and unmanipulable reality that only opens up in death and is called God. In it there becomes visible sacramentally the community of those who acknowledge and seal our promise to let ourselves fall together with Jesus into this unspeakable mystery.

If we praise the eucharist of the church in this way as the center and highest actualization of the church and of our Christian lives, then we should not forget that this is primarily true of the eucharist insofar as, and "only" insofar as, it is the supreme and most central *sign of* unity with Jesus Christ in the church, which has to be received and lived in the midst of the gray ordinariness of our lives. Certainly Jesus is present among us in this eucharistic celebration in a completely unique way,

---

*Homily given on Holy Thursday, 1976. Previously unpublished. From the Karl-Rahner-Arkiv, Innsbruck. Trans. Frederick G. Lawrence, Boston College.

and is giving himself to us for our own. But this powerful presence of the Lord in this celebration is again only a sign of the presence of Jesus in his Spirit, which is always given throughout our lives and, because lived ever anew, has to be acted upon and suffered.

Only when these two modes of presence — the sacramental and the pneumatic (if we can put it so) — meet and mutually condition each other, do we celebrate the eucharist of Jesus as it was intended. Only when we emerge from this presence of Jesus in his Spirit in the midst of the gray ordinariness of our lives, only when we discover there our common destiny with Jesus, only when we undergo there the experience of his forgiving, liberating Spirit, can we authentically realize what happens in the eucharist we are celebrating, and what lends this unity with Jesus in his Spirit its sacramental tangibility as well.

We must be able to encounter the Lord in our lives: in his scriptural word; in our brothers and sisters; in our love for them that comes forth without counting the cost; in the everydayness of our duty, which takes us out of ourselves; in our experiences of disappointment; in the taste of death which codetermines our lives; and even in our guilt. Only when we discover Jesus and his destiny in every dimension of our existence will his eucharist we are celebrating with him and among ourselves also really be more than a mysterious rite, which we might fear we can no longer celebrate genuinely, even if, to the contrary, this sacramental event of itself can lead us into the true understanding of our life that we always and everywhere do and suffer.

Out of the ultimate depths (usually repressed by us) of our everyday lives into which God in his Spirit has already irrupted, we must and we can look with the eyes of faith to *Jesus'* last meal the way it shows itself to these eyes, and at *our* eucharistic community. Ultimately, the two are one and the same meal, and whatever we say about one holds true also for the other. So in the presence of both we can say: he is sitting at table with those he loves and calls his friends and so are always the new beginning of a community that believes in him, and in this faith possesses salvation, of the community that is supposed to embrace everyone at history's end.

He sits with them at the meal, because as human we are most intimately together with our many loved ones when our community of loyalty and love is also embodied in the common sharing in the bread and the drink taken from the one earth, from which everyone lives. He always sits together with them as if for the last time, because he knows that in himself and in his own he is always on the move in the voyage that, lonely and alone — in himself and then in his own — heads into the outermost darkness and solitude of death. And this death, his own in himself and that of his friends, stands before him. His death in himself and in us.

The absolute mystery of the unfathomable. The death of the living one, whose nature — in itself and by reason of his solidarity with us, also in us — is not like that proper to our nature taken from its own perspective alone, but always stands in a mysterious harmony with the collapsing fragility, the contradiction and the nothingness into which guilt seeks to escape. Before Jesus, who celebrates his and our eucharist, stands death, which is the bodiliness of guilt, and which is our fate that we both enact and suffer at once as the simple unique deed that is our own, and that, in the manner in which we do it, overpowers us destructively, once we have done it. It is the deed in which there comes about what is most our own and what is most alien to us. Jesus accepts this death in himself and in us; he goes to meet it, lets his life of absolute unity and purity fall into this abyss of hellish meaninglessness with which he has no community at all, either in his earthly life or now in his Spirit in us.

Because the incomprehensibility of the one whom he calls his Father even in his hour of death so ordains it, because he, the infinite mystery of obedience and love, worthy of adoration was able, even in this boundless emptiness and loneliness of death, to remain one with God and with us — this death is our fate. And with this death he receives into himself and in us everything else that also pertains to the infinity of this deadly and death-dealing doctrine: the obtuseness of the hearts of the disciples, of our hearts; the unbelief still at work in us; the pain, the betrayal; being rejected by his people, the brutal stupidity of the politics that kills him; the collapse of his mission and his active life.

When we celebrate the eucharist in faith, Christ takes the bottomless chalice of his life, then and now in us, and looks into its opaque depths and places it to his lips, already anticipating and saying yes to everything we call his passion, the passion of the Son of man, his death taken simply, which was always at work in human beings already from the beginning of the world. All this had its apex and its victory in the cross of Jesus, and it keeps on going until the final human life has been suffered to the end.

This acceptance of the unacceptable, this identification of life with death, this embrace of guilt by holy, obedient love, this thrusting of the light inextinguishable into the darkness — all this occurs during the easy and unobtrusive openness of a human life which, knowingly and prepared, heads toward death; and it happens in Jesus, and as in him, so also in us — this is the redemption of the world. It is our salvation; it is our last judgment that bestows grace on us; it is the tangible revelation that even we who horribly get ourselves caught in our guilt with no way out are accepted and beloved.

World history is at once the story of the guilt-ridden estrangement from God and the story of the passion that in Jesus' cross brings about the historical comprehensibility of the world's redemption. This passion — Jesus' and our own — that is redeemed and redeeming, gives notice of itself in the Holy Spirit and in the holy word of this kind of eucharistic celebration. This celebration asks of us whether we want to share the passion of Jesus in our lives, and provides also the power for such a sharing, until Jesus' life, death, and resurrection are also brought to completion throughout all the spaces and times of our very own lives. We celebrate now the passion of the Lord in sacramental sign, that it may be lived in the deed and truth of our lives.

48 • Good Friday*

The day we are commemorating seems far away, yet actually it did not begin in history and has never come to an end. For it began with history itself and is still present in our own life today. For what finally comes to light in the darkness of the first Good Friday is, in the words of St. Paul, the ever-valid and ever-new scandal and folly of the cross, though the apostle adds at once that just this is the wisdom and power of God for those who believe.

True, we do not always feel this. It is even a good thing that we realize our condition only rarely, else we should not be able to bear it. But on this Good Friday we ought to consider of our own free will the terrors of life, so that we may stand fast when we must face the abyss and endure it. For we all are gathered round the cross of the crucified, whether we look up to him or try to look past him, whether we are at the moment quite happy and merry (this is not forbidden) or frightened to death.

We are standing under the cross, being ourselves delivered to death, imprisoned in guilt, disappointed, deficient in love, selfish and cowardly, suffering through ourselves, through others, through life itself, which we do not understand. Of course, if we are just quite comfortable we protest against such a pessimistic outlook which wants to take away our joy in life (which is quite untrue); when we are vigorous

---

Grace in Freedom, 123–24.

in body and soul we refuse to believe that this will not last forever. Yet we are always under the cross.

Would it not therefore be a good thing to look up to him whom they have pierced, as scripture expresses it? Ought we not to admit what we have suppressed and to *want* to stand where we actually do stand? Surely we ought to have the courage to let our heart be seized by God's grace and to accept the scandal and absurdity of our inescapable situation as "the power of God and the wisdom of God" by looking up at the crucified and entering into the mystery of his death.

Many certainly do this without being aware of it by their way of life which accepts death in silent obedience. But we may also fail to do this. Hence it is better expressly to celebrate the Good Friday of the Lord by approaching his cross and speaking his last words with him. They are quite simple, everyone can understand and say them with him. This is the abyss of existence into which we fall. And we believe that there dwell love and life themselves. We say, Father, into your hands I commend myself, my spirit, my life and my death. We have done all we could do — the other, the ineffable that is salvation will come too.

49 • Good Friday: "Behold the Wood of the Cross . . . "*

One part of the Good Friday liturgy of the church is the unveiling of the cross. The priest unveils a large cross, and kneeling down sings the following words three times: "Behold the wood of the cross, on which hung the savior of the world; come, let us adore!"

What takes place in the simple power of liturgical gesture is only a shadowy image of what actually happened and is happening in the history of humankind. The cross of Christ has cast its shadow over all time. To be sure, historically speaking, the cross was erected only once in a definite place — on that hill of execution near the gate to the city of Jerusalem; and at a definite time — in the year 33, under the emperor Tiberius. And it was all over in three short hours. And then, no more.

But all time had waited for this moment that seems so short. All that had gone before flowed together into this moment. It was the hidden meaning and goal of all the long centuries that passed before the event of the cross. The ages of the early fathers, of the patriarchs and of all

---

*The Eternal Year, 79–86.

races were impregnated, darkly and in a concealed way, by the power of this event.

Invisibly and without notice, but directed by the hidden wisdom of the Lord of all history, all roads led to this place, all the roads that human beings, weeping and with bloody feet, had traveled since the first day of humankind's history, usually without knowing where they led. All the events of universal history could only ripen to their hidden fruit that is eternity, when this event took place in the fullness of time. If, previous to Christ's coming, people went astray, then it was because they did not know the one terminus of time, the cross, which alone remains while everything else changes. When they went the right way, then it was because they were already being led by that power that draws all persons to the one who is lifted up on the cross.

Yes, the ages before Christ were overshadowed by the cross. They were mysteriously mapped out to be a part of that divine and universal drama of the history of humankind, in which the cross of Christ, the glorification of the Lord on the cross, is the deciding word.

However, what was already mysteriously at work in the heart of these ages was concealed from them just as the ultimate meaning, the ultimate importance and the real impression produced by a word that we ourselves speak, is only really revealed when a response comes back to us from some other quarter. But before the word was actually spoken from the cross, no one knew what answer God would give to all the words of human history, to the cries of guilt and of need, of yearning and of complaint, and of urgent petition. Before the cross, no one knew definitively and unequivocally what God would say to us.

Now, however, God has spoken his final word in this world and in its history, the word that is the cross of his Son. And in the two thousand years since the cross, human beings have been advancing in a never-ending, drab procession to meet this unveiled cross — whether they knew it or not — in all the tangles and meaningless twistings of their path through life. Yet they have been advancing with a formidable resoluteness toward this unveiled cross. Persons from the beginning of their history, and of their misfortune, had been marching toward it, always in the dark shadow of the veiled cross. And in the two thousand years since the crucifixion, what came to pass during those three hours — when the cross on Golgotha pierced the heavens and the man thrust out upon it died — what took place then, happens again and again, continually. Many pass by, and many remain.

Many pass by. Their glance lights by chance upon him who hangs on this gibbet. Then they hurry on. For they will have nothing to do with such a one. To help is impossible. Even to stay there demands being well-disposed. All things considered, it comes down to this one person, the crucified. That's that. And you can't make a man who is nailed to the cross into the world's turning point. No one need seriously consider that. Many pass by. Perhaps they glance back and take one final look; they shake their heads, they laugh, they blaspheme.

They may even be saddened; in any case, they proceed to their daily agenda, declaring that Bacchus is a better symbol of the meaning of life than Christ crucified. They pass by, perhaps white with hate for the crucified, who will ostensibly rob them of the pleasure of life. They pass by regretfully, perhaps, like Cleophas: "But we had hoped that he would redeem Israel and now it's already the third day." Many pass by. On and on. Am I among those who pass by? Who pass by the truth of life, pass by God, pass by the true salvation? Am I in the procession that flows past the cross and spills into the darkness? Even those who wear Christian garments and who use Christian gestures, even pious Christians can hasten past the cross of Christ. Past, until all is past. Many pass by the unveiled cross.

Many remain. Because they belong there. Because here they have found everything. They stay. They kneel down. They kiss the scars. Sinners — we are all sinners — kneel down before this cross. For we have crucified him. Because our sins were laid upon him. Death is born from our sins, the death that overpowered him. He suffered from the sins we have committed. Sinners kiss the wounds that they themselves have caused. The murderers flee from their guilt to the murdered one, the executioners to their own victim. And so I go to him. And sinners, who themselves are crucified with him on the cross of their own guilt, speak: "Lord, think of me when you come into your kingdom."

The dying lie at his feet. For they suffer *his* destiny. They die because he died. True, everyone must die because of sin. But God has allowed this deadly guilt in his kingdom of this world for a reason. He held this world embraced in his love for his incarnate Son, in whose death he was so able to overcome sin through greater grace that the world could not escape his mercy. And therefore death, which we ourselves caused and which we suffer as the wages of sin, is first, last, and always only the death that causes the death of sin.

Those who suffer weep before his cross. What night of need was not his night? What fears are not sanctified by his? To be raised up in hope, what grief needs to know more than that it has been borne by the Son of man, who is the Son of God?

Before him the children kneel. For he has loved them, and although he knew what is in each person, he relied on them and threatened with his woe whoever scandalized one of these little ones.

Before him kneel the old people, who — let us be honest — have nothing more in sight and can count on nothing but to die. They kneel before their dying God. And they know that the greatest grace and hardest act of their lives are still to come. Only the one who dies in him and with him receives this grace rightly and carries out the act perfectly.

Before him kneel the homeless, and they gaze upon him who willed to die abandoned by his own people, outside the city near the highway, after living a hard life, not knowing where he would lay his head, poorer than the foxes, who have their dens.

The lonely kneel silently before him. For, as he was dying, the loneliest man of all, he knew them in the solitude of death and of abandonment by God. And he allowed all their bitter loneliness into his own heart, until everything else was driven out, except love for the abandoned.

Widows and mothers who have lost their sons and daughters kneel before him, weeping. For his eyes still look lovingly and with concern through the dark shadows of death that surround him, upon the mother whom he must leave lonely.

Lovers prostrate themselves before the crucified. For with him is all the strength of love and all the strength that turns the disillusion of love into that love which is stronger than death, into that unique love of Christ that can feed on its own fire and stay alive.

Before the cross the scholars and wise of this world kneel. They learn thereby that all wisdom that does not burn in the blessed foolishness of love is vain; they learn thereby that the logic of the cross, which to the Greeks is folly and to the Jews a scandal, is God's wisdom and God's strength for those who are saved by it. And they learn that it has pleased God to save the world through the folly of the cross, before which every mouth is dumb and all the wisdom of the world humbles itself — before the folly of divine love.

God's priests kneel before the cross, because they have to preach the cross and they are always drinking from the chalice of his failure. They kneel there because, with their sins and weakness, they are always putting themselves between God's light and human beings, because more than all others they need his mercy. The account demanded of them shall be whether they prized the blood that today flowed from the wounds of the Son of man.

It is also possible for those who think they cannot believe to remain standing there and to look at him. If they are humble persons who long for the light, and if they do not run away from the light in their greatest need — and today there are many like this — then they are such that suffer with Christ without knowing it. They should look upon the one who, as he was dying, cried out, "My God, my God, why have you forsaken me?" They should have the courage to love as their brother the one who (since he was the eternal Son of the Father) came into the dim, deadly darkness, in which a person has God only in the complete abandonment of everything, even of himself or herself. They should recognize their night as part of the Son's Good Friday. If they have dismissed from their hearts the impression that God is dead, then — if they only grasp it with faith — they share God's destiny of death, who himself willed really to die for them, who willed to be dead so that they might live and believe that even the furthest distance can be outreached by the silent love of their God.

Before his cross "I" kneel. Do you kneel there, solitary, ineffable ego that does not even know itself, that is a wavering spark between the abyss of nothingness and the abyss of eternity? If I do not know myself and my origin, if my destiny is hidden from me, if I stand in fear before myself and before the chasms of my heart — where should I stay, if not before the cross, in which the incomprehensibility of human destiny becomes the revelation that God is truly love. I kneel before him. And I am silent. For what shall I tell him, except what I am? And if I have never understood myself, what else can I do except surrender myself to him completely, to him whose love, loyal even to death, alone has understood me? And if this ego silently loves and lovingly commits itself, then it perceives that it finds its true essence and its genuine likeness precisely in the crucified.

So all who have come to know the mercy of God kneel before the cross that invisibly towers up through all space and all time. They prostrate themselves. They are silent. They weep. They adore the crucified. They adore the life that was given for us. They adore the death that brought us life. They adore the love that loved to the end, the obedience that was strong to the point of death, even to death on a cross. They adore the mystery that contained the answer to all questions. They look on him whom they have pierced and they understand the sins that they have committed, and the righteousness which the Son has satisfied, and the justice which came over sinners as mercy.

They gaze at him who forever stretches his hands out toward a stubborn and rebellious people. They want to be close to the Son of the Father, close to their dead brother who sacrificed himself for them. They want to be close to the one door through which the path leads into God's freedom, away from the slavery of finiteness and from the shame of sin. They want to possess him who alone proves that God loves to the end, the sole proof that by itself prevails against the thousand judgments of God that seem to testify to his wrath. They attend to the pledge that has value even in God's sight. They tend the sacrifice that alone penetrates through all heaven. They praise the consolation of their weary soul and the strength of their weak heart. They want to hear him who, in the torment of his agony, prayed for his enemies; who, in the shadow of death, thought of his friends; who promised paradise as he died; who committed his soul into the hands of the Father.

They want to hear him who can say that he fulfilled all things. They see with anxiety that he is no longer veiled from them, for they know, when they see their naked crucified Lord, that they are looking at the end result of all sin and all agony. For only light and happiness can come after this, the lowest depths of all calamity and terror.

They wait — if necessary, for a lifetime — until he, with lips that burn from thirst, also speaks a word to them. Let it sound as it will, it is a word of his mercy and of his love. This is enough. So those who are redeemed, those who weep and those who love, kneel under the cross of the world.

Do I kneel thus below the cross for the three hours of my life, until everything is also fulfilled in me and through me? Am I one with the crucified? My soul thirsts for God my savior. I want to rise up and I want to see him who has drunk the most bitter cup of this world. The most bitter, for in comparison what is the little bitterness that we feel, we who are sinners and so indifferent to it all? I want to kiss his bloody feet, the feet that pursued me even into the most monstrous inextricability of my sins. I want to see the pierced side of him who has locked me in his heart and who therefore took me with him when he went home, passing over from this world through death to the Father, so that I, too, am now there where only God can be. I want to see the wood of the Cross, on which the salvation of the world, my salvation, hung. Come let us adore him.

50 • Good Friday: The Cross—The World's Salvation*

Good Friday is the day on which the church — that is, we ourselves — proclaim the death of the Lord as our salvation. *The* death. But let us say first of all, quite deliberately, *a* death; and, before that, a dying. A dying. It was something normal inasmuch as everyone has to die and at every moment dying is going on in the world in almost innumerable instances; and the different instances of dying become more and more similar, the closer each one comes to death, so that when death is actually present it is no longer possible to distinguish one instance from another.

---

*Opportunities for Faith, 25–30.

The death of which we are speaking was not entirely normal, since it was a violent death freely and sinfully decreed by others. It might indeed be said that society with all that it involves cooperated anonymously in *that* death and even in those aspects which appear to be quite normal. But we should not put everything on the same plane: not every death is the same as that of Jesus, a political-religious murder.

This death certainly has a religious cause, the opposition of the people represented by its leaders to Jesus' claim; and it has a unique depth, which is involved in the nature and self-understanding of Jesus. But we orthodox Christians should not settle down too quickly with this final understanding of Jesus' death; for, if we pass over the penultimate stage, there is a danger of misunderstanding the last stage of all. But this penultimate stage, in which the ultimate significance of Jesus' death is revealed, takes the form of losing his life through being murdered when he is involved in an absolute conflict with the political-religious society.

To put it somewhat bitterly and cynically, we certainly cannot, as people quite often seem to do nowadays, reduce christology to the proposition: Jesus wore his hair long and was against the establishment. But neither should we regard his death as a nonpolitical affair, involving a conflict merely between religious ideologies which a priori have nothing to do with society as such.

This is not the time to begin to interpret the death of Jesus in the light of what is known today as "political theology." But this aspect of Jesus' death does compel us to ask whether we share truly and vitally the death of the Lord, whether we too can live in opposition to the maxims of a society or whether we are cowardly conformists, merely reflecting the conventional outlook. To be a nonconformist when necessary, in accordance with one's conscience, does not always involve physical danger; perhaps it does so very rarely. But what happens then is always really something of a death: a sense of solitude, of the futility of keeping faith, the uselessness of respectability. And vice versa, true nonconformity in face of the leaders of a perpetually impious and sinful society can be perceived by the fact that it is not a theatrical gesture, not a harmless game, not childish self-importance, but a readiness for activity which receives no internal or external reward, is unrecognized, and leads a human being already into that silence where death dwells.

It is impossible to generalize about how the active nonconformity required from each individual coexists with the life-style and the maxims of his or her society. It can exist in opposition to current patterns of moral behavior; it can imply the renunciation of a personal advantage which society and its laws would grant without question; it can grow into a fight, when necessary, against society's institutionalized injustice and lack of freedom.

At the point where this nonconformity seems hopeless, the folly and the powerlessness of the cross begins.

This is strange. Someone who begins his imitation of the crucified with this apparently penultimate and external stage of the death of Jesus will soon observe that such imitation is a gate through which he or she can enter into the innermost recesses of life, into a participation in *the* death of Jesus, which redeems us for the freedom of the children of God.

Jesus once said, "As you did it to one of the least of these my brethren, you did it to me" (Mt 25:40). These words imply a mysterious identity between the Son of man and every human being. They permit us to go from the Son of man to any other man or woman in order to perceive the ultimate depth of his or her apparently banal, ordinary life. But they permit us also, on the other hand, to perceive something of the mystery of the Son of man in the light of the experience of the unfathomability of any person. We are certainly justified in varying these words on Good Friday: Wherever you come across someone who is dying, you find me, the one dying on the cross.

Were we ever present where someone was dying and in such a way that we were really alert to what was happening? Perhaps we were, although we are glad today to banish death into the solitude of an impersonal, efficiently run hospital where the people whose profession it is to cope with the dying may be trusted not to take it all too tragically. If we really are present, however helplessly, when a human being is dying, we are justified by this variation on the words of Jesus in surmising what his dying and his death were, without disputing or obscuring their radical uniqueness and incomparability.

What is our experience at any person's death? Someone goes and leaves behind an empty place. Whether she knows it or not — at least if death is voluntarily accepted, something that happens more frequently than we observe — to make a place is an act of love of neighbor: it is done for others. The dying person makes a place and disappears in utter powerlessness. It is really impossible to help her.

She is radically alone; she dies her death, which no one takes from her, her death which is at once wholly unique and the most universal event in human life, so that this solitary abandonment yet again unites all, and each one in every death can catch sight of her own destiny, which quickly comes upon her, for she began to die at the very moment of her birth. And then death appears and the deceased person is entangled in a mute, abysmal mystery. All that we see now is an enigmatic death mask which indicates, almost derisively, that someone was here and has gone, and we ask ourselves what there is in this infinite mystery into which the dead person has fallen: the emptiness of nothing or indeed precisely that ineffable, holy, judging, and sheltering incomprehensibility which, helpless as we are, we call God. And we ask further, without being able to give a firm answer, *how* the dead person accepted this mystery: as the one *or* the other, as what seems to us so ambiguous.

Jesus died as we do and we shall come to understand his death only if we grasp the fact that it was the unique, incomparable, and redeeming death precisely because it was the most absolutely and radically human to a degree which *we* never quite attain: we, the very ones who irresistibly fail to measure up to ourselves and thus also to the absolute radicality of death. He went to his death and accepted it also as an act of love for others, for all. He accepted death face to face with that mystery which in death is inescapable and which even for him appeared as incomprehensible ambiguity, so that he spoke both of the void created by God's abandonment of him *and* of the mystery enveloping him as of the Father into whose hands he delivered up unconditionally his life and his death.

In the light of his life, his death, and his resurrection, we have the courage to believe that he really succeeded in dying this radical death. Hence there was nothing in him that was not yielded up in utter freedom to God's incomprehensibility, without any reservations and without cherishing any illusions which might have rendered this abysmal incomprehensibility less bewildering or innocuous to a degree at which we might in the end come to terms with it. He also accepted completely just this utter unfathomability as the protecting mystery of love. He succeeded in both: enduring to the very last the contradiction which tore his heart and entering into a unity reconciled and reconciling. When we acknowledge what is never completely intelligible to us, the radical nature of Jesus' human death, we have acknowledged him already in his death as the Son of God. For this radical death can occur only if God makes it, like this whole man, his own reality.

If we want to reflect a little more on the Christian theology of death, we must first of all make the obvious remark that the familiar statements of Christian dogmatics sound quite mythological at first hearing. Sacrifice of the cross, reconciliation with God through the blood of Jesus, suffering that offers satisfaction to the offended deity, the wrath of the holy God which falls on Jesus in our place: such expressions do sound at first like mythological statements, the meaning and truth of which can be grasped by us only with difficulty or not at all — quite apart from the fact that it is very difficult for us to understand how we can depend on another person at the very roots of our existence, as on our own inalienable decision and on God himself in his divinity, in which our freedom also remains enveloped.

We can and must interpret such formulas in the sure conviction that this well-intentioned interpretation does not lead us away either from the testimony of scripture or from the faith of our fathers. We are bound to strive for such an understanding, since it is only in this way that we can honor today's mystery.

First of all it is obvious that Good Friday does not mean changing the mind of an angry God who is disavowing human beings, but that this redeeming act itself proceeds from the pure initiative of God's holy love and is in no way effected by anything outside God.

Neither does it mean that God, in a kind of new, second approach, brings order again into his world which had been reduced to chaos in a way that was surprising and unforeseen even for God himself. From the very beginning, sin in human history was allowed by God to enter the world only because and insofar as he knew it to be overcome by the victorious power of his absolute love. Nor is it the case that Christ's saving deed at a definite point of space and time in history somehow impaired or rendered superfluous God's free act of grace *always* and *everywhere* sustaining the *whole* dark history of humankind or the freedom of human beings turning to God and liberated by God's grace, without which there is no salvation as consummation of freedom. Salvation and redemption are accomplished through the entire single history of all human beings and through their freedom.

What remains then of the meaning of the one cross on the unique Good Friday? The world, we might say, is sustained from the very beginning by the victorious self-communication of God always and everywhere, in the movement of a self-surpassing toward God, toward him as its consummation. Everywhere, that is, where there is not a final no to put a stop to it. And even this no — this is the Christian hope which cannot be reduced to theory — is constantly overcome and unmasked as powerless precisely by this God of victorious self-communication. But this very history, in which God is the innermost power of its movement and the goal of the world, has its climax at which there is revealed and made evident the direction in which it is moving, the source of its power, and the goal which sustains it and is irreversibly established within it.

This climax of history, which does not bring history to a close, but makes known its meaning and the victorious finality of its goal *within* history itself, is the cross, the death, and the resurrection of Jesus in one. Here God's yes to the world and the world's to God become historical, unambiguous, and irrevocable. Since we can always say that

the goal of a movement sustains that movement itself as its secret acti-
vating force and does not merely come at the end, we can and must say
that God gives himself to the world *because* of this event of the cross.
For God directs toward this event the history of his self-communication
to the world and the person's history of freedom, both of which are sustained always and everywhere by God himself. There is a point in this
movement at which God's movement toward the world reaches the
latter's lowest depths: in the individual's death, which God accepts as
his own and in which the world accepts this radical descent of God
into death simultaneously as his supreme manifestation and as that
which is most its own.

If we allow history to be history, a single one-track movement sustained by a goal in which the meaning of the movement itself becomes
historically evident, then the message of the cross as salvation of the
world loses all suspicion of mythology. In Jesus' dying and rising, salvation history, which is always and everywhere, reaches its unique
climax and therefore this cross is the salvation of the world.

51 • Good Friday:
Gratitude for the Cross*

In commemorating the death of Jesus as the ground of our salvation
and of our final hope for life, we should not at the outset overlook the
fact that it is in the ordinariness of life that we hope that we are saved
and redeemed and set free. Here already is a reason for gratitude for
the cross. The ordinariness of Jesus' destiny, which we believe to be
our redemption, became in fact saving because it was accepted by
God. It did not fall through death into the void but was caught up and
given definitive meaning in the loving and blessed incomprehensibility
of God. And thus an ordinary life, so like the life that we ourselves
experience, witnessed in a conclusive way to the self-giving love of the
mystery we call God.

In and through his death, Jesus' life was marked by an unimaginable dreadfulness that he alone as someone who gave himself in trust
and love to God could experience. All the terrible things that led to his
death, the injustice done him, the execution by the political and religious powers of the time, the brutality he suffered, were finally only

---

*Herausforderung des Christen, 42–46. Trans. Daniel Donovan, University of Saint Michael's College, Toronto.

preliminaries to a death that we all die and which everywhere in its incomprehensibility and in the final loneliness and impotency into which it leads is equally terrifying.

Although there can be enormous differences in our experience before death, the terror of death itself is the same for everyone. If by God's grace this terror did not bear within itself the hope of an incomprehensible life, and if this inner mystery of death had not become believable for us through the death of Jesus understood as the coming of the definitive love of God and as a passage into that fulfillment, which we call the resurrection, then we might well despair. Through the death of Jesus, ordinary death, which is common to us all and which we share with him, has become full of blessed hope. That death which is the fate of everyone, which reveals everything as provisional and passing, and which seems to involve all things in one and the same process of destruction, has itself become a sign of limitless hope and gives to all the rest its final dignity and meaning.

Everything that in its meaning, glory, and blessedness seemed to reach only to the fast approaching border of death has now an infinite glory and promise which no death can any longer limit. If all our days are ordinary because they lead inevitably to that great equalizer that is death, they have also become for those who in faith rightly understand the death of Jesus feast days in which the event of an eternal life is celebrated and the banality of this life receives an eternal dignity. Everyday life can thus become gratitude for the cross.

Although there are many grounds that might be mentioned for gratitude for the cross, our reflection about it is rooted in the experience that in Jesus God appeared and that through God's act the redeemer and the redeemed are one and the same. To carry this reflection a step further, this unity of redeemer and redeemed is intended, through the grace of God which comes to us from the cross of Jesus and which leads on to the universal triumph of his resurrection, to become a reality in us. What is characteristic of our gratitude for the cross consists precisely in our identity with the crucified one.

What constitutes the saving act of Jesus on the cross? To this question a thousand right answers might be given because what is being asked here sums up in itself all the incomprehensibility of God and of humankind, an incomprehensibility that no single formulation can exhaust. The scriptures offer the most varied answers to our question. It is not my intention to list them here. In dying, Jesus stood as a human being before that abyss of death that puts everything into question and renders it impotent. He let himself fall into it, accepting it in faith and hope. Through the true mystery of death, which we call God, that last cry of despair, which alone we humans of ourselves can bring to death, was transformed into a final and free abandonment of self in faith, hope, and love. In this abandonment the incomprehensibility of the God of the abyss dawned as pure blessedness.

Naturally Jesus' death has a meaning and a dignity that we cannot attribute to our own. It was the once and for all, irrevocable and unrepeatable word of God's power to us, the act of *the* Word of God. As fundamental as this is for Christians, it remains true that his abandonment of self in faith and hope into the incomprehensibility of death in which God dwells is also demanded of us in our death. In us too the redeemed and the redeemer must become one; salvation by another and salvation by oneself, when seen in their ultimate significance, do not represent contradictions for a Christian. Self-abandonment in death will only escape being an act of despair if we do it in the power of God's act in us, in the power of the Spirit which made possible and perfected Jesus' own self-abandonment. His death becomes for us the promise that the same Spirit will effect in our death this marvel of transformation of doubt into an acceptance of the incomprehensibility we call God. We cannot simply *know* that this marvel of hopeful self-abandonment is taking place in us, but we can firmly hope that it is.

It remains true that the saving self-abandonment of Jesus reaches out, if we allow it, to embrace us. We die in him and with him. This self-abandonment, of course, has to be exercised in ordinary, everyday life, in the unavoidable and yet calm acceptance of the renunciations that it entails, with its banality and barrenness, its hidden and thankless moments of bitterness. If in this way we learn how to die with Jesus and thus go to meet the hoped for miracle that in our death through the Spirit of God who bestows God's acceptance we will willingly abandon ourselves, then our life will become in its sober ordinariness an act of gratitude for the cross.

Many will give thanks through the calm sobriety with which they embrace life and death as these come to them without explicitly knowing that their very calmness is the result of God's grace or that they are reenacting the redemptive pattern of the life and death of Jesus. Those who in explicit faith have encountered the crucified Christ, the one who has gone through death into the life of God, know that they can expect something more and something different from their death than a despairing muteness, the beginning of a definitive and silent emptiness. For Christians the blessed hope of infinite openness that is present in both life and death becomes a duty, which finally God is and the fulfillment of which he gives us.

Christian spiritual literature often affirms that the pious must and indeed *can* accept with gratitude and even joy the bitterness of their life, its disappointment, pain, and hopelessness, the slow and yet inexorable approach of death, as their "cross." This affirmation and demand are incomprehensible. Gratitude for the cross is certainly anything but a self-evident possibility. That we accept bravely and without self-pity the harshness that is a part of life, together with its vitality, strength, and glory, is a demanding aspect of life that is by no means easy. But where what might be called the "cross" really enters into our life and begins to dominate it, where pain no longer affirms strength, where effort is no longer the price that we willingly pay for achievement and success, where trials and disappointments are the precursors of death which itself can promise nothing more than a fall into emptiness, there gratitude for the cross becomes incomprehensible. Gratitude seems to take its possibility and its strength from life, whereas what is now being asked is that we give thanks for life's destruction.

It would appear that in life we can only give thanks through life for life and not for death, but that in fact is what both the cross of Jesus and our cross primarily are. In this rather hopeless situation we might at least take consolation in the thought that when nothing further can be done, we are free from all obligation. This, obviously, would include gratitude for the cross. To Christians, however, and to those who in the depth of their being are anonymously but truly Christians, a great and finally incomprehensible promise has been made. In death they will not only be saved, as it were, from without by God's power, but this saving act of God will enable them to save themselves. Through an act that is both theirs and God's, they will be able in death to abandon themselves and thus experience gratitude for the cross. Such gratitude consists ultimately in the acceptance, through God's gift, of Christ's cross and of our own. The Christian hope is that God himself with his power will be with us in the abyss of our powerlessness at the moment of death so that not only will life follow death but death itself through God's power becomes our own act by which life is created. Willing self-abandonment is a deed that creates eternity.

Because God and human beings are not in competition with one another, dividing up, as it were, our reality between them, this pure act of God on our behalf is at the same time our own highest act. The acceptance of death which brings salvation and in which God gives himself to us is thus itself the perfect form of gratitude for the cross. Death which is our own cross and our sharing in the cross of Christ is not just an event at the end of life but is something that takes place throughout the whole of life. Every awareness of limitation, all bitterness and disappointment, every decline in our powers, experience of failure, emptiness and barrenness, pain, misery and need, oppression and injustice, all such things are precursors and even parts of that one death that we die throughout life.

The willing and hopeful acceptance of the many experiences of death in life are a part of that one experience of gratitude for the cross which we both suffer and do by dying in self-abandonment. Gratitude for the cross thus becomes a blessed part of everyday life. It does not consist in profound theories, eloquent words, or elevated feelings. Nor does it forbid us to struggle courageously for life, freedom, and joy wherever we can. True gratitude for the cross is the calm and honest acceptance of that slow process of dying that takes place throughout life. Such gratitude is basically simple. Because everyone, even if only anonymously, encounters the cross of Christ, all are asked whether they are willing to express their gratitude for the cross.

52 • Good Friday: Faith, Hope, Love, and Christ's Cross*

We look at the cross with faith, hope, love, and these three basic attitudes of Christian life should also set for us the themes and the order of our three meditations on the cross of Christ. If we place faith, hope, love in series, we are of course aware of the fact that with the inner limitation of these three fundamental actuations of the Christian person to a single meditation, we are always considering the totality that faith, hope, and love perceive as they look upon the cross of the Lord. Obviously such brief spurs to meditation can actually only hint at but a little of the unspeakable fullness of the mystery.

Faith looks at the cross of the Lord. What this cross first says to believers for their own lives is the simple yet frightening fact affecting the whole of life that the cross (though people may want to name it differently) has to do with things in people's lives which they cannot escape in the long run. In the life of Jesus himself the cross was unfathomably terrifying and unique due to its circumstances. However, not only in the frightful course of history are there repeatedly and everywhere, down to the most recent days, occurrences before whose darkness and horror we are struck dumb, without a clue, just as we are in the face of Jesus' death by execution. In the final analysis, there are not happy *and*

---

*Herausforderung des Christen, 36–41. Trans. Frederick G. Lawrence, Boston College.

unhappy persons, winners *and* losers, but (if we think of the one life of humanity including its end as a whole) only the vanquished: people who have been cast into that killingly silent unfathomability that renders us lonely in a thousand ways — poverty, illness, failure, cramped existence, frightful societal injustice. In Christian terminology we designate this unfathomableness with the hackneyed and pious-sounding word, cross.

We cannot avoid the cross, it leaves its imprint on our lives until it gets conquered in death; and it is planted on our grave as the sign of our having been vanquished. Of course we can and we have to defend ourselves against every evil in social and individual life. Of course the message of the cross should not be misunderstood as a call to nonaction and as a consolation for others in situations where we are supposed to fight for them. But all this does not change the fact that we all are the ones headed toward death, which is concealed in the interstices of our lives in their solitariness and unfathomability.

Yet our faith, when it looks upon the cross of Jesus, is challenged as to whether it will withstand this insight into the inescapable character of the cross. This realism without any illusion in relation to life is clearly the first thing required when Christians are bidden to take up their cross and follow Jesus. But how greatly both individuals and society constantly are tempted to cover over their own situation in its inexorability, and to suppress the word of the cross. Repeatedly in life and in society we have achieved — often great — partial victories over the cross. Already for this reason we should be joyful; the power of life, of the Spirit and of love make us happy; whenever it is possible for us, we should hope again and again for new partial victories. But all this should not suppress the knowledge of the cross. All life's victories ought to be united mysteriously with this knowledge in which we willingly accept the word of the cross.

At this point our reflection passes over into the question that each person must put to himself or herself in silence: Where is the cross in my life that I do not see and do not willingly take upon myself, and yet which becomes only a cross of Christ's blessing if it is seen and voluntarily assumed? Each person is asked, and each person has to give his or her own response. If a mature human being were to say, this question does not come up at all in his or her life, this person would be either one in whom the power of Jesus' cross has won its victory, perhaps in complete anonymity; or he or she would be one who in awful blindness has not yet at all broken through to the real question of life. All of us are asked, each for ourselves.

Hope looks upon the cross of Jesus. This shall be the content of the following deliberation.

Before we turn directly to this theme, a preparatory remark is needed. We want to speak about the one all-encompassing and all-supporting hope whose meaning and force is God — a hope that realizes it is promoted and justified at once in view of the cross of Jesus. Its opposite is absolute despair, which can also be quite soberly, quietly, and even possibly freely and guiltily in a person's life. But wherever a person has been torn apart by suffering, struggle, and death, and robbed of his or her free self-possession and of any real self-determination, a kind of despair can be present that has nothing to do with guilt and despair in the personal sense, in which a person goes from being an agent to being just a victim from whom God has removed all responsibility in order to take that responsibility upon himself and his unfathomable mercy, even though, when regarded from our perspective, the fate of a person in such desperation may appear to be as horrible as can be.

We have many hopes in our lives that fade, and the question arises whether we also have a hope given by God himself that underpins and embraces everything; a hope that does not perish, but lasts through all our other hopes' undertakings. We have many hopes: for health, for victory over sickness, for success in life, for love and security, for peace in the world, and thousands of other things to which the life impulse reaches out. They are all good in themselves; we also experience repeatedly the fulfillment of these hopes in part and for a period of time. Finally, all these hopes get disappointed. They fade and pass away, whether they have been fulfilled or not; because we are headed toward death, and along this path our hopes are taken away one after another.

What then? What even now when we are overpowered by the ultimate hopelessness of our hopes in an hour of quiet, or in the midst of life's turmoil? What, when the lights of our lives that illumined our every day are extinguished one by one? When evening and night come and everything melts into a silent unreality? Is there just despair at the death of every hope, a despair that clings to itself, perhaps without a word, and yet is the only thing remaining? Or does there occur then the event of the one and only, but all-encompassing, hope? Christians witness the experience that in the death of all hopes hope can surge up and conquer. Then we have no single thing to hold onto; the one unfathomability embracing all, and called by the true name of God, silently receives us. And when we let ourselves be taken and fall, trusting that this unfathomable mystery is the one blessed homeland, then we experience that we do not have to hold on in order to be held, we do not have to struggle to win, we do not have to pursue now this thing and now that in order to possess the one hope that is unfathomable, and which to a certain extent is suspended in itself, and yet shelters in itself the unspeakable fulfillment.

But there is something else to Christian hope — a hopeful knowledge of Jesus' victory in his defeat. And in Christians these two moments, the letting ourselves fall into God's unfathomability as into our ineffable happiness, and the confession of Jesus' victory in his mortal defeat, mutually condition and support each other. And together they form the one Christian hope. Because when people in the experience of their own banality and guilt could despair of themselves on the basis of their own resources, they realize in view of Jesus, so selfless and holy, that they should at least not let this life fall desperate into vacuous meaninglessness, but instead must confess him together with his life's destiny as the one living with God forever. And they themselves ought to have a hope because this crucified one loved them even till the end. Then the experience of God in the defeat of our hopes as the hope and the confession of the crucified as the conqueror converge in one Christian hope. Do we have this kind of hope, the only hope? In Holy Week we pray: *Ave crux, spes unica.* Hail, cross, our only hope.

Finally, love is called upon to look upon the love of the crucified for us. The reciprocal love between Jesus and Christians in view of the cross is our theme, a theme that cannot be sounded completely, because the love meant here in itself can alone be understood by the lover in love; and all reflection upon it has to fall short. And this makes sense, especially when it is a matter of the love of the crucified Son of God, and we are dealing with the love that is supposed to be the salvation of our existence in its entirety. Though we are not able to sound the depths of our theme, only two questions may be asked modestly and humbly: Did the crucified one love us, or indeed me, on the cross? Can I really love him?

Has Jesus loved me on the cross? Could he know about me in my concrete, unique existence? Could he know about me in the godforsaken darkness and terrible impotence of his death? Was there room for me in this dying Jesus? And does this love extend to me over such great spaces and times to where I must live and die? To this question we have to answer a shocking but believing yes, even though it remains obscure to us how love is possible in the heart of a finite human being and in the darkness of death. The scriptures attest to it out of their living experience of the Spirit of Jesus: he has loved me and given himself for me. Erudite theology seeks to elucidate the possibility of this love attested to by the scriptures by pointing to the most radical unity of the divine Word and the human reality of Jesus, and to the conjunction of the divine consciousness and of human consciousness, for this union in Jesus also makes possible a knowledge of each and every person in his human consciousness.

Perhaps we can get a little sense of this possibility from another perspective. The dimensions and levels on which people enter into relations with each other and so enable love are very disparate. So, too, there are the most diverse modes of love — superficial, everyday, and love as the most radical element in the innermost core of a person's existence. The mere fact that we are in bodily proximity and friendly feelings pass back and forth between us does not necessarily mean that the absolute love which really unites and lasts in the ultimate depths is present. But whenever anyone, whether in blessed light or in mortal night, really lets go, lets themselves fall, and gives themselves unconditionally over to the unfathomable mystery, which tears them away from themselves, and enables ultimate love (which is giving ourselves away), which at the same time is the origin and goal of all realities and of all people, precisely then do the kind of people who love themselves away attain the innermost ground of all reality which is close to everyone. Jesus loves everyone, he loves me, because he has totally forgotten about himself and so, out of the unfathomable center of all reality, definitively has come close to me and to everyone in death.

Can I love Jesus? Or is this kind of love only a rare, unreal ideology, a pious introvertedness and substitute for the love we owe any real, concrete human person who encounters us in everyday life? This question has to be responded to with the Gospel of Matthew, chapter 25, and with the first epistle of John. According to the witness of scripture, one can only truly love God and Jesus in the measure that one really loves the concrete neighbor. If one loves the neighbor truly, without reservation and at the risk of one's whole existence, then such love is already, expressly or unreflectively, a breakthrough to the very reality in which God and human beings are irrevocably one, in which God guarantees the possibility and the happy outcome of the risk of human love. And in this reality, God does not allow it just to be a risk that falls through in the end, but makes it possible in this unity for human beings to love God himself humanly in a human being.

However, this unity is called the Godman Jesus Christ. Love for others, which in itself is defenseless against suspicion of being an absurd risk, is thus a breakthrough to the love of the Godman wherever it still enters into love's radical risk, whether we are explicitly aware of it or not. The Christian, however, knows this. When he or she tries really to love the neighbor, he or she should hope to be loving Jesus too, and to make this love in prayer and hope into the explicit center of his or her life.

The gaze of love rests on the crucified one and the Christian knows: I am embraced by an eternal love in the midst of my disappointments, my misery, my having been consecrated for death, my guilt. And the Christian knows: I am myself liberated by this love that encompasses me into the possibility of being able to love human beings and God.

53 • Holy Saturday*

Holy Saturday is a strange day, mysterious and silent. It is a day without a liturgy. This is, as it were, a symbol of everyday life which is a mean between the abysmal terror of Good Friday and the exuberant joy of Easter. For ordinary life is also mostly in between the two, in the center which is also a transition and can only be this.

Perhaps the worst in life is already behind us. Though this is not certain, and perhaps not even radically true. For the very end is still before us. Nevertheless, maybe we have "come through"; perhaps the old wounds are no longer bleeding; we have become wiser and more modest in our desires; we expect less from ourselves and others, and our resignation is not too painful.

This may be just as well. We cannot always have everything in one exercise, as a medieval mystic says. We need not always be horrified by the incomprehensibility of life nor entranced by its glory, we need not always celebrate the highest liturgy of life or death. Ordinariness, too, may be a blessing. But this ordinariness of the in-between must be understood as a transition, the transition from Good Friday to Easter.

The human being, especially the Christian, has not the right to be modest, she must maintain her infinite claim. The fact that her pain is bearable must not be allowed to replace her blessed duty to hope for the infinite joy of eternity. Because God *is,* he may demand all, for he is all. Because death has died in Christ, our resignation must also die.

The Holy Saturday of our life must be the preparation for Easter, the persistent hope for the final glory of God. If we live the Holy Saturday of our existence properly, this will not be a merely ideological addition to this common life as the mean between its contraries. It is realized in what makes our everyday life specifically human: in the patience that can wait, in the sense of humor which does not take things too seriously, in being prepared to let others be first, in the courage which always seeks for a way out of the difficulties.

Grace in Freedom, 124–25.

The virtue of our daily life is the hope which does what is possible and expects God to do the impossible. To express it somewhat paradoxically, but nevertheless seriously: the worst has actually already happened; we exist, and even death cannot deprive us of this. Now is the Holy Saturday of our ordinary life, but there will also be Easter, our true and eternal life.

EASTER AND PENTECOST

54 • Risen Victorious
from the Tomb*

Meditation for the Easter Vigil

It is Holy Saturday evening. We are looking forward to the feast of Easter. We can have a living Christian faith in the exultant proclamation of this feast only if we try to understand the content of this faith as intrinsically related to our life at the present time. This does not mean that we measure God's word by human standards, that we can believe only in what is expected and calculated in advance, but not in the all-transforming miracle. It means only that we are bound to strive so to assimilate God's word that it is really understood, even though we know that our effort to produce the necessary horizon of understanding of that word is itself called forth by God's word and must be sustained by the light of God's grace within us.

If then we want to understand what is meant by the permanent mystery of Jesus' resurrection, it is a good thing to leave out of consideration the division of the human being into body and soul. We are not questioning here the validity of this dualism within its limits. But if we were to make it the basis of our inquiry and assume that we could ask questions about one "part" of the human person which would produce no answers about the other part, we should in fact be obstructing any understanding of the resurrection of Jesus.

"Resurrection" as it is understood here is that of an integral human being, the final state of the one person, not a revival of his or her biological reality or even a return to that biological life which we experience in ourselves in conditions of space and time and in its death instinct. If resurrection means the final state of the one integral human being, then it is clear once again that we cannot a priori exclude our bodily nature from this state, even though it is beyond our power to understand positively *how* this bodily nature shares in the final state of the one whole person.

Resurrection then implies simply the redeemed finality of the one integral human being in which his or her experienced plurality, in spite of its diversity and mixture of opposites, remains in itself solidly one

---

*Opportunities for Faith, 31–39.

with a unity that is not dissolved and interconnected elements that are not dispersed.

Resurrection then as a *general* term in itself implies nothing about a future for that material reality which we know as the corpse left behind, since the final, redeemed state of the one human being can also be conceived and can exist without the material elements abandoned in a kind of total change of material: these are his or her own only as long as they live with the life of the whole person. Therefore, resurrection in general, as the final destiny of all of us, in which we profess our faith in the Apostles' Creed, also does not imply the image of an empty, emptied grave, nor even a decision about the time relationship between the resurrection and our continuous succession of time: that is, whether it may be conceived as supervening at the moment of each individual death or only at the very end of time.

In regard to the resurrection of Jesus there may be special reasons why the later statements of the New Testament speak not only of that resurrection but also of the empty tomb. But in any case it must be said that the mere establishing of the fact of an empty tomb is not a sufficient reason for believing in the resurrection of the person who had been buried there; it must also be said that resurrection as a general term does not necessarily imply the emptying of a grave.

We have thus reached an horizon at which it is possible to understand something of Jesus' resurrection. *Our* infinite claim to our finality, to the redeemed state of the one whole person, is this horizon. For we can say: I am, I shall be, I shall remain, I don't sink into the void of nothingness and meaninglessness, and I can't escape the enormous burden of responsibility for my life by slipping away from reality into the emptiness of having existed. And this is equivalent to saying: I shall rise.

It may certainly be the case that this absolute claim to one's own resurrection must be and is sustained itself by God's grace, which is the grace of Christ. It may be the case that this absolute claim in depth of one's own existence can be given conceptual expression as a claim *precisely* to resurrection only in confrontation with the biblical message of the resurrection. This alters nothing in the *mutual* relationship between the resurrection of Jesus and our own claim which is conditional upon it. It is possible to believe in the resurrection of Jesus because the claim to our own resurrection is alive in us, if only we understand what is meant by resurrection in general.

In our hope for ourselves we look for the sign in our history which authorizes us to hope: to hope, that is, for an existence with a totally human, eternal validity, for what we can call our "resurrection." We look hopefully for the sign which authorizes this hope. For, however much we feel obliged to hope in this way and to resist the utterly skeptical attitude which we *might* also choose to adopt in regard to our life, there is an inward threat to our hope which drives us to look for its authorization in our history. We cannot of course say that someone whom God finally rejects will succeed in taking refuge in pure nothingness. But we are in fact looking toward God for our finality and can therefore conceive what we call our eternal, totally human validity — that is, our resurrection — only as acceptance by God, from whom the sins of our life threaten to separate us.

Life commands us (in virtue of God's hidden grace) to hope for resurrection and at the very same time our sin makes it questionable. Where then, we ask, is the sign that we may and must still hope, in spite of the darkness of sin which continually produces a new sinful hopelessness?

The sign lies in the fact that a person who has entered into a radical solidarity with us and has accepted the darkness of our sinful existence is the risen one, whom God accepts in his wholeness. This sign that we have been seeking is called Jesus of Nazareth, crucified and risen. The manifestation of this sign is called Easter. The assurance that this sign of hope appears just *here* constitutes the content and singularity of Christianity. It is significant — and by no means to be taken for granted — that nowhere among humankind has anyone been bold enough to assert that a person has risen, apart from and independently of Jesus. People have venerated not only mythical figures, but also historically unmistakable persons, as wise and good, as masters of life after they were dead, but no one has ever ventured to look beyond their grave in order to say that they exist and live and have become for themselves and us even more powerful in their final reality than they ever were on earth.

The very fact that humankind found the absolute courage to assert this only of Jesus provides food for thought. If, while cherishing hope for ourselves (and not in any other way), we look to Jesus, we see, not indeed that we have to believe, but certainly that we can believe. We *can* believe with that intellectual integrity which is the inner light of the supreme, free, but pregnant decisions of our life, even though it flickers and dies apart from these.

We look to Jesus: in the light certainly of the disciples' Easter experience, but to Jesus himself. In him, we then discover, is that distant reality which threatens our hope and renders it uncertain: this is sin, by which a person selfishly cuts himself or herself off from God and neighbor. *He* has suffered the ultimate of what constitutes our life: God's simultaneous closeness and remoteness. Looking into the devouring abyss of utter abandonment by God, he says: Father!

And, together with his disciples, we have the courage to believe that this word in death penetrated to him for whom it was meant and was heard. We have courage because we do not first have to invent him, but we believe within the community of believers, and because we see that the hope we cherish for ourselves would be destroyed if we were to give up this courage of faith in the resurrection of Jesus. We certainly need not and may not emancipate ourselves from the Easter experience of the first disciples. And why should we do so, we who in fact received *their* faith transmitted to us, and thus and only thus found in history the testimony of our hope. But, while all this is true, we Christians too can say: We also have known him as alive in our lives and his cause lived on in us.

It lives on precisely in the hope, which is incomprehensible even to ourselves, of the redeeming and redeemed finality of our existence, the hope which makes us singularly free from all powers of death, of sin, of disappointment, free from all that otherwise enslaves us. Persons who hope, at least at the final basic decision of their life, even if they cannot give thematic expression in words to their hope, really believe in Jesus' resurrection. Why then should we not do this expressly and celebrate Easter?

Anyone who has ever really celebrated the Russian Easter liturgy with the faithful or has allowed the *Exultet* of the Roman liturgy to touch his or her heart knows the meaning of paschal joy. It is the subjective aspect of Easter: the joy of liberation, of overcoming death, of sheer victory. It can certainly be said that, if the objective Easter event did not exist, its victory would not be effective in Easter *faith;* if, then, objective and subjective did not here form an indissoluble unity and if Easter faith is joy (what else could it be?), then Easter (understood quite subjectively and thus alone really objectively) and joy (understood as perfect) are two words for one and the same event. But if somebody says this we are deeply shocked.

Where then with us Christians, who claim to believe in Easter, is this joy which reaches its consummation at Easter? Where is the jubilation, where the unconquerable, radiant confidence? Where is the laughter, where are the tears of pure and redeemed joy? Where, among us Christians, is that spontaneous cheerfulness which is in fact characteristic of those who have overcome, who *know* that the gate to infinite future can never again be closed against us, leaving us locked in the hell of our own finiteness and futility?

It is the Christian Easter which puts Christians to the greatest test. As Nietzsche said, people should be able to see us as those who are redeemed. But I fear that we show no sign of this. How then are we to come to terms with the Easter we are celebrating? Or, better, how does Easter come to terms with us Easter-less Christians?

First of all, there is no point in concealing this situation of ours with speeches that are supposed to sound inspired, like those of a loud-mouthed party secretary when the election day draws near on which his party finally loses. If for Christians there is a way of access to the joy of Easter, then today certainly it can only be through admitting that we are not very enthusiastic (privately and ecclesially) about Easter. Christians know too that they cannot select at random the point at which their momentary situation is registered in Christ's life and destiny. The feeling of paschal high-spiritedness can never be a participation in the life and victory of the Lord. For he was certainly not in a paschal mood when he cried out in the darkness of his death: "My God, why have you forsaken me?" The light of Easter shines only for the one who has accepted and voluntarily endured to the end the darkness of Good Friday. Is it then so surprising that we don't seem particularly full of paschal joy when we are afraid of the darkness of Good Friday and don't want to accept and endure it to the end?

If we accept our darkness, if we don't explain it away either by a tortured pretense of joy or by taking the darkness for granted (as the absolute skeptic tries to do), then in a sense we experience the empty form of Christian joy, the longing for joy, the desire for it, and therefore the readiness to accept it whenever it is disposed to come upon us, in whatever form, in whatever measure. If we admit our arid joylessness, if we don't try to numb it with drugs — which a despairing person is ready to accept only too lightly in the most varied forms — then a first experience of joy does indeed come upon us, a sense of Easter.

This sounds very abstract. We have to try to give up endless reflection and to put into practice what has been said. For example, we can forget our own joylessness and try to create a little joy for others. If we succeed, it might mean becoming even more acutely conscious of our own joyless state. But for that very reason the otherwise dead joylessness nevertheless comes to life. And in this lively pain we begin to suspect what paschal joy might be and we wait patiently until God puts it into our heart as his gift, as that which alone enables us to rejoice with the joy that is identical with Easter.

55 • Our Easter Faith*

Why are we so lax and resigned? Why do we often struggle as if we only externally wished secretly to put off the conceded defeat? Why do

---

*Was Heißt Auferstehung, ed. Albert Raffelt (Freiburg i. Br.: Herder, 1985), 42–48. Trans. Frederick G. Lawrence, Boston College.

we so stingily offer up in Christ's service only a couple of pennies as though it were too insecure for us to risk our whole life, all our strength, and the last drop of our heart's blood for that service. Is Christ, or is he not, risen from the dead?

We believe in his resurrection! Is this true? Do we believe all that is involved in this?

He is the living one. He is the victor over sin and death. He is not one who ascended into heaven in order to disappear from world history as if he had never been in it. He ascended to heaven after he had descended into the last depths of sin, death, and the lost world, and came out of this abyss, which contains everything, alive. More: there in the ultimate lostness, whence all viciousness springs and where all streams of tears have their origin and where the last source of all hatred and self-seeking abides — that is where he has won victory. He won not by shoving the world from himself and heaving it away, but by the fact that, losing himself, he forced his way into the innermost center whence its entire destiny springs forth, seized this center, and accepted it for eternity.

And so he has already transformed the world. Conquered it inasmuch as he transformed it. By becoming the *heart of the world,* its ultimate finality, its most secret and inward strength. And so in his resurrection he has not gone away from us. He has actually come to be present in it with us all our days. We no longer see his shape. It flashed only briefly, as it were, in order to show us that he is with us forever. With us by means of his divine Spirit, who has become the hidden Spirit of the world, and, since the death and resurrection of Christ, inseparably united with him, never again separable from him, because *he* has been inseparably united to that piece of the world which we call the transfigured humanity of Christ, which has itself become "open" to the world in its entirety in virtue of his death and resurrection.

Christ in his Spirit is installed already in the center of all things as its authentic and true essence and heart: in the expectation of all creatures for a share in the transfiguration of the body of Christ, in tears as the hidden jubilation, in beggars to whom we give as the eternal wealth in which we will share, in our impotence as the power of God, in the "folly of the cross" as wisdom, in death as the life no longer threatened by death, in the wretched defeats of his servants as the victory that is God's alone, even in the midst of sin as the ready mercy of eternal love even to the end of the world. He is even present in the indifference and unreceptivity of many for our message in order to discipline us, his useless servants, for our lukewarmness, or to let us share in his lack of success by which he redeemed the world. He is with us like the day's light and the air we do not notice; like the hidden law of a movement we can't properly grasp, because we only experience too small a piece of this motion into which we have been caught up. He is present as the innermost structure of this world which still triumphs and prevails when all the world's orders seem to be disintegrating. He is with us who proclaim his resurrection: in our words, when they sound empty and tinny even to ourselves; in our blessings, even when they come forth with strain and difficulty from our lips; in our sacraments, even when they no longer *seem* to harbor any strength in them.

When someone shuts the door on us and his good news, they cannot keep him out. He climbs into every heart ever anew to make them restless with hunger for justice and truth. He fills them with the hunger and longing that belong to him, because he is love and justice, life and truth. He has become the eternal restlessness of this world. And wherever this world seems to get changed into a monstrous chaos, wherever all the dams seem to break, this seeming is in truth a sign that he is in the center of this erupting volcano and that his day is near. He is in the ship of time, and yet he stands at the same time on the shore of eternity. The storm that threatens to sink the ship is only the sign that he will now arise — "and there arose a great stillness" — or that the ship will be lifted safely from the storm of time onto the shore of eternity. In each century the world declares that Christ's kingdom is perishing from weakness due to old age, and people can pass over now in peace to the order of the day; and the paroxysm of the frenzy of this same world against Christ is released ever again as the sign (which the blind do not see) that he is always still living in this world.

He is risen. And the *world* with him. It is already transformed with him, and soon — quickly and ever more quickly — our weak flesh will see what has already happened. For *us,* the moment between its transfiguration and the revelation of this change just lasts a long and bitter time. We call this moment the history of the world since Christ, or our lives. We go away like the disciples between Good Friday and Easter: " ... but we had hoped.... " Ah, we are still hoping. We await in trembling the outcome of the battle, whereas in reality, if we had the eyes of faith, for these eyes the triumphal procession is already forming, in which nature and history as the victory of Christ are supposed to march into the eternal kingdom of the Father. We lament when his hard grip presses upon us, and pulls us through the dark and narrow door of his suffering into the land of the light and of the infinite wideness of his Father. We lament and our lamentation overtakes us so that we have more trust in the obscure twilight of our earth than in the light of the risen one. But he does not ask about out petty whining. He brings us along: When there shall occur that which has already happened, you will also comprehend it!

Has the risen one descended into the expectant waiting room of *my heart* in order to proclaim the redemption there, too; and also to transform everything there? If only I had the whole Easter faith that compels everything else! Then I would notice that I do not fall when I give up the crampingly violent inner anxiety about myself and the success of my mission; that I am not desperate when I finally have despaired of myself and my strength. Then I would suddenly — as by a miracle that has to happen anew every day — notice that he is with me. He, the risen one. Then I would realize that I do not at all have to seek him in heaven, because he dwells in me and in me he lives out his homeward journey to the Father. Then I would experience that *I* do not live enough (although I could do so) out of the already transformed center of my heart; that I — not he — am far away.

If only I had the whole Easter faith! Why should I not have it? I do have it because his grace is in me, because I have been baptized and confirmed. In baptism I have received his Spirit in order to radiate the triumph of Easter in word and deed into his world. So I will prepare myself to live this faith. Daily I will let Paul (2 Tm 2:8–11) say to me: "Remember, Jesus Christ, risen from the dead, descended from David, as preached in my gospel, the gospel for which I am suffering and wearing fetters like a criminal. But the word of God is not fettered. Therefore, I endure everything for the sake of the elect, that they also may obtain the salvation which in Christ Jesus goes with eternal glory. The saying is sure: If we have died with him, we shall also live with him."

56 • "The Lord Is Truly Risen!"*

On Easter Day and in a celebration proclaiming the death of the Lord and extolling his resurrection, the preacher can only do just that: bear witness to this resurrection. In this connection, bearing witness means acknowledging the reality as independent of my thinking *and* at the same time accepting it as the firm basis of my own life. Obviously only a very little can be said about this basic reality and truth of Christianity, when the sermon has to be so short.

We are professing our faith in Christ's resurrection and celebrating it. To make it present in our lives in this way does not mean that the crucified and dead Christ has returned to this earthly sphere of expe-

---

*Opportunities for Faith, 37–39.

rience, to this earthly world and history. It means the very opposite. The empty tomb, attested by the earliest tradition, is not the starting point but an elucidation of the Easter faith, if only because, considered in itself, it does not imply any resurrection and in principle has nothing to do with resurrection as the final salvation of the whole human being from the fate of his or her former materiality. Jesus' resurrection means that in the concrete he is the one who, through and in God, is eternally redeemed.

If we understood *what* is truly and exactly the "cause" of Jesus and *if* we grasped the fact that this cause cannot be separated from his person, then we could also say: Jesus' resurrection means that his cause is not finished with. But, since for the most part we don't consider and recognize this double "if," a formula of this kind is worse than misleading. Nevertheless, Jesus' resurrection does not mean that we ought to try to visualize his bodily condition, that we ought to localize the risen Christ within the sphere of our experience, that we ought to think of successive duration as the continuation of *our* time after death, and so on.

If that were possible, he would not have risen to the final consummation with God, but would have been revived merely for our biological life which is subject to death. If God is the absolute mystery, then our final consummation into this mystery is likewise beyond our understanding. Jesus' resurrection simply means that this man Jesus, whom we cannot split up into body and soul each with its different destiny, is the definitive person, the one received by God into eternal bliss, the one whose history does not fade in the empty nothingness of the past, but has its end in the final consummation.

Are we bold enough to believe in the resurrection? Or do we regard it on Easter Day as merely a myth and leave it at that or try to find a new interpretation? Why do we believe? Why can we be intellectually sincere in our belief? We can. It is a question of course of affirming in *faith* and not compelling assent in a rationalistic fashion. We can be intellectually sincere in our faith in Jesus' resurrection even if we have not entered into all the problems of modern exegesis in regard to this question.

Why? We can ask in turn: Can I be intellectually sincere in believing in my *own* "resurrection?" That is, may I base my life on the assumption that what constitutes that life — freedom, responsibility, love — has a final significance and does not disappear into the abyss of futile nothingness? But if I do build on this and at the same time know that I cannot break up into two heterogeneous realities called matter and spirit, which have wholly distinct and separate fates, then I believe in *my* resurrection.

For I cannot and must not split up the spiritual-corporeal unity of my life and ascribe a different fate to each of the two parts thus formed. I, the concrete human being, believe in my finality and consequently in my resurrection, and what I mean by this resurrection is precisely that finality, without attempting to describe it in the inadequate terms drawn from experience of the present world. Even someone who has thought it all out and thinks that death is the end of everything, but at the same time displays in one's life an absolute respect for human dignity, affirms in practice what one denies in theory: that is, precisely one's "resurrection." If this is one's situation what reason could there be for denying the resurrection of Jesus?

Even if I am skeptical in regard to *myself*, considering myself a pretty worthless specimen among the enormous numbers of people, not venturing to think it would be easy to find anything of eternal worth in myself, this is not the case when I look at Jesus. When I consider his life and his death, am I not bound to admit that *he* — if anyone — is wholly and really of eternal worth? He it is who really loved unselfishly and voluntarily accepted the horror of this life up to the point of being forsaken by God in death.

And have not innumerable people, beginning with his disciples, professed their faith in this resurrection of his? Was not this the disciples' experience, in spite of their own mistrust? At the same time, I think I may say that we too can have this experience of the permanently real validity of Jesus, if we seek with mind and heart that human being for whom death is victory, if we take that person absolutely seriously without reducing him to a mere idea. We do not thereby become independent of the testimony of the first disciples, since it is only through their testimony that we know by name and in his history the person whom we discover in this way.

If we were not to believe in Jesus' resurrection, although the explicit testimony of all Christendom has reached our ears and hearts, could we then still seriously say that we were hoping in faith for *our own* resurrection? At the point where we stand, we who have encountered Christianity, faith in Jesus' resurrection and hope in our own, have become *one* reality, the elements of which are mutually dependent.

When shortly we profess our faith in the fact that "he rose from the dead" and declare, "I look forward to the resurrection of the dead," we are really professing in *one* article of faith our belief in the *one* reality, the beginning and manifestation of which took place for us in Jesus, which lays hold on us and reaches its end in the future consummation of world history: the redeemed, transfigured finality of the *one* world in spirit and matter. The celebration we are now beginning is a profession of faith in this consummation and its anticipation in the form of a sacred sign.

The Lord is truly risen.

57 • Easter and Hope*

At the start two things must be said. First, I am — at least I hope I am — convinced in faith of the truth of the Christian Easter message. With the Christian churches I confess that *the Lord is truly risen:* that and nothing else, however much I am aware that at all times and therefore also today one must meditate on what it means. I do not intend to speak of it in a way acceptable to all: that would be to say nothing of value. I think nonetheless that such a clear confession is still worth thinking about for *all* people today — because of the subject, naturally, not because of the writer.

And second, the following is not an attempt at a prose poem or Easter hymn. Believers who can leave despair and the disillusionment of life behind them, who believe and who, freed by this inner blessing of their lives, confess what they believe, sing that hymn. My purpose here is not so much to speak of this hoping Easter faith itself as to offer a modest meditation at its margin, at its threshold, on its meaning and credibility. Belief and such reflections on it are not the same thing.

Many (perhaps most) people *live* an ultimate conviction because of which they in fact live the truth which sets us free. Many of them, however, cannot "objectify" it, either for themselves or for others: when they begin to reflect on what they are living discreetly and unobtrusively in the responsibility, love, and loyalty of the everyday, they find they cannot articulate it in a formal expression of their beliefs.

They become confused and begin to doubt whether so lofty and sublime a thing as that expressed in religious and perhaps even metaphysical statements about the ultimate meaning of human life could exist in their lives. Perhaps many are given only in the obscure ground of their existence what others — religions and other interpreters of the human being — also dare to say expressly. That is in principle perfectly justified, because where it is successful it can purify and clarify the (so far unspoken) realization of life and give courage. If this silent ground of life and its free, responsible realization is successfully interpreted in a Christian way in my present reflections, then my subject matter con-

*Christian at the Crossroads, 87–93.

cerns something that the Christian can (and even must) grant as an unreflected event even in one who, in his or her own reflections does not acknowledge such speech as an accurate statement of what he or she lives, or at any rate doubts the appropriateness of such discourse.

There are plenty of anguished atheists and people who doubt the eternal worth of a responsible life. Their systems, however, do not enable them to explain adequately whence such radical grief can enter the desert of existence, and their grief proclaims the opposite of what they understand in the dimension of their reflective interpretation of life. On these premises, I venture to add that where a person lives his or her life in unconditional, selfless love, in an ultimate loyalty that goes unrewarded, in responsible acceptance of the dictates of autarchical conscience — solitary and unsung as it is — he or she is living out a hoping belief in his or her permanent definitiveness, whether he or she reflects about it, manages to objectify this conviction verbally, or not.

Whoever stands before the graves of Auschwitz or Bangla Desh or other monuments to the absurdity of human life and manages neither to run away (because one cannot tolerate this absurdity) nor to fall into cynical doubt, believes in what we Christians call eternal life, even though one's mind does not grasp it, and whether one can tolerate this statement of radical courage or not. One can live radical love, loyalty, and responsibility, which can never in the long run "pay," *and* "think" that all human life ends in the empty meaningless void, but in the very act of such a life the thought is belied, and it is contradicted by one's deeds.

Basic acts of life like these place their hope in definitiveness, in the ultimate salvation of life; they affirm the first and final condition of such hope, which we call God. Only such belief enables us to be responsible for human life, if life is otherwise doomed to perish, and prevents it from becoming no more than the fertilizer of a future which itself is destined to drop into the void. Persons who say that this definitiveness is already present in life, since we become certain of God's love and faithfulness *here and now*, cannot, if they are logical, then commit such certainty to destruction. Persons who experience eternity in time must, precisely because they do so, not let destructive time carry the day over their experience of love for God and neighbor.

We need not "visualize" or "picture" this definitiveness — given in radical hope — of our history and person. We know of it nothing but what is given in the unconditioned hope. We are not, of course, permitted to think of it as an extension of our time into which new things are introduced at pleasure. It is the definitiveness of our history in the presence of God, the definitiveness of a life which took place here in time, and even though in a hidden manner contained enough of what is worth existing definitively, "forever."

This hope applies concretely to the whole human being, and consequently is already a hope for what Christians call the "resurrection of the body." A platonic Western tradition has been accustomed, it is true, to call the inner ground of the person's permanence "soul" and the ground of his spatio-temporality "body," and to imagine the content of the individual's ultimate hope as the immortality of a *part* of the human being, namely the soul, and then to relegate the person's "resurrection" (of the "flesh" which the human being is and not only has) as expressed in Christian hope to the end of collective history as a supervening event of consequence only to the "body." Today we should not criticize these platonizing conceptual schemes too disdainfully, partly because they have constantly been used in the doctrines of the Christian church to clarify the content of Christian teaching.

We may, however, also say that the (joint) Christian and human *hope* concerns the salvation of the entire person and therefore is a hope which cannot first of all exclude the "body" and then learn something about *its* destiny only from a special, separate doctrine. This may be said even though we do not need to deny that the one definitiveness of the human being must be thought of as taking effect variously, depending on the several aspects it contains, without our being able to picture this difference perhaps of "glorification" of "body" and "soul" more precisely.

Ultimately, therefore, it is not a question of faith whether what we call the resurrection of the body in the narrower sense takes place at the end of collective history or is thought of as a simultaneously occurring moment of the one process by which a person achieves his or her definitiveness at the time of (his or her own) death. As early as the Middle Ages, theology could conceive of a "resurrection" of the human being independently of the question of what happened to the corpse left behind in death. The human person is one, who has a hope for himself or herself; this hope is radically posited in the act of responsible assumption of his or her existence and enters the reflecting consciousness in what we call the "resurrection of the flesh" (and also embraces the "soul" in the latter's redeemed, beatific immortality).

It is only in such hope that we can treat of the question of Jesus' resurrection. Such hope is the locus of this latter belief. The hope at the heart of existence (it is indifferent here whether it is made one's own in freedom or rejected in despair, which is a real possibility even though it means the person's perdition) scans history for its tangible pledge; for the event in which it can dare to say: something happened there which I hope also happens to me; for the event in which it is offered its own self-objectification and from which it draws the courage to confess itself. Christian faith finds this event in Jesus. Hope for us is a hope which, in denying Jesus, would disown itself.

This is not the place to set out everything the Christian faith professes about Jesus. We can only say briefly that faith presents this Jesus, his life, his work, his claim on us, and affirms: he lives. His cause did not perish, was not invalidated by his death. If he himself had perished, if he were not alive now, his cause would be not he himself but a mere ideology which we could have even without him. We could not call this event, of which our hope is in constant quest, Jesus, unless reports had come down to us through the apostolic witness to him, his work, his life and death, and his definitive permanence in life (called resurrection). Even given all this, we can experience for ourselves in our encounter with him that he lives: in the liberating power of his life and death which took place in God, and in the testimony of his Spirit, without which we could not believe, even in his resurrection.

We are not (and could not be) as dependent on the "eyewitness" of the first disciples as those people who learn only by report of an event which occurred quite outside the circle of their own experience. The evidence of the disciples *and* our own inner evidence of the experience of the living power of Jesus (of Jesus, not of an ideology associated arbitrarily with his name in the final analysis) together form one testimony: he lives. Some people say with a shrug of the shoulders that they experience in themselves nothing of this witness of Jesus' "Spirit" who witnesses to him as living. Those people are to be asked whether they have ever willingly exposed themselves to Jesus' challenging call which concerns life and death (that is, love for God and neighbor in one) and then is experienced as inseparable from his person.

With regard to what is usually meant by Jesus' resurrection, we know no more than what we hope for ourselves: the permanent, effective saving of his life through God. We do not need to visualize to ourselves the peculiar nature of his physical risen existence, because we cannot. Nor do we need to see in the "empty tomb," which could not on its own guarantee any resurrection, the proper reason for belief in his resurrection.

We could, if we were so inclined, read the reports of the risen Christ's appearances in scripture as secondary clarifications of an appearance of the risen Jesus which properly lies *behind* these visions, because we do not have to put these visions on a par with the kind of visions familiar to us from the history of mysticism.

We do not regard the resurrection as an event that takes place only in our faith; but we do say that it belongs to the permanent victory of

Jesus and his cause that it must be perpetuated in our faith. If his resurrection was nowhere going to find faith, it would never have happened, because it was to be God's victorious self-promise to the world. In any case, Jesus' resurrection is not the return of a deceased man to our space and time with all its limitations, it is something quite different of its very essence from the raisings of dead people to life recorded in both Old and New Testaments.

The risen Jesus announces the fact that he has been saved forever and his life accepted by God, but he does not return to the world which stands under the law of futility and death and must be conquered with our hope. We simply look on this living and dying of Jesus', as the first disciples did, experience his liberating power in us and then say: we should be denying our own hope of resurrection if we did not affirm of *this* Jesus that he lives, that he is therefore risen, if therefore our own hope did not know that it was empowered and liberated in him for that act in which the individual person also accepts his or her ineradicable hope in freedom and lets it enter his or her consciousness.

As far as other people are concerned, if we take the guilt in human life as seriously as the hope, we should not perhaps dare to believe in a beatific redemption of life, even though we, the guilty, must fear more for *ourselves* than for others, whose guilt we can never know so well as our own. If, however, there has ever lived a person whose courage confutes the skeptical opinion that humankind, so questionable and evil, should be wiped off the face of the earth as soon as possible as a failed experiment, that person is, according to the evidence of Christianity and way beyond the frontiers of ecclesial Christendom, Jesus. One may even say, if one so wishes: he must be God for the life of this Jesus not to have foundered. Why should this life not give as good a "proof of God's existence" as the world, in which atoms conduct their ghostly dance by "chance and necessity" and the human person lives as a frightful question?

It can, of course, be asked what sort of situation the individual is in if ultimately everything is based "merely" on hope, and even Jesus' resurrection is based in the final analysis "only" on the hope in which we also hope for everything for ourselves. To this we may reply with unimpeachable logic that the ultimate in the human being as a complete person (unlike the functional satisfaction of particular needs in life) consists in the movement which we call hope. Hope sustains, gives reality, *when* and as it happens. And outside itself it needs no justification.

Apart from hope there is only despair. We can certainly try to dismiss despair and suppress it, but without hope it is sure to return, and without freely accepted hope it does return. And despair has no justification in itself, even though it might often seem easier to someone than hope, because in despair one has only to let oneself fall. We may ask: Where, then, does this hope in the resurrection exert its world-shaping and world-conquering power, when, despite all the Christians who pretend they hope (but then stop all too willingly at the tangible which one can possess even without hope), human history is still a hopeless mixture of stupidity, evil, and death and against it we can do no more than squeeze by in the enjoyment of the higher or lower ephemeralities?

That, however, is to miss the real question of hope. The person who asks such a question wishes not to hope but to enjoy now what is hoped for. She wants an already transformed world, not to work the transformation of the world by her hope against hope (as scripture puts it). She in her turn must be asked where her alternative is (one that can serve as a life principle), and she should ask herself whether in the final analysis she does not still accept a world which seems tolerable to her because in it other people still hope, with or without their fully knowing it.

The Christian may legitimately ask (as he must also ask himself) the person who says that his life consists in an incomprehensible "nevertheless" of selfless love (for example, in firm certainty that this world would be a little more bearable with a little more freedom and justice) whether the reality of his life really corresponds to some extent to these heroic words, and especially whether he is also willing to summon up not only the courage of hope (which he has if he really loves) but also the courage to confess explicitly the hope he summons up covertly *if* he loves selflessly.

If hope is not to belie its own essence, it can tolerate no definitive limits. But where it exists and sustains the whole person, takes the whole person out of herself into this mystery we call God, it can and must also believe in Jesus' resurrection: if it knows him and if it does not imagine resurrection to be something that does not in fact belong to the content of the Christian Easter faith in the resurrection.

In the liturgy of the Orthodox church (provided that it too, like our own church in all too many cases — through our own fault — has not degenerated into a philistine ritualism), believers embrace each other at the Easter Vigil in tears and jubilation: Christ is risen, he is truly risen. That cannot be organized and catered for in liturgy: but on Easter night believers (that is, those who think and hope they believe, but do not know it with the same certainty) and "unbelievers" (that is, those who think they do not have such Easter faith) embrace each other as those who hope together against all hope and despite everything.

The unbeliever must be glad that his believing brother and sister hope he believes, even when he himself thinks he has to interpret that belief as the most prodigious moonshine (he does not thereby imagine, we trust, that his unbelief is utterly certain and reliable). And the believer must still have the courage to tell her unbelieving brother and sister (all the time praying himself: I do have faith, help the little faith I have): the Lord is risen, he is really risen. And she may, indeed must, hope that this unbelieving brother or sister of hers is in fact a believer in the hope which is unconditionally accepted in freedom. The Christian believer may certainly not suppress the demand also to believe expressly, which is incumbent on all. But on Easter night she must be glad above all that Jesus rose among many who hope, without being able to say what has already been said by the resurrection: in other words, all that it implies.

58 • Easter: The Beginning of Glory*

If someone had already lit the fuse for a tremendous explosion, but was still waiting for the explosion which will follow with dreadful certainty, that person certainly would not say that the lighting of the fuse was an event of the past. The beginning of an event, which is still in course of development but is moving inexorably and irresistibly toward its culmination, is not past but is a kind of present, and already contains its future; it is a movement which continues by comprising past and present in a present real unity. These concepts must be clear if we are to attempt to say something meaningful about the Lord's resurrection.

Easter is not the celebration of a past event. The alleluia is not for what was; Easter proclaims a beginning which has already decided the remotest future. The resurrection means that the beginning of glory has already started. And what began in that way is in process of fulfillment. Does it take long? It lasts thousands of years because at least that short space of time is needed for an incalculable plenitude of reality and history to force itself through the brief death agony of a gigantic transformation (which we call natural history and world history) to its glorious fulfillment. Everything is in movement. Nothing has an abiding place here.

We are gradually finding out, at least in outline, that nature has its own oriented history, that nature is in movement, that it develops and

---

*Everyday Faith, 71–75.

unfolds in time and by an incomprehensible self-transcendence behind which there stands the creative power of God, attains ever higher levels of reality. We are gradually realizing that human history has its purposeful course and is not merely the eternal return of the identical ("there is nothing new under the sun"), that the nations are summoned in a certain sequence and have each their definite historical mission; that history in its totality has its pattern and an irreversible direction.

But what is the goal of this whole movement in nature, history, and spirit? Is everything advancing toward a collapse, to meaninglessness and nothingness? Are we only going to lose our way? Is what happens ultimately only the demonstration of the emptiness and hollowness of all things, which are unmasked in the course of the history of nature and the world? Are all the comedies and tragedies of this history mere playacting which can only deludedly be taken seriously while they are still going on and are not yet played out?

How far has this history already advanced? Has its meaning already emerged in this game of limitless scope? Has the ultimate, all-decisive keyword already been spoken which gave all that came earlier its meaning, and already clearly contains the outcome of the whole drama?

We Christians say that this whole history of nature and humankind has a meaning, a blessed and transfigured, all-embracing meaning, no longer mixed with meaninglessness and darkness, a meaning which is infinite reality and unity comprising all possibilities and glory in one. And when we invoke the absolute meaning in this way, we call it God. God as he is in himself is the goal of all history. He himself is at hand.

All the streams of change in us flow toward him; they are not lost in the bottomless void of nothingness and meaninglessness. But when we say this, when we declare infinity to be the meaning of the finite, eternity the meaning of time, and God himself (by grace) to be the purport of his creature, we are not speaking simply of a distant, not yet wholly realized ideal, which we hope vaguely may be realized one day but which for the moment and for an incalculable time is still a distant future existing only in thought.

No, we say Easter, resurrection. That means, it has already begun, the definitive future has already started. The transfiguration of the world is no ideal, no postulate, but a reality. The history of nature with all its developments and self-transcendence has already — though for the moment only in its first exemplar — reached its unsurpassable culmination: material reality which, wholly transfigured, is for eternity the glorious body of God. The most tremendous and definitive self-transcendence of the material world (through the grace-given power of God alone, of course) has already taken place. It has leapt beyond itself into the infinity of God's spirituality and, in this upward flight into God's immeasurable flame, it has not been consumed but has survived, definitively transfigured.

If we thought about it correctly, we Christians would really have to say that we, not the others, are the most radical materialists, for we say that God's pure and substantial self-utterance (the divine Word of God) has a true body for all eternity. The history of humanity, so we say when we celebrate Easter, has already reached its goal in a representative or, rather, in *the* representative of this whole history (in him and through him for the others).

And this has happened where not simply spirit and glorified soul, but the one human being in his totality who acted and suffered this history of his, attained perfect fulfillment, where everything abides, nothing is lost, and everything is disclosed as meaningful and glorious. This end, which is the beginning of the fulfillment of all things, has arrived and has manifested itself to humanity still advancing through history just as the front of a procession which has reached the goal calls back with cries of triumph to those still marching: we are there, we have found the goal and it is what we hoped it would be.

The place at which such a beginning of the end and completion has appeared is called Jesus of Nazareth, crucified and risen. Because his tomb is empty, because he who was dead has shown himself to be living in the unity of his whole concrete humanity, we know that everything has already really begun to be well. Almost everything is still on the way. But on the way to a goal which is not a utopian ideal but an already existent reality.

The human person likes to give half answers, likes to escape to where he or she does not have to make a clear decision. That is understandable. We are travelers and consequently in a condition in which everything, meaning and meaninglessness, death and life, is still mixed together, half finished, incomplete. But it cannot remain so. It is moving on. And the end cannot be other than clear and plain. Consequently, reality compels us, whether we wish or not, to give a plain answer in our own lives.

And so the question is put to us: Death or life? Meaning or meaninglessness? Ideals which are nebulously inconclusive or real facts? If by faith and action we plainly decide for meaning and life as facts, and consider life and death as mere *ideals* to be inadequate, if we affirm life and meaning as a fact, not halfheartedly but wholeheartedly in endless magnitude and scope, then whether we know it or not we have said Easter. And we Christians know this. We know that the reality of Easter is not simply the essence hidden in the depth of our life but is the truth and reality of our faith called by its name and explicitly professed.

And so we comprise the whole history of nature and of humankind in a celebration which in rite contains the actual reality celebrated, and we make the ultimate statement about it: I believe in the resurrection of the body (flesh) and life everlasting. I believe that the beginning of the glory of all things has already come upon us, that we, apparently so lost, wandering and seeking far away, are already encompassed by infinite blessedness. For the end has already begun. And it is glory.

59 • Easter:
A Faith That Loves the Earth*

It is difficult in well-worn human words to do justice to the joy of Easter. Not simply because all the mysteries of the gospel have difficulty in penetrating the narrow limits of our being and because it is even more difficult for our language to contain them. The message of Easter is the most human news brought by Christianity. That is why we have the most difficulty in understanding it. It is most difficult to be, do, and believe what is truest, closest, and easiest. For we people of today live by the tacitly assumed and therefore to us all the more self-evident prejudice that what is religious is purely a matter of the innermost heart and the highest point of the mind, something which we have to do for ourselves alone and which therefore has the difficulty and unreality of the thoughts and moods of the heart.

But Easter says that God has done something. God himself. And his action has not merely lightly touched the heart of some human being here and there, so that it trembles at the inexpressible and nameless. God has raised his Son from the dead. God has called the flesh to life. He has conquered death. He has done something and triumphed where it is not at all a question merely of interior sensibility but where, despite all our praise of the mind, we are most really ourselves, in the reality of the earth, far from all that is purely thought and feeling, where we learn what we are — mortal children of the earth.

We are children of this earth. Birth and death, body and earth, bread and wine — such is our life. The earth is our home. Certainly for all this to be so and to be splendid, mind has to be mingled with it like a secret essence, the delicate, sensitive, perceptive mind which gazes into the infinite, and the soul which makes everything living and light. But mind and soul have to be *there*, where we are, on the earth and in the body.

Everyday Faith, 76–83.

They have to be there as the eternal radiance of earthly things, not like a pilgrim who, not understood and himself an alien, wanders once like a ghost across the world's stage in a brief episode. We are too much the children of this earth to want to emigrate from it forever one day. And even if heaven has to bestow itself for earth to be endurable, it has itself to come down and stand over this abiding earth as a light of blessedness and itself break forth as radiance from the dark bosom of the earth.

We belong here. We cannot become unfaithful to the earth, not out of autocratic self-will, which would not suit the sons and daughters of serious, humble mother earth, but because we must be what we are. But we suffer from a secret and mortal sorrow which lodges in the very center of our earthly nature. The earth, our great mother, is itself in distress. It groans under its transitoriness. Its most joyful festivities suddenly resemble the beginning of funeral rites, and when we hear its laughter we tremble in case in a moment tears will be mingled with it. The earth bears children who die, who are too weak to live forever and who have too much mind to be able entirely to renounce eternal joy. Unlike the beasts of the earth, they see the end before it is there and they are not compassionately spared conscious experience of that end.

The earth bears children whose hearts know no limits, and what the earth gives them is too beautiful for them to despise and too poor to enrich them, the insatiable. And because the earth is the scene of this unhappy discord between the great promise which haunts them and the meager gift which does not satisfy them, the earth becomes a fertile source of its children's guilt, for they try to tear more from the earth than it can rightly give. It can complain that it itself became so discordant through the primordial sin of the first man and woman on earth, whom we call Adam and Eve.

But that does not alter the fact that the earth is now an unhappy mother, too living and too beautiful to be able to send its children away even to conquer a new home of eternal life in another world, and too poor to give them as fulfillment what it has contributed to give them as longing. And because the earth is always both life and death, it mostly brings neither, and the sad mixture of life and death, exultation and lament, creative action and monotonous servitude is what we call our everyday life. And so we are here on the earth, our home, and yet it is not enough. The adventure of emigrating from what is earthly won't do, not out of cowardice but out of a fidelity imposed on us by our own nature.

What are we to do? Listen to the message of the resurrection of the Lord. Has Christ the Lord risen from the dead or not? We believe in his resurrection and so we confess: he died, descended into the realm of the dead and rose again the third day. But what does that mean, and why is it a blessing for the children of the earth?

The Son of the Father has died, he who is the Son of man. He who is at once the eternal plenitude of the Godhead, self-sufficient, limitless, and blessed as Word of the Father before all ages *and* the child of this earth as son of his blessed mother. He who is both the Son of God's plenitude and the child of earth's need has died. But the fact that he died does not mean (as in a really unchristian way we "spirituals" shortsightedly think) that his spirit and soul, the vessel of his eternal Godhead have freed themselves from the world and the earth and, as it were, fled into the immensity of God's glory beyond the world because the body which bound them to the earth was shattered in death and because the murderous earth showed that the child of eternal light could find no home in its darkness. We say "died" and immediately add "descended into the realm of the dead and rose again." And this gives the "died" quite a different sense from the world-forsaking sense which we are tempted to attribute to death.

Jesus himself said that he would descend into the heart of the earth (Mt 12:40), that is, into the heart of all earthly things where everything is linked into one and where in the midst of that unity death and futility sit. In death he descended there. By a holy ruse of eternal life he allowed himself to be overcome by death, allowed death to swallow him into the innermost center of the world so that, having descended to the primordial forces and the radical unity of the world, he might establish his divine life in it forever.

Because he died, he belongs in very truth to this earth. For although the human person — the soul, as we say — enters in death into direct relation to God, it is only when the human body is laid in the earth that the human person enters into definitive unity with that mysterious single basis in which all spatio-temporal things are linked and in which they have, as it were, the root of their life.

The Lord descended into death into this lowest and deepest of all the visible creation. He is there now, and not futility and death. In death he became the heart of the earthly world, divine heart in the very heart and center of the world where this, prior even to its unfolding in space and time, sinks its roots into God's omnipotence. It was from this one heart of all earthly things, in which fulfilled unity and nothingness could no longer be distinguished and from which their whole destiny derived, that he rose.

And he did not rise in order finally to depart from hence, not so that the travail of death which gave birth to him anew might transfer him to the life and light of God and he would leave behind him the dark bosom of the earth empty and without hope. For he rose again in his *body*. That means he has already begun to transform this world into himself. He has accepted the world forever. He has been born again as a child of the earth, but of the transfigured, liberated earth, the earth which in him is eternally confirmed and eternally redeemed from death and futility.

He rose, not to show that he was leaving the tomb of the earth once and for all, but in order to demonstrate that precisely that tomb of the dead — the body and the earth — has finally changed into the glorious, immeasurable house of the living God and of the God-filled soul of the Son. He did not go forth from the dwelling-place of earth by rising from the dead. For he still possesses, of course, definitively and transfigured, his body, which is a piece of the earth, a piece which still belongs to it as a part of its reality and its destiny. He rose again to reveal that through his death the life of freedom and beatitude remains established forever within the narrow limits and sorrow of the earth, in the depth of its heart.

What we call his resurrection and unthinkingly regard as his own personal destiny, is simply, on the surface of reality as a whole, the first symptom in experience of the fact that behind so-called experience (which we take so seriously) everything has already become different in the true and decisive depth of all things. His resurrection is like the first eruption of a volcano which shows that in the interior of the world God's fire is already burning, and this will bring everything to blessed ardor in his light. He has risen to show that has already begun. Already from the heart of the world into which he descended in death, the new forces of a transfigured earth are at work. Already in the innermost center of all reality, futility, sin, and death are vanquished and all that is needed is the short space of time which we call history *post Christum natum,* until everywhere and not only in the body of Jesus what has really already begun will be manifest.

Because he did not begin to save and transfigure the world with the superficial symptoms but started with its innermost root, we creatures of the surface think that nothing has happened. Because the waters of suffering and guilt are still flowing where *we* are standing, we think the deep sources from which they spring have not yet dried up. Because wickedness is still inscribing its runes on the face of the earth, we conclude that in the deepest heart of reality love is extinct. But all that is merely appearance, the appearance which we take to be the reality of life.

He has risen because in death he conquered and redeemed forever the innermost center of all earthly reality. And having risen, he has held fast to it. And so he has remained. When we confess him as having ascended to God's heaven, that is only another expression for the fact that he withdraws from us for awhile the tangible manifestation of his glorified humanity and above all that there is no longer any abyss between God and the world.

Christ is already in the midst of all the poor things of this earth, which we cannot leave because it is our mother. He is in the wordless expectation of all creatures, which without knowing it, wait to share in the glorification of his body. He is in the history of the earth, the blind course of which in all victories and all breakdowns is moving with uncanny precision toward his day, the day on which his glory, transforming all things, will break forth from its own depths. He is in all tears and in all death as hidden rejoicing and as the life which triumphs by appearing to die. He is in the beggar to whom we give, as the secret wealth which accrues to the donor. He is in the pitiful defeats of his servants, as the victory which is God's alone. He is in our powerlessness as the power which can allow itself to seem weak, because it is unconquerable. He is even in the midst of sin as the mercy of eternal love patient and willing to the end. He is there as the most secret law and the innermost essence of all things which still triumphs and prevails even when all order and structure seem to be disintegrating.

He is with us like the light of day and the air which we do not notice, like the hidden law of a movement which we do not grasp, because the part which we ourselves experience is too short for us to discern the formula of the movement. But he is there, the heart of this earthly world and the secret seal of its eternal validity.

Consequently, we children of this earth may love it, must love it. Even where it is fearful and afflicts us with its distress and mortal destiny. For since he has entered into it forever by his death and resurrection, its misery is merely temporary and simply a test of our faith in its innermost mystery, which is the risen Christ. That this is the secret meaning of its distress is not our experience. Indeed it is not. It is our faith. The blessed faith which defies all experience. The faith which can love the earth because it is the "body" of the risen Christ or is becoming it.

We therefore do not need to leave it. For God's life dwells in it. If we seek the God of infinity (and how could we fail to?) *and* the familiar earth as it is and as it is to become, in order to be our eternal home in freedom, then one way leads to both. For in the Lord's resurrection God has shown that he has taken the earth to himself forever.

Caro cardo salutis, said one of the ancient fathers of the church with an untranslatable play on words: the flesh is the hinge of salvation. The reality beyond all the distress of sin and death is not up yonder; it has come down and dwells in the innermost reality of our flesh. The sublimest religious sentiment of flight from the world would not bring the God of our life and of the salvation of this earth down from the remoteness of his eternity and would not reach him in that other world of his.

But he has come to us himself. He has transformed what we are and what despite everything we still tend to regard as the gloomy earthly residue of our spiritual nature: the flesh. Since then mother earth has only borne children who are transformed. For his resurrection is the beginning of the resurrection of all flesh.

One thing is needed, it is true, for his action, which we can never undo, to become the benediction of our human reality. He must break open the tomb of our hearts. He must rise from the center of our being also, where he is present as power and as promise. There he is still in movement. There it is still Holy Saturday until the last day which will be the universal Easter of the cosmos. And that resurrection takes place under the freedom of our faith. Even so it is *his* deed. But an action of his which takes place as our own, as an action of loving belief which takes us up into the tremendous movement of all earthly reality toward its own glory, which has begun in Christ's resurrection.

60 • You Are with Me*

Fourth Sunday After Easter (A), 1 Pt 2:21–25; Ps 23

Today, the second Sunday after Easter, is often known as Good Shepherd Sunday. The reason is obvious: the Gospel of the day is in the tenth chapter of St. John, verses 11 to 16; and the epistle, taken from the second chapter of 1 Peter, has the same theme — Christ the good shepherd. Here Christ is called the shepherd and guardian of our souls. So St. Peter is echoing an expression that the Lord himself uses in St. John, where he says that he is the good shepherd.

The image itself comes from the Old Testament. It was usual in ancient times to call princes, those who ruled the nations, the shepherds of their people. The image was perfectly intelligible to the people of that time. They pictured a person going before his flock, feeding and guiding them, leading them to pasture, defending them, looking after them. And the people of that time modestly pictured themselves as the ones led and protected by a higher wisdom and a higher power.

---

*Biblical Homilies, 172–75.

No one thought the image was degrading; people knew that they were in good hands; and so in Psalms and elsewhere in the Old Testament God is called the ruler and governor of the people, the creator and the Lord, the provident, faithful, loving, mighty prince, the shepherd of the people.

And Jesus, coming from the Father, Jesus the presence of the divine shepherd, calls himself the good shepherd. Thus he himself refers to the Old Testament; accordingly, if we would understand a little better what is said in the epistle today about the shepherd and guardian of our souls, we may quite properly go back to the Old Testament and meditate for a while on the twenty-third psalm. It is the psalm about God our shepherd.

We all know this psalm, and yet one can read it again and again. It says: "The Lord is my shepherd." The Lord, Yahweh, he who entered into a covenant with this stiff-necked people and thought of us too as part of his people — for he had in mind the eternal covenant that we enter into, that we are called to — the Lord who has come close to us in Jesus Christ, is our shepherd forever, the one to whom we must keep returning, as St. Peter says in today's epistle.

And the psalmist goes on: "I shall not want." Do we really feel that about God, the eternal and incomprehensible? Can we confidently say: He is my shepherd whom I can trust. I belong to him. I feel his hand governing all my life. His providence watches over me. He is close to me. He feeds and guides me. I lack for nothing? Do we not often feel quite the opposite — indigent, deprived of many things?

But here the psalmist says to God: You are my shepherd, I lack for nothing. He says it calmly and boldly. He says it almost in defiance of the lessons of his life simply because it is true, though it is a truth that transcends our own experience: God is our shepherd and so we lack for nothing. So he goes on to paint what seems to be a bold, optimistic, cheerful picture of his life: "He makes me lie down in green pastures. He leads me beside still waters; he restores my soul. He leads me in paths of righteousness for his name's sake."

Dear God, can we pray like this? Is this how we think of our life — resting in God's resting places, our soul restored, led along the right path? Do we feel that God does all this, and must do it, for his name's sake, because his name is the kind and the eternal, the God of all consolation, the almighty, the shepherd of the world — of scattered reality which must be gathered into one — because his name is "my shepherd"? Well, it is true, says the psalmist. For his name's sake there must be green pastures in our life where we can lie down and rest, where we can be restored and led along the right path.

Is the psalmist a foolish optimist, imagining such things? By no means. For he continues: "Even though I walk through the valley of the shadow of death" — so he has his feet on the ground, he can see human life in human terms: He is walking through the valley of the shadow of death and there seems to be no way out of it: this path that he has just called the right one, onto which the divine shepherd has led him, is the valley of the shadow of death, and it seems to get darker and darker.

But he goes on: "Even though I walk through the valley of the shadow of death, I fear no evil; for thou art with me." The good shepherd accompanies us along the paths that seem dark. He is with us even where we seem to lie in darkness and the shadow of death and not in green pastures. Thou art with me. On this path the psalmist knows that he, poor little lost sheep, will be attacked by the wolves of this life, by famished vultures circling in the sky above an earth that seems to be just a graveyard; and so he remembers that the shepherd he trusts is armed with a rod and a staff to protect his flock from their enemies and get them through all the narrow passes, if need be to force them gently through; and that is why he says: "Your rod" — we should say "club" — "and your staff, they comfort me."

Can we pray this psalm about the good shepherd? Yes, we can. For when we walk in the valley of the shadow of death, there is no salvation except the words: You are with me even here, and it is your rod and your staff that comfort me.

Then the psalmist changes his image a little and, as it were, turns his good shepherd into a hospitable master of the house: "You prepare a table before me in the presence of my enemies; you anoint my head with oil, my cup overflows. Surely goodness and mercy shall follow me all the days of my life; and I shall dwell in the house of the Lord forever." We always dwell in the house of the Lord. We keep coming to his table, and the cup of life overflows not with gall and wormwood but with consolation and blessing, even when the case seems to be quite otherwise.

Goodness and mercy, divine goodness and inexhaustible mercy shall follow me all the days of my life, says the psalmist. That is his way of telling God that he believes God is the good shepherd in Jesus Christ our Lord, the shepherd and guardian of our souls. For he has accompanied us through the darkness of this life on the way of the cross even unto Golgotha. That is why he is the good shepherd who laid down his life for us, so that we should believe that God is truly our shepherd in this life.

Shall we not say once more to him, confessing that it is our own experience: "The Lord is my shepherd, I shall not want"?

61 • God in You Desires God for You*

Saturday of the Sixth Week of Easter, Jn 16:23–30

Let us try to meditate on an idea in today's Gospel which is particularly brought out in the first verses but really pervades the whole — the idea of praying for things in Jesus' name.

Jesus tells us to ask for things in his name; he says that such prayer will be heard, that the Father even anticipates it because he knows — if we make our petition in Jesus' name — that it is a prayer of love for him and of faith. Jesus says: If we are heard because we pray this way in his name, then our joy will be full.

Petition in Jesus' name. If we do not hastily assume that petition must mean explicitly praying to God in words, explicitly thinking of him, but consider what we are like in our ordinary lives, in our secret moments, we shall see that we are all desire and longing, ever on the lookout for something new and different, that we are hungry and thirsty for the good things of life, one cry for a fulfillment we do not yet possess. These desires, which are almost identical with ourselves, which we live and are, reach out here, there, and everywhere. It is strange. They contradict each other; they seek the noble and the sublime, and the most concrete of earthly things; they seize us by turns, the longing, the crying out, the yearning, the desires, the wishes, the hungers, begging and imploring. Now it is one thing, now another; we are practically one vast chaos of appetites.

There is no help for it, even if we want to be orderly and lucid, well coordinated and balanced; we can be nothing else but a multiplicity of desires, and they simply do not, of themselves, present any clear outline, they have no inner cohesion, they are not one harmonious whole in which we could find ourselves and perfect fulfillment. We need someone to straighten out the tangled desires that we are, to infuse them with tranquility and an inner light and joy.

Once everything within us is well-ordered, peaceful, and coherent, we are a petition, a desire, that can be heard. For how can our prayer be answered unless our desire, however manifold, is concentrated on one thing? That is why we must ask in Jesus' name; which does not mean that we invoke him verbally and then desire whatever our turbulent,

---

*Biblical Homilies, 84–87.

divided heart or our appetite, our wretched mania for everything and anything, happens to hanker for.

No, asking in Jesus' name means entering into him, living by him, being one with him in love and faith. If he is in us in faith, in love, in grace, in his Spirit, and then our petition arises from the center of our being, which is himself, and if all our petition and desire is gathered up and fused in him and his Spirit, then the Father hears us. Then our petition becomes simple and straightforward, harmonious, sober, and unpretentious.

Then what St. Paul says in the letter to the Romans applies to us: We do not know how to pray as we ought, but the Spirit himself intercedes for us, praying the one prayer, Abba! Father! He longs for that from which the Spirit and Jesus himself have proceeded: he longs for God, he asks God for God, on our behalf he asks for God. Everything is included and contained in this prayer.

Not as though we must not ask him for everything that will in any way ease, clarify, or illuminate our lives; not as though we must not ask for our daily bread, and appeal to the eternal Father in our daily necessities and pain. These things we should do. But it should all be caught up into the one great prayer of Christ's Spirit, in the name of Jesus. Then we shall see that God really answers our prayer, in one way or another. Then we shall no longer feel that this "one way or another" is a feeble excuse offered by the pious, and the gospel, for unanswered prayer.

No. Our prayer is answered, but precisely because it is prayer in Jesus' name; and what we ultimately pray for is for the Lord to grow in our lives, to fill our existence with himself, to triumph, to gather into one our scattered life, the thousand and one desires of which we are made.

He answers our prayer, for he gives us himself. Of course we must accept the gift and not clutch at a thousand other things. If we reach for the gift — we have Jesus' word for it — God gives us everything else that we really need besides. He makes our clamant poverty wealth and abundance once more. We have only two alternatives: either to ask the Father in Jesus' name for the good Spirit — as Jesus says in St. Luke — or to be a confusion of centrifugal desires which divide our heart, rend our life asunder, and finally run down in death.

But to pray in Jesus' name is to have one's prayer answered, to receive God and God's blessing; and then, even amid tears, even in pain, even in indigence, even when it seems that one has still not been heard, the heart rests in God, and that — while we are still here on pilgrimage, far from the Lord — is perfect joy.

Always Jesus can say to us: Hitherto you have asked nothing in my name. You have tried to, you have meant to, you have started to. But you see, I who gather everything together and reduce everything to one even in your life, I must become the strength and the burden of your prayer, its blessing and its answer. Ask now in my name, as you pray with me the prayer I said on the cross: "Father, into your hands I commend my spirit"; when I knew that I was returning home to the Father and that on my homecoming he will pour forth the Spirit in your heart, God in you to ask for God for you so that your prayer may be answered and your joy may be full.

62 • Christ's Ascension*

He has departed from us. It is alarming that we feel no grief. He must have intended that we be consoled; but our barren and shallow hearts are astonished at this kind of comfort. First of all, we must reflect for a long time before we begin to grasp the fact that we are supposed to be inconsolable over his going away. Yes, it is true: to be comforted, we actually would have had to detain him here on earth.

A shocking fear of the emptiness that he left behind must have come over us. At last there was in our midst someone who was not superfluous; someone who did not *become* a burden, but who *bore* the burden. Because he was good, so unassumingly good, we almost took it for granted! Someone who gave a name to the incomprehensible puzzle behind all things — he called it his Father — and did so with neither incredible naiveté, nor with tasteless presumption. Indeed, he almost led the world into the temptation of taking it for granted, when he allowed us, too, to whisper into the divine darkness, Our Father. It was God's mercy and his eternal wisdom in our midst.

At last we were able to imagine something about God besides the abstractions of philosophers. At last there was someone who knew something, and yet did not have to speak with clever eloquence. Someone we needed only to touch, someone we dared to kiss. Someone we slapped on the shoulder in a friendly way, and he did not get all upset about it. And in these trivialities we had everything — everything incarnate: we had God, his mercy, his grace and his nearness. The eternal Word of the Father had compressed himself into our flesh. Oh, that he did not shudder at this incomprehensibly foolish undertaking — to make God's life a resident in the stall of this world.

And now he is gone away again, and we accept it with indifference.

The Eternal Year, 97–104.

Perhaps we secretly imagine that he could not stand it in our midst. Naturally not, when they crucified him. Dear God, I surely would have done it too, had I been there. Can I (just as I am right now) seriously consider myself better than they? I would be absolutely forsaken, if Christ had not prayed for his enemies, and so for me. That's the only consolation, the only certainty. For only those who are lost are unaware of this consolation. Can a person like me believe in you and love you? I hope so, Lord. Have mercy on me!

Or did he put up with it all and endure it even to the extent that he has taken up to heaven what he assumed in the incarnation? Actually, it would not have been good for us if he had stayed behind here on earth. For even we cannot endure it here forever. Yes, we die. Somewhere, and in some manner, some of us even willingly. We die either from despair or from yearning after freedom: we choose either the death of death or the death of life. But to stay here forever! That would be the wandering Jew in eternal hell.

It was therefore right, quite right, for him to go away. He certainly did what could be done here on earth (pardon me, what only *he* could do here). For the sake of this earth, in boundless love for this terrible earth — did he confuse it with his Father, or is this confusion precisely his mystery, justified because the Father gave it to him? — for the sake of this earth, he let his heart be pressed out to the last drop, like a grape. He let all his heart's fullness flow down into this earth. Greedily the earth swallowed it up, until the fire of guilt and terror in her innards was quenched, and her inmost cavity was filled up with the blood of God himself.

He did what he could do here. It was not his affair that the Father, in his kindness, did not let the earth burst into flames immediately. That was his Father's business. He was pleased that *we* should still have something to say and do. Christ himself insisted on this delay for "a little while." What bold courage! What a trusting heart! He had to go away; there was nothing more for him to do. For everything was fulfilled ever since he turned the dark night of Golgotha into the bright shining day of his love. Afterward, he whispered swiftly to his intimate friends that this is the way to triumph. (Lord, help my unbelief!)

He has taken away with him what he had assumed, the frail flesh, the trembling heart, the human mind (which in the death pang blacks out and knows no more answers). What I am, he assumed: this cramped hovel, full of darkness, where questions and the failure really to understand slink around like squealing rats and find no exit. Naturally, I am aware that one can talk about him with more elegant, more pleasing words if the human being is looked at from God's point of view. You who are irritated at this anthropology, are you just as keenly aware that you, too, are actually judging human beings from God's perspective: and he saw that all was good? Or do you live the lighthearted life of wood lice, who so easily tolerate themselves? Why do you still want God, if you already think that you yourselves are so respectable?

Let us not quibble about this. Your faith and my faith firmly establish that human nature is misunderstood, if it does not as soon as possible attain to God once and for all. Such a "nature" the Son has possessed, "consubstantial with us." And precisely because this nature belonged entirely to God he was aware (really aware, as an individual) of the person's natural state, as long as this nature did not run away from itself into God and seek to be completely dissolved in God and absorbed in the divine nature.

This nature of ours the Son has assumed, and he has taken it with him. He has taken it to that place where we might have thought that nature must completely dissolve into nothingness, if it wants to venture the step across to the beyond. He has taken it to the only place where it can be, if it is not to find its hell right here. I need no fashionable explanation or demythologizing to know that I cannot imagine human nature's behavior "there," or what it does "there." I am not so spiritualistic that I find it easier to imagine a "soul" there than a body. How ridiculous are those Christians who fancy that they can think of Mary in heaven with only her soul, rather than complete with body and soul. In this regard, the few Catholic "heretics" of today who put everyone who dies in God's grace in heaven with body and soul would be more correct than these others.

Therefore I do not suppose that I can picture in my imagination a finite spirit that endures in the presence of God himself — precisely there and only there. But I do know that under pain of eternal damnation we are forbidden to be less demanding and to strive after a more modest place of happiness, or to renounce completely an eternal existence. And I do not know what a body does there. I do not know what both body and soul do there for the length of an eternity. Of course God is eternally meaningful. But how about us? How about us with bodies and souls (or however it may be depicted)? Here on earth we do not last for very long, and we cannot imagine the beyond. Or is, perchance, the beatific vision, the contemplation of God, no longer an absolute mystery in our faith? And have you already taken the trouble to picture in your mind exactly what a glorified body is?

And so my faith and my consolation are centered on this: that he has taken with him everything that is ours. He has ascended and he sits at the right hand of the Father. "I see the Son of man standing at the right hand of God." The absolute Logos shall look at me in eternity with the face of a man. Those who theorize on the beatific vision forget this. As yet, I have read nothing about this in any modern tract in dogma. How strange! At this point pious ascetics read into the silence of the theologians some sentimental anthropomorphism about joy. And what is more, they even dare — on their way to the beatific vision — to bypass the humanity of Jesus. As though we can do this so casually! Whoever "imagines" things this way obviously is not sufficiently aware that God's revelation was a man.

Jesus has taken with him what he was, and what we are, to such an extent that he himself, Jesus of Nazareth, abides forever. We must be more important than we thought, of more permanent value and of more substance, when we consider that this is feasible in spite of our foolish or despairing pride. One could reduce all Christianity to this one formula: it is the faith in which God so surpassed the pride of human beings that the person's grossest imaginings of his own worth are degraded to sinful disbelief and almost brutish timidity.

Moreover, when one indulges in "pantheistic" imaginings about God's existence, on closer inspection one certainly does not make oneself into God, but rather God into oneself. Pantheism is no objection against what has been said above, for what does the incarnation, what does grace and glory mean except that the human person can endure in the midst of God, in the midst of this absolute fire, in the midst of this incomprehensibility. He or she can endure directly before one who is so exalted above everything that is outside of him that it is simply inexpressible. This is, nevertheless, the most unlikely truth. And it is celebrated in Christ's ascension. For in his ascension this truth has been definitively realized.

He has taken ourselves with him. No wonder, then, that we can imagine nothing concerning this, that we today can picture less about this than the ancients could. They had Christ ascending to *caelum empyreum.* In the world of their physical science they had a place for heaven, and they had it, presumably, *even before heaven (as it really is) came to be: by means of Easter and the ascension.*

Nor is this surprising. The breakup of the picture the ancients had of the physical universe was fundamentally a very Christian occurrence. Although understandable and unavoidable, the ancient notion was fundamentally very unchristian, because it made heaven exist before and independently of Christ and the events of his death and resurrection. In this view, moreover, Christ was the gate-opener of heaven rather than its founder. Whoever wants to take the *aperuisti credentibus regna caelorum,* "you have *opened* the kingdom of heaven for the faithful," so literally that Christ has done nothing except open heaven, would say too little about him. *Condidisti...,* "you have *established...,*" would be more accurate.

Space controlled time and history. And all this was not so Christian that we today must demythologize merely because formerly this was not correct. For today, since the world and even space itself are seen to be finite, there is "room" enough even for a corporeal heaven, even though this can no longer be thought of (as with the ancients) as an ultimately homogeneous piece of our space, nor as an upper border on the edge of our space. And if this quite modern natural science is a unique focusing of the thought of the unimaginable on matter, we shall also learn anew to "think" of heaven simply as bodily glorification, and thus we shall learn to take seriously its reality.

The ontology of the beatific vision was indeed a very abstract matter, and we can still learn something about it from the ancients. Their gift to us is not obscurity, and indeed they believed, and knew with faith. It would not, then, be at all "modern," but worse than the ancient way, if we were to act as if we could not take the ascension (his and ours) seriously, simply because we could not picture it in our imagination.

Is he far away from us because he has ascended above the heavens? When is someone close to us? When we can touch him and kiss him, like Judas kissing the Lord? Or do gestures like these really belong to the category of those tapping signs which prisoners use to transmit by code their walled-in loneliness from cell to cell? In order to be really near, don't we have to die, and start to live "far away"? Isn't it necessary for us first to have descended through death down into the heart of the world, in order to be near everything, near because in death we begin to live at the secret root of all things? Is not the body of flesh which we now carry around with us the limitation to a narrow here and now in this finite space and time, so that the only one who can be really close to all things is the person who by dying strips off this mortal flesh in order to put on the heavenly body?

But he seems to be far away from me, and indeed, he himself said that he would leave us. No, not really; he was speaking only of relinquishing that earthly nearness, which, ultimately, is really distance. He was telling us that he would give no more tapping signs, that he would not need to, because he is no longer close by in the dungeon of his passible, unglorified body. But now, through death and glorification, he is right in our midst, right here where we are, and not beside us, not merely next to us. "Behold, I am with you all days!"

And when he tells us through the apostle that he is with us in his Spirit, through which he lives in us and we in him, when he lets us "put on" himself, he does not mean his holy commandments, nor his dispositions and attitudes, nor his theories and the prospects which he opens to us, but rather his actual spirit, the Spirit that proceeds from him as the living, given reality of his divine life. This is the life that streamed forth from his heart pierced in death, the life that penetrated into the innermost core of the world and the innermost core of our hearts.

Because he wanted to come close to us definitively, he has gone away and has taken us with him. Because he was lifted up (on the cross of death and to the right hand of the Father), he and everything in him have become near. The reason for this is that his Spirit — the Spirit in whom Christ is near to us, the Spirit upon whom Christ from eternity to eternity bestows the eternal fullness of life from the Father, the Spirit over and above which there is nothing that Christ could give in all eternity — this Spirit is already in us now. He is in us as the basis of the nearness of eternal contemplation, as the basis of the transfiguration of the flesh. We notice nothing of this, and that is why the ascension seems to be separation. But it is separation only for our paltry consciousness. We must will to believe in such a nearness — in the Holy Spirit.

The ascension is the universal event of salvation history that must recur in each individual, in our personal salvation history through grace. When we become poor, then we become rich. When the lights of the world grow dark, then we are bathed in light. When we are apparently estranged from the nearness of his earthly flesh, then we are the more united with him. When we think we feel only a waste and emptiness of the heart, when all the joy of celebrating appears to be only official fuss, because the real truth around us cannot yet be admitted, then we are in truth better prepared for the feast of the Ascension than we might suppose.

He takes on our semblance only to give us his own reality — the eternal, inexpressible reality that he received from the Father, that he gives us in his Spirit, and that we can receive because he, returning home with all that is ours, made it possible for us to share in God's own life.

63 • "... Why Do You Stand Looking into Heaven?"*

Acts 1:9–11

We want to turn our attention meditatively to this text of the New Testament that contains the most explicit and picturesque report of

*Herausforderung des Christen, 47–50. Trans. Frederick G. Lawrence, Boston College.

Jesus' ascension. But we have to leave out of consideration most of the questions and reflections that are evoked in us by this report of Jesus' being taken up into heaven: the relationship of this report in Luke-Acts to those in Mark and Luke's Gospel; and the significance of the lack of such accounts in the rest of the Gospels; the hermeneutical principles for the interpretation of this kind of account; the question of the relationship between what we call the resurrection of Jesus and what we call his ascension; and in general and overall, the question as to what the ascension of Jesus means according to our faith. All this is presupposed as having been given due consideration.

Here we turn our attention to only one verse of our text, 11: "This same Jesus, who was taken away from you into heaven, will come in the same way as you saw him go into heaven." In this sentence the sameness of the trope of Jesus' going away and coming again is spoken about. However one is to interpret this eleventh verse of the first chapter of Acts taken by itself and read in its narrowest context, I think, without wishing to decide the issue, that one should interpret and play variations on the verse in terms of the New Testament as a whole. The same Jesus who was removed from us by *death* and is only genuinely believed in as such will also be the one who comes, the one who for our salvation comes into our lives, into our deaths, and into the completion of the world as the one swallowed up by death into the unfathomability of God, and who can only come in this way if we share in performing the movement of his passage in faith, hope, and love.

Jesus has departed from us by his death. In *this* way he redeemed us. If, by God's free disposition, no finite entity created and bestowed by God is supposed to be the fulfillment of our existence, but God himself in his unending unfathomability, then the act of receiving such salvation by a world that is finite and closed by guilt can only occur if the reality of a life in the grip of the incomprehensible — in a word — dies. Because such an act of unconditional acceptance of the deadly unfathomability of God as our salvation happened in Jesus and was accepted by God as the promise of the same acceptance for everyone, Jesus is the salvation of the world. But for this reason, too, it could only happen in virtue of his death. Because this is the only way for human beings really to fall into the abyss of their absurdity or into the abyss of God's unfathomability, which makes us happy without another, third, mediating, or provisional moment being possible.

Yet in this way, too, Jesus is also undeniably the one taken away from us by death. We can say that precisely by reason of his death he has become close to us in his Spirit, who emerges out of his devastated heart as the spring of living water. But when we thus speak of "Spirit" as his proximity to us, then this means precisely that he is only close to us if we let ourselves in for that movement from God called (exactly) Spirit. In this movement we allow ourselves to be drawn beyond everything conceivable and manageable by us ourselves into the untracked and unmapped unfathomability of God and his will; and we receive this measureless reality as our happiness. Jesus, the one who has died, is near us in our willingness to be baptized into his death ever anew.

As this one who has died, Jesus is the one who comes. This is precisely to say that his death is not a past episode revised and eliminated by his coming, but precisely the law of his coming. Indeed he comes by taking us and not by being present again where he once was and where we are; he comes by taking us away into the unfathomability of God by the passage through death; and he is the one who has come when this process of deadly transition into the power of his Spirit from the comprehensible and from our mastery into the happy unfathomability of God is perfected.

Are we the ones who await *this* Jesus? Are we the ones who effectively accept the event of his coming, the event of his headlong plunge into death? The question hanging directly over us is: do we truly await this Jesus who has gone through death and who at the same time comes to us? Or do we attempt to lead and to defend a life which in no way accepts death as the really radical situation in which faith, hope, and love attain fulfillment?

What is involved in the answering of this question for each individual in his or her private existence, each person has to deliberate on for himself or herself. But this question is always newly directed to the church as such. For the church is not the institution of salvation which can remain stabile on this earth and which discharges, one by one, into God's incomprehensibility only those whom it has embraced with its saving care. Rather it is the pilgrim people of God who, as such, await the coming of Jesus and stand under the law of his Spirit which redeems and triumphs only through death.

But when we put this question in this way to ourselves as the church, then we can only hear it with fear and trembling. To be sure: laws, institutions, offices and competencies, sacramental signs, and all the other things that go to make up the body of this earthly church, have to exist. They also pertain to the earthly body of the incarnate Word of God. But all this bodiliness of the church is still only the incarnateness of the Logos in Jesus when it is surrendered ever anew to his death, when it accepts its own death ever anew; and so and only so does it await the coming of Jesus in the all-consuming glory of the unfathomable God.

But do we live, build, and bear this bodiliness of the church *as* something that has to pass through death? Do we not glorify or blame (both amount to the same thing) this concreteness of the church as if it were eternally valid and would not have to pass away so that the eternal kingdom of God can come? Aren't we too interested in restoration, too anxiously worried about the letter of the law and of dogma? Too anxious in the face of the novel and the unusual? In the face of the dangerous and the not yet secure? As if we had to defend a church that itself were already the definitive kingdom and not just the tent (that needs ever again to be dismantled and put up again provisionally) of the pilgrim people of God, which, with inexorable courage, is even now in the period of time heading toward that point where there will be no church?

Aren't we secretly and without admitting it to ourselves on a march into the ghetto, which means nothing except that we build up a church that is dogmatically, juridically, and liturgically as perfect as possible, without seriously asking ourselves if contemporary people also can and want to live in this church? Aren't we people, who with backs bent over, busily construct the little fields of our plans without ever standing up straight and looking out for the coming of Jesus, who approaches out of the unfathomability of God as one who has died, and who through his death and our dying along with him, breaks up dogma, law, and rite (without abolishing their historical significance) and so liberates us into the freedom of God?

"Men of Galilee, why do you stand looking into heaven?" Only if we look to Jesus, the one dying and the one who died, as the one who comes in the freedom which only his death bestows on us, are we Christians. Only so do we have also the right relationship of nearness and distance to our Christian mission in this age which is supposed to serve in its own way not only the letter but the Spirit of Jesus.

64 • The Message of Pentecost*

Pentecost completes Easter, for Pentecost is the completion of the saving events celebrated during the Easter season. We celebrated these events by recalling the sacrificial death of the Lord, his victorious resurrection, and his entrance — by means of his ascension — into his Father's eternity. All these events took place so that the Holy Spirit might become our portion. All these events have but one goal: to

---

*The Eternal Year, 105–12.

redeem the world and the human beings in it, and to give God himself to this redeemed world.

That is why Pentecost is the fulfillment of Easter. The reason why the glowing love of the Father and of the Son has descended into our hearts is that the Father's own Son has brought our humanity back into the Father's light. The reason why one can live God's own life in the Holy Spirit is that the Son of man died according to the flesh. The Holy Spirit of the eternal God has come. He is here: he lives in us, he sanctifies us, he strengthens us, he consoles us. He is the pledge of eternal life, the earnest of absolute triumph.

The center of all reality, the innermost heart of all infinity, the love of the all-holy God has become our center, our heart. True and absolute reality now lives in our nothingness; the strength of God vitalizes our weakness: eternal life lives in mortal human beings. The only thing that nightfall really means now is that we cannot grasp the meaning of the day that has dawned on us since Pentecost — the day that will see no sunset. The tears of our despair and of our ever-recurring disappointments are nothing but trivial illusions that veil an eternal joy.

God is ours. He has not given us merely a gift, a gift created and finite like ourselves. No, he has given us his whole being without reserve: he has given us the clarity of his knowledge, the freedom of his love, and the bliss of his trinitarian life. He has given us himself. And his name is Holy Spirit. He is ours. He is in each heart that calls to him in humble faith. He is ours to such an extent that, strictly speaking, we can no longer say what the human being is if we omit the fact that God himself is the person's possession. God is *our* God: that is the glad tidings of Pentecost.

That is the good news of Pentecost, the glorious, radiant message, the tidings of strength and of light and of victory, the message that God loves us and has blessed us with himself. That is the message. But do we give ear to this message, and do we grasp it with faith? I do not mean to ask whether we doubt it intellectually or whether we admit its validity with slightly less than full consent. But rather, has the message penetrated our hearts? Is it really there — in the bloodstream — and not merely there as one of our maxims (we have so many!), which we readily cite while living by entirely different standards? Is the good news of Pentecost in our heart of hearts as the light and strength of our lives? Or is it merely stirring rhetoric, pious words for the feast day, when we can treat ourselves to such ideals, because on feast days we are virtuous and do not have to work?

Do we live by the message? And, not only that, do we talk about it? Is our heart submissive enough to welcome as sheer grace the gift which is God himself, the gift which we can receive only on our knees in mute trembling before such a merciful God? Or is our heart so proud and self-assured that we think it only proper that God should visit us with his own personal life? Is our heart so haughty that it presumes to take such a grace for granted? Or is it so timid and despairing, so weary and empty, that it can really be satisfied only by its own poverty and weakness, because these things can be experienced, while possession by God's Spirit must be grasped by faith? In short, do we believe in the message of Pentecost?

Do we not have to cry out with the man in the Gospel, "I believe, Lord, help my unbelief" (Mk 9:24)? We must keep on asking, together with those who heard St. Peter's Pentecost sermon, "Brethren, what shall we do?" (Acts 2:37). What shall we do, so that the Holy Spirit will be our portion, so that he will remain with us always, and continue to increase in us? Peter gave the answer to this question, and his answer is still valid for us: "Repent and be baptized every one of you in the name of Jesus Christ for the forgiveness of your sins; and you will receive the gift of the Holy Spirit" (Acts 2:38). The order of these two requisites may be reversed for us who have already been baptized; the demand itself still remains the same: baptism and, every day, a new conversion.

We are baptized. This is the first thing that God has done for us, and this assures us that he has willed to give us his Holy Spirit. Like the wind, the Spirit of God blows where he will, and in his loving patience he roams, no doubt, through all the streets of the world, in order there to touch us. And, in the omnipotence of his grace, he may find many to touch. Yet this grace always strives to bring such persons home to its kingdom, the church, and to incorporate them into the mystical body of Christ, whose soul is that same Spirit.

But when his action takes place tangibly, in time and space, when it occurs not merely in the depths of the heart, but also in sign on the body, in word and water, when baptism is bestowed, then we know that here God surely lays his hands on us (if the individual does not obstruct his action) and he says: "You are mine." Here God stamps his indestructible seal in the heart of human beings. Here, in the very depths of our being, the Father plants his Holy Spirit, his sacred strength, his divine life.

And this has happened to us. We are baptized. God has touched us, not merely by ideas and theories, not merely in pious moods and feelings, but by his own personal, incarnate action, which he works in us in baptism through his ordained servant. This is our consolation and our conviction: that God has already freely and openly spoken to us and poured the Spirit of his life into our hearts from the first days of our life. This clear testimony on the part of God is more impressive than the ambiguous testimony of our own heart in its weariness, weakness, and bitter emptiness. God has spoken in baptism: "You are my son and the holy temple of my own Spirit."

Compared with the divine word, of what value then is our every-day experience, the practical experience that makes us appear to be poor, God-forsaken and Spirit-forsaken creatures? Our faith is in God rather than in ourselves. We are baptized. And the delightful Spirit of God's life is in the depth of our being where we ourselves, perhaps, with our smattering of psychology, have not reached. There in those depths the Spirit speaks to the eternal God and says: Abba, Father. There he addresses us: Child, truly beloved child of everlasting life. We are baptized.

But if our baptism is recorded on the first page of the book of our life, we are not released from the second demand made by Peter on Pentecost: Repent. We can quench the Spirit, we can cause him grief, we can hinder him from bringing the blessed fruit of eternal life into us. And that is why we must open ourselves again each day to this Spirit of the Lord, turn to him again each day, be converted to him again each day.

We so-called good Christians may often have the agonizing impression that the Spirit of God has forgotten us. In our own lives and in the life of the church, that great dwelling and temple of the Holy Spirit, we may often think that we are too little aware of the Spirit of God and his free but powerful sway. We may feel that we detect in and around us much of the letter and little of the Spirit, many commands and little freedom, much of eternal work and little heartfelt love, much fear and trembling and little bold trust, much duty and little charisma, much timid fear before God and little joyous confidence in his goodness, much love for the world and little for eternity.

In short, we may think we find in and around us too much of the spirit of the world and too little of the Spirit of the Father. While these impressions may frequently be valid, there is usually something false in them, too. Something false, I say, because the human eye cannot detect the Spirit in us and in the church. And if we feel how little we are truly persons of the Spirit, we are usually once again ensnared in a false idea of God's Spirit and of his work in the church. And that is the reason why daily conversion and reflection are especially necessary.

Ostensibly we seek the clarity of a faith that never falters, but in reality we want only a freedom from doubt that waters down our faith and its decision. We think we are seeking the Spirit of faith; yet instead of the certainty of the Spirit, who dwells in the darkness of faith, we are seeking only the clarity of earthly truisms.

Ostensibly we seek the power of the Spirit who overcomes the world, while in reality we desire a decisive triumph for the kingdom of God on earth, a triumph that would spare us from being patient and constant, even to the end. We think we seek the Spirit of divine power, but we desire the glory of the world instead of the power of the Spirit, who through patient love courts the hearts of human beings and their freely returned love — even to the end.

Ostensibly we seek the freedom of the children of God in the Spirit of freedom; but we really desire free rein for our laziness and our earthly tendencies. We think we are seeking the Holy Spirit of freedom, whereas we are seeking only the non-Spirit which binds an individual in the fetters of her own selfishness, isolating her from other people, instead of drawing her into the freedom of the Spirit by first ushering her into the selfless love of God.

Ostensibly we seek the Spirit of holy joy, when in reality we desire leisurely entertainment that saves us from sharing in the tears of Christ and from shedding tears of repentance.

Ostensibly we seek the Spirit who gives life; yet in reality we desire only the non-Spirit who lies to us about life to lure us past the life that is gained only through death, to lure us where there is nothing but death.

We must reflect on all this, over and over again, every day. We must not interpret our experience of life falsely, and think that the Spirit of God has become distant and weak. Rather, we must learn from these experiences that we are always seeking him in the wrong place and in the wrong way, that we are always ready to confuse him with something else. If we reflect in this way, then we shall perceive over and over again with trembling joy that he is there, that he is with us: the Spirit of faith in darkness, the Spirit of freedom in obedience, the Spirit of joy in tears, the Spirit of eternal life in the midst of death. Then we are filled, in all the insignificance and silence of this world, in all the sober realism of everyday life, with the holy conviction that he is there, he is with us. He prays with unspeakable groanings in each one's heart. He consoles and strengthens, he heals and helps, he gives the certainty of eternal life. But we must reflect anew, each day.

Daily conversion enjoins yet a second activity: to pray for the Holy Spirit. The church was in prayer when the Holy Spirit came on Pentecost. He is the Spirit of grace — of grace that cannot be merited. He is the unfathomable marvel of God's love. Our deeds do not force him down from heaven, nor can the despairing cry of our distress compel him. He is and he remains, always and in each moment, the free gift from above. In the very moment when we decide to seize upon him as something which belongs to us by right, he will withdraw.

On the other hand, when we wait, expecting nothing from ourselves, when we reckon with the incalculable, when we call to one who has no name, when we are confident without referring to anything that is in ourselves, then we pray, we pray for the Holy Spirit. And then the Holy Spirit comes, gently perhaps, and unnoticeably, but really. He comes not because we pray, but because God wills to love us. Then the Holy Spirit comes, because the Spirit of God himself, praying in us, has called out to himself. If we realize that we are unprofitable servants — how hard this is, and yet so obvious — then the reward of unprofitable servants, the Holy Spirit, is already there. If we confess our weakness — how hard this is and yet so obvious — then we are praying, and then the strength of our weakness, the Holy Spirit, is already with us.

Everything that we are, therefore, prays in us for the Holy Spirit of the Father and of the Son. The recognition that we are outcasts before God, our weakness — even our sinfulness, which causes us to lose God's word through carelessness, our poverty, weakness and darkness, even our coldness toward God and his holy love — everything that is in us prays in mute expectancy for the Holy Spirit of the Father and of the Son.

Come, Spirit, Spirit of the Father and of the Son. Come, Spirit of love, Spirit of sonship, Spirit of peace, of faith, of strength, of holy joy. Come, secret joy, into the tears of the world. Come, victory-rich life, into the death of the earth.

Come, Father of the poor, support of the oppressed. Come, love, who is poured out into our hearts. We have nothing that can force you; yet on that very account we are confident. Our hearts stand in mysterious awe at your coming, because you are selfless and gentle, because you are something else than our heart. Yet this is for us the firmest promise that you are nevertheless coming. Come, therefore, come to us every day, again and again. We put our trust in you. Where else could we trust? We love you because you are love itself. In you we have God for our Father, because you cry out in us, Abba, Father. We thank you, quickening Spirit, Holy Spirit, we thank you for dwelling in us, for having willed to be in us the seal of the living God, the seal that stamps us as his property. Do not forsake us in the bitter struggle that is life; do not forsake us at the end when everything else will abandon us. *Veni, Sancte Spiritus.*

65 • Pentecost: Fear of the Spirit*

We are told in the Acts of the Apostles (19:1–2) that Paul found some disciples at Ephesus and asked them: "Did you receive the Holy Spirit

---

Opportunities for Faith, 40–45.

when you believed?" They answered: "We have never even heard of the Holy Spirit."

Many Christians today, if they were faced with the same question, ought really to answer: We were told about the Holy Spirit in our religious instruction at school, we were baptized and confirmed, but that's about all we've had to do with the Holy Spirit; we've not yet seen any trace of him in our lives.

In fact, in this age of technology, of rationally planned leadership of human beings, of mass media, of rational psychology and depth psychology, it isn't easy for people today to discover within the field of their experience anything they might venture to call the efficacy of the Holy Spirit. There seems to be no scope for anything that is not secular within a "system" of intramundane causes and effects, without exit or entrance.

If we want to get rid of the impression of a secular world, in which there is nothing like a Holy Spirit, then we shall have to stop looking for him only under explicitly religious labels of the kind to which our religious training has accustomed us. If we look out for inner freedom in which a person, regardless of herself, remains faithful to the dictate of her conscience; if someone succeeds, without knowing how, in really breaking out of the prison of her egoism; if someone not only gets his pleasures and delights, but possesses that joy which knows no limit; if someone with mute resignation allows death to take her and at the same time entrusts herself to an ultimate mystery in which she believes as unity, meaning, and love: when these things happen, what we Christians call the Holy Spirit is at work, precisely because in these and similar experiences what is involved is not a controllable and definable factor of the world of our experience. The Spirit is at work precisely because this world of experience is delivered up to its incomprehensible ground, to its innermost center which is no longer its very own.

We Christians least of all need to think of this nameless Holy Spirit, "poured out upon all flesh," as locked up within the walls of the church. Rather do we form the church as the community of those who confess explicitly in historical and social forms that God loved the world (not merely us Christians) and made his Spirit the innermost dynamic principle of the world, through whom everyone finds God as his absolute future, as long as he does not cut himself off from God through the deep-rooted sin of a whole life. If we see the gift of the Spirit to the world in this way, then it is perhaps not so difficult to find in this world the Holy Spirit in whom we profess our faith at Pentecost as our innermost mystery and even more as God's mystery.

We in the church would be able to discover and experience the Spirit of the Lord more easily and more powerfully if we were not afraid

of him. He is in fact the Spirit of life, of freedom, of confidence, of
hope and joy, of unity, and thus of peace. We might therefore suppose
that the human person longs for the Holy Spirit more than anything
else. But he is the Spirit who constantly breaks through all frontiers in
order to make these gifts, who seeks to deliver up everything to the
incomprehensibility which we call God; he is the Spirit who gives life
through death.

It is not surprising that we are afraid of him. For we always want
to know what we are involved in, we want to have the entries in our
life's account clearly before us and to be able to add them up to a figure
that we can clearly grasp. We are frightened of experiments whose outcome cannot be foreseen. We hate to be overtaxed and like to measure
our duty by what we are prepared to accomplish without great efforts.
We want the Spirit therefore in small doses, but he won't put up with
this. We trust him only insofar as he is expressed in literary form, in law
and tradition, in institutions that have proved their worth. We want him
to be measured by these standards, to prove his identity as *Holy* Spirit
through these, although in fact it should be the other way round.

We are afraid of the Spirit. In a word, he is too incalculable for us.
We believe only in theory and not in practical life that God is infinite
incomprehensibility into which the Holy Spirit wants to hurl us. We
make our permanent home in what should be merely the starting point
or take-off runway for this movement of human beings through faith,
hope, and love, into the immense incomprehensibility of God.

It is no better when we give the name of church to this country
which we don't want to leave, when we forget that the church too
has validity before God and human beings only to the extent that she
produces through word and sacrament this hope and faith and the
love in which human persons entrust themselves unconditionally to
the Holy Spirit of God.

Even in the life of the church as such this fear of the Holy Spirit can
be found. Fear can be perceived among the "traditionalists." They fear
risks and experiments the results of which are not known in advance.
They don't want to hear any formulations of faith with which they have
not been familiar from childhood onward, as if a proposition and the
Spirit which it attests were simply identical. They want to have unity
in the variety of the church in such a way that they can thoroughly
understand this unity and take it under their own control. The tradition
which they defend — as such rightly — is for them the land of the
fathers, now definitely acquired and only needing to be inhabited and
governed, not a station on a pilgrimage, beckoning them on further,
even though of course in the direction in which they had hitherto been
moving. And if they admit and profess in theory the doctrine of divine

unrest in the church, known as the Holy Spirit, it is only in order really to have the right to refuse the demands of this incalculable Spirit in practical life.

On the other hand, we get the impression that those also are often afraid of the Holy Spirit who proudly call themselves or are suspected by others of being "progressives." For real confidence in the power of the Holy Spirit in his church implies also the hopeful faith that he constantly prevails in this church with his power of renewal. But why then are these "progressives" so often irritated and impatient? How is the faith in God's Spirit constantly renewing "the face of the earth" of the church compatible with the peevish threat to leave the church if she does not soon undergo a thorough change, while granting her somewhat optimistically a brief period in which to become again a home which they don't have to leave?

Don't the "progressives" also dictate to the Holy Spirit where he has to be active? Namely, at a critical distance from the church which is identified with office and tradition, in purely social commitment, in the will for the unity of Christians at all costs. Not, however, in worship of God, in love for a real, concretely existing neighbor, in fraternal patience and magnanimous understanding for those of his brethren who have to serve the church in an office to which they never quite do justice (how could it be otherwise?), with goodwill and an open mind even toward initiatives which emerge from official sources in the church, in an open-mindedness without which, whether we admit it or not, we remain complacently and autocratically entangled in our own subjectivity. Are the "progressives" not often afraid of the Holy Spirit when they fear death, which means here fear of the mute, unrewarded sacrifice in the service of the church and of her mission, a sacrifice which cannot be justified in terms of a will for a merely intramundane future?

If the question is put to "traditionalists" and "progressives" in this way, as to whether they are not both afraid of the Spirit, the double question must not be suspected as a cheap, dialectical reconciliation of the two standpoints, nor be misused by professors and, today, by bishops who are inclined to advise a cheap "both this and that" or a "golden mean." Of course there are appropriate middle ways, and certainly the extremes of the *terribles simplificateurs* are stupid and can lead only to disaster. Certainly among the Christian virtues are moderation, patience, and the realism which is not fanatical and does not want to turn the world too quickly into a paradise soon to become a concentration camp of universal forced happiness.

But the Holy Spirit is simply not a compromise between intramundane antagonisms, not the golden mean, not the holiness of narrow-minded mediocrity. The Holy Spirit in particular must not be understood as one side of a dialectic, the other being made up of the letter, the law, the institution, rational calculation. Rather is he the one who constantly blasts open all such empirical, dialectical unities of opposites (although these have their justification) and sweeps them into the movement directed toward the incomprehensible God, who is not merely another particular factor in the world and in the counter-and interplay of its forces.

If, then, all are asked if they are not afraid of the Spirit, this does not mean striving after the golden mean with the secret intention of smoothing everything out so that all remains as before and each one sticks to his opinion and attitude. The prayer to the Holy Spirit, the appeal to leave everything to him, means rather a readiness to admit into life the incalculable, the new that becomes old, the old becoming new; it often means having no clearly worked out answer in the concrete situation, but, with a secret confidence on which adequate reflection is impossible, leaving the existing and enduring question itself to count as the answer; it means continuing, because the past provides enough reason for hope, but in fact only for hope.

The word of the Holy Spirit does not provide prescriptions which we merely need to carry out. It commands boldness, experiment, decision, which cannot be justified by general principles (the law and the letter). The word of the Holy Spirit is the question to each individual in his irreplaceable uniqueness as to whether he has the courage to venture, to experiment, to endure the opposition of the great mass (whether traditionalist or progressive); whether he trusts in something which in the last resort cannot be rationally proved, but which is of course supremely rational wisdom — that is, in the Holy Spirit.

With this courage everyone in the church must do his own part, even though at first sight he is not in agreement with what the other does for his part. Each must do this conscious of the fact that her gift and her mission are different from the Spirit's gift to others. But if the unity of the Spirit in the variety of his gifts is to be maintained, there are in fact *many* gifts. An antagonism, a dispute, among these gifts in the church simply cannot be avoided. For if these gifts were unambiguously and palpably already reconciled for us, there would be no need of a Holy Spirit who is of himself this unity; and, because not comprehensible and controllable by us, this unity escapes us.

This duty exists for us only if we blast open what the Spirit has given us for our own — so that we do this and not something else — in the loving hope that all these gifts are one, even though we cannot see into and control this unity, even though we must bear witness to our faith in this incomprehensible unity in terms of the sort of unity that we ourselves can achieve in humility and a willingness to adapt ourselves.

But *how* this courage in regard to our own gift of the Holy Spirit *and* the will for the unity of all gifts in the church can coexist at the same time is in the very last resort once again not a question to be solved by the principles of systematic reasoning, but the gift of the Holy Spirit who gives himself to us in a way that does not place him under our control. We should have no fear of this Spirit, we should admit him, each of us being critical in regard to ourselves. Then the Spirit's improvisation, which we call the church, is more likely to succeed than seeking to form the church only according to the principles which we have taken under our own control.

66 • Nature Abhors a Vacuum*

Pentecost Monday, Jn 16:5–14

Today's Gospel is taken from the words of the Lord at the Last Supper, as given in Jn 16:5–14. Jesus speaks of the future, he takes his leave of the apostles and consoles them. It is difficult to deal with this text in order because in a very deep and authentic sense Jesus keeps saying the same thing — all there is to say. We might say that the fourteenth chapter has to do with consoling the apostles over Jesus' departure and with the promise of the Spirit; and chapters 15 and 16 might be summed up in his words: Abide in me, and I in you. Chapter 17 can be called Christ's high priestly prayer.

Again we might say that chapters 15 and 16 comprise two parts: the first, chapter 15, could be entitled: the fellowship and destiny of the disciples; and the second, chapter 16, consolation of the disciples in the Holy Spirit and in the prospect of soon seeing Christ again.

Today's text belongs to this latter part. We might also entitle the first fifteen verses of chapter 16: the Holy Spirit and his work. For from verse 4 onward Jesus says something about the relationship of the Holy Spirit with the world, and in the following verses something about the relationship of the Holy Spirit with the disciples of Jesus. Let us briefly consider these verses together and see whether they may not bring a little light and consolation and seriousness into our lives.

Biblical Homilies, 76–79.

Jesus is speaking of his departure. He says that he must go and that of all this mysterious process whereby Jesus dies, seems to leave the world, and returns to his Father, the disciples understand only the absence of their Lord, only the emptiness compared with the presence he has been to them. Only distance and separation. That is why sorrow has filled their hearts.

Do we not have this experience of parting, time and again; of some person or something that is dear to us leaving us, taking our very selves away? Our heart is filled with sorrow; we are threatened with a deadly, killing grief — a this-worldly grief that knows no hope. Because I have said these things to you, sorrow has filled your hearts, says the Lord. He does not blame them so much for this as for not asking where he is going, for not asking him to tell them the true nature of this going. My going, Jesus tells his disciples, is the coming of the Father and existence in the Holy Spirit.

We must not take this superficially, as though Jesus simply said, Yes I am going, but to console you I shall send you the Holy Spirit. He does do this, but we shall only understand the passage if we apprehend — at least by faith — that, as the Lord says here, his going actually is the coming of God's Spirit. We might put it this way: there is no such thing, either in the world or in the heart, as literal vacancy, as a vacuum. And wherever space is really left by parting, by death, by renunciation, by apparent emptiness, provided the emptiness that cannot remain such is not filled by the world, or activity, or chatter, or the deadly grief of the world — there God is.

When he is in the heart in this way we call him the Holy Spirit, because he is revealed to us out of the fullness of the Godhead, by the mercy of the Father, and sent to us as the Spirit of the Son. If Jesus takes from us what seems to us his palpable presence, what we in our folly think of as his only real palpable presence, takes from us the consolation of the utterable and the tangible, of what can be seen and possessed, then, if we believe in him, he comes to us in the Holy Spirit.

That is why he says: "It is to your advantage that I go away; for if I go, I will send the Spirit to you." But the Spirit cannot come into hearts that will not open themselves to this awful emptiness, as it seems to be, which is filled by the Spirit of God; hearts that are unbelieving, that are the "world" in the sense meant here. What happens in such hearts shows us the negative counterpart of the Spirit's dominion. When he comes, Jesus says, he will convince the world of sin and of righteousness and of judgment.

How does the Spirit do that? By this sinful sorrow — even if he protests against it — the human person knows in her heart that she is not in the truth, not in righteousness, but in sin. She perceives her sin because she does not believe in Jesus who is given in the Spirit. The despairing emptiness within tells the human being that somebody has gone and that true righteousness exists when one loves the world enough to reach out, unafraid, beyond the world, has the courage to leave oneself open to the unutterable, when one believes that one possesses everything although one seems to have lost everything, that one has conquered although in this going of Christ one seems to have been defeated.

And so the emptiness that is deadly because it is not filled by the Spirit of God convinces the world that the only righteousness consists in acknowledging that the Son goes to the Father and is no more seen; that no one is right who does not accept this fact. By this darkness which will not allow itself to be illumined by that unutterable light, the prince of this world is already judged. For the judgment is that the person who does not abandon himself to trusting faith has already judged himself in this deadly emptiness, in this despairing darkness. But with you, my disciples, Jesus says, the case is different: the Spirit comes ever anew, ever more abundantly, in this experience that seems so dark.

When Jesus seems to have nothing more to say to us, then he is telling us what he wished to tell us but was not able to when he was tangibly present — the secret of his death, which is life; of our death, which is eternal life. That is why he says: "I have yet many things to say to you, but you cannot bear them now." But when the Spirit of truth has come — that is, I who now take leave of you — then I shall lead you not into this or that partial truth, but into all truth.

For the Spirit does not speak of something or other; he speaks of me who have entered with your own destiny into my Father's infinity. He declares what he hears — ultimately, what he is — the eternal wisdom of God himself which blossoms in silence, in the experience of our own crucifying finitude. He will not speak on his own authority, Jesus says, but whatever he hears he will speak, and he will declare to you the things that are to come — God himself. He will glorify me, for he will take what is mine and declare it to you.

We are always approaching the ascension of Jesus, and it always seems to us to be a parting. This thing that happened to Jesus keeps happening in our own lives. As we pilgrims journey on toward the parting, let us look squarely at it. So long as we believe, and accept what we undergo as the lot of the Lord and his disciples, the Holy Spirit will always come with his life, with his righteousness, with all truth, and lead us into God's eternal life and light.

67 • The Spirit of Truth Accuses the World!*

Pentecost Monday, Jn 16:5–14

Today's Gospel is taken from St. John, chapter 16, from Jesus' farewell to his disciples at the Last Supper. Verses 5 to 16 of this chapter form a unity which we might entitle: the Paraclete, the Spirit of truth accuses the world and instructs the disciples; for it deals with these two subjects. Let us consider the first part, because it is rather difficult to understand even from a textual point of view. May God give us the grace to understand the holy Gospel a little better and let it speak to us.

First Jesus observes — this is how our passage begins — that the disciples are sorrowful because he has said that he is going away. But in their sorrow, he says, they do not ask where he is going. If they understood that he who has come to redeem the world is returning to the Father, that his going, his death, his loss to them is acceptance by the Father, entering into his glory, the triumph of his redemptive work, then, Jesus says, their heart would no longer be filled with this earthly, wild, despairing sorrow; they would realize that it must be so, and that by departing from them and returning home he is only the closer to them in his Spirit. Then Jesus explains that this work of the Spirit who brings them closer to him consists in judging the world and leading the disciples into all truth, even such truth as they do not yet understand.

St. John pictures a trial conducted before the tribunal of God — the trial of the world by the Paraclete, God's consoler and advocate, the Spirit of truth. This trial will not await the end of time; it begins now, because the Spirit of God, set free by the death of Jesus, is at work in the world through the pneumatic preaching of Jesus' witnesses.

Jesus says that if the Spirit does not convert the world to the disciples' preaching, at least he will convince it to the extent of showing it what it is in three respects: in respect of sin, of righteousness, and of judgment. There we are, and Jesus explains what these three things mean. He will convince the world of sin: because, the Lord says, it does not believe in me. The term of sin then is always unbelief, failure to believe in him who departed in the weakness of the cross and precisely so enters his home, returns to his Father, precisely so bestows the Spirit through his heart, perforated by the sins of the world. We really must examine our sins to see whether they are not a denial that Jesus has gone to the Father. It is a sin, Jesus says, not to believe me

*Biblical Homilies, 80–83.

who have gone to the Father through the shame and humiliation of death on the cross.

Whenever we sin, we flee the cross of the Lord, we do not believe in his going to the Father. And whenever we do not understand that truth, we are sinners. Now the Spirit is meant to teach us, to convince us who would not accept the scandal of the cross — not in our own lives, not in the church, not in the world — that the Holy Spirit of God, of truth, of power, of love, comes in the cross, and that any other opinion is a sin, is a refusal to believe in the crucified and risen Lord who has returned to his Father.

Moreover, Jesus says, the Spirit convinces the world of righteousness — convinces it that Jesus is right at this trial which is universal history, where the world and the crucified stand together before the tribunal of the Father, each accusing the other. The righteousness we speak of here is being right, is the very triumph of Jesus at this trial, before this tribunal of world history.

The Spirit convinces the world of righteousness: because I am going to the Father, because I am the one whom the Father accepts in death, because I am the one — Jesus means — who having placed his soul in the Father's hands through this frightful death, truly reaches him in what seems to be the moment of defeat, of ruin and disaster. Wherever the folly of the cross is, there he goes to the Father, he is accepted even though we no longer see him, and there he is right. That is what the Spirit convinces the world of: of his being right, of his righteousness.

And third, he convinces the world of judgment, because the prince of this world, Jesus says, is already judged. In Christ's return home redemption is complete, the powers of darkness are stripped of all their real power, the world and all the world rules is already judged. Perhaps this discourse of Jesus' seems remote and abstract to us. But if we examine our own lives, our sorrow, our dissatisfaction, our skepticism, all that our heart may be full of, then I think we can well reread these few verses and by God's grace they may touch our hearts.

Then Jesus would say: You are sorrowful because I who am the nearness of your God seem to withdraw into the shadow of death, into infinite distance, because you think I have gone away. But I have gone home, and only so can the Spirit dwell with you, he who can convince you too that not believing in this truth of my going to the Father is the ultimate basis of your sins, and that my going, my being right pronounces judgment even in this world upon the powers of sin that would hold you captive. Believe. Call on the Spirit, call on grace, and the Lord is with you, the Lord who forgives and delivers, frees and sanctifies, and amid the darkness of this world sets up his everlasting kingdom in your heart.

YEARLY FEASTS

68 • Corpus Christi*

The procession is both the most external element connected with the feast of Corpus Christi, and it is also its distinguishing factor. When, however, what is external springs entirely from within, as it does here, then the external is also the revelation of the inner kernel. And that is why it is possible to contemplate the mystery of this feast from the point of view of the procession.

The Corpus Christi procession originated in the last part of the thirteenth century. At the beginning of the fifteenth century, it had already become a universal custom. It is a relic of the late Middle Ages and of their unity of faith, and so it is not a demonstration of faith against a non-Catholic world. It originated from the general custom of having field-processions. The people who marched in these processions brought with them the tools of their everyday life. They carried the "holy ones" (the relics belonging to the church, even to the "most holy One") into every aspect of their life.

Because even in their diversity all these people sprang from *one* root and aspired to one end, in the procession they intertwined the spheres and activities of their lives. The wide open spaces became their church, the sun became the candles for the altar, the fresh breeze joined with the songs of the people to make one choir, the altars stood at the intersection of everyday life. The solemn gathering of people standing before God became a colorful, happy procession of marchers, and the carefree birds of the air winged their flight through the prayers that rose from the troubled earth — prayers that already were almost transformed into pure song of praise. Thus the procession is both the visible expression of the human being's movement through the space of her existence toward her goal, and the shining forth of the holy one, who is himself the support of this procession, who steadfastly stays with it, and who leads it to its proper goal, who is God.

From this point of view, we come to the significance of the feast of Corpus Christi: to the significance of the eucharist. Certainly this sacrament reaches its full significance when it is received. Even when we keep it on our altars and when we carry it through the regions where we live, uplifted and in full sight, still it is always the food which we wholly make our own only when we eat it. Yet this sacrament is

*The Eternal Year, 113–119.

227

an enduring sacrament that can and should be preserved, shown, and worshiped, just as in daily life we are ready to eat the food that we long for and that our eye sees. And so the essence of the sacrament of the altar also shows forth when it is seen and honored as the sacrament that endures, even if what it contains does not appear so clearly as it does when we receive the sacrament in sign and reality.

Seen in this way, what is the first thing that the Corpus Christi procession tells us? It tells us — or rather through it we remind ourselves — that we are pilgrims on the earth. We have here no lasting dwelling place. We are a people who change, who are restlessly driven on through time and space, who are "on the way," and still seeking our real homeland and our everlasting rest. We are those who must allow themselves to be changed, because to be a member of the human race means to let oneself change, and perfection means to have changed often. The movement of the procession makes perfectly clear our dependence on time and the stratification of the sphere of our existence.

But this procession is not merely a throng, and its motion is not only the mass flight of those who are hurrying through time and the barren desert of earthly existence. A procession is a holy movement of those truly united. It is a gentle stream of peaceful majesty, not a procession of fists clenched in bitterness, but of hands folded in gentleness. It is a procession which threatens no one, excludes no one, and whose blessing even falls on those who stand astonished at its edge and who look on, comprehending nothing. It is a movement which the holy one, the eternal one, supports with his presence; he gives peace to the movement and he gives unity to those taking part in it. The Lord of history and of this holy exodus from exile toward the eternal homeland himself accompanies the exodus. It is a holy procession, one that has a goal, both before it and with it. From this point of view, we can understand the specific significance of this procession.

It tells us of the eternal presence of human guilt in the history of humankind and in our own history; yes, even in the history of my life. With us on our march we carry the body which was given for us. The cross of Calvary goes with us, the sign that the guilt of deicide weighs upon humankind. The body and the life that we all have crushed in death goes with us. This procession of sinners tells us that in our journey through time we always have the crucified one with us.

When we walk down our streets, past houses where dwell sinful luxury, sinful misery, and darkness of hearts, then we are walking past new manifestations of this sin of the world. When we walk right into the midst of these manifestations, then we are proclaiming his death, which we are all guilty of, and our death. Through this procession, which is accompanied by the crucified one, we acknowledge that we are sinners and that we have to suffer our own guilt and that of all humankind. We confess that again and again we walk down the path of error, of guilt, and of death, the path which the sinless one also walked for us and always continues to walk with us — in the sacrament and in the grace of his Spirit. This path has mysteriously become redemption for those who believe with love, who understand this sacrament, and who take it with them on their dark path.

The procession tells us of the abiding presence of Christ, our reconciliation on the paths of our life. He goes with us, he who is reconciliation, he who is love and mercy. During all the time that we call life, as we trudge along the streets of this earth, he is there, right behind us, pursuing us in the obstinacy of his love. He follows us, even when we walk down a crooked path and lose our direction. He seeks the lost sheep even in the wilderness, and he runs to meet the prodigal son. He walks with us on the pilgrimage of our life, he who walked down all these streets himself — *quaerens me sedisti lassus* [In searching for me, you sat wearied — *Dies irae* sequence] — from birth to death. He therefore knows how we feel on this endless journey that is so often trackless. He is near at hand, visible and invisible, with the mercy of his heart, with the patient and full and merciful experience of his whole human life. He, salvation itself, and the propitiation of our sins. We carry the sacrament through the fields and wilderness of our life, and give testimony that as long as he goes with us we have with us the one who can make every way straight and purposeful.

The procession tells us of a blessed wonder: since the incarnation and death and resurrection of Christ, our movement in the procession is not only toward a goal, but we already move right in the midst of the goal itself. Indeed, the end of the ages has already come over us. Yes, we wandering pilgrims already carry in our hands the one who is himself our end and our goal. We lift up the body in which divinity and humanity are already indissolubly united.

We carry the glorified body (although still hidden under the veils of this world) in which the world, in a moment that belongs to it forever, has already begun to be glorified and to tower up into the eternal, inaccessible light of God himself. The motion of the world, so the Corpus Christi procession tells us, has already entered upon its last phase, and as a whole it can no longer miss its goal. The distant goal of this motion of all millennia has already mysteriously penetrated into the movement itself. It is there not merely as promise and as a far distant future, but as reality and presence.

We sing, *Et antiquum documentum novo cedat ritui* [The new law's new oblation ends the form of ancient rite]; we should also grasp all that this means. Gone is the alliance of promise, of experiment and of provision; gone is the history that is still open and still experimentally seeking its goal by trial and error. The eternal and definitive one, God himself, is already there. There is a mysterious moment when time and eternity, earth and heaven, God and humanity — two poles, separated by an eternity, yet coming up to meet one another — even begin to penetrate each other. In this moment and in this place, the procession that carries the body of the Lord takes place; it is the expression of this moment and of this point.

Novum Pascha novae legis Phase vetus terminat [*Lauda Sion* sequence]. Through the new covenant, the new Paschal lamb brought the old alliance to an end. This procession carries the already glorified body of him who forever is inseparably God and man, and thus it tells us that our motion has already — mysteriously, yet really — taken into itself its definitive goal. This procession also tells us about the unity that exists between the persons walking in the procession.

Humankind moves through all the vast spheres of its histories, its cultures, its states and wars, its summits and abysses. Yet this motion is more than human beings running helter-skelter in confusion and chaos, more than the chaotic haste of those who, throughout their whole life, are pursued by the bare necessities of life, by utopian ideals and by diabolical powers. They already have unity bestowed upon them, freely and graciously, both among themselves and in their motion.

According to St. Paul, we are all one body, we who eat of the one bread. Sign of unity and bond of love, is what Augustine calls the body which the pilgrims of history in loving faith carry into the marketplace of their lives in this holy procession. They lift it in blessing over the earth — the earth from which they can scarcely earn their bread. They lift it over the earth which greedily drinks their blood and their tears, so that eventually (but only provisionally) the body will have to pass away into the seemingly aimless history of nature.

We carry the body of the Lord in holy procession and by this action we proclaim that we are one, that we are walking the same path, the one path of God and his eternity. The same power of eternal life is already working in all of us: the one divine love is already our portion. Our share in this love binds us together more deeply and more inwardly than anything that could unite or even separate us in the past. The sacrament of the unity of the church and of all the redeemed — this is what we carry throughout life. We thus give witness to the love that moves the sun and the other stars, to the love that is impelling both humanity and the entire cosmos toward that goal and into that one kingdom in which God will be all in all.

We are pilgrims and aliens who have here no lasting dwelling place. We are still seeking what is to come and what is to abide forever: the supreme goal and the everlasting rest which is, quite simply, life itself. But we are pilgrims whose success is accompanied by the mercy of God, pilgrims who already have their goal in their possession, since what we already have and already are has only to be made manifest. We are pilgrims of an unending motion toward the goal and in the goal, pilgrims of a single goal, who are one in love through the one bread of eternal life.

Let us walk indefatigably, today and forever, on all the streets of this life, the smooth and the rough, the blissful and the bloodied. The Lord is nearby; the goal and the strength of the way is there. Under God's heaven a holy procession moves on the streets of the earth. It will arrive at its goal. For already — this day, in fact — heaven and earth join together and celebrate one blessed feast.

69 • Corpus Christi: Feast of Our Daily Bread*

Corpus Christi is a strange feast. It celebrates what is celebrated every day in the unassuming silence of our churches: the mystery of the altar. It displays in festive procession what is not only shown every day but received, the holy bread of eternal life. It lifts up outwardly what is received elsewhere, the heavenly manna. It is almost as if the feast were attempting specially to celebrate what in fact happens every day, and yet fails to do so because ordinary life can celebrate more fittingly than the high festival what is ultimately in question: the fact that we receive this bread of eternal life as pilgrims between time and eternity, each day anew until the journey is at an end and God unveiled becomes for us the eternal bread of glory. Whether this is so or not, we celebrate this feast in order that the everyday round may not allow us to forget too much what we celebrate each day: the meal of those who are pilgrims to eternal life.

How exactly this meal suits our needs! We are still traveling as pilgrims, never settled, always moving on, in the provisional. Consequently, we walk among shadows and symbols in the darkness of faith. That is an unavoidable lot and its pain is salutary and should not surprise us. The highest is, after all, furthest away and remains a prize

---

*Everyday Faith, 85–89.

promised only to voluntary fidelity in what is provisional. Yet we should like to have this highest at once even now although, or rather precisely because, we are wandering in search of it.

For how could we go on pilgrimage if we were not already aware of the powers of eternity in us? How could we hope, if what we hope for were *only* far away? One can only seek God with God, and we should not seek if we had not yet already found, if he himself did not permit himself to be found by us day by day. And so the promise and the possession must both be true: way and goal are simultaneously present, God is with us, hidden under the veil of his own creatures.

If therefore the holy banquet of eternity is prepared for us here in time, it is in a way which the sober humility of pilgrims such as we may expect: simple and ordinary, hidden under the signs of commonplace, everyday earthly life, under which the real meaning has to be believed and firmly held in hope and love.

And so the Lord has prepared this meal: for the senses a sign, in appearance a little bread and wine, such as usually nourish our bodies and cheer our minds. But when at his command, by his power and with his words *the* commemoration of his last meal is celebrated, and this latter is truly brought into our own present moment, then the inner truth and reality of these signs is himself in his flesh and blood. He becomes the bread of limitless strength and the wine of inexpressible joy. He himself makes his body a sign for us in our time of what he wishes to be for us in his Spirit: God giving his own life to his poor creature. He becomes for us now as we receive the bread of the altars, what he is in himself: the earthly reality by which God's eternity has entered into the narrow limits of our finitude.

A person's head bends over what looks like an ordinary piece of bread — over what in fact merely looks like a semblance of real bread — his hand reaches for a cup such as usually contains merely the drink of this earthly life, and then there happens what is the innermost goal of *everything* that happens. God and the believing heart each from their own side break through all the sinister walls which at other times so infinitely separate them.

They meet in him who is both, in whom such a unity already occurred definitively and corporeally, in the Lord, who in one person is the eternal Word from on high and the son of the earth from the Virgin's womb. We hold the body of this earth which was born and was sacrificed in pain; we penetrate once more into the depth of what he suffered long ago, when we hold what he took from us. And we are abidingly where we and he have remained, in the center with God. Sacred banquet in which Christ is received, the memory of his passion is renewed, the soul is filled with grace and the earnest of future glory is bestowed.

Yet we commonplace people make this mystery of eternal life in this dying time so commonplace! Look how the priest performs his sublime office — morosely, impelled by objective duty, as though he were carrying out some duty of this world and not the liturgy in which the light and blessedness of heaven are contained. Consider the narrow and barren hearts into which the Lord descends and which at best do not know what to say to him except the few selfish desires which make up their everyday round.

Alas, we Christians. In this sacrament we receive both the pure blessedness of heaven and the refined transfigured essence of the bittersweet fruit of this earth. We receive it, to be sure, as though wrapped in the hard shell of custom but nevertheless in all truth. And we receive it as though nothing were happening. Weary and lazy we take the same heart back home from the table of God into the narrow rooms of our lives where we are more at home than in God's upper room. We offer the Son in sacrifice and want to refuse our hearts. We play the divine game of the liturgy and we are not in earnest about it. We have perhaps a good will but it has so little power over the dull heaviness of our heart.

But perhaps even this belongs to the sign, when God is already hastening toward his creature even here in time, and when even now the banquet of eternal life is celebrated in advance. If the supper of eternal life is prepared in the narrow houses of time, it is not surprising that the needy come to it, and that their small minds and meager hearts do not yet realize at all what is to be theirs. It is understandable that we are rather disturbed and feel our strength overtaxed and, as it were, almost driven to irritated reserve by such lavishness on God's part. For it is after all still grace, his blessed grace, if we come at all, if we do after all have supper at his table, if we only come, if we only drag ourselves to him, we who are dreary, bent, weary, and burdened.

He welcomes us even if he does not find in our eyes radiant joy at his presence. For he has of course descended into all the abysses of this earth; it does not offend him to have to enter the dull narrowness of our hearts, or if only a small spark of love and goodwill glimmer there. In the patience which God has with us weaklings, the highest sacrament is meant to be the sacrament of our every day.

But because that is so, because we only come from so far away, because we make the feast a burden and an effort because it is a daily one, it is right for us at least once in the year to celebrate a feast of those feasts which we celebrate every day. A feast to celebrate the fact that what is usual is most unusual, what is done every day is the substance of eternity, the humble bread of earth, God's coming among us, and the beginning of the transfiguration of all earthly reality.

Let us therefore celebrate on Corpus Christi in mourning but with consolation the fact that every day we so unfestively celebrate the mystery of the Lord, a feast of joy that despite this he is with us all days until the end. Let us keep a feast of the past which is present in the commemoration of the supper and death of the Lord, which truly annuls all distance of time, a feast of the future which under the veil of the sacrament already even now has what all the future is to bring, the presence of the God of eternal love. Every day God prepares his feast for us, the holy supper of the Lord. On the feast of Corpus Christi, we ourselves ought in some way to prepare a feast for God in warm gratitude for his giving us every day that festive meal in which we pilgrims receive strength and joy so that here on the roads of time we may arrive home for the banquet of eternal life.

70 • Corpus Christi: On the Way with the Lord*

The church today carries its sacrament in festive procession through all the fields of human reality. Joyfully singing hymns it walks through the streets of the world and shows to this world with an almost frightening exuberance and exultation its most intimate possession, the blessed presence of its Lord. In this solemn action, procession and singing, the church apparently does not pay much heed to whether we ourselves feel festive and joyful, or whether we are really able sincerely to do what we are called upon to do on this feastday.

The church is bold enough each year on a certain particular day to hold a procession of a kind which one can only really hold if one is joyful, free, inwardly unhampered by the burden of ordinary life. For that reason alone one might perhaps be disturbed. Can I join in the celebrations? Is my own heart not too heavy? In fact when we hear the rejoicing, see the solemn ceremony and at the same time consider what is being shown there, our very heart misgives us. Not that one is condemning this festive rejoicing, God forbid. Where else should we hold festival if not here, when we profess that we sinners, weak, empty, and fettered, are liberated, given the freedom of the holy glory of God?

*Everyday Faith, 90–95.

What is frightening and inconceivable about these people singing and holding festival is that it is death they are celebrating with such jubilation. For it is written, as often as you do this, you proclaim the Lord's death until he comes. The Lord instituted this sacrament on the night when he was betrayed into death. He said: Do this in remembrance of me, so that we should celebrate in perpetual remembrance the sacrifice in which his body was shattered and his blood shed and he allowed his forsaken soul to fall into the hands of the incomprehensible God.

It is true indeed that our very heart misgives us. For jubilantly under the blue sky in the scent of the flowers and of incense, under arcades of sacred song, we bear the sign of a person's death, and not just any individual's, but the death of him who was the Word of God made flesh. How incomprehensible is the human being and his or her existence that there can be an event in which the utmost darkness of plunging into a bottomless grave can be a festival of childlike, innocent joy.

We are proclaiming the death of the Lord until he comes again. Do not let us forget that today. Remembrance of that death is not death to joy, but its unfathomable root, from which the true joy of this day indescribably flows as though from an inexhaustible spring.

Look at these people walking in procession! In festive clothes, they are singing and moving forward almost as David once did when he danced before the ark of the covenant. Where are they going? If one has the courage to ask and the courage to answer the question seriously and in all its aspects, completely and without illusions, can one avoid one answer, even if it is only a part of the complete answer: they are going forward to death?

For the place of their procession is, of course, time which never stands still. And where time is, death sits, the end of the matter, even of the movement in time. So when those who are walking have finished their festive procession, they are already inexorably a few hours nearer to death, their own death, precisely so much nearer than if they had bitterly wept during those hours.

And after this solemn procession, of course, things do not cease, life goes on. For those in the procession go further, on other paths. But these paths or those, these stony ways and those wide roads are nevertheless only sections of one and the same road. And this leads to where there is no going on, where everything that moves and advances has an end, the one end.

It is strange that those who are walking in this way and on this day have decorated the outward road of their interior journey to death, bear on this serious walk through the festive streets precisely him who died just as they must die, who died for those who have to die, who died for them because they have to die. It is he they have with them on their way. They carry the one who was slain, toward their own death.

Why do they do this? Are they not taking death to their hearts if they bear this dead man, whereas they are after all moving in order that the stop, the end, may not happen too quickly? Why do they hold this procession of people destined for death, with him who was slain, to the accompaniment of songs instead of tears of hopeless despair?

Precisely because he died. Because it was the Son of God, who is life itself, who died. Because with them they have him who shared their lot, though he is the God whom nothing befalls. Because it is he who gave his life voluntarily, though none could take it from him, because it is he who could overcome death in death, because it is he who went down into the ultimate void in order to fill it with eternal life. Because they have him with them on the *via dolorosa* of their life, they may laugh and sing and transform part of their serious journey into a Corpus Christi procession.

They can also weep. They can take part just as they are, dusty from the main roads of life, rather tired and dull, not really inclined either to laugh or cry, existing as it were halfway between the lowest depths and the blissful heights of existence, traveling like pilgrims on a road which it is impossible to identify either as *via triumphalis* or *via dolorosa.*

They may and can be all these things if they go forward and he is there. For if he is there, it is as one who has wept the tears of their death for them, who has gone down into the lowest depth of death, where no mortal except him has been. While he accompanies us now in the sacrament (as he does every day in the grace of his Spirit) those who walk invoke him who suffered under Pontius Pilate, died and was buried, descended into hell.

But this is said of him who is the eternal Word of the Father, who is wisdom, light and strength, life and resurrection. When the sign of the ultimate and most terrible death is raised in blessing over those who are on their knees, it means that in the sign of death which blesses mortal human beings on their way to death, life is present, not death, the life which made of death itself the victory of life.

And so, once a year for us Christians our road becomes a *via triumphalis* and we walk behind one who, bearing life in himself, became our life by sharing our death. He goes on ahead. His sacrament announces his death. And also ours. Since he goes on before us, he does not delude us with any stupefying trivialities. He says, you share my fate which you proclaim in this sacrament; you share its hardship, difficulty, and inexorability. And by this solemn procession, we proclaim that his fate is ours too. And in its entirety, of which it is written, "I died and behold I am alive for evermore, and I have the keys of death and Hades" (Rv 1:18).

We cannot grasp all at once the immeasurable significance of a procession like this with him who died and who lives. Who could comprehend God and the world, life and death, time and eternity united as they are in this festival? We can only go on walking through life, led through ever new realities, and this walk today is only a symbol of them. Sometimes the way is a pleasant one, a high road to distant destinations, another time it is a way of the cross. Sometimes dusty field paths, in open country, but barren; sometimes forest tracks leading one knows not where.

To all of them the words of scripture apply: the human person is not the master of his or her ways. But all ways ought to form one way, one of God's paths, as the psalms often say. All should link up into stretches of road leading to a goal, whether they pass through joy or death. All paths ought to lead into the free incalculability of God where there are no more paths because one has come to the end of perfect fulfillment, and this is at once trackless immensity and familiar home.

If we see the sacramental path of today's procession, we shall not forget the other paths of which today's walk is only a sign, a profession of faith and a promise. During it we shall not forget the other paths, those of our own lives; the ways of those who are weary, poor, and burdened and perhaps do not know what the hidden goal of this apparently erratic and aimless wandering is; the way of those who, ruled by the enemies of Christianity, are not allowed to make joyful processions — but have to follow the real way of the cross of faith behind him who bore the cross.

We will remember and pray God to give us some day the grace that at our end a very small procession, even if it only consists of a silently praying priest in everyday clothes, will turn into the street of our life in its last moments and so become the provision for the journey, the viaticum, of eternal life for us at the place where our course goes no further. Then in the sacrament or, if it so pleases God, at least in the grace of the sacrament, the Lord will come with us at least the last stretch of our way. Then the pathway of this dying life in imitation of Christ will become the blessed road of eternal life leading into the unutterable glory of God.

71 • An Earthly Mysticism*

Second Sunday in Ordinary Time (C), Jn 2:1–14

When John narrates the life of the Lord, he always sees the eternal within the everyday, since the earthly occurrence is supposed to reflect the heavenly events that are being enacted in the earthly. There is a marriage feast. People are drinking and laughing. The waiters scurry about, and the wine is good. It is truly congenial, and everyone contributes joyfully and without inhibitions to the expansive mood. The quiet woman from Nazareth (one couldn't omit her from the invitation list) makes no disturbance, though one had worried a bit about that. In fact she is only concerned that the feast keep up its spirited pace. (She even notices a danger in this regard before anyone else suspects it. How humane are the true children of heaven!)

The Son of this woman is there too with his friends. This is a "the more guests, the merrier" kind of celebration. Like his mother, he too is mysterious. But a remarkable thing: he fits into the context, although today one intends simply to be completely very jolly. No, he is no killjoy. Who would have ever thought that! One had feared perhaps a bit of heavy preaching. And look: where earthly joy threatens to run out along with the wine, he works his first miracle. Quietly and unobtrusively, so that even a miracle of God does not disrupt a human celebration.

He loves human beings. He who is himself human. He loves them, their earth, and their joys, the flavor of wine, and the carefree laughter from childlike hearts. (Later on, people who cannot stand themselves will even call him a carouser and a drunk.) This is the start of his signs. He will make an end of this beginning — a fulfillment. He will drink the earth with its blood in the reality of the cross and under the sign of wine. He will change the water of bitterness into the wine of eternal joy. He will preserve the earth, the body of the human being. They will be transfigured, not done away with. When the radiance of the divinity shall finally break through, then the earth and the body will not perish under this radiance, but be properly confirmed for the first time. For always and ever!

He did not come to lead spirits out of a dark dungeon that holds them fast, but to redeem the flesh forever into its complete, transfigured being. This is why the Son of man goes to the wedding feast, for there he raised up the flesh anew in order to affirm it. He takes the drinking cup, fills it with the wine of the earth, drinks it, and extends

---

Der Volksbote (Innsbruck), 12 January 1950, p. 13. Trans. Frederick G. Lawrence, Boston College.

it to all these young people who do not know what is going on. It will be a long time before the earth and all human beings are redeemed. It will cost his tears and blood until the earth is pure, and before people dare to believe they can be human beings for all eternity without becoming either animals or angels. It will cost his blood before human beings comprehend and become capable of living up to the fact that we can love the earth and God. God, because without him the earth is as nothing; the earth, because it is the sacrament of God. He works a miracle with regard to the wine of the earth for a childlike, happy moment in the present. His eyes look ahead, and his heart longs for that day in God's kingdom when he, with all who are blessed of his Father, will drink afresh and eternally of the harvest from the vineyard at the wedding feast of the lamb, then, when there shall be a new heaven, but also a new earth.

72 • The Mystery of the Heart*

"CRIMSON MYSTERY OF ALL THINGS" — the church speaks in a hymn by Gertrude von le Fort — "solitary Heart, all-knowing Heart, world-conquering Heart." According to the metaphysical dialogues of Hedwig Conrad-Martius, the heart is

> the center of the human person. His whole being, as it gives birth to itself in soul, body and mind, unfolds and gushes forth. It is again taken up into and established in this one center. Here, as it were, it is tied together and fastened centrally; the whole "bloodstream," every path of personal life, runs together into it, in order to go out again from it. One can say, will, and do nothing as a total person that does not spring from this center in which alone his whole being is established in unity. In a personal sense, all else is empty, unsubstantial, and unreal.

The "heart" is the name we give to the unifying element in the human person's diversity. The heart is that ultimate ground of a person's being. Her diversity of character, thought, and activity springs from this ground. All that she is and does unfolds from this source. Her diversity, originally one in its source, remains one even in its unfolding, and it ultimately returns to this unity.

The "heart" is the name we give to the inner ground of an individual's character, wherein a person is really himself, unique and

---

*The Eternal Year, 121–28.

alone. The human being's apartness, his individuality, his interiority, his solitariness — this is what we call the heart. This characteristic of the heart reveals and at the same time veils itself in everything that the person is and does. For the human being's total diversity in being and activity would be nothing if it did not blossom forth from the heart as from a living ground, and at the same time veil this hidden ground. It must be veiled because its water doesn't flow on the surface of what we commonly speak of as the human person's being and activity.

An individual's uniqueness, her individuality, is her heart. That is why one is always alone and solitary — alone and solitary in the meaning that everyday life gives to the words, in the idiom of the marketplace, which no longer suspects the abysses concealed in human words. For there is a realm where the person is entirely himself, where he himself is his solitary destiny. In this realm where he can no longer bring himself and his fragmentary world to the market of everyday life — in the realm, therefore, where his heart is — the person is alone and solitary because of this apartness of his being and his activity. He is alone because the heart is never a generic concept, never a coin that can find its way through many hands; because the heart belongs always — yes, only — to itself and to the God who created it.

And that is the reason why only the *heart* knows in the full sense of the word. For the person properly knows only what is proper to her. Whatever else she knows, she knows only because it is this sphere of her own being, the world, into which she pours out the diversity of her life, or because it is the mystery of her unique heart, the mystery that is God. That is why really interior knowledge, knowledge that really grasps something completely and is more than a list of indifferent facts, is knowledge of the heart, the human being's center, which knows by experience and by suffering — her center, where spirit and body, light and love dwell together undivided in one chasm. The heart is all-knowing in its apartness because all that it knows it knows in *one*, because it is in possession of itself.

But what is this solitary, all-knowing human heart in which the world is perceived and concentrated, the heart that is the ground of a person and of all his activity? Is this being perishable or is it substantial? Shadow or reality? Death or life? Is scripture's final word on the heart (it is mentioned in about a thousand places) the bitter wisdom of Ecclesiastes (7:4): "The heart of the wise is in the house of mourning; but the heart of fools is in the house of mirth," *or* is it the faith of Peter (2 Pt 1:19) that the morningstar rises in the heart and that peace exults eternally?

When a person collects himself in his heart, when all being and doing finally flow back from dispersion into that one ground that we call the heart, what happens there? What does the person experience when in his heart he experiences what he possesses as his own, what he really is? Is this ground nothingness or fullness? Is there fullness and reality only in diversity, and is apartness only a pitiful loneliness? Does the solitary heart border on infinity, or is it, as the end of all things and all reality, the place where apartness comes to itself in order to trickle away into its own finiteness and come to despair?

Does heart mean the mouth of all the brooks of our being, the mouth that leads into eternity, or is it the gate through which all dying reality is pressed down, weak and tired, to everlasting death? Is the flowing together of all our diverse activities into the heart the end of the delusion that we might be something, because diversity that is not gathered up causes us to fail to notice that all this diversity really adds up to zero?

Doesn't it seem that a person can appear all the more constricted and empty — even in the experience of daily life — the more collected she is; and all the richer, the more dispersed and diffused she is? Doesn't it seem that whoever possesses himself has just himself alone, and only he who loses himself can possess another? Is not gathering to the one heart in this manner the dispersion of everything, and is not dispersion into everything the only gathering possible to it? Is there, then, no apartness, and is the only apartness that exists the apartness of an empty heart?

This, then, is the ultimate need, the innermost misery, the misery of the heart: that the human heart (the ultimate center of the world) only seems to be the place where the human being's own poverty is frightened concerning itself, and the place where, at best, the finitude of all things — which could never be all in one — is unmasked. Do we have to *love* and *seek* our heart, because only in this way are we in possession of ourselves? Or do we have to hate and flee, because we possess in our ground, the heart, only the nothingness of our own being?

Of course we are ready with a quick answer. So quick that it would perhaps be better if we did not have it at hand *so* quickly that as a result we no longer understand the question. We answer: "God." Yes, this is the answer, the whole answer, supposing only that we understand it. Indeed, he is the apartness, who is fullness and not emptiness, who is life and not death. He is the central point, the heart of the world, in whom all reality is gathered up and yet is not pressed together in a stifling corner.

He is the unfathomable womb, in which everything shines brightly, however. He is the unity which is not purchased at the price of denial.

Down from his mountains all waters eternally gush in a torrent, and the chambers of these mountains stay just as eternally full. He is not, as we are, merely the heart of one solitary person, but the heart of all reality, the all-in-one inwardness of all things. He exists before all multiplicity and dispersion, and he never needs such multiplicity, to be everything. He can be of one mind without being unilateral; he can be all without being all-common.

But have we found an answer for the distress, the misery, the need of our heart? If we say that "God" is the answer, have we really named the heart of our hearts? Does that answer of itself tell us that the apartness of *our* heart, too, is fullness and not emptiness, reality and not despairing loneliness? Does that answer tell us that the inner awareness of our all-knowing heart embraces the infinite and not our nothingness? Doesn't our heart, the center of our being, run into extreme danger precisely through this answer, given so quickly? For if he is the heart of our hearts — even though as philosophers we quickly and confidently say that he is — is the need of our hearts then banished, or have we just named its ultimate need?

So easily do we explain God as the heart of our hearts with worldly wisdom, and fancy that by saying this we have said that the full oneness and the one fullness is ours, the fullness that fills our empty oneness, without its having to go out in complete dispersion.

But even if we say that God is the mystery of our hearts, the salvation of our heart's need, then, if we reflect rightly, it may appear to us in fear and trembling that it is most frightful to have God as the center of our center. For is not his own infinity, in which everything is the same, bearable only for him? *He,* of course, is always everything in each of his attributes and in each of his works. He has his *whole* heart in all that he is and in all that he does, so that with him everything is always fruitful and *at the same time* inward.

But what if he comes to us in this way? Then he would be "all in each" for *us* too. When he enters into our life he does not need to be particularly concerned that the lightning flash of his omnipotence should also be for him the soft light of his wisdom. He can let his *whole* being roar into our life in its power, and yet his waters have flowed from nowhere at all and have released no possibility that he does not fill with his reality. He can overpower us as inexorable justice, and to his ear the eternal judgment to damnation is still the jubilation that praises his boundless goodness.

But for us and for our narrowness it is precisely this that is frightful and terrifying, it is just this that causes all the seams of our finiteness to sag apart. He is always his whole self. He is always his heart, in whatever way he may treat us — whether he loves us or passes us by, whether his power or his goodness is revealed to us, whether his justice or his mercy comes over us.

But precisely because he thus is and remains the *one,* the all-one infinity of all being (however he may manifest himself to us), when we appeal to his all-one infinity, *we* do not know how he will act toward us. When we boldly declare that he is the heart of our heart, we do not know whether justice or grace will become the center of our hearts. Just when we want to use his heart so that the needed calculation of our heart will come out right, we write the enigmatic number of his ambiguous infinity and the figuring of our heart becomes all the more a really insoluble riddle. How insane it would be to ponder over him and count up his attributes, if we could not know whether they fall on us as an annihilating flash of lightning or as a dew that brings blessing. All the wisdom of the world cannot know this. For it has never known about God's judgment, under which we have all fallen. But without this all truth remains either tragic naiveté or malice.

The center of our hearts has to be God; the heart of the world has to be the heart of our hearts. He must send us his heart so that our hearts may be at rest. It has to be *his* heart. But it must not be the heart that embraces each and every thing in unfathomable unity. He must make as the center of our being a heart that is really the heart of the infinite God, and that *nonetheless* is a heart that is not everything, a heart that does not signify only *one,* a heart that is not only the ground of *one.* For the mortal fear over his ambiguous infinity and for the need of our hearts to depart from us, he has to let his heart become finite. He must let it become the unequivocality that is our life. He must let it enter into our narrow confines, so that it can be the center of our life without destroying the narrow house of our finitude, in which alone we can live and breathe.

And he has done it. And the name of his heart is: Jesus Christ! It is a finite heart, and yet it is the heart of God. When it loves us and thus becomes the center of our hearts, every need, every distress, every misery of our hearts is taken from us. For his heart is God's heart, and yet it does not have the terrifying ambiguity of his infinity. Up from this heart and out from this heart human words have arisen, intimate words, words of the heart, words of God that have only *one* meaning, a meaning that gladdens and blesses.

Our heart becomes calm and rests in this heart, in his heart. When it loves us, then we know that the love of such a heart is only love and nothing else. In him the enigmatic mystery of the world's heart which is God becomes the crimson mystery of all things, the mystery that God has loved the world in its destitution.

Only in this heart do we know who God wills to be for us. Only by it, the heart of Christ, is the riddle, into which all the wisdom of the world leads us, changed into the mystery of love that gladdens and blesses. In the heart of Christ our heart is all-knowing because it knows the one fact without which all knowledge is vanity and spiritual nuisance and without which all the practical experience of our heart causes only despair: in the heart of Christ our heart knows that it is one with *the* heart of God. It knows that it is one with the heart of God in which even the thief and the murderer find pardon, one with the heart in which our deepest, darkest nights are transformed into days, because he has endured the nights with us. It knows that it is one with the heart in which everything is transformed into the one love.

If he is our heart, our diversity can enter into the apartness of God without being burned to nothing in it. In him our dispersion can be collected without being confined and constricted, our heart can gush forth into the expanse of the world without being lost. The heart of Jesus is God's heart in the world, in which alone the world finds its God as its blessed mystery, in which alone God becomes the heart of our hearts, in which our being finds its center: at one and the same time unified and all-embracing.

73 • A Thing That Is Transparent Must Be Empty*

Fourth Sunday in Ordinary Time (C), 1 Cor 13:1–13

Our text today is taken from the thirteenth chapter of St. Paul's first letter to the Corinthians. Chapters 12, 13, and 14 deal with supernatural gifts that had been bestowed on the Christians of Corinth: prophecies, the gift of tongues, and other charismata of the Holy Spirit which God's Spirit had given for the building up of that young church.

But for all these gifts, certain disorders had arisen. So Paul writes lest the charismatic gifts themselves should lead to confusion. He speaks of right order and the limitations of these gifts; he explains how they should be properly used for the benefit of the community. But to show Christians who attached great importance to charismata that there is something more vital and basic in Christian life, Paul says in the midst of

---

*Biblical Homilies, 121–124.

his discussion of special graces that he will show them a more perfect way.

This "canticle of love" has three parts. First the apostle says that without this love everything else in human and Christian life — God's charismata, even faith, even martyrdom — is worthless; that without love we are nothing. Next Paul enumerates the characteristics of this love, which — though he does not explicitly say so — unites us with God and other human beings alike. And finally he says that love is the supreme good because it is the ultimate and all-embracing thing and never ends.

In these few minutes it will not be possible to expound this song of songs. We should not do justice to St. Paul's words. One must read them oneself, meditate on them and take them to heart. But for today we might just consider the relation between knowledge and love. At the very outset of this song of songs St. Paul says: "If I understand all mysteries and all knowledge, but have not love, I am nothing." In the third section he says that our knowledge is imperfect, that we only know in part, and that this remains the case so long as we are here on pilgrimage, far from the Lord; we know as children do, in childish terms; we see in a mirror, dimly and in parables.

In the second section Paul has said that love rejoices in the truth. So all through this song of songs St. Paul is thinking of the connection between knowledge and love. We, then, who profess to seek the truth, who write on our university buildings that the truth shall make us free — we are told that our knowledge is fragmentary and that love is what really matters. Indeed, if we examine our text with care, we shall see something which is generally overlooked or misinterpreted: Paul means that even in the consummation to come knowledge is perfected only when it is done away with, so to speak; when it abandons itself, so to speak, in love.

True, Paul says that then we shall know face to face, not in a mirror, not in riddles and parables, not in shadows, but just as we are known. Yet if we weigh the faith as a whole, we shall realize that Paul does not mean that mystery will cease to be mysterious, that we shall comprehend God and, as it were, exhaust his infinity. We know by faith that even when we see face to face we shall gaze on the incomprehensible God.

To that extent, Paul means, faith and hope remain. For if we translate rightly, he does not say that faith, hope, and love remain "now" as contrasted with "later," the consummation; he says: "but now" — this is the particle which introduces a proof — "but now faith, hope, love abide, always abide."

Of course this faith becomes a faith that sees face to face, and this hope becomes possession; but because this vision is the vision of the incomprehensible God and because this possession is the possession of the infinite God who must ever give himself anew in his sovereign love, there always remains something that can be called faith and hope — at least in the sense which Paul means here.

Now the apostle says that love is greater than faith and hope as they remain even in eternity, even in the vision of God face to face; even where mystery is close at hand, where it is looked upon, the human being's happiness can only consist in that vision — he or she cannot cease gazing into endless, unutterable mystery.

Love rejoices in the truth because that truth is the disclosure of love's ineffable incomprehensibility even when one sees it face to face. Only where truth is transmuted into love, only where love can rejoice over truth because truth as it were hands over to love, only where knowledge is the affirmation of incomprehensible mystery — only there are consummation and beatitude, God and human beings with the mysterious secret they share: love.

That is why Paul says: "So faith, hope, and love abide, these three: but the greatest of these is love." Then he adds one thing more: "Make love your aim," seek the mystery that lies beyond all dull knowledge; seek the mystery that nobody can understand because a mystery understood is one no longer and a thing that is transparent must be empty and futile. Make love your aim because that is the only perfection.

Of course one may ask: What is love anyhow? And the answer must be: Everything, the all-embracing, that which comprehends all things and is not comprehended, God who is love, the person who has attained to God in love, the unutterable. If we did not already know from experience what it means, no one could explain to us this saying: "Make love your aim." It would be Greek to us. But since God has already poured forth the Holy Spirit of his love into our hearts, these words mean something to the individual who is sick with longing, who grieves over darkness, who rejoices in the truth, who struggles toward mystery and light inaccessible, so that it may one day be accessible and she may look upon it. If she reads the song of songs in faith and love, a stronger desire for the love that abides and is best of all will awaken in her heart. Make love your aim.

74 • Love Sees the World
as a Parable*

Fifth Sunday in Ordinary Time (C), Lk 5:1–11

This story is found only in St. Luke. Matthew and Mark merely state briefly that Jesus told Peter and his companions to follow him and become fishers of men and women, and that they followed. But Luke tells of an incident that preceded this call.

I think that in the case of this story we can do nothing better than read it in silence and recollection. It is a marvelous story. When we look at it, we are struck by how much is contained in these eleven verses. The sea is here and the land, the crowd and the individuals, the labor and the preaching of the word of God, the failure and the miraculous blessing on the renewed labor, the daily round of work and the call to a divine mission, the intimate familiarity of men and women with Jesus and the shiver of realization that he is the holy one and that we are sinners.

We might say that this little incident contains everything, the whole of human life, all its reality, all its experience. Day and night are here, failure and success, bitterness and blessing. We are here and the Lord is here. And all these things are woven together in the quietest and most natural way. Each opens on to the other, one referring to another, none is, as it were, sealed off from the rest but every one relates to the whole and the whole is only the little things of everyday life preserved and confirmed and filled with blessing.

This is not just an artificial impression. Something like this must have been in the mind of the Lord. He sees the boat and decides to teach from it. This certainly has a practical reason: it makes it easier for him to speak to the people who are pressing all around him. But it must also have occurred to him that it was Peter's ship he was going into. How else would he have come to see the calling of Peter under that figure of speech which here finds its reality: a fisherman on the sea?

Jesus himself sees all the incidents which are here joined to make a single whole. They are open to him and to his heart. This heart, which unites all things in its love, knows of no divisions. The fishing of these fishermen, who have caught nothing all night long, is so important to him that he crowns it with a miracle. If they here learned to labor the

---

*Biblical Homilies, 38–40.

night long, catch nothing, and still obey the command of Jesus, they learned something for their new calling of fishers of men and women.

Something like this will have to happen in us too and in our lives, which will have to find their unity in love. The unity of a love that despises nothing and shuts out nothing, the unity of a love that endures pettiness and remains open to greatness, a love that sees the world as a great parable, not a parable that is separate and apart, but a parable that is itself drawn into the great reality it represents. Our daily round of work is full of holy significance, a preparation for greatness. And it is in the midst of this daily round that what is holy happens.

But in this relaxed, almost serene unity of the world, our lives, and our callings, only those who are loving and patient can see and recognize the likeness of their own life. Those who hear the word of God from the midst of the crowd and feel that this word is addressed to them in the inmost solitude of their heart, those persons who gratefully accept the things of earth from the hand of God and know themselves to be loved by Christ in spite of everything, each of them who says: "Depart from me for I am a sinful man," is the one who is called to the closest intimacy and the holiest imitation.

It seems to me that in this small incident in the life of Jesus, a few verses, we can read the secrets of our hearts and come to understand that all the love of the heart of Christ is found in one event: we are called, we follow, and in our failure we are blessed.

75 • The Eternal Word of God Is Our Companion at Table*

Saturday of the Fifth Week in Ordinary Time, Mk 8:1–9

When we listen to the Sunday Gospel we would do well to remember from time to time that it is being read during holy mass. The liturgy of the word, including the proclaiming of the Gospel and its interpretation, is meant in the holy mass to form a part of this whole sacred event as well as being a preparation for the celebration of the Last Supper of Jesus, the holy sacrifice of the church.

---

*Biblical Homilies, 31–34.

In the case of today's Gospel we must admit that many exegetes hold, seemingly with good reason, that this Gospel account of the multiplication of the loaves is not intended by the evangelist to refer immediately to the eucharistic meal. But when we remember that at least St. John explicitly regards the multiplication of the loaves as a holy and symbolic event pointing to the Last Supper, when we further observe that the writers of the synoptic Gospels depict Jesus in the same attitude as at the Last Supper, taking the bread, giving thanks, blessing it, breaking, and distributing it, then we should surely see in this account of the miracle of the loaves a foreshadowing of what we are to celebrate during this sacred time: the meal in which the Lord gives strength to his own in the desert of life through the hands of his apostles, so that they may not faint from weariness on their journey to eternity. Without drawing any farfetched analogies or artificial allegories, we can still see that this Gospel is describing that relationship between Jesus and humankind that reaches its highest point and finds its deepest reality and truth in that bequest of the Lord, his Last Supper.

Let us look a little closer at this Gospel. Jesus teaches in the desert but the word which he preaches and wishes to preach is really his revelation of himself as the kingdom of God's mercy come upon earth. Thus this word of Jesus tends directly to the end that what he reveals — namely, himself as the grace of God made flesh — enters really into the being of the human person, not just in thought but in all truth, in his spirit, in his grace, and in their historical manifestation, the sacraments and the sacrament.

And when these people are here in the desert, when they are in need, when Jesus himself says of them: "Some of them have come a long way," then all this is no more than one accidental manifestation and exemplification of the common condition of us all — that we are in need, that we cannot of ourselves provide the bread we need for our existence. We are those who are on a journey, we are those who have come a long way. We are those of whom Jesus has said: "I have compassion on the crowd." We are those who must endure long days with the Lord, and hunger also, until he takes pity on us and gives us strength. We must — like these people in the Gospel — listen to the word of God and listen again and again, until it really enters into us through the miracle of God's grace and becomes the strength of our lives and the light of our hearts.

When Jesus gathers the apostles around him and makes them the instruments of his mercy to the people, he is calling them to be the foundations of his church, the distributors of his grace, the preachers of his word. In this Gospel he uses them as dispensers of the earthly bread and he will appoint them to dispense the heavenly bread to their brothers and sisters. Hence if we see in this activity of the apostles a foreshadowing of that future activity of theirs, which will be to join with the people of God in anticipating the feast of eternal life during this pilgrimage through time, we will not be straying too far from this Gospel and its primary meaning; for what happens in this Gospel is also intended by the Lord to happen today, at this particular hour, in this particular place.

The Lord is the center of this event both here and in the Gospel: he takes the bread, he blesses it, he gives thanks to God for this gift of earth. He does it as the head of the household used to do it in the Old Testament, in the name of all those who were gathered around his table; but when the eternal Word of God prays to the Father in our flesh and as our companion at table, when he thanks him for the gifts of earth, blesses him and his name for all his mercy and love, then such an action performed by him who is Son of man and Son of God has dimensions that are infinite: the eternal high priest in the name of all his brothers and sisters offers the adoration of the world and of all history forever and ever, while he offers himself through his death to the eternal Father.

If the evangelists have stylized this Gospel scene in order to match the story of the Last Supper, then we in our turn can read into this Gospel what happens in our own lives: the Lord is in our midst as the great giver of thanks for us all, for our lives, for our destinies, and as the great offerer of sacrifice who includes us and our being in that great liturgy that embraces time and eternity and offers all things to God. If we go in faith to the table of the Lord, then we will be like the people of whom today's Gospel says: "They ate, and were satisfied."

We will hunger all the more for the eternal banquet with God himself, we will be satisfied so that we will not faint on the way even though we have come from afar and the road to eternity is long. He gives himself to us, with his appointed death, with his cross; but also with the victory won by the cross which has saved us and our lives. This bread, which is he himself and which he offers to us, is the food of eternal life that gives strength for eternity. Through it there comes about what we see in the Gospel: a fellowship of pilgrims, a fellowship gathered around the apostles, a fellowship of a meal that includes everyone, a fellowship of one single pilgrim path to God. When we read this Gospel from the eighth chapter of St. Mark, let us pray God to bring about in our midst and at this hour what is but faintly foretold and shadowed and promised by today's Gospel.

76 • We Know Ourselves
Least of All*

Eighth Sunday in Ordinary Time (A),
1 Cor 4:1–5

About the year A.D. 55 at Ephesus, St. Paul wrote his first letter to the church he had founded at Corinth on his second missionary journey. This letter deals with the practical concerns and difficulties of the new community, surrounded as it was by a pleasure-loving pagan metropolis. First Paul describes certain abuses which had crept in. Then he takes up questions of a more theological nature that had been put to him by the community.

The first abuse, which Paul addresses himself to in the first four chapters of his letter, was a certain factious spirit within the community: some adhered to Paul; some to a preacher named Apollos who had arrived there later; some claimed to be special followers of Cephas — Peter; some again of Christ. Paul denounces this partisan attitude and says: "When all is said and done, we are all of us only servants of the Lord and stewards of God's mysteries."

We have but one commission from one Lord; that commission we must faithfully carry out; and if we do so faithfully we need apologize to no one, we need take no heed of any human condemnation; our judge is the Lord. It is nothing to us if you judge us or differentiate between us, as though one of us were something more and the other something less, as though one were more important to the Christian body than the other.

Well then, our text tells us something that is of great importance. Paul writes that it is a small thing to him to be judged by any human court. His judge is the Lord, and it is the Lord he must please. Here, as it were to reinforce his point, he says that he does not even judge himself. Now such a statement needs to be interpreted with care, according to St. Paul's own mind. In the same fourth chapter of 1 Corinthians, which contains this strange statement, Paul stresses the fact that he is an apostle, that the Corinthians can learn something from him, and he explains in detail how he has become a spectacle to the world, even to angels, and to human beings. So he knows what he is and he is emphatic that his conscience is clear. He says that he has worthily

---

*Biblical Homilies, 113–16.

carried out his apostolic office; and therefore he does judge himself after all.

In one sense this is perfectly natural: the human person is a free, spiritual being; he is responsible for his manner of life, and so inevitably he looks back at his past from time to time and considers whether he has been found a good and faithful servant. We ourselves do this. Yet Paul says that he does not judge himself. What does he mean?

What he means may be of no small importance to us personally. He knows that the ultimate, irrevocable judgment, which exposes everything and judges everything, is not the human being's to pass but God's. God judges; at the end of the day it is he who knows our hearts and not we; he searches out all that is hidden, as Paul says, and brings it to light. That is something beyond us, even if we are meant to have a clear conscience and must often examine ourselves, as St. Paul says elsewhere in this letter that someone should examine herself, for example, before approaching the sacrament of the eucharist.

Important as it is, however, this examination can take us only part of the way. There comes a point where we are the people least known to ourselves. There comes a point where we can no longer act as law and judge, prosecutor and accused, all wrapped up in one. And because this is so, our self-examination is something tentative and we may tranquilly leave God to be the judge. Sometimes we human beings are too anxious. We may be trying to get everything too tidy, to get the bookkeeping of our interior life right to the last farthing.

Of course there are people who do too little, who are superficial and too readily satisfied with themselves, who gloss over the dark side of their lives with a few facile excuses. But there are also the fretful, the anxious, the scrupulous, who somehow or other seem to think they must defend themselves against God. Whereas all we can do is flee to God and his mercy. Poor helpless frail creatures, we can only beg him to make the crooked straight, to bring low the mountains, to make the darkness light.

Let us really listen to the message of the gospel, that God is kind, that he is coming to us in his incarnate mercy, and that when he comes he — not we — will bring what is dark into the light, bring what is hidden into God's day. This day is the day of God's mercy, love, and faithfulness toward us. God stands by us even if we cannot always be said to have stood by him.

He loves us, even if we are sometimes strangely forgetful of him in our daily lives, even if our heart seems to be more attached to many things than to him, the God of our heart and our portion forever. He is the one who is faithful to us, good to us, close to us, merciful to us. He is our light. He has come, and always longs to come to us more abundantly. We should be optimistic about God and his mercy; for we have no right to entertain a low view of God and his mercy. We do not judge ourselves. If instead we let him judge us, being patient with him and with ourselves, faithful to him, accepting the life that he himself accepted when he became flesh, trusting in him, then his judgment when his day comes will be grace and peace from God our Savior.

77 • To Be Sober and Yet to Love*

Friday of the Eighth Week in Ordinary Time, 1 Pt 4:7–11

If we preface today's epistle with a brief passage from St. Peter's letter and append another brief passage to it in the spirit of this letter, then we shall have a complete pericope. We shall begin with the statement: "The end of all things is at hand," and end with the verse: "To him be the dominion forever and ever. Amen."

Let us briefly consider this text together, just as it comes. From chapter 3 onward Peter speaks of certain motives for leading the Christian life he has commended in the preceding chapters. He cites the example of the crucified; he speaks of our dying with Christ and then — here today's passage begins — he thinks of the day of judgment: The end of all things is at hand.

That is always so. It is so no matter how long the history of the world may go on. For our life, our brief and finite life, impinges directly on the eternal God. It is temporal; it is ordered to an end; and the distance between what now is and the end, is inconsiderable. The end is at hand. We live only once and irrevocably; we do not know how much time is left to us. We do not know whether we are young or old. We must look beyond our fleeting life; for as the letter to the Hebrews says, it is appointed for human beings to die once, and after that comes judgment. This thought prompts St. Peter to give us two guiding principles for our life: We are to keep sane and sober, and love one another.

Now one might suppose that only the former of these two principles followed from the fact that the end is nigh. If one knows that everything will soon be over, then of course it is well to be sober; then our whole life in this world, everything that we have done and suffered, everything

---

*Biblical Homilies, 179–83.

that has delighted us or busied us, ceases to be trivial: it all assumes an enormous importance; it becomes weighty simply because it was once lived and because our life is lived out within so small a compass; it is all relative, but in the literal sense — related to the end, to eternity, to the judgment, to the ultimacy of our existence.

Then one is sober; for whoever contemplates and weighs things as they are, as the *Imitation of Christ* says, is both sober and watchful and, as St. Peter goes on, knows how to pray. For when can one pray? When contemplating God, when grasping the reality and earnestness of life, realizing that all we are and have and experience is ordered with deadly certainty to God's judgment. Then one holds out one's life, one's heart, one's joys, and one's sorrows to God; then one prays.

It is less easy to understand why the apostle connects the end of all things with the admonition: "Above all hold unfailing your love for one another." And yet someone can really love only if he is free of himself, only when he has anchored his mind and his life in God. Only then can he look at things from outside himself, only then can he truly love; and it is perfectly true that those who truly love their neighbor also love God, even if they are not aware of the fact.

Be that as it may, anyone who knows the span of her life in God and faces it in God is free of herself and able to love her neighbor. "Above all hold unfailing your love for one another," says St. Peter. And then he says something, something consoling, that must have been a familiar saying in ancient Christianity, that Peter did not invent himself, that is based on a saying in the Old Testament, that occurs in St. James and elsewhere in early Christian literature. He says: "Love covers a multitude of sins." If we feel that we are sinners, if we find ourselves wanting in many respects and falling daily, let us say to encourage and console ourselves: Love covers a multitude of sins. It is almost as if scripture were being vague and lax; but that is what it says; and we may take it on God's word.

What else? "Practice hospitality ungrudgingly to one another." In the conditions then prevailing this was a very important and practical admonition, which may seem less important to us now that there are so many hotels and restaurants. And yet it may be that we now live in greater isolation than ever; perhaps our ability to make contact, as they say, is less than ever. Well, we should at least seek out our neighbor spiritually and entertain him spiritually, take his worries and difficulties and joys into innermost depths; then he will more easily find his way to our house and our table and will perceive that there he has a home and a country of his own in the love of Christ.

Next Peter considers human beings in their variety and says to them — and really this is another source of consolation for us — that each should love the other with the gifts that she has. Not everyone has every gift, and so we cannot all be useful to each other in every possible respect. Certainly we cannot give many people all the help they need. God meant somebody else to do the rest, without a doubt. What we have to do — it is a consolation and an admonition — is serve our neighbor with our own gift, small as it may be, odd as it may be. Serve one another with the gift of grace that each one has received. God often does not require what we imagine he requires for the service of our neighbor; but he bluntly demands that we use the gift he has given us.

Let us ask ourselves: What talents have I that I may be hiding away in a napkin like the unprofitable servant in the Gospel, not allowing them to benefit others because I am self-centered, because I love my ease, because I want to be left in peace, because I do not want to serve as the apostle tells us to? St. Peter makes another application of the same ideal. Perhaps he is thinking of the church's priests and deacons when he says: "Whoever renders service, let him render it by the strength which God supplies."

However that may be, we must take our orders, and then we hear the consoling reminder: no more is expected of you than what you are able to do, whatever the distress of the world and even of your neighbor may be. Only be sure you use your gift in the strength which God supplies, in God's sight, on God's errand, in his grace, with him in view, as a person responsible to him, so that you may serve your brother and sister, thus truly loving him, and stand firm when the end of everything has come.

In that spirit St. Peter concludes this passage: "So may God be glorified in everything through Jesus Christ." The motto of the Benedictines, *Ut in omnibus honorificetur Deus,* is taken from this epistle. It could well be our motto: In everything I experience, think, do, or suffer, and in my dying, may God be glorified through Jesus Christ who lives in us, who has given us his strength to live and die with, so that in us too the Son may be glorified before the Father. Peter closes: "To him be the dominion forever and ever. Amen." That is the end of all that Peter wishes to say to us today, all that our life should say: To him who alone is blessed, to the great and everlasting God of our life, be dominion in our Lord, in the power of the Holy Spirit who is poured forth in us, forever and ever.

78 • God's Truth
in Search of the Moment*

Monday (II) in the Eleventh Week
in Ordinary Time, 2 Cor 6:1–10

Let us consider together the first three verses in the sixth chapter of the second letter to the Corinthians. Only these. Paul says: "Working together with him, then, we entreat you not to accept the grace of God in vain. For he says, 'At the acceptable time I have listened to you, and helped you on the day of salvation.' Behold, now is the acceptable time; behold, now is the day of salvation."

These are the opening verses of today's text. In the second letter to the Corinthians St. Paul defends himself against adversaries that he has discovered in the church of Corinth. In his first seven chapters he celebrates the dignity and holiness of his apostolic office, and without any thought of self-praise candidly emphasizes the becoming attitude which he has shown in the sight of God and human beings in discharging his duties.

Chapters 8 and 9 are a digression; here Paul discusses the collection that is to be taken up at Corinth for the church in Jerusalem. And in chapters 10 to 13 St. Paul again joins issue with his opponents at Corinth. Describing the dignity of the apostolic office in these first chapters, he exalts it as a ministry of reconciliation and says that he not only preaches Christ but beseeches them on behalf of Christ to be reconciled speedily to God.

So Paul does not merely preach some general reconciliation with God; he knows that he is proclaiming God's word in a very particular situation, at the right time on the day of salvation. His office has an extraordinary weight and urgency because the word cannot be preached anytime and anywhere, because it is not a truth for all times and therefore for none, but a truth that has come from God in search of a particular moment — the Christian moment — and therefore has found and ushered in that moment.

Quoting Isaiah, chapter 49, in the Greek translation, St. Paul uses a very precise Greek word that does not simply mean "time." He says kairos. The word was familiar to the Greeks of that period. There was even a god called Kairos, whose statue stood at the entrance of the

---

*Biblical Homilies, 125–28.

stadium at Olympus — the god of the right moment, of the ephemeral situation where time must be seized by the forelock, as we say.

Naturally, Paul does not believe that such a god exists. But he does recognize the existence of this crucial, fleeting moment that God gives us, the moment of decision in human life. We all know that we only live once, and that this one life produces the fruit of eternity. We Christians know that this irrecoverable time is God's gift. We are called into a particular age and given a time there whose length God alone determines. We have no say in that. Every moment of this time is precious and unique, for no moment is ever really repeated.

And since we Christians are called as Christians into the age of Christ, when God's revealed word about his redemption, his love and mercy, is preached to us, and since God's incarnate Word belongs to this our age, the day of salvation is really here; this is the right moment, the acceptable moment, the "psychological moment" (as Paul's word might be rendered). So Paul says and the church says, now is the right time, now is your kairos, now is the day of salvation. This now will not last forever, this now is transitory, this now is a gift beyond our control. We may still have a long life before us, but all the same every moment of our life is precious, and every one is a gift of God.

We often wish we were living at some other period of history or of our own lives. Perhaps we are going through a time of distress and long for a time of joy. Perhaps we should be glad of a time for greatness and instead are tied down to some paltry, weary, monotonous job that seems to have very little point. Yet scripture says of every one of our moments: Behold, now is the acceptable time, now is the day of salvation — the day that you have now, the hour that is given to you now.

We should keep begging God with all our strength: Give me the light and strength to see the time I have as you do, to recognize it — though it may be distressing or wearisome or bitter, may even be the hour to die or to endure a lingering death — as your hour and your gift, as the day of your salvation.

If we could begin every day in this spirit, could accept each hour from the hand of God (for that is where it comes from), if we did not complain, if we did not beat our heads against a stone wall, but said with faith and humility, in the power of the Spirit and the light of the Lord: Now is the day of the Lord, the hour of salvation, the moment that can produce my eternity — then should we not understand our lives better? Then would not our days, however empty of human consolation, be fuller, brighter, nobler, ampler, blessed with the secret blessedness that the Christian can know even in desolation, even on the cross?

Let us say once more with the apostle: Behold, now is the right moment; behold, now is the day of salvation. O God, by your grace give us light and strength to recognize and endure the day and the moment that you keep giving us as your gift, your grace, and our appointed task, so that this time, the time of salvation, may produce your eternity.

79 • In Two Ways Humbled*

Saturday of the Twelfth Week in Ordinary Time, Mt 8:1–13

The eighth chapter follows immediately after the sermon on the mount and, together with the ninth chapter, forms a section in which St. Matthew sets a seal on the Sermon by relating some of the Lord's miracles, the cure of the leper and the healing of the centurion's servant at Capharnaum. We shall consider the second of these two miracles and in order to deepen our understanding of the story of the centurion of Capharnaum beyond the merely miraculous aspect, we shall have to look a little more deeply into the background.

Capharnaum was a border town between the territories of Philip and Herod Antipas, who had divided between them the kingdom of their father Herod. As a border town it had a customs post, where we meet Matthew, and a garrison. We know from the Gospels and also from the literature of the time that the troops of Herod Antipas consisted for the most part of pagans. Thus it happened, as we see more clearly from the seventh chapter of St. Luke, where the first ten verses recount the same incident, that this centurion was a pagan and a foreigner, a man who was a member of the occupying forces, a man who was cut off by his culture, his politics, and his religion from the people of the place.

We might describe him in the language of the Gospels as a man who did not belong to the children of the kingdom, who was not one of those to whom the Judaism of that time would allow any right to the promises of God or who was subject to the law of the living God. He was one of those who stood outside. That is how the Jews of the time must have looked on the centurion and they must have disapproved of him all the more since he was not only a heathen but, as we have

---

*Biblical Homilies, 17–21.

said before, a representative of the forces of oppression. That is one side of the picture.

On the other side, we learn in the seventh chapter of St. Luke that this centurion had showed himself very friendly toward the Jewish people. There the Jews themselves say about him: he loves our nation. And there is something more they can tell the Lord in his favor, something which hardly seems to match with the status of a junior officer, one who commanded a century, the smallest military unit of the time. He built our synagogue, they say, the synagogue of Capharnaum, the synagogue where Jesus preaches his wonderful promise of the bread of life in the sixth chapter of St. John.

This centurion had also undoubtedly a sympathetic understanding of the Jews, of their religion, their promises, their expectation of a coming kingdom of God to be ushered in by the messiah. But while he sympathized, he knew he did not belong to their nation. He shows his respect for this dividing line by a simple but significant gesture. A Jew never entered the house of a pagan unless he had to. The centurion knew this. He did not resent it. And therefore he said to the Lord: I am not worthy to have you come under my roof.

This is not so much the expression of a personal humility in face of the contrast between his private person and the Lord, the wonderworker, radiant with holiness and greatness. It is rather the gesture of humility of a man who carefully regards the religious views of another, who as a matter of course and with what one might call the tolerance of humility takes into account the mentality of another, respects it, refrains from wounding it — even, it may be, at the expense of his own feelings.

So with reverence and respect for the Jewish people, but with respect also for the distance that separated him from them, the centurion looked on Jesus and believed in him, believed in the dignity of his person, believed in his claim, believed in his power to work miracles in proof of his mission. He is also a man who stands faithfully by his servants. So he sends the leaders of the synagogue — this we learn from St. Luke's account, fuller and more accurate than St. Matthew's — to ask the Lord for a miracle, the curing of his servant.

The Gospel story emphasizes the wonder and astonishment of Jesus at this faith. One might almost say that the centurion's attitude is matched by a similar attitude on the part of Jesus, but on a divine scale. He also is the child of his people. He also respects the limitations imposed on his earthly life, for he knows that he is sent primarily only to his people, to the lost sheep of the house of Israel. And in St. John's Gospel he says that salvation comes from the Jews. Hence: "Truly, I say to you, not even in Israel have I found such faith."

This practical demonstration, evidently genuine and spontaneous, that outside the people of God, outside the covenant, outside what was for hundreds and thousands of years the special field of God's activity, there existed more faith, more loyalty, more respect for what was good and valuable, this single demonstration is broadened by Jesus to the extent of saying that many will come from east and west and from north and south — as St. Luke adds — and sit down with Abraham and Isaac and Jacob in the kingdom of God at that everlasting divine banquet, while the sons of the kingdom, those who thought that their descent from Father Abraham would give them a right to this eternal kingdom of God, are thrown into the outer darkness, where there will be weeping and gnashing of teeth.

It is clear that for St. Matthew the whole point of the miracle is that it was worked on behalf of someone who did not belong to the chosen people, since he includes in his narrative this saying of the Lord which Luke in his thirteenth chapter assigns to an entirely different and more likely occasion.

Does all this not have some meaning for us? It is certainly possible that we could fail to put a high enough value on the grace of Christ found in the church, but it is also possible that we could fall into the opposite error of thinking that we alone are the chosen ones, we who are inside, the sons of the kingdom.

Jesus by his example is saying this to us: You must be the kind of people who will not hesitate to recognize the truth, to recognize goodness, honesty, virtue, loyalty, courage, wherever they appear. You must not be partisans. You must see the light wherever it shines. It may be anywhere, without prejudice to the truth of the church. We know from our faith that God's grace is not confined to the visible church of Christ, that God's grace comes and goes through all the alleyways of the world and finds everywhere hearts in which supernatural salvation is wrought through this faith and this grace.

So we Catholics should not fall into the mistake of thinking that because we are the children of the true church, there can be no divine grace or love except in our hearts. We must be told again and again what this Gospel tells us, that the children of the kingdom can be among those cast out, while others who did not seem to be chosen will come from the four corners of the earth and be numbered among the elect.

The grace of the true church should make us feel humbled in two ways: first, because we must admit to ourselves that we are perhaps not all that we could be if this grace were fully alive and true in us; second, because it brings us no certain guarantee of election. So let us follow the example of the Lord and be open and generous in recognizing whatever is good, whatever is noble and active and admirable and alive, wherever it may be, in recognizing that grace can work also outside the visible church. Let the grace we have received make us all the more humble and so prepare us to enjoy its fruits in eternity.

80 • The Ship in the Storm*

Thursday of the Thirteenth Week in Ordinary Time, Mt 8:23–27

From the earliest times of the church fathers, a picture of the destiny of the church has been seen in today's Gospel. The boat of the church travels with the Lord over the sea of time and an eternally restless history, till it lands at last on the shore of God and his eternal life. It is the Lord's boat, his voyage, and his destiny. But he is sleeping. At that time and today his disciples cannot help perceiving this sleep as a sign of his leaden fatigue and his lack of sensitivity to their plight. He is asleep in the boat of the church. But the storm rages, and by sober calculation the little boat has to perish. The disciples become excited about such inopportune calm. How can one, having shoved a pillow comfortably under one's head, sleep, when they are about to be shipwrecked? (How can one celebrate a Holy Year† with great pomp and busyness, and think about such unrealistic things as declaring the assumption of the Virgin Mary a dogma, when the world is getting shipwrecked?)

The good disciples in the boat of the church today are still nervous and excited. They seem to have every reason to be, as well. The storm of history is still ever on the increase. The boat is weak (held together by nothing but "zeros," as the wide-awake disciples snidely remark). When they can no longer reproach the master for sleeping, then they upbraid their fellow crewmembers on the boat for all their heavylidded drowsiness and even more petty things. They think it is the fault of the boat, its cargo, and the passengers themselves that the storm plays so malevolently with them.

---

*Der Volksbote (Innsbruck), 26 February 1950, p. 12. Trans. Frederick G. Lawrence, Boston College.

†A year during which the pope grants a special indulgence to all who visit Rome or designated local churches and perform works of penance and charity —Trans. ed.

If they had taken another course (in terms of church politics, social, or apologetic issues, and so forth), they would have had a better trip, and been able carefully to steer clear of the storm zones of history. It is true: many do fall asleep, and all too wrongly, out of laziness or dullness, they have slept on the boat of the church during the storm. Because it affects each person on the boat, we all need to be aroused from our humdrum ways, from our complacency and slackness of heart. Truly, our calm and our caring is not always that of Christ. When we ourselves, instead of praying and doing penance, bury our heads in the pillow of a complacent optimism, this is no guarantee that the storm will soon stop, or that its waves could not quite dangerously cast the exhaustedly asleep sailor overboard from the boat's deck.

Not just anxiety, but even sleep can be of very "little faith." But aren't the Lord's good crewmembers on the boat also nervous? Don't they often think too quickly and ultimately mistakenly that the storm would no longer be a threat if everything were in order on board? The storm is not dispelled by cries and excited accusations back and forth. And also not by surprising proposals of another route. The storm belongs to the voyage of the boat through history. In retrospect, peaceful calm has proven every time to be the most dangerous times in the church. Then there is more sleeping than at any other time.

Only one who is not astonished at the storm and places his or her hopes in nothing earthly should be intending to improve the church. (The earthly realm stretches from the atomic bomb to the holiest of reforms, inclusively.) Only then does that person have the sure vision and the calm hand for doing his or her share rightly for the improvement of conditions on board. We all should not be surprised if people shout and sleep during the storm. Both are human. We do one or the other ourselves, too. Maybe alternating both. But the boat keeps on going. It is always on the verge of sinking; it becomes instead full of the bitter water of the ocean; its position gets ever more critical (regarded on the whole, this is what has been predicted by the scriptures themselves). But it travels onward, it does not sink, no matter how much of its cargo is tossed overboard, or how many of its passengers disembark. The storm will only cease when the boat lies on the shore of eternal calm. It will bring with it all the true yields of the history of this temporal state. Even us and our lives, if — in spite of sleeping and shouting — we believe in the Lord, who makes the voyage through world history in the ship of the church full of divine peace.

81 • A Universe Made to Our Measure*

Fifteenth Sunday in Ordinary Time (A), Rom 8:18–23

The letter to the Romans is the longest and most pregnant of the apostolic letters in the New Testament, and the eighth chapter, which contains today's text, is the climax of that letter. St. Paul devotes his first eight chapters to showing that a human being is not justified and sanctified by his own efforts, by independently fulfilling the law of God, but by God's grace. Grace must precede anything the person does in that order, it is in no way due to the individual, it is given him by the sheer goodness and benignity of God; it and God's Holy Spirit — on whom one lays hold by believing in this gracious, unmerited doing of God — make the human being holy and just, snatch him from the dark powers of this world, give him the victory over them, enable him to look confidently toward his future.

This is what St. Paul is saying here, once he has shown the sinfulness of all humankind and its need of redemption; once he has said that this justice which comes not from human beings but from God, must be steeped in faith, and transforms a person. Now chapter 8 describes this justice.

It is approached from two points of view: Paul tells us what someone now is through the spirit of sonship that is poured forth in his heart; and he tells us where the human being, thus justified, is going. Inasmuch as an individual is now a child of God, he is already a new creature. Inasmuch as he has just begun his course, is journeying toward the true fulfillment of what he already is, the human person remains subject to the premessianic age; he is in transition. The past and the future meet within the framework of his existence. He finds himself as it were on a bridge, crossing over from this sinful life that is forfeit to death and the law, into God's freedom. That is why he is still exposed to the sufferings of this world, why he still groans with this age, this world, that is subject to corruption.

But he knows that is entirely provisional and transitory, that it will all be done away with; and so Paul says: "I consider that the sufferings of this present time are not worth comparing with the glory that is to be revealed in us." It is a glory which we already possess in germ in

---

*Biblical Homilies, 91–95.

the Spirit of God, a glory which has only to be revealed in due course, which must burst forth from the center of our existence, seize upon every sphere, every dimension of our earthly being, and transform it, subject it to this higher law of God, this glory of God. And so what we have still to suffer in this passing age is not to be compared with the glory that is to come, that is to be revealed in us.

Now Paul turns from the individual Christian. What she suffers, after all, is only a share in the nature of existence, in the destiny of the world as a whole. Because we are earthly, fleshly human beings, because we are still subject to this our time, to this aeon, we must suffer. Sickness and death are not simply forces that murderously fall upon us with one accord. According to St. Paul, they are dark, cosmic powers, ultimately the spawn of sin, at work everywhere in the world. In the whole of nature St. Paul sees this darkness at work, affecting us individuals almost incidentally.

So he goes on to say: "For the creation waits with eager longing for the revealing of the sons of God." We people of today see things quite differently. We feel that we have been thrust into a world that is alien to us, alien to us and our lot. But Paul sees the world in the light of God, which means that he sees it in relation to the one creator of heaven and earth, of all things visible and invisible, of all time and of every age. And since he sees the world in relation to its single origin, he recognizes that it has been designed in accordance with a single, coherent, intelligent plan and that this plan, to put it briefly, is humankind — or rather, the Godman and those who are his.

Whereas we feel that we are simply may-flies in a huge world which is blind and deaf to human beings, Paul sees God, the creator, and his first thought, and that is his Son who is to become a creature, a man, and those who belong to him. And therefore the whole world was designed in view of this man, centered about him — designed too in view of human beings who God knew would use their freedom to become sinners in need of redemption. So that all God's creation was arranged from the first to suit this poor humanity, this sinful humanity. Hence Paul says that this creation was subjected to futility, but hopes to be set free from its bondage to decay and obtain the glorious liberty of the children of God.

Natural history — as we might say — and the history of humankind, natural history and the history of salvation and damnation, were ordered to each other from the first by the one God and Lord, who will not dismiss even sinful human beings from his service, who contrives to turn even the no of his free creature into the greater yes of God and his mercy. That is why God was able to subject this earthly world to nothingness, bondage, and futility, because all this nothingness and futility, this mortality, this finitude, this death, is girt about by God's mightier power, which has instilled into this hopelessness the hope of a blessed freedom and a glory destined by God's grace for those who shall have been his children, brethren of the incarnate God, fellow-heirs of Jesus Christ.

So it is that with an eye and an ear which have been opened by God's revelation, Paul is able to gaze into all creation, listen to it, perceive its nothingness but also its yearning for the final glory which it is to share with the redeemed, transfigured sons and daughters of God. So he says: "We know that the whole creation has been groaning in travail together until now." Only it? No, we as well, although we are the sons and daughters of God.

Within us too is this groaning and desire, because we have not yet reached the consummation. "And not only the creation, but we ourselves, who have the first fruits of the Spirit, groan inwardly as we wait for adoption as sons, the redemption of our bodies." Thus for Paul the human heart, the heart of nature, and revelation are all agreed; the ultimate promise, ultimate light, unbounded hope are already rooted in our heart and in all nature. But everything is still at its beginnings, still in transition. Everything is still in the birthpangs of the new and perfect creation.

Is this what we feel our life to be like? Or does this "unitary" sense of existence that the apostle has and that binds together the blessedness to come and the anguish of the present in one elemental act of redeemed creation — does it disintegrate with us, so that at one moment we enjoy creation as though it were the ultimate thing, and at another moment suffer on its account as though it bore no hope in its entrails?

All too easily that can happen to us. We either snatch at the cup of the joys of this life as though nothing else existed for us to desire, or we curse the cup of sorrow, distress, and death as though it were not the only cure for those who must recover for eternal life.

Let us learn from St. Paul, through this eighth chapter of Romans, where we really stand. We are redeemed souls who must make our way through an earthly world and see it for what it is: a world which is to share in the glory of the children of God and therefore even now is full of promise. But we must go further and have the courage to believe, be vigilant, and long for the glory of the children of God which is yet to be revealed in us. That is why — as St. Paul says elsewhere — we are to rejoice; and even when we weep we must not weep as they do who have no hope. We must be composed, integrated people, because it is in us, the children of this earth who have the Spirit of the eternal God, that the world itself is integrated, knit together into a good world which is one day to find beatitude with God in his everlasting life.

82 • Love of God
and of Those Furthest Away*

Fifteenth Sunday in Ordinary Time (C), Lk 10:25–29

As a matter of fact: the love of neighbor is not one of the many concerns we pursue secondarily as well — compared with what is of more importance — because in the end there is nothing else at all. This love is rather the most authentic dimension of life, even though it mostly but not always is done through things that a normal person would do in any case.

Those who love their neighbor have fulfilled the Law, say the scriptures (Rom 13:8). Surely it is the case: we ought to know God explicitly in order to serve him and to love him. But if we really love our neighbor and break through an express or hidden egoism, we know God even though we think we know nothing of him. One can find eternal life even if we have not explicitly known or called upon God [Vatican II: Dogmatic Constitution on the Church, no. 16; Pastoral Constitution on the Church in the Modern World, no. 22], if through no fault of our own we fail to discover this relationship explicitly. But no persons find their salvation and their God who have not explicitly loved their neighbor in word and deed. And whoever are of the opinion that they have to do with God expressly in their thoughts and feelings, but do not love their neighbor, they know nothing in a saving manner about God and how to be related to him.

If therefore Christians who by their love of neighbor are supposed to witness to the unfathomable reality that God loves us, then they should not thereby forget that today everyone in the world is to be in solidarity with each other, if it is simply supposed to proceed on. Then they have to love in deeds, and not just in convictions and words, also those far away, whom Christians and the situation of today's world have turned into neighbors for us. A World Mission Sunday is therefore an admonition to deeds of love, which are no arbitrary luxury which we still perform as an afterthought, even as Christians. Maybe we do not have to be concerned about Mission Sunday as such. But its warning holds good for all Christians even if they heed this warning elsewhere. If we respond to this admonition, we have loved God, and the remote neighbor, and the nearby neighbor all at once. But that is Christianity.

---

*Herausforderung des Christen, 55–56. Trans. Frederick G. Lawrence, Boston College.

83 • Technology Multiplies the Loaves*

Seventeenth Sunday in Ordinary Time (B), Jn 6:1-15

What happens in the Gospel that is read to us today? We hear of people driven on by a hunger for God. They follow Jesus into the wilderness. They follow him there because they realize that their own life is a wilderness, because at the bottom of their hearts they know that the human person needs God and God's word. They are looking for a prophet, they hunger for God's word, they demand more than their ordinary life is able to offer them.

So they go; they go into the wilderness; they leave the places where they have their homes and the bread of their earthly existence. And strange to say, while they are hungering this way for God, an earthly hunger seizes them. While they are looking for God, they perceive that they are human beings, who must have their earthly bread, who must try to defend their earthly existence. Hungering for God, they find themselves hungering for earthly life.

The situation becomes still stranger: the man that they are following, so that he may break the bread of eternity for them, the man from whom they expected nothing but the words of eternal life, gives them earthly bread, looks after their earthly existence, fears that they may perish in the wilderness. Stranger and stranger, they halt and sit down, they are fed, their hunger is satisfied, and in verse 26 of this chapter Jesus tells us what happens next. "Truly, truly," he says, "I say to you, you seek me, not because you saw signs, but because you ate your fill of the loaves." At the end of today's Gospel, chapter 6, verse 14, we read: "When the people saw the sign that he had done, they said, 'This is indeed the prophet who is to come into the world!' "

And so they want to make him their king. Because they sought the bread of eternity, God also gives them the bread of this world; and because he gives it to them, they begin to lose interest in him and his eternal life and to seek earthly bread once more. They want to make their God the king of their earthly life. When they have eaten their fill, they are more eager than ever for the bread of this life; and what was only meant to give them leisure and freedom of mind for seeking God,

---

*Biblical Homilies, 68-71.

becomes a temptation, tempts them to covet earthly well-being and the joys of earthly life and even to pervert the gift of God.

And then, we are told, Jesus withdrew into the hills by himself. Because they were that way, because they perverted God's gift, because eating their fill only made them those who hunger for the things of this world, God, who had given them even their earthly bread, withdrew from them. Now this is only a parable of what constantly happens in the life of humankind and of the individual, particularly in our technological age.

God gives us technology in order that we may have our earthly bread and be able to multiply it so as to feed the great multitude in the wilderness of this world. This miracle, whereby technology multiplies the loaves, is granted us so that we may have time to desire God's bread and satisfy our hunger for eternity. And we, like the people in that other wilderness, are tempted by the miracle to want still more and to make God king of our technology.

But he withdraws from us. He stays by himself on the mountain of his eternity and will not lend himself to our scheme. And once again we find ourselves alone, in a still more savage wilderness despite the twelve baskets of miraculous bread with which we are still encumbered.

Let us not say that technology, civilization, a rising standard of living, comfort, the wider scope that is opening up for our earthly existence, presents no special temptation to us personally. We may not be the most self-indulgent people of our age; perhaps we have not really had our fair share of the bread that technology passes on to us from God. But we are the very people who are tempted, and who (perhaps without committing any discernible sin) often succumb to the temptation.

Is there not something to the quip that people can be divided into two classes, those who have a car and those who wish they had one? Are we not often the ones who covet things, who remain inwardly dissatisfied even though we really have enough of the bread of this life and ought to desire God more? Have we often given up earthly things that we could have, simply to show God that we love him? Do we not condemn this demonic technological world only when we must do without something that we covet in our heart of hearts? Do we modern Christians live considerably below the heights, or even in the very abyss of this age, because we are incapable of anything better? Have we the clarity of mind and the stout heart to develop a soundly Christian pattern of life, in the midst of a technological age that we affirm and accept as our lot — one that will uphold the right scale of values not only in theory but also in day-to-day reality? Or must Christ say to us too:

You do not follow me because you recognize your age as a token of God's goodness, but because you have stuffed yourselves with bread and want still more?

Ah, today's Gospel has much to teach us about our age, about our intimate selves, if we will only face our life and take its true measure: life in the age of technology, which as a whole, if not in every detail, is willed by God because he means it to multiply the loaves. Otherwise, though nothing is said about this in our hymnals, we too may become involved in a mysterious way in the sinfulness of our age. Everyone contributes something to the spirit of the age. And everyone is called upon to live in such a way, for his own part, that his age may be one when God can rely on our clarity of mind, on the love of our hearts for him, and give us the bread of this world, so that in the wilderness of this life we may receive the bread of everlasting life for eternity.

84 • We Have Not Far to Seek*

Twentieth Sunday in Ordinary Time (B), Lk 14:16–24; Jn 6:53–56

Today's Gospel tells us the story of the great supper which God himself has prepared in his church for those whom he has invited to the supper of eternal life. Today's text, therefore, gives us an opportunity to turn our attention to the mystery of the eucharist.

It seems to me that out of the immense fullness of truth and reality of this sacrament there is just one thing that we should keep in mind — that we receive the body of Christ. In the course of her doctrinal development the church has concentrated her gaze more and more on this one fact, that Jesus Christ is wholly present in this sacrament, with his divinity and his humanity, with his flesh and his blood, with his body and his soul, truly, really, and substantially present, and that we receive him as the complete master of our lives to be our food for eternity.

This is so true and so important that, while we may very rightly follow the mind of the church in meditating on this presence, celebrating it, receiving it, praying to it, praising it, and loving it, it still remains true that the Lord gives himself to us by granting us, in his own words, his

---

*Biblical Homilies, 50–53.

body as food and his blood as drink. There must be some significance in the fact that the Lord speaks of the presence in this sacrament, not just of his person but of his body and his blood.

If we turn to the discourse promising the Eucharist in the sixth chapter of St. John, the discourse which Jesus delivered to his disciples in the synagogue at Capharnaum after the miraculous multiplication of the loaves, we find that it is about his flesh and his blood that he speaks. Jesus here does not use the word "body" which he will use later in the words of institution at the Last Supper; he uses the word "flesh." There is no doubt that this Johannine discourse is meant to refer back to the same word in the prologue of St. John's Gospel, where we are told that the Word of God became "flesh."

When we ask just why Jesus should give us his body, we should keep in mind this Johannine reference to the flesh in which the Son of man has come. When John talks about the flesh he means first of all what scripture always means by this word. In Semitic usage it always means the whole human being, not just a part of him, not just what we nowadays in an almost medical sense refer to as our body in contradistinction to our spiritual soul. The flesh and the body mean the whole person, but especially the tangible person, that takes its place in this earthly environment, that can be touched, that has a meaningful reality when one touches it and says, "This is it," that is, not merely spirit and concept and truth and abstract thought, but a concrete human being.

Thus John says: "The Word became flesh." By this he means: Yes, it is here where we are; it is among us; it shares our life; it shares space and time; it shares our existence; here we can and must seek the everlasting God. And now Jesus says to us: "Take and eat: this is my body, my flesh." Again and again the earth offers its most desirable possession, the pure and lowly bread and the wine of rejoicing.

From the Last Supper there stretches the unbroken chain of all those whom Jesus has sent out on his mission with his word. Link after link falls into place in this succession of the living bread and the earthly wine, this chain of human words and human signs. Through these mysterious, modest, simple proceedings, we receive not merely the truth of God, not merely or primarily his eternal divinity, but the flesh and blood of the Son of God, which he eternally took upon himself, from which he shall never be parted, in which he has immersed himself, so that this godless world might be filled with the eternal radiance of the Godhead.

So we receive the body and the blood of the Lord, that body, true, real, earthly, which tasted death, that transfigured body which heralds the eternal transfiguration of the world, to which this body continues to belong even when it has been transfigured into the life of God and sits at the right hand of the Father. We need not seek any further; we have him here where we are; we can point to him; we can look on him; we can receive him bodily.

And when we are oppressed by the almost overwhelming feeling that we are so far from God, that our heart is empty of God, when it seems that all the thoughts and feelings of our heart cannot find him, when we have the impression that we are here and that God, the true God, the inaccessible light, the incomprehensible, is so far away — then at least we will want to receive physically the body of the Lord.

It is true that unless the flesh and blood are received in faith and love they avail us nothing; they are received for our condemnation. But when we who are poor and hungry, beggars and cripples, blind and lame, when we who have been called in from the highways and hedges of the world, where we thought only to look in from outside on the splendor of God, when we who are all too conscious of our poverty and need, of our pilgrim existence, nevertheless enter in as invited guests to this physical banquet of everlasting life, when we can eat the bread of this earth and drink the wine of this land where we live, because we know that it is filled with the eternity of God, when we enter in trustingly and say we want to receive even once the body of the Lord, then God must and will make everything different.

Then he fills us with his grace and his strength, with his light and his life, even while we think ourselves to be empty and dark, dead and wretched without God. "Take and eat: this is my body." And the Lord says: "He who eats my flesh has eternal life." He has come to us in our flesh and gives us this flesh because we do not know how to come to him. Because he is here, because he himself has come in the flesh of this earth, we want to receive the bread of life, his flesh which is our flesh, and we want to drink the cup of his blood, in which our blood, the blood of our race, has been assumed and eternally redeemed. And because we feel so poor and empty, he gives us what is our own, where we are at home, what we understand, and calls it the pledge of his own divine life.

That is why we can always have confidence in him as our feelings tell us, and enter into this banquet of eternal life, because he is where we are and we have no cause to fear that he is far away; for he has given us his body and blood which are eternal life.

85 • Real Christian Morality*

Friday (I) of the Twenty-First Week in Ordinary Time, 1 Thes 4:1–7

St. Paul wrote this letter at Corinth, in about the year A.D. 51 during his second missionary journey, soon after he had founded the church at Thessalonica. The first part of the letter treats chiefly of his personal relations with the community, and then in chapter 4 he passes on to admonitions and definite doctrine. The doctrine has mainly to do with the second coming of Christ. We have already discussed the first part of the section mainly devoted to morals, chapter 4, verses 1 to 7.

Paul has exhorted the Thessalonians to be upright, chaste, and honest in all they do. These things call for no special comment. But I think that when we read these admonitions, listen to them, hear them solemnly preached in church, we may find them rather a bore. To be blunt, moralizing, constant exhortation, all that sort of thing rubs us the wrong way. It may even scandalize us. Now we might give this subject a little thought.

Why does this happen? For one thing because we have so often heard it all before — in the catechism, at school, from our parents. It is ceaselessly inculcated by the spokesmen of bourgeois morality. We have heard it in the confessional, in sermons, in pastoral letters — always the same admonitions that we find Paul addressing to us today: be chaste, be honest, practice the other virtues, in short keep the ten commandments. We have heard it all so often that despite ourselves we find it a little tiresome, old-fashioned, and hackneyed.

What is more, we may well reflect — and here is another stumbling block — this is not what Christianity is really about. Of course these are things that must be done. Agreed. But on the whole we do them, and all the exhortation is beside the point. Anyhow — we may well reflect — Christianity has to do with God, his grace, his glorious life, looking forward to eternity, the way eternity infringes on time, acknowledging the infinite, exalted, holy God of eternal life.

Compared with these things — with the fact that God himself has shared our existence by becoming man in his divine Word, with the prospect of everlasting life in the company of God himself — petty moralizing really seems a little grotesque. Not that we doubt or deny those moral duties, but surely they are relatively unimportant compared with the great truths that we are taught, after all, by faith, by God's own

*Biblical Homilies, 159–63.

word. After all, the pedestrian morality that is so earnestly preached is rather obvious. What else is it but what they call the natural law, which we can discover simply by the light of reason?

We are interested in God's mysteries and God's beatitude. We want to rise above this everyday morality, to know God and his eternal life, mysteries that are inaccessible to the feeble light of natural reason. And so we may even be scandalized by these admonitions.

A third reason might be adduced. All this moralizing is about *how* to live an upright life. But as to what one must actually do, what the real content of life is, the moralizers leave us none the wiser. They seem intent on restricting our lives; they point out the ditches on the right- and on the left-hand side of the road; but what our life and work really are, what contents our hearts, they do not say. All these rules, these prescriptions, all this scolding, these warnings always being volunteered by unenlightened, petty-minded pedagogues and educators do not tell us what is to be done, where our heart and mind are to find fulfillment in this life on earth.

Well, what about it? Must we be scandalized, or have we something to learn all the same when God's own word, scripture, and the church, keeps preaching these things day in, day out? Yes, God's word is right. In the first place it is marvelous what we do not happen to hear. We say we know all these rules, all these warnings, by heart; and indeed we preach them often enough ourselves to other people — to children, to adolescents, to people about us — in so many words; or at least implicitly when we think of our environment in unflattering terms.

Yes, we know these rules and admonitions. But when we ought to act according to them in our own concrete life they often do not occur to us. And when they are preached, we are likely to hear everything but what speaks to our condition. We think of how the exhortation applies to others. We are always ready with a big "if," a "but," an "on the other hand," to water down God's word to us.

Do we ever ask ourselves: When did I last look at the Bible, listen to a sermon, do any spiritual reading? How often do we admit with remorse and contrition: yes, that is so; I do not act as I should? When have we really allowed ourselves to be convinced by God's word, really capitulated to his admonition and admitted that it applies to us?

The human being has a remarkable facility for failing to hear these rules. That is why God keeps coming with the good seed of his word, even with the seed of moral considerations, back and forth across the stony field of our heart, keeps sowing in the hope that one day something may grow there.

We must say one more thing. Morals, even ordinary morals, bourgeois morals, decency and integrity, sincerity, uprightness are all included in true morality. Pedestrian virtues, perhaps; but, so long as they are something more than mere respectability, singularly dear to God. A person who in the inmost depths of her heart is really devoted to God's will, an individual to whom God's word is law, hears a voice even in the most ordinary moral prescriptions that is the voice of her God, and not of purely human reason. Someone who really and honestly obeys her conscience, not resorting to a thousand ruses to make the voice of conscience sound gentler, works for eternity in time; her humdrum days weave the fabric of a divine life.

Of course these moral rules that tell us how to do things must be constantly related to the concrete content of our work, of all our earthly task. Morality cannot simply be like a motor idling on its own, for its own sake. It is a way of doing what God has given us to do — all that we have to do in relation to our neighbor, to our work and our prayer, to our life with its joys and sorrows, to God.

But if we do all that in the way God commands, then these very earthly things will become heavenly, the temporal will become eternal, and the fruit of everlasting life will grow in the field of this present time. Because that is so, because small things become great and time becomes eternity, and because it only happens if we faithfully keep God's small, perhaps awkward commandments, even when we would gladly overlook them — these admonitions in the Gospels and in the letters of the apostles are meant for us as well as for the rest.

We cannot bypass them to busy ourselves only with God's great glories. We must let God tell us who we have to be and what we have to be like, so that we may be true children of light, heirs of eternity, beloved brothers and sisters of the Son of God, who condescended to share our life and set us an example so that we might act like him: obedient to God's commandments and the prescriptions of morality, which are not meant to be a stumbling block to us but a means to eternal life.

86 • The Supreme Challenge*

Twenty-Second Sunday in Ordinary Time (B), Jas 1:17–21

Our text for today is taken from the first chapter of the letter of St. James. We might divide this chapter into two main sections, so far

---

*Biblical Homilies, 164–67.

as this pithy letter of moral admonition can be divided at all. After the greeting, the first eighteen verses are an exhortation to steadfastness in time of temptation. Verses 19 to 27 call upon Christians to practice in their lives the gospel which they listen to in faith.

Let us consider the last few verses of this first part of St. James's letter. They say: "Every good endowment and every perfect gift is from above, coming down from the Father of lights with whom there is no variation or shadow due to change"; and the next verse says: "Of his own will he brought us forth by the word of truth that we should be a kind of first fruits of his creatures."

If we would understand these verses aright, we must look at the context in which they occur. In chapter 1, verse 13 of this letter, so as to fortify us when we are faced with temptation and danger of death, St. James has roundly declared that God tempts no one: God cannot be tempted with evil and he himself tempts no one; but, he goes on, each person is tempted when he is lured and enticed by his own desire. And then sin follows.

It is in this connection that he says that every good endowment and every perfect gift is from above, coming down from the Father of lights. Now this statement may seem rather obvious. But what of St. James's statement, a moment ago, that God tempts no one? It will not seem so obvious if we scan the Old and New Testaments. Does not God himself try our hearts? Is he not the Father of all things? Of all ages? Does he not hold all things in his hand? How then can anything attack us which does not come from him? How could he try our hearts if he did not lead us into temptation? Would there be any reason to pray: "Lead us not into temptation" if it were clear from the first that God does not tempt anybody?

What then does the apostle mean by saying that God tempts no one, as he himself is not tempted by evil? It is certain that God places us in this life, subjects us to trial, only because he wants our own good, wants us to be approved, wants us to receive even his gift of eternity by our own free doing in this life. He does not will darkness and evil; he does not try to involve us in sin; he places us on probation in this life so that we may have the glory of freely choosing God and eternal light.

And there is no greater or more perfect gift than being allowed to do this — to be the maker, as it were, of one's own eternity, though by the grace of God. That is what God wanted human beings to be. That is how noble and exalted a creature God wanted him to be. And therefore however much of a temptation things may seem to be for us, all that comes from God is a good endowment, a perfect gift. It is sheer light because it comes from him.

So St. James says in this first verse: "Whatever comes from the Father of lights is a good endowment, a perfect gift." He means that it depends on us what happens to the sheer light which eternal love has given us. Of course we are often tempted, heavy laden, provoked by evil, often in danger of being enticed by our desire and giving birth to sin, as St. James has just said — sin that brings death with it. Well, if that happens then we have turned God's sheer light into darkness — so we must interpret this way God has of dealing with the human person, mystery though it must always remain. For whatever comes from him must be a good endowment, a perfect gift. And now we ought to examine our lives and see whether we accept all that comes to us as God's good endowment and perfect gift, coming down from the Father of lights who, like a changeless sun, sheds nothing but eternal light in the empty gloom of all that is not God.

Where is the bitterness in our life, where is the cross, the heart-break, the enigma, the crushing burden, the harshness, the despair? Do we stand firm against it? And do we say, believing the gospel: this too is a good endowment and a perfect gift from the Father of lights? This text of St. James, then, is a weighty one, a challenge to do the greatest thing that can be done in a human life; and if we do it, then we shall never look at anything in isolation, so that it might become unintelligible, a provocation to sin, a temptation.

We must never look at creatures apart from God and the intention in which he gave them to us. Only then shall we truly see them as a good endowment, a perfect gift, and really understand what St. James means when he goes on: "Of his own will he brought us forth by the word of truth that we should be a kind of first fruits of his creatures." This does not mean some truth or other; this means the truth that turns darkness into light, the cross into a good gift, the narrowness and darkness of the creature into boundless light of God.

If we accept everything just as it comes down from God the Father of lights, if our eyes are enlightened so that we can see this light, then we are the true children of that Father of lights, begotten by the word of truth; the enlightened, adult children of God who interpret all things according to God; who have room and to spare in their hearts and can fit everything in there in due order, all the good endowments and perfect gifts; then we remain free for God, open to him, and our life remains open to God's glory; we are really a kind of first fruits of his creatures as we are meant to be.

In many respects, I fear, we have yet to be thus brought forth by the word of truth, yet to become children of the light, a kind of first fruits of God's real creatures. The beginning was made when we were baptized and believed, but it is not yet complete; this beginning is only perfected when we ourselves have been perfected, when we have accepted everything that comes to us as a perfect gift from above, when our shadowed, mutable being, because we have thus accepted it, has entered into eternal light.

87 • Two Paradoxes*

Twenty-Second Sunday in Ordinary Time (B), Jas 1:22–27

Verses 22 to 27 in the first chapter of the letter of St. James belong to the second part of that chapter which we have already mentioned. It is the part which tells us to be doers of the word of the gospel and not simply hearers.

We shall select only two thoughts from today's text. Though there may be very little connection between them, each one merits some attention.

In verse 22 St. James says: "But be doers of the word, and not hearers only," and then he adds, "deceiving yourselves." The word he uses here occurs only once elsewhere in the New Testament (Col 2:4). Literally translated, this Greek word means to "think past" a thing, to delude or beguile ourselves with all sorts of excuses, qualifications, and sophisms, as the text of Colossians says. Here James tells us to beware of thinking past reality in that way. The image he uses, if we look squarely at it, can only mean that the human person has the ability to shy away from hard facts, by her own fault, and thus deceive herself.

Now it is a very strange assertion to make, that someone cannot only deceive others but can also deceive herself. Looking at the matter from the point of view of ordinary logic and common sense, we might well say that such a thing is impossible. How can the deceiver and the deceived be the same person? Yet our own experience confirms what scripture tells us here, that it is indeed possible. We think of a pretense, we find it persuasive, we say we are convinced, and then we conclude that we are in good conscience. And yet we are deceivers, and we contrive to deceive ourselves.

We shall not inquire further, at the moment, into the psychology which makes such a thing possible. Let us simply learn a lesson from what St. James says about talking and thinking ourselves round and

---

*Biblical Homilies, 168–71.

past reality. Let us be suspicious of ourselves, of the many good reasons we seem to have for avoiding something unpleasant in our Christian lives, or for not honestly doing our duty, or for blaming others instead of ourselves, or envying others their apparent good fortune, or refusing to be put upon.

In these and a multitude of other cases, let us heed the apostle's warning and ask whether we are not in danger of deceiving ourselves, of guiltily distorting the knowledge that we have and suppressing the truth, as Paul says in the first chapter of Romans — God's plain, unvarnished, inexorable, perhaps humiliating truth that makes demands on us. "Do not deceive yourselves," says St. James.

The second thought which we shall briefly consider today is found in verse 25 of this first chapter. Here the apostle — he who warns us to be doers of the word and not hearers only, he who tells us later in his letter that we must not only believe but also produce the works of faith — speaks like St. Paul of the perfect law of liberty. And he thinks that this idea embodies the heart of Christianity.

The perfect law of liberty: that in itself is a strange expression, well nigh a paradox. Law and freedom seem to be mutually exclusive. Where there is a law, surely, freedom ceases: and where there is freedom there surely is no law. We can gather, then, that our author is thinking of a freedom which somehow frees us by binding, and of a law which frees us by reclaiming us from a servitude in which we should otherwise be languishing and which — deceiving ourselves — we should imagine to be freedom.

What St. James says means something more. We human beings, one might say, by way of quasi-definition, are those strange creatures who perceive that they are finite and therefore, not free, who are prisoners of their finitude: unable to determine how long we shall live, unable to control the situation in which we find ourselves, prisoners of our limited knowledge, of the needs of our heart, of bodily sickness, of our environment, constantly exposed to death. Not only are we finite in all these ways; unlike other creatures, we know that we are finite and we feel ourselves oppressed and trapped by finitude. And along comes the apostle talking of the perfect law of freedom.

The word "perfect" in Greek, as in English, implies that an end has been reached. The perfect law only exists complete and glorious when we ourselves have reached our end, have ceased to endure this finitude and are perfected in the unveiled freedom of God's children. Then we are wholly liberated. But James says that we are to live even now in the perfect law of liberty. And so that law must be given to us in this world, to us poor, indigent, suffering, limited, finite souls in this poor world. Yes, it is already given to us, for God's Spirit, the Spirit of infinite freedom, is already given to us — in faith, of course; in hope; and in that love which will never end.

If then we feel enslaved, imprisoned, distressed, and heavy laden, that is an admonition to descend deeper into our hearts, to where God already dwells in his Holy Spirit of boundless freedom. It is an admonition to pray: I believe in the perfect law of liberty, I believe in eternal life, I believe in God the liberator, in the truth of God which sets human beings free, in the love of God which is free. Then, doing the works of faith, we shall not feel distressed to be still in chains, because in our heart of hearts we are already liberated, and so we know that everything which still keeps us unfree is transitory, and that the perfect law of freedom endures for all eternity.

88 • What We Must Give Away*

Twenty-Third Sunday in Ordinary Time (A), Rom 13:8–10

The text set before us today says:

Owe no one anything, except to love one another; for he who loves his neighbor has fulfilled the law. The commandments, "You shall not commit adultery, You shall not kill, You shall not steal, You shall not covet," and any other commandment, are summed up in this sentence, "You shall love your neighbor as yourself." Love does no wrong to a neighbor; therefore, love is the fulfilling of the law.

Reading over that text, we do not find it particularly hard to understand. It does not seem obscure. All the same, if we ask exactly what St. Paul means when he says that love is the fulfilling, the fullness, the perfection of the law, we shall find that the matter is not so simple after all. And even if we reflect a while upon these three verses, we shall not really be able to say that we have got to the bottom of them.

Perhaps we can understand these verses better if we glance at what went before. You remember that the third part of the letter to the Romans, chapter 12 to chapter 15, verse 14, deals with the moral duties of Christians. In the first seven verses of this thirteenth chapter St. Paul has spoken of the duties of Christians toward civil authority, widening

---

*Biblical Homilies, 103–7.

his horizon in the last verse to consider our duties toward humankind in general.

Thus he says in verse 7: "Pay all of them their dues, taxes to whom taxes are due, revenue to whom revenue is due," and now taking the wider view, "respect to whom respect is due, honor to whom honor is due." A very comprehensive precept, a dictum recalling that of the old Latins, "to each his own." Owe no one anything. Give everyone his due. If someone can rightly claim a tax from you because he is an official of the state, well and good. The state shall have its tax. If you owe a person respect, show him respect.

Now we might be tempted to say: once everyone has had his due from us, there is an end to it. We owe nothing more, we have given all that can be claimed from us. We may well think to ourselves: fine, now be on your way. All accounts are settled. You have had all you can require of me, and I have probably had all I can require of you. That is that.

Oh no, says St. Paul, you have not started yet. When I have treated the next person fairly, paid my bills, refrained from stealing her property, respected her, perhaps helped her in one way or another as she can expect me to do, says St. Paul, then my obligations to her begin. Now what can I still owe a human being once I have given her everything to which she has a right?

Obviously the remaining obligation must be of quite a different sort. Paul says: "Owe no one anything." Let us try translating the text somewhat differently, say as follows: Pay every person his due in tangible terms, and something will still be owing. What is that? Brotherly love, says St. Paul. Now if we examine our consciences and allowed our real thoughts expression, we should probably say: I am already practicing this love. I have paid my taxes, been respectful, given people due honor, done this or that work of mercy, contributed to the support of my pastors, given a shilling or two for the refugees, and so forth.

What more is expected of me? Paul says: Pay every human being his due, and something will still be owing — agape, true love of our neighbor. Now how is that debt paid? In the case we are envisaging there is nothing more I can give; all that I have given is gone, the other individual has tucked it all away — from bills and taxes to respect, honor, and even reverence.

Supposing that I do still have to love him as my neighbor, as St. Paul says, what more can he expect of me than I have already given him? Yourself. Only if we meditate on this can we understand Paul's saying that when all debts are paid and nothing is left outstanding, we still owe the other person fraternal love. It is true that we do. For this agape — a word which the Greeks do not seem to have used in this Pauline sense at all — this love, has its origin, its being, and its prototype in God, of whom St. John says that he is love, agape, and of whom St. Paul says that his love, his agape, is poured forth in our hearts.

What is this divine love? It is God's surrender of himself to us. He not only gives us his gifts, he gives us himself. And if we are to love our neighbor with such agape, then our obligation is never satisfied. It keeps growing as we pay. We have never done with it. We can never say: now be off, you have had all you can expect of me.

If I must give myself to the next person, can I say that I have done it? Obviously not. Why not? Well, to look at the matter from below, as it were, we are human beings, capable of this act of love toward men and women only in space and time, in earthly and tangible terms, wrapped in the payment of other debts. If only for this reason, our love remains something imperfect. When we look into our own hearts, how difficult the whole thing is; we cannot seem to get away from ourselves, we are always turning back to ourselves, we do not seem able to give our hearts away. And sometimes when we think that we have done it, is the truth not that we want the others to give themselves to us but have no mind to give ourselves to them just as they are?

Now looking at the matter from above, we see that we must be growing, as it were, always absorbing infinities into ourselves because it is our business to remain open to God. For having given us himself in his agape, he belongs to us. And so our life, our being, is full of endless potentialities that we exploit only by degrees, step by step, piecemeal. If we keep enriching ourselves in this way, accumulating grace and blessing, ever more selfless and more faithful, absorbing God who gives himself to us, then we begin to see the kind of love we could give away to others, simply by giving away ourselves, still half-grown, still tentative, still imperfect though we are. At best, our achievements in this world remain so fragmentary, we are so pitifully imprisoned within ourselves.

When we give to others it is usually from afar, to show them that we really do want to love our neighbor. And when we try to give from nearby, try to show with words, or sacrifice, or faithfulness, that we want to love one another, it all remains so elementary. Now perhaps we understand a little better what St. Paul means when he says: This love is the surpassing fulfillment of the law. Where laws are nothing more than laws, they can only represent a kind of rough-and-ready justice, distinguishing what is mine and what is the other fellow's, showing the individual what concrete goods and services she owes her neighbor.

But exact calculations and legality are superseded when love enters the picture, when someone gives himself with all his divine infinity to his neighbor, or at least tries to start doing so. Then he is no longer a person accomplishing something or rendering a service; he does more than comply with an objective norm which is equally binding on us all; he is a person perfecting himself by being the unique creature he is meant to be, perfecting himself because God has given him his own divine self in a unique way.

And because what is involved here is a person, unique and irreplaceable, a person who achieves and perfects herself by lovingly giving herself away to others, all mere legality is superabundantly fulfilled and left behind. Thus love is the fulfilling of the law and the bond of perfection, as Paul says — that which will not pass away. That is why Paul can actually say: such a one has not only kept the law but more than fulfilled it, has passed beyond it and arrived at what must be the human being's destination.

For if we truly love our neighbor in God — only in God are we able to give ourselves away to our neighbor — we really need not trouble about anything else. Law, with its demands, its overharsh requirements, lies behind us. We have entered upon the blessed freedom of God's love for us, of our love for God, of the love that by God's grace we have for our neighbor. Only when we have got that length — not by our own powers but by the grace of God — shall we have reached our fulfillment in God.

89 • What If There Were Nothing More to Do?*

Twenty-Third Sunday in Ordinary Time (A), Rom 13:8–10

Today's text is taken once again from St. Paul's letter to the Romans. It comprises only three verses of chapter 13. Between chapter 12 and these verses Paul has spoken of the duties of Christians toward authority, saying in that connection — so we might well sum up his teaching — "Pay all of them their dues, taxes to whom taxes are due, revenue to whom revenue is due, honor to whom honor is due."

Now he adds a few important admonitions about the Christian love of our neighbor. We have often spoken before of this love of our neighbor; but the apostle and the church tell us the same thing again and

*Biblical Homilies, 108–12.

so we shall listen to these verses. They can always teach us something useful. If the repetition should seem boring to us, we can recollect what the beautiful tradition [from St. Jerome, *On Gal.,* 6.10] tells us about St. John. He used to keep saying, "Little children, love one another — " and when his disciples asked why he always preached the same thing, he replied that it was the commandment of the Lord and that that was enough.

If we would meditate on the theology these three verses contain, we might again try rearranging them. In verse 10 St. Paul says that love is the fulfillment of the law. Now first of all that simply means that someone who loves her neighbor and does what love bids her do has done what the law requires of her; she has observed and fulfilled the prescriptions of the law.

And so love is the fulfilling of the law. Looking at love from this point of view we might think to ourselves: It is only a general term that comprehends the individual commandments and the various duties we have toward God and, in particular, toward our neighbor. We might suppose that this commandment merely tells us to give him what is his due, as Paul says. If we owe him attention, then attention; if we owe him taxes, then taxes; and once we have discharged these individual duties, so that we owe our neighbor nothing more, we might suppose that we have fulfilled the other commandments and have done with them.

No doubt St. Paul means by verse 10 that we must at least do those deeds, acquit ourselves of those tasks of love, and — why not say it — that it is always suspicious when we appeal to our good heart and good intentions in order to get out of doing the deeds of love. What we must do is love in such a way that our love does fulfill the other commandments.

But Paul says something rather different about love in verse 9. He says that it sums up the law. Here he uses a Greek word that means providing something with a head or a summing-up. Only in one other passage of the New Testament does this word occur — in Ephesians 1:10. There Paul says that the Lord, Christ, unites the universe in himself because it has pleased God to unite all things, the universe, in the incarnate Word of the Father as in their one head. Christ sums up the history of God's redemption, God's mercy, the church, and the whole of creation: In him all things subsist and hold together, are united, have their ultimate meaning and orientation, their salvation and their end — in him, because he is at once God and a creature.

Now it is in this sense, says St. Paul, that love is the head, the summing-up, of the law. Only in love do the various individual prescriptions, rules, provisions, and demands find their ultimate meaning, are they united and transcended. For Christ is more than the sum of all other creatures. He is the supereminent head. He is the summing-up which is more than the sum of all other things that are summed up. And so love is more than the sum of the commandments, more than the sum of all the things that we must do for our neighbor. It is all-embracing — because it is the love of God which he gives us and which we give him in the power of his Spirit.

And so this love is really the very mystery of God, who is love. And because it draws God into its own being as its own source and goal, it is always something more than the rational order of the universe; more than the sum of tangible, calculable duties that we owe our neighbor; more, we might say, than the rules for keeping the machinery of this world and human life running smoothly.

It is the unspeakable and the overwhelming, that which takes one into the depths of God himself. It is something that cannot be explained in terms of anything else. Though it does demand concrete deeds of loyalty and kindness to others, the core of it cannot be recast in any other mold. If we speak of God, or love, or the mystery of human life, or eternity, we are speaking of one and the same thing, in which everything is summed up as in its head. And so, as verse 9 says, love sums up the law.

Now we can also understand verse 8. There Paul says, pursuing the train of thought in the previous passage that I have already discussed, that we are to owe no one anything; as he has said, we are to pay taxes to whom taxes are due, honor to whom honor is due — in short, to pay our debts. And then do we owe no one anything further? If we examine our lives we are likely to discover that our attitude is that of the man in the Gospel: "Friend, what do I owe you? Take what belongs to you, and go." We have often said this, not only to our neighbor but even to God: Take what belongs to you; there you are, and (perhaps we do not add aloud) leave me in peace. This is often our attitude toward our neighbor and God and our life and our work — toward everything.

There is a great deal that we are compelled to give; we have never done with paying taxes. So Paul says: Give this person what is due him, and the other person what is due the other. And then he says: Owe no one anything. But no sooner has the apostle said that than he stops short, and then goes on: "except to love one another." For we always owe this love. Such is Paul's mind, and that is why he says at this point that all things are summed up in Christ and in love. Not as though we did not have to give proofs of our love; but it is an unlimited and endless duty, done only when we loved God and our neighbor with our whole heart and our whole strength forever.

Love is what we always owe. We can never really pay off that debt.

Yet after all to realize the fact is not a grief, but a joy. Where should we be if once no more love were expected of us and we had done everything? We should be drained dry, finished, at the end of our rope. We should be dead human beings, nothing anymore. But if there is such a thing as a love that never ends so long as God demands it of us, never ends because he always demands it of us, because he gives it to us so that we in turn can give it; if he promises through his very demand that he will give us this boundless love for him and our neighbor; if God's word is more reliable than our experience of our own niggardly, dying hearts; if it is true that over our lives there hovers a boundless love which is never exhausted, which gathers everything into the infinite mystery of God, then we can believe and hope and love. Then what St. Paul says is true: Love never ends. Then we can always owe God this love, and he will give us all eternity to go on loving him.

90 • How Powerful Is the Seed of God?*

Saturday of the Twenty-Fourth Week in Ordinary Time, Lk 8:4–15

In the eighth chapter of St. Luke we find the parable of the sower, as it is generally called. It could also be called the parable of the different fates of the word of God. This story must have been specially close to the heart of the primitive church. It is found in all three synoptics: Mark has it in chapter 4 and Matthew in chapter 13. Scripture has also preserved for us the Lord's own explanation of the story. For that reason the preacher feels reluctant to add anything to these words of the Lord which are so clear. The parable is one that we understand at once.

If, however, we should desire to delve more deeply into this well-known parable, we might begin by asking ourselves why Jesus tells this parable and why he tells it to us. We could first ask ourselves why Jesus, seen in human terms, should have told this parable. We are entitled to think of the Lord in this truly human way because he is truly human. And therefore the things that he says come from his heart and reflect his inner feelings.

---

*Biblical Homilies, 41–44.

If we ask why Jesus thus considered tells this parable we will have to answer: because he cares so deeply about the fate of what he is speaking of. He comes, he speaks, he preaches, he distributes the words of God. They are strength, light, grace, they come from his very heart. He is wholly involved in what he says. He gives at the same time the full force of his heart, his love, and his grace. He speaks from the source of final and definitive words, because he comes from above and does not speak human wisdom but proclaims that light that comes down as God's grace and salvation on the hearts of men and women to illumine them on their way to eternal light.

But when Jesus speaks and preaches in this way, what does he see? His word is not accepted, he finds deaf ears and cold hearts, he finds men and women who answer him with refusal, with self-complacency, with contempt, with evasion. And from the depths of his disappointment and the pain of this experience, he asks: How is it that this word bears so little fruit in this world? He tells himself the same parable that he tells us: "A sower went out to sow his seed." He turns his gaze to nature, to what his Father has made, to where reality comes closest to what God had intended. He sees that the seed that is sown there meets with different fates. The end does not always correspond to the beginning. Fashioned and given by the Father, it meets with different fates, even though it was created by God — or perhaps (who knows?) because it was created by God.

This consoles him. This renews his courage to go on proclaiming the message entrusted to him by his Father, to go on working, to go on walking the fields of this world, sowing the seed, tirelessly, patiently, persistently, to go on in all weathers, no matter what fate the seed may meet, to leave everything else to the decrees of the eternal Father, to the mysterious providence of God.

We go on to ask our second question. Why does Jesus tell this parable to us? Why does he tell us of what consoles his heart? The answer must be that we are in danger of taking scandal at what happens to God, to his grace, to his church, in ourselves, in history, in our surroundings, in everything we see. More, are we not tempted again and again to think that this cannot really be the seed of God, that it cannot be his word, his grace, his power, his design, his handiwork, his church, his sacrament, if the results it meets with are meager, so wretched, so precarious, so continually rejected and destroyed by the world?

Do we not keep asking ourselves — or are we afraid to ask ourselves — this question: Where is the finger of God to be found in our lives and in the history of our time? Do we not have the feeling that God's word should be more powerful, that God's power should be almighty in the history of our time, that God's light should shine more clearly in our hearts and in the world, that God's comfort and strength should more fully possess our poor, dry, cold, tired, dull hearts? Do we not, like Jesus, ask ourselves in our hearts: What are we to make of the fate of what claims to be the seed of God in this world, God's life and God's own fate?

Are we not then the kind of people to whom Jesus needs to tell this parable? But, we may ask, is this story then an answer to our question? Look: an answer to this question, if it is to be a true one, can only be given with diffidence, and silence would be a better answer still. Certainly Jesus tells us in the parable that it is not the seed of God that is at fault but the ground, the stony hearts, those who, in Jesus' words, spring up among thorns, among riches and pleasures — it is their fault that the life of God bears no fruit in dry and hardened hearts, in blind souls.

But — one might be tempted to answer against this parable of the Lord — is all this not part of God's plan too? The stony hearts and the hard ground and the thorns and thistles of this world and the devil and the hard-trodden pathways of our time? Is all this not foreseen and willed by God? Or if he merely permits it, is he not still responsible for it? We can easily be tempted to blame God for the different fates that the seed of God meets in the world.

If we are tempted in this way, then it is time to let this parable of Jesus speak to us, this parable told us by someone who knows God because he comes from him, for he himself has felt the pain of this question and the temptation of every human heart to cry out in protest. No, he tells us, each one of us, you must take the blame for the different fates of the word of God upon yourself, in your own heart, because you are a sinner, because you are hard of heart, because your soul does not seek after the light of God as it should be sought after.

Only when you confess that you bear a responsibility for the fate of God and of his grace, a responsibility that cannot be removed or lessened or transferred or excused, only then will you be what you should be in the sight of God, only then will you find favor and justification with God. We must keep tilling the soil of our poor hearts, we must leave there no beaten track for the endless traffic of the world and its affairs to pass over, monotonous and incessant. We must prepare good soil in our hearts for the seed of God; if we do this and ask for nothing more, then this seed of God will surely bring forth fruit in our hearts, thirtyfold and sixtyfold and a hundredfold. If we recognize our responsibility, we will see God in his mercy once more enabling us to be good soil for his seed. Then we will see that all is grace and the eternal mercy of God, who gives both the seed and the growth in his infinite generosity.

91 • Profiting from Every Situation*

Twenty-Fifth Sunday in Ordinary Time (C), Lk 16:1–9

Today's Gospel is one we have often read, and probably often wondered about. For it is really strange that Jesus should choose a story like this, drawn from the shabby workaday world, as a parable of the sublime, of his own message, of the kingdom of God that he came to bring us. Here is a rogue — we may as well call a spade a spade — who has been swindling his employer; and when he is about to lose his job because he has been found out, he contrives a masterstroke that will leave him comfortably off for life.

Jesus uses this unsavory story as a parable — an image or comparison — of the way we should act in the kingdom of God. Jesus, the holy one, infinitely sensitive, who alone was actually able to ask, "Which of you convicts me of sin?" he who alone really knew evil, as we can never know it, regards this earthly, shabby, mean, nasty little affair with perfect detachment, so casually that he can make of it another comparison with the kingdom of heaven.

Be frank. Are there not times when we feel oppressed by the gloom, the meanness, the petty egoism, the spite, the gossip, all the things that make up our routine? Are we not often grieved to find that people are so crude, so unprepared to be understanding; that even good people, who are struggling and praying to become compassionate, fail to understand us, pass coldly by, unmoved by our distress?

The world often seems so bitter, so narrow, so heartless; so mean a place. On closer examination, of course, we see that we often grieve over the wretched world when it causes us pain, but much less often when it does not. But however that may be, perhaps we could to some extent imitate Jesus in this matter — even ask him for an attitude very like his own. He has told us that his heavenly Father allows wheat and weeds to grow in the one field which is the world. He was patient and long-suffering, a sober realist — which is why he puts up with us. Must we not imitate him a little and bear with his world — our environment, our fellow men and women, our church — so that God may also bear with us? For if he does not, what is to become of us?

I think there is a second thing we can learn from this parable today. What exactly is the prudence of the dishonest steward which his master praises and which Jesus himself sets before us for our imitation?

---

*Biblical Homilies, 58–61.

We might say that he is prudent in contriving to turn every situation to his own advantage. While he was steward he lined his pockets; and now that he is to be dismissed he profits from his new circumstances, though they are the opposite of what he has been accustomed to.

As long as he was steward, it would presumably have been disadvantageous for himself to reduce the debts that were owing to his master. Now he seizes the opportunity which could not present itself then. He is prudent because he derives advantage for himself from every situation. That is his prudence. An earthly and vulgar prudence, but the Lord uses it to teach us the heavenly prudence we should have. What does this mean for us?

Our life is a series of vicissitudes. The landscape of the soul is exposed to every kind of weather. By turns we are happy and unhappy; now lively, now weary; now pleased with our surroundings, now disappointed and hurt; now young, now old; now encouraged by success, now crushed by some bitter failure; now grateful for all the benefits we receive, now wounded by the thought of all that is denied us. Ups and downs, like those of the steward in the Gospel. But are we as prudent as he was? Have we the faith, the stout heart, the humble mind, the docility to God's good pleasure, to see in the most contrasting fortunes of our lives a chance to bring forth fruit for eternity, to prove our love for God, to be patient and courageous, unassuming and devoted; or do we insist on having our own way in the service that we offer God, are we prepared to find him only in the particular situation we have chosen?

Before we know it, he has sent us a different situation; and we have not the magnanimity, the willing, loving, uninhibited prudence to perceive God's call, his work for us, in the different situation, to accept it with a will, to get on with it, to be well content with God's good pleasure for us. We are not so prudent as the steward in the Gospel. And yet we should be. If the heart is really kept open and ready for God, anything that may happen to us in life can be accepted as a grace and a blessing.

Of course this means having a heart that is well-disposed and humble, that listens and obeys. But why not ask God for that gift? Could we not pray instead of complaining, call on God instead of accusing others? Somewhere in the life of every human being is a wound that has never healed. For we should be saints in the literal sense of the word — holy people — if always and in all things we were at one with God and his will.

It is because we are not that the parable of the Christian's heavenly prudence concerns us all. If we will only look a little more closely at our lives, we shall find situations, relationships, burdens, here and there, that can only be seen for what they are, can only be coped with, if we are prudent enough by God's grace to acknowledge with a heavenly prudence: This too is a word of God's eternal love; I must be loving and courageous and answer yes.

92 • The Denarius Stands for Us— and for God*

Twenty-Fifth Sunday in Ordinary Time (A), Mt 20:1–16

It seems to me that this Gospel of the laborers in the vineyard, even though we know it so well, appears stranger and more incomprehensible each time it is read. That every person receives the same reward surely does not hold true of eternity. Nor can we conclude from this story that God does not render to everyone according to his works, for it is written in scripture that he does. What then, we may well ask, is this story really telling us?

We have here a parable of the Lord that demonstrates what is true of all his parables, namely, that one must concentrate on the message of the story as a whole and not try to find an application for every detail of the story in the religious and supernatural sphere, in the relationship of human beings to God.

In this parable we should not ask who those are who were called at the first hour and those who were called at the third, sixth, ninth, and eleventh hours. We should not seek any special significance in the fact that the latecomers were paid first or in other similar details. At God's eternal judgment there will be no grumblers. All these details in Jesus' story were put in only to throw into relief the central message, which is all that really matters. But what is this central message?

To understand the parable we must remember in the first place that at that time the usual wage of a hired laborer was one denarius for one day's work. So when the householder offered one denarius to those who were willing to work in his vineyard and who went and did the work, and when he had them paid a denarius at the end of the day, he was giving them the wage that was normal, accepted, fair, and — to use modern terminology — in accordance with social justice.

---

*Biblical Homilies, 22–25.

They have no reason to be surprised at it. When they started the day they expected no more. Therefore it is clear that when the householder has a denarius paid out to each of the latecomers, there is no longer question of a wage which they have earned. He had not even promised them this denarius, for all he said was that he would give them what was right. And they certainly did not expect to be given so much. The householder expressly asks the grumblers whether he has not the right to be generous. What he gives to these latecomers, therefore, is not an expression of wages which they have earned or of the justice which applies to masters and servants; rather it is an expression of his own generosity, that free generosity — and here we are coming to the point of the whole story — that incalculable mercy, that grace which cannot be reckoned up in terms of wages and justice, that generosity and mercy which ultimately prevail between God and us.

This story does not deal with the question whether any individual is rewarded by God's judgment according to his works or not. In this parable Jesus is saying something else, something far wider, something especially significant in view of the way in which the Jews of that time were preoccupied with rewards; he is saying to us that between God and us there prevails something quite different, something that cannot be calculated, that cannot be expressed in terms of justice, something that is in fact the mercy and free disposition of the eternal God.

This is a truth which at first humbles a person, for it tells her that she is not someone who can confront God with claims in justice which she has established through her own efforts. She is not someone who can calculate with God. But this truth, that everything depends on the free mercy of God, is also a truth which comforts us and raises us up and frees us from a burden. For if we were to calculate with God, then God would calculate with us and question our claim. In that case we would inevitably come off second best.

No, it is certainly better that everything should depend on God's free mercy. For it means that whether we begin to serve God early or late, we can always be of good heart, and no matter what demands are made upon us, we can say to God: You are the God of mercy and consolation, the God who bestows grace and who makes payment with the denarius that no one can earn by his own efforts, who makes payment to us who are such poor sinners and unprofitable servants.

Where it is that this mercy of God enters our life, where it is that he shows himself to us as one freely disposes of us and does not negotiate, is an entirely different question. We cannot find the answer to it in this parable. We cannot make an unjustified application of the details of this parable to the divine reality. We can only say that in the last analysis everything we can earn and must earn in the way of wages depends on the free disposition of God, who gives to us as he wills and ordains our beginning and our ending according to his pleasure. From this there follows something which can never, I think, lose its importance for us.

The thing which God freely disposes of, the thing we cannot negotiate or calculate about with him, is ultimately our own selves. Our own selves, just as we are: with our life, with our temperament, with our destiny, with our surroundings, with our time, with our heredity, with our family, with everything that we happen to be and cannot change. And whenever we grumble and complain about others with whom God has dealt differently, we are really refusing to accept our own selves from the hands of God.

This parable teaches us to say: we are those who receive the denarius, we ourselves are the denarius. For we receive ourselves, with our destiny, with our freedom certainly and whatever we choose to do with that freedom, but ultimately what we receive is ourselves. This we must accept, not just without grumbling, without inward protest, but with a good will, because it is given to us by the God who asks: "Do you begrudge my generosity?" This, then, is our great life's work: to accept ourselves as the mysterious and gradually revealed gift of the eternal generosity of God.

For everything that we are and have, even the painful and mysterious, is God's generous gift; we must not grumble at it but must accept it in the knowledge that when we do so God gives himself with his gift — here again the parable falls short of the reality — and so gives us everything that we could receive. To do this is the wisdom and the chief work of a Christian life. If we look into our own lives we will find that we have not always done it. All of us, young and old alike, are really latecomers. And yet God is willing to give us everything if we will only accept it — ourselves and himself and life without end.

93 • The Past Is the Key to the Future*

Monday (II) of the Twenty-Eighth Week in Ordinary Time, Gal 4:22–31

St. Paul wrote the letter to the Galatians round about the year A.D. 55 while he was at Ephesus. We are not quite sure to which

---

*Biblical Homilies, 129–32.

churches in Asia Minor it was addressed. In any case Paul had visited these churches twice, and after his departure certain Jewish Christian preachers arrived and taught these gentiles that they could not really be complete Christians unless they accepted circumcision and other prescriptions of the Jewish law.

Now Paul declares in chapter 1 of this letter that his gospel — the gospel of freedom from the law of the Old Testament — comes from God. In chapter 2 he says that his gospel agrees with the gospel of the original apostles at Jerusalem. And then he shows that according to God's Old Testament law itself, outwardly observing the law, observing the law without grace, does not justify a human being; that only faith in the Holy Spirit, only the grace of Jesus Christ, justifies someone. Our text is part of St. Paul's effort to prove by the Old Testament that Christians are freed from the yoke of the Old Testament.

If we read these verses we must admit that it is difficult for us to see Paul's meaning. He uses a type of theological proof which was a commonplace among the Jewish theologians of that day. He draws a parallel; he cites an antetype in the Old Testament which clarifies and illustrates something in the present dispensation, the New Testament.

We might say that he sets up two sides in the Old Testament: on one side he has Hagar and her son Ishmael, on the other Sarah and her son Isaac. These are types of the two testaments or covenants: the old covenant, the law which was given on Sinai and the new covenant, the new law of freedom and the Spirit — corresponding to the earthly Jerusalem and the heavenly. Paul concludes that those who belong to the old covenant are in bondage to the law, whereas we who belong to the heavenly Jerusalem and the law of freedom and the Spirit are free in Christ.

Now this kind of reasoning may seem strange and artificial to us. But the basic idea ought to be quite comprehensible. It is an ancient one. When God acts, when he has acted, throughout the course of a long history, then we naturally expect this whole action of his to have a particular style, a continuity and coherence. God, who has thought out this single history, brought it into being, shaped and guided it, governs all its thousand details and vicissitudes so that everything fits into place. The future will always be new and startling; we shall not be able to foretell it by studying the past. But once it is here we see that, new as it may be, it is still of a piece with the past; there is a normality about it, an inner bond, that makes it part of the totality of that history we are speaking of.

We are justified, accordingly, in discovering prototypes and like-nesses of the present in what has gone before. At the same time this history is ever maturing, ever disclosing more of what it means, leaving the past behind as a halting analogy, a feeble foreshadowing of the fulfillment we know.

Our present is Christ Jesus. Within the unity of God's historical action, within the one vast work of the God who gives all grace, what has gone before takes on a significance that is surprising and yet consistent with the rest. So in this strange doing of God there was one man who was the son of promise and another, the son of the bondwoman, who simply fell heir to his mother's lot. Here Paul can see a parable of the way God in the new covenant calls human beings into the freedom of the Spirit, pardons them, delivers them from the yoke of a law imposed from without, giving them the inward Spirit of power, grace, and love whereby an individual is able to satisfy the law superabundantly and interiorly, so that he is no longer the slave of the law but a son, doing what God's law in the Old Testament really intended, because of the intimate understanding, the empathy, he has with the Giver of the law.

Can we not discern such a continuity in God's gracious governance of ourselves and our lives? We too are always being startled, always having to enter situations we had not foreseen or reckoned with, we too must keep saying: I am never prepared for the way things turn out. But if they turn out as God, who is greater than we are and more mysterious, planned for us, and if we have accepted them and not frustrated God's design by indocility of heart, then we shall suddenly sense that it all fits into the mysterious pattern of our lives.

Of course our life is still incomplete, a kind of jigsaw puzzle. If we study its composition we cannot really see how the pieces fit together or what the finished picture will look like. But if we look at our life with candor, humility, and love, we shall not fail to discern the unity of God's work in us. What once seemed glaring contradictions have already been reconciled. Much that once seemed hopelessly dissonant has already settled into harmony, thanks to God's goodness and mercy.

This higher harmony may have been unexpected, it may be still incomplete, but at least enough of it is there for us to be able to feel confident of the rest. And much in the past can serve as a type and allegory of what now is and what is yet to come. Paul once said to his Christians: "I am sure that he who began a good work in you will bring it to completion." That is the motto of God's harmonious work within us. Because we know from experience that he is kind and forgiving, the God of enlightenment, mercy, and all consolation, we can rightly read the present and the future in the light of the past. We too find types in the past of what is and what is to be. And when everything is over, it will all have fitted into the one, great, holy loving idea God had when he fashioned our being and our life, when he called us by name.

94 • The Essence of Christianity*

Twenty-Ninth and Thirtieth Sunday in Ordinary Time (A), 1 Thes 1:2–10

On the second missionary journey, when he first visited Europe, St. Paul came to Salonika. Not long after founding the church there he had to move on, attacks by outsiders making it impossible for him to stay in that large and busy port. He journeyed to Athens and then on to Corinth, where he wrote this first letter to the Thessalonians some time between the years A.D. 51 and 53. When we read the opening verses of this letter, therefore, we can reflect that they are probably the first words of the New Testament to be set down in writing. And we shall notice that they contain the essential truths of the faith. Here in these few words of introduction Paul tells us, out of the plenitude of his faith, what our Christian life means. We cannot examine all Paul says here; we must select certain subjects to discuss. Let us leave aside what Paul says of his apostolic commission and of the community's apostolic work. We shall only touch on three points.

At the very beginning, in verses 2 and 3, Paul speaks of faith, hope, and love. It is only later, in the first letter to the Corinthians, that he expressly mentions these three as a special group of Christian virtues. But here we see that he is well aware of their existence. He says that Christians practice the work of faith, the labor of love, and the steadfastness of love. Now in some sense that is the whole of Christianity. When God speaks to us and calls us, and we do the work of faith throughout our lives, and if we really love God and our neighbor through this faith — do not merely feel an emotion but love them in actual deeds of sacrifice — and if we are steadfast in hope because we know that we are pilgrims and that ultimate reality still lies ahead, if we practice this self-sacrificing love, active faith, and unshakable hope — then we are genuine Christians.

Then what Paul says a few lines later of the Thessalonians can be said of us: You received the word in much affliction, with joy inspired by the Holy Spirit. In the divine Spirit that is poured forth in our hearts; we shall then be able to endure joyfully the affliction, the bitterness, the difficulties, the trials of our lives, of which Christians have not less but more than other people. For the Christian is a strange kind of person who simultaneously experiences tribulation and the joy of the Holy Spirit, which is deeper and more penetrating than any tribulation; joy

---

*Biblical Homilies, 155–58.

that is strong and active and endures unto the end. That is the first thing St. Paul says about faith, hope, and love.

The second thing that we shall note in Paul's description of Christian existence is a single word: election (*eklogē*). It is a difficult word for us to hear, for us Christians of today precisely because we are Christians of today. Contemporary persons have a way of losing themselves in the crowd. They do not want to attract attention. They want to be everyman and everywoman. Now there is something to be said for this attitude. It may even be thoroughly Christian: being plain and ordinary, unobtrusive, patient with the monotony of an average, undistinguished life. Yet this odd instinct to be retiring — and it is odd — may conceal a form of cowardice.

To the Christians of those other days, who were few and persecuted, whom people looked on as eccentric outsiders, Paul says: You have a vocation, you are chosen, you are called forth by God by his grace and his election. There is no need to go into the question of where others stand. Here we can apply what Jesus said to Peter: If it is my will that you follow me, why should you concern yourself with the affairs of others? Even if God saves the rest, and we can confidently commend them to his boundless mercy, our own business is to answer his call, to be convinced that he is calling us and that there is nothing for it but to follow him blindly, with no questions asked. We must realize that if we are indeed God's chosen ones, as Paul says, it means that God and his grace have done this thing, and not we ourselves. And so we must give ceaseless thanks to God, thank God always.

The third thing the apostle speaks of is the quintessence of Christianity. He says that Christians have turned from the idols, the false gods of their past life, to serve a living and true God; that they wait for his Son from heaven, whom he raised from the dead, until he comes again to take them into his glory, to deliver them from the wrath to come.

Now that is really all Christianity is about: knowing the living, true God who has called us, who is more than all the idols of this life that we are constantly tempted to raise to altars of our hearts. For we too, just like the people of those times, are always in danger of worshiping idols, though we no longer make graven images to worship.

Idols may still stand on our altars: the idol of success in this world, the idol of pleasure, the idol of recognition by others, perhaps even idols that we do not believe in, that we consider a devouring nothingness. For as well as benevolent duties human beings have often worshiped dark and vicious ones; perhaps we are tempted today, in the gloom of our existence, to worship such malevolent deities.

These too would count among the idols that we have been chosen to turn away from, so as to serve the true, living God, the God of everlasting life; for he has called us in Jesus Christ his Son. God's history and God's works have only just begun and we have been drawn into them, and therefore we still await the end of that holy history into which our life has been taken up, and we confess that he will come thence to judge the living and the dead, to judge us and, we trust, everyone at the tribunal of his mercy.

There we have a few of the things Paul tells us about our Christian existence on the oldest page of the New Testament.

Let us beg God for the work of faith, the unflagging labor of love, and the steadfastness of hope; these three. If we have them, we have enough. For them we are God's chosen ones, who have turned from idols — from the idols of life — to the living God, and we wait for his Son, the eternal Word of his love which shall be spoken to us in heaven to make us happy forever.

95 • The Chance of a Lifetime*

Tuesday (I) of the Thirty-First Week in Ordinary Time, Rom 12:6–16

The first eleven chapters of the letter to the Romans are of a doctrinal nature. From the twelfth chapter onward, as is his custom, St. Paul admonishes Christians about their moral obligations. Our text belongs to this second part of the letter. In itself it does not call for much explanation. It is intelligible and beautiful; it describes Christian life as it should be, in St. Paul's view. We shall only add two brief observations.

In verses 6 to 8 Paul says, giving certain concrete examples, that we ought to have a bold confidence in our own mission and vocation. He has already said in verse 4: "For as in one body we have many members, and all the members do not have the same function, so we, though many, are one body in Christ, and individually members one of another." And then our text begins: "Having gifts that differ according to the grace given to us, let us use them." Then Paul says: "If prophecy, in proportion to our faith; if service, in our serving; he who teaches, in his teaching; he who does acts of mercy, with cheerfulness."

Now when Paul says that everyone has her own gift, her own vocation, it is a truism. Every individual has her own quite particular character and experience, her own history, her own age, this or that

---

*Biblical Homilies, 96–98.

sex, her own education and training, her own quite definite place in human society and — as Paul says — in the church of God. But are we always well content with this place, this vocation and mission?

The vocation and character that we have been given need not relate to the spiritual offices St. Paul speaks of here. A person with the most secular and earthly of jobs to do is as much called by God as anyone; she is following her vocation. So these first three verses say to us: Do your job, accept it, do not look for anything else, do not dream of something you have not got and can never have. Do what you are called to by the reality of your life, perhaps even by the sheer force of your circumstances. Thus St. Paul speaks to slaves in 1 Corinthians. Do that, he says. If you must admonish, then do it; if you have to speak, then do it. St. Paul says this to us, who try to escape ourselves and our real lives. Whatever we have to do is a vocation from God. It is the chance of a lifetime; our one chance to be Christian.

What Paul says in verses 9 to 16 — I mean his second observation — is also an appeal for bold confidence that ordinary, daily life is the stuff that makes up real Christianity. When he tells us here: "Rejoice with those who rejoice, weep with those who weep. Live in harmony with one another. Contribute to the needs of the saints. Be patient in tribulation. Rejoice in your hope. Serve the Lord," what else is this but a picture of our daily life, our daily life well-spent, to be sure, accepted with its joy and its tears, with the tribulation and distress of others, with the hospitality we extend, with the situations we would gladly escape, where we are expected to do plain little things and are tempted to dash out far beyond our depth.

Is our love not often pretense? Do we honor one another? How zealous are we? Are we not often lukewarm? Do we serve the Lord in all things? Or are we not often glad to be able to shut the door behind us and leave others to shift for themselves? Have we ever actually prayed for our enemies, real or supposed? Do we rejoice with those that rejoice, or do we expect others to rejoice in our own joy? Do we weep with those who weep, or do we avoid becoming involved in other people's pain, saying to ourselves that our own burden is quite enough for us to bear?

In these plain verses St. Paul tells us: Love ordinary things and ordinary life. Let life carry you along, with its ups and downs, its people, its laughter and its tears — all the variety that God's providence means it to have. Let love be genuine, and then you will be Christians. If we would only accept our gift and vocation, accept our ordinary life as God's charisma, our burden would be eased and we should be happy in this world.

96 • There Is Something Mysterious about the Kingdom of God*

Tuesday of the Thirty-First Week in Ordinary Time, Lk 14:16–24

Today's Gospel comes from the fourteenth chapter of St. Luke's Gospel, verses 16 to 24. A similar parable is found in St. Matthew in the twenty-second chapter, verses 1 to 14. Here in St. Luke we have the parable of the banquet which a man arranges — so the evangelist tells us — and to which he invites his guests. In the twenty-second chapter of St. Matthew we have the parable of the royal wedding feast which the king holds for his son and to which he invites his guests. The exegetes ask whether these two texts refer to a single parable told by Jesus or whether he in fact told two different parables with a similar theme. Whichever may be the case, the basic thought in the two parables is the same.

To this royal banquet of eternity, to the kingdom of God, the first people to be invited are those who seem to us to have the right to be invited first, since they have the necessary qualification for such an invitation and will therefore accept the invitation — but in fact they do not accept it. Then others are invited to this royal banquet of eternity, people who seem to us not to possess the qualification that would fit them for this invitation and who should therefore refuse it — and yet we see that they accept it. They become the guests of the householder or the kin at this feast which — translated into reality — stands for the eternity of blessed fulfillment.

In each case there is the basic thought which our Lord seems to be expressing that those who were first invited but refused are the Pharisees, the party of the pious, the orthodox. And those who do not seem to be called and yet accept the invitation are the tax collectors and the sinners, those who in the estimation of the pious of that time were shut out from the messianic promise, from the covenant which God had made with his chosen people.

When we apply this parable of Jesus to ourselves, then — let us make no bones about it — it can frighten us; for if we accept these two great classes into which Jesus divides people and ask ourselves to which of them we belong, we must answer that we belong to the first invited. We are Catholics; we are baptized; we belong to the one, true, holy church; we are to all appearances pious. Now it does not, of

---

*Biblical Homilies, 54–57.

course, follow that our history must develop in the same way as today's Gospel. But we must plainly recognize that what is set down here may easily happen to us, because we can be one of the first invited who made their excuses.

And it is true that the kingdom of God does not consist merely in those things which we certainly are: baptized Christians, churchgoers, people who do not come into any open conflict with the church and her commandments — all this is relevant but it is not identical with the kingdom of God. So we too, who already seem to be inside, are invited to enter truly and to belong to the royal banquet of the true and interior kingdom of God. Here we can really be among those who excuse themselves.

The invitation to the kingdom of God and to its royal banquet of eternal life is not something that is given once for all time: it happens again and again that God calls us to obedience to his will, to resignation in the face of his decrees, to self-denial, to his love, to the carrying of the cross, to the unrewarded daily grind, to silence when we want to speak bitter words, to a thousand things which are invitations to the royal banquet and do not seem so.

Here the parable breaks down. Here in order to meet the invitation we must remember that it will not of course come in the form of a holy message from the eternal God, nor will someone come to us in great splendor, obviously sent from God, who will expressly inform us in clear and unambiguous terms that this is something that concerns the eternal kingdom of God. No, this happens without pomp or circumstance; this happens in the depths of our conscience, this usually happens almost incidentally. It is then that we may be among those who say: "Hold me excused: I have something else to do."

We have no farm to buy and no oxen to examine and no earthly wedding to celebrate; but when we receive these secret, interior, hidden, obscure, invitations to God in his cross and in his love, we have a thousand other things to do which seem to us much more pressing: business, work, worldly success — I cannot say what it may be, but each one must examine her own heart and she will find enough things there which she uses as excuses with God to avoid accepting his invitation. Where and when this happens, no one can say to another, unless the other bares his conscience in detail and his adviser has a true eye for God's will through the light of God.

But can we not ask ourselves another question, prompted by today's Gospel: can we not ask where and when we make this refusal to God and with such apparently good reason? When we reflect on the text of the Gospel we see that the reasons given seem good ones. Or can a person never miss some meal or other and excuse himself because he has bought a farm or a pair of oxen or because he is celebrating his own wedding?

Jesus has so constructed his story that one is almost forced to make a charge of unreasonableness against it: Can this householder be angry with these first invited guests for not coming when they have such important things to do? In other words, applying it to ourselves, must we be always reminding ourselves of the danger of using excuses that seem to us good and valid? Is there anyone who has never said: "I could never stand for that"?

In fact he could but did not want to, and so with these words reproduced exactly the sentiment expressed here in the Gospel: "Hold me excused," meaning that this excuse must be accepted even if it means a refusal to be called deeper into the mystery of the kingdom of God, for instance, through the silent suffering of injustice.

There are a thousand excuses which have been used by us poor sinners, cowardly and complacent earthlings. In this form or that, on this occasion or that, the kingdom of God passed us by and may well have found instead those whom we judge to be wicked, impious, sinful. There is something mysterious about the kingdom of God. We can only beg God to call us in such a way that our ears will be opened, that we will hear his call and come. We can only beg him to give us the strength of a brave and unselfish heart, so that we will not make excuses that, in the sight of God and in the pitiless light of his eternity, are no excuses at all.

In today's prayer we say: "May God grant us a holy fear and love of his name, since he does not deny his leadership to those who are grounded in both." If he gives us the pure and holy fear of rejecting his invitation to us, and the love that is stronger than all our self-seeking, then he will lead us to find the right road now and in the future and to attain to the eternal banquet of living happiness.

97 • Christ the King: There Stands the Truth*

Jn 18:33–37

Today we celebrate the feast of Christ the King, the sovereignty that belongs to Christ, the Godman, over every created thing, over human beings and their history, and especially over the human heart.

---

*Biblical Homilies, 88–90.

When we read today's Gospel, which is taken from the passion, it strikes us as an odd choice for this feast. Christ stands there before a proconsul of the Roman Empire, a ruler of this world, accused by both the religious and the political authorities of his nation, and is condemned to death. Scourged and crowned with thorns, he stands there, and Pilate says with a gesture of pity but full of disgust: Here is the man. And the man whose servants do not fight for him, who is handed over to a pagan power, is presented to us as our king. And when he announces the kingship with which today's Gospel has to do, he says to us: "Yes, I am a king. For this I was born, and for this I have come into the world, to bear witness to the truth. Everyone who is of the truth hears my voice."

Of course his kingship embraces more than we are told of in today's Gospel. But Jesus is king precisely because he has come to bear witness to the truth. What truth is meant here? We can only understand the verse if we realize exactly what St. John understands by truth. This Johannine truth has no plural, and is not the same thing as truth in the sense of a set of propositions. It means the antithesis of the world: For this I was born and have come into the world.

What is this world in St. John? Here we must be precise. It is not the world which provides a house for our life, which we like, where we feel at ease. The world in St. John is something different, whatever it may mean in other contexts. For him the world is darkness which shuts God out, which will not receive the light. The world is what is dying, what is perishing; the world is sin, anguish, and judgment.

Johannine truth is the antithesis of all this. It is the thing that is one, wholly compact, unchanging, reliable, the thing that comes from God, that he must disclose, whose coming still has a history in this dark world, that is only there if God reveals it. Truth with John is one of those ideas, like light and life, that say everything and embrace everything which is our salvation, which comes from God, which he reveals, which is only there if he takes us into this reality.

So John says in chapter 17 that the devil is not in the truth. We do not have the truth, we are in it. That is why verse 37 says that everyone who is of the truth hears his word. It is this truth we are dealing with here, this deed of God, this revealed reality. And Jesus says: Because I bear witness to this truth I am the king of this world.

Now to understand this saying we must bear in mind Jesus' conviction that he himself is this truth that has come into the world. Because he is there, because the Son — his quintessence — is there, because his sinlessness has appeared, because his love has revealed itself even unto the cross, therefore God's truth is there and bears witness to itself. He is king because he is this truth, brings it to us, attests it; because this divine truth undergoes that fate in the world which we read of here in the Gospel.

The self-revealing truth of God's faithfulness, of his saving mercy, stands there in the person of Jesus: accused, scourged, crowned with thorns, soon to be pierced by the lance of this world. There is God's truth and his reality, exposing itself to such a fate, bearing triumphant witness to itself by submitting to the humiliation which the lying world holds in store for it.

We say we are university people and deal with truth, and we inscribe our buildings with the text: "The truth shall make you free." If we do not understand this truth, this kingship of Christ, we may be clever, we may be scholars, but we are not in the truth which alone is light and salvation, life and eternity. We must understand this truth of the cross, this self-abasement unto death, if we would understand anything about truth and not just about the theses of the learned. And we must also bear witness to this truth by what we sacrifice and what we venture. We must want to be witnesses of Christ and subjects of his kingdom, and have the courage to accept abasement.

Right and truth are not necessarily what seem noble and glorious, what the world will accept and heartily applaud. No, the light shines in the darkness and the darkness has not comprehended it. In us too there is that darkness. That shrinking from the light is part of our own heart, and so Jesus the man of sorrows stands before us and says to us: "Everyone who is of the truth hears my voice."

Without making pronouncements about the church and her power, without thinking of the church in terms of party politics, could we not make room in our hearts and say: Disperse the darkness of my heart and allow your truth, which is humility, faithfulness, hoping against hope, blessed truth, to be in me, so that your power may triumph by drawing everything to you, as you hang there, lifted up upon the cross — even my poor heart.

98 • The End of the Church Year: The Christian and the Inevitable*

Mt 24:15–35

We are at the end of another year of the church's time and another year of our own. Therefore at this time we should give thanks to God —

---

*Biblical Homilies, 26–30.

and not just for this grace. For he has also kept us in the kingdom of his Son. He has preserved the light of faith for us and he has not taken his love from us, and so this year has passed to the glory of God. What seems over and done with has been laid up in the future for us by God's mercy.

It is no accident that the church reads in today's Gospel the passage that comes in the twenty-fourth chapter of St. Matthew, verses 15 to 35. It is part of the Lord's discourse about the future and last things. In a mysterious way the discourse mingles the end of the world with the destruction of Jerusalem. Whether this is to be ascribed to the author of the Gospel or to the Lord himself is not of fundamental importance. For in spite of it we can see clearly the distinction between the two.

Verses 15 to 28 deal with the destruction of Jerusalem and the ending and abolition of the part played by the old covenant in the history of salvation.

Verses 29 to 31 deal with the second coming. Earlier the ending of the Old Testament salvation history was spoken of, now the ending of salvation history as a whole is described. It is not strange that the two are surveyed at the same time. Not that there is not an immeasurable length of time between the two, but still they belong together in their inner theological sense.

In verses 32 to 35 questions about the timing of the first-named events are dealt with. And about the end of Jerusalem we are told: "This generation will not pass away till all these things take place." And the question about the timing of the absolute ending of the history of salvation is answered when we are told that no one knows it except the Father himself. So already from these two answers we can see that the Lord draws a distinction in time between two events. Generally these sayings about the last things are regarded as though the Lord were here showing his powers of prophecy.

But I think that these words (verses 15 to 28) can be looked at in another light. These words foretell times of historical catastrophe. But the prophecy is not made merely to show that the Lord knew all these things beforehand and that he too had some knowledge of them; rather he is giving rules by which a person is to conduct himself in times of catastrophe.

This too contains useful lessons for us. He is saying something obvious, which human beings nevertheless ignore. They should know the signs of the time, they should not turn their gaze from the historical situation, they should draw all the radical consequences; namely, that he who is in the field should turn back, that he who is outside the house should not go for his mantle.

Naturally not all of this applies to our case. But can we not also say that we should not deny the soundness of the earthly instinct? What then is our situation? Is it not true that everything is dark in our time, full of direst catastrophe with all the talk about war and destruction? And yet we look away from it all and try to arrange our lives again in domestic comfort.

We do not want to be those who have been told in what kind of times they live. We do not want to be the ones who draw the Christian consequences. Or are we people who remind ourselves that we must trust in God in this time of ours, that we must live from the deepest source of our being — in God and in our hope in him and in our love for him? If we saw our situation clearly, we would not fear catastrophe but we would be patient and resigned in doing and suffering whatever each day might bring us. We could do what has to be done in spite of the future: we could do our duty and whatever the present demands of us without heeding the threats of the future.

This question can be understood only by the individual who believes and has confidence that God is the future and he alone.

The second thing of which Jesus reminds us in this text is prayer: pray, he says, that your flight may not be on a sabbath. Once again the command is not applicable in its context. But the Lord is foretelling a future which he says will be full of terror and in which part of the history of God's love is swallowed up in God's anger.

He foresees inevitable catastrophes, he foresees them with resignation, and he tells us that prayer will still have its meaning there. How infinitely powerful he considers prayer to be, how realistically he appraises its effect! He says: These things will happen. He does not say: You can prevent them. But he does say: Pray, because that alone makes sense. We cannot estimate the possibilities of the future and we do not know what earthly results this prayer may achieve and what is denied to it by God's will. It is for us to trust in God and to pray also for an earthly future. If in an earthly situation a great deal is laid down as inevitable so that the Lord can say to us: This or that will happen and cannot be avoided — still we must listen to Christ's admonition in the Gospel, that prayer is still meaningful for history and even mandatory.

And the Lord says a third thing which follows from the others: For the sake of the elect those days will be shortened. For their sake: were it not for them, no one would be left alive in the whole area of this historical situation of which the Lord is speaking. He also tells us: There are elect. Here again he means: You cannot make a heaven on earth, you are not the representatives of a utopian dream future. But you are the blessing of God for this point of history and it will not be until the last judgment that we will be able to assess what the blessed of the

Father in heaven have meant for this point of history and for the ability to endure it.

How often will we too say: For the sake of the elect these days have been shortened. So the Lord tells us with sober realism that no matter what circumstances of catastrophe may exist, we can never have the right to believe only in the darkness of this earth. When they come, they must find us believing and loving, people who know that every trial is a pathway to God. God's word and God's power have laid on us the duty of becoming freely and willingly the elect for this our time. In the second century it was said: "For the sake of us Christians this era exists." The early Christians had this proud awareness of themselves. We have, must have, an equally strong belief in our mission.

If we are persevering in our faith, if we are the children of God and hence the children of his eternal election, then we should always pray with the hope that the days of darkness will be shortened. And always, whether we live or die, we must shine like stars in heaven. That is our duty, to act in the sight of God in heaven and of our historical age on earth in the way the Lord has told us to act: in sobriety and resolution, in prayer and in the awareness that we are the elect for whose sake the blessing and the promise have been given.

FEASTS OF
THE LORD AND
OF THE SAINTS

99 • Thomas Aquinas:
Monk, Theologian, and Mystic*

28 January

When we celebrate the feast of Thomas Aquinas, the patron of our theological studies, then this does not mean just a historical recollection about intellectual history. What we do is (or should be) a process that only a Christian in the community of saints can enact. Those in heaven are not dead. They are alive. They live in the fulfillment, that is, in the true reality that is powerful and present. Those who can be called by name are the true reality; they are what is to the point, more than theoretical principles and abstract maxims. That they exist; that they are with God; that they love us; that we love them; that in the eternal liturgy of heaven they intercede for us, their brothers and sisters; that the quintessence of their love, because they are eternally saved, remains established in the primordial source of all reality, out of which the history that came before and comes after them also constantly lives; that at the profoundest level they do not belong to the past, but are only past to the extent that they have hurried on before us into the future, which is still only coming upon us: *dominus cum sanctis suis* [the Lord, with his saints] — all that is more real than we are.

In comparison with this reality, the time-conditioned dimension of the saints, what is really past about them, is in itself meaningless. But we earth-bound people can only know what is eternal and heavenly about this present reality inasmuch as it is given to us in general, by looking back into their past, into their lives which — even though they have been transfigured — have entered into eternal validity with God. Otherwise we would contemplate the abstract dimension and miss the genuine reality: the concrete person, the unique and yet eternally valid reality, the one loving and praising, the one blessed and saved.

I would like to say three things today about Thomas: he was a monk; he was a theologian; he was a mystic.

---

*Korrespondenzblatt des PGV [Priestergebetsvereign im Theologischen Konvikte] (Canisianum) zu Innsbruck 86 (1952): 89–93. Trans. Frederick G. Lawrence, Boston College.

Thomas was a monk. This means: he was one who denied himself. This is a hard saying that stirs up scandal. One can say it differently: he was a person who let go of the smaller thing to discover the greater thing; who let go of the world in order to have God. But one does not remove the scandal that Christianity essentially is. The scandal that in this eon we cannot have everything all at once; that we have to decide; that a split runs through us; that we have to let go to find, have to die in order to live, have to become poor in order to possess; that only if we give up much in this world can we believe in God, who is everything.

Because he, the saint, knew this and wanted to realize it, he became a monk: one ordinary, poor, unmarried, insignificant, and fitted into the confines of a community. It would not have been necessary for him. His monastic vocation meant no "social climbing" for him; it was not the resentment of a life fallen too short, not the dishonest apotheosis of human unreliability. He was of such mature and powerful humanity, like his pugnacious brothers who were thoroughly confident that he would fit into their circle. He was not a religious fanatic who possessed no understanding and no vision, no sensitivity for the enchanting glory of this world.

In fact, he held this earthly reality much too much in esteem, and in contrast to the theology before him. And yet he became a monk. Because he wanted God and knew he was called to this path. Because he had the believing realism of Christians, who know that the disorder of sin is the order of this world, and the order of the cross (this squaring of the circle), which alone is the promise of eternity, is not there now: that he be able to take in all at once and totally into his heart in an unrestricted way God and world, heaven and earth, the blessedness of human beings and that of God as well.

He decided, and set himself apart from the world. He departed without despising what he left behind; he went, knowing that he would discover everything again. He gave it all up, truly soberly and nobly, but without any of that fanaticism of people who — in an uncreaturely way — would have the mad notion that they could only live in this world by renouncing it. Although he did not intend this, still, he knew that in each and every Christian, the path leading to the world comes to a point where the cross stands. And because he wanted to be a Christian, he held his vocation to be that of a monk (without imposing this vocation on others and without being misled from his own vocation by the contrasting stances of other Christians).

At the very least, a priest of the Western church, even if he is not a monk in the canonical sense, is a monk without needing to exist as a monk in this sense. He is a monk in a deeper theological sense. For he is unmarried, and a person who in the broader sense has entrusted the say over his own life to the bidding of his bishop; he is a person who can no longer live for himself. Whoever wants to be a priest should not deceive himself in this matter. He has to — no, he ought to deny himself. There are thousands of things, pretty, vital, healthy, joyful, and enjoyable, which in themselves are forbidden to no one, and as long as they do not entice us unquestioningly away from the destiny that comes from God.

But the priest has to be able to pass them by. Left behind, without any hatred or resentment, in such a way even that he does not let it be noticed that the renunciation really costs something, although it is only a costly renunciation for the precious act of faith, and not the rejection of what does not really matter. This Christian renunciation, this incarnation of faith, which priests have to live out in public as rendering testimony for the grace of the world, has to be practiced. They practice this in the sobriety of the everyday, in the confines of the seminary, in the dryness of scholastic study, in the honorableness of the renunciation of the dear little joys of life that are so fitting for those called to marriage, in the enduring of surroundings one did not seek out for oneself; in the obedience that soberly and resignedly even can give up one's own — perhaps even better — insight because, in the end, nothing depends on it but the self-assertion of our selfish ego, which is supposed to die. If we want to become priests, then we have to learn to become monks in a theological sense: the one in solitude with God, for whom God alone suffices, even though he has to do without the rest, until there will be a new heaven and a new earth.

Thomas was a theologian. He was a member of an order for which the priesthood and apostolic mission were no accidental appendages, but in which instead the monastic life was built on the priesthood. Therefore, at the same time he was a secular priest in a quite theological sense — a priest for the world — along with his monasticism. And that is why he wanted to be a theologian. Because he knew he was sent to proclaim the joyful message of the gospel, he knew he had to be a theologian. For one can only make known as life witness what one has oneself made the true center of one's own spiritual existence.

Contemplata aliis tradere [to hand the realities one has contemplated on to others]. *Contemplata.* But for authentic contemplation which is supposed to be transmitted by preaching and theology, theological study is normally the indispensable presupposition. And so Thomas was a theologian. A theologian who had no need of stirring up cheap emotions, and for whom it was always and everywhere a matter of reality. He was one who under certain circumstances renounced going to choir for the sake of study. He was one who studied and taught with the kind of objectivity that is the sign of the greater hearts, who love the subject matter more than their subjectively selective curiosity. He had the courage for clarity where clarity was possible, and the courage for mystery. He could distinguish in order to unify. He could muster the courage to contradict the traditional opinion (without being a sensationalist or making novelty the criterion of truth); he could even, whenever it had to be and no better solution could be found, stick with the traditional opinion, although he may have perceived its obscurity and its insufficiencies. He spoke in his theology about God and not about himself. He is prosaic even though he is a person who can also write poetry. He is a speculator and would trade Paris for John Chrysostom's *Commentary on the Gospel of Matthew.*

As a flexible theologian, he can also learn something new and revise his views. He thinks things out from the perspective of the whole, and yet he still (to the extent an individual can) has an understanding of and an immersion in the particular issue. He speaks his opinion without any stridency or acting as if his opponents were stupid. Rarely does any sharp word come from him. He is great in his theology, not because he would be the unique and all-encompassing theologian or considered himself as one, but because he thinks *in medio Ecclesiae* [in the midst of the church], and stays open for anything that moved the past and his own age.

One becoming a priest must be a theologian. Not a schoolboy who snakes his way through examinations because otherwise one won't get ordained. We don't need to be theological geniuses. But we have to be human beings and Christians who love theological knowledge, who are there for it with mind and heart. For us there can in the long run be no really spiritual life without an intellectual life. In theology we have to allow ourselves to be challenged as whole persons with all we are, with mind and heart, with the whole weight and seriousness of existence in our times, with all the experience of our lives. Not only what is written in schoolbooks belongs to theology.

But theology only can be pursued as preparation of the whole priestly person preaching later on, if there flows into it and there is elaborated in it whatever moves or what ought to have moved a cultivated person in the age in which God has placed us without our asking. Just as Thomas did, so must we. If the living God has spoken to us, and if theology is nothing but the exact listening to God's revelation with every means of grace and nature available to a person, then we have to be theologians, or we are not in general what we should be. For us, theology is simply a part, an inner moment of the work of salvation on our own existence and that of others. Not just an academic affair.

Thomas was a mystic. In this connection I do not mean that Thomas was ever in ecstasy, or a mystic of extraordinary phenomena, or a person who in the style of the Spanish mystics was almost a bit introvertedly absorbed by his own subjective experiences. There is little or nothing about this to note in his writings. But he was a mystic insofar as he knew about the *latens Deitas: Adoro te devote, latens Deitas* [Devoutly I adore you, hidden Deity]. About the hidden God of orienting silence, about the God beyond what even the holiest theology is capable of saying about him, about the God who is loved as unfathomable. He knew about this God not only in theory but in the experience of the heart, so much so that in the end this experience left him dumbstruck, so that finally *suspendit organa scriptionis: paleae sunt, quae scripsi, frater Reginalde* [He dropped his writing tool: "The things I have written are straw, Brother Reginald"].

In the end he abandoned even the house of life in which the light of theology burned, and slipped away into God's boundless wideness, "when it was also night." He stammered a little of the Canticle of Canticles about love, and went silent. Only in order to let God speak, before whom the human words Thomas spoke to us are shadows and images. How right and fitting that this came only at the end, and that this came at the end. It has to be so. But what is supposed to come at the end, not before, but then, must already be immersed from the beginning as the hidden core in that husk in which alone he can ripen: in the monastic renunciation of life and in the struggle of theology for the light of God, in the struggle for the light rewarded by the crucifying and blessed experience of the night of God, which is the unique rising of eternal light.

We are not yet at the end. Consequently, we should not strike the pose of having the final experience of the mature saint. But we can also practice in our lives the final experience in which the human being is struck dumb, and all the lights go out, so that only God speaks and his light alone illuminates. To practice. If we live in dark times; if theology is tedious and its fruit remains paltry; if faith has ever again laboriously to subdue the deep, unadmitted lack of faith on the part of mind and heart; if deception has to be repeatedly disillusioned; if we have done everything and still remain useless servants; if every empowerment is only once again the beginning of agony, as with the Son of man in the garden; if all enthusiasm is always transformed again into the irksome duty of everyday, then we are headed each hour along a straight path on which we, holding the empty straw of our lives and of our scholarship in our hands, obtain as beggars the eternal realm, which is then really and truly God himself. We practice if, like Thomas, we are monks and theologians, joyful people of honest renunciation and knowledge-hungry hearers of the word of God.

Thomas lives on. He may appear remote to us. But he is not. For the community of saints is near, and the apparent distance is mere illusion. The saints may appear as extinguished in the face of the dazzling radiance of God into which they have entered, as if they disappeared into the distance of lost centuries. But time ripens eternity and God is not a God of the dead but of the living. Whatever has returned to him lives. And so Thomas lives. We are asked whether our faith is alive, a faith in which Thomas also, among a thousand times a thousand of all the saints, can become a piece of our lives.

100 • Thomas Aquinas: Patron of Theological Studies*

28 January

When we are celebrating the feast of St. Thomas and, as is right and proper, are thinking about the patron of theological studies, and ponder on him in our meditation, perhaps the first thing we might consider for a moment is Catholic veneration of saints in general. It is a specifically Catholic thing within Western Christianity, and rightly so. But we must understand what this honor paid to saints really means. Then we shall realize that on this point we are not at all as Catholic nowadays as we perhaps think we are.

Veneration of the saints is not merely historical remembrance of a past which is important from a human and ecclesiastical point of view. It is a real and genuine relation to a living person who has attained perfect fulfillment and therefore remains present and powerful. Veneration of the saints is faith, hope, and love; it means being drawn into the kingdom of God in its perfect fulfillment which has already dawned.

And this is where probably all or at least most of us have difficulties. That does not attract us at all for our part today. Religion for us has become concentrated in a very remarkable way on God. The absolute mystery is unique, and religion for us has come to mean appearing before that abyss of radical infinity and incomprehensibility.

For us the dead are very dead and remote. The world of human beings has become fragile, strange, finite, and above all secular. As a result, the saints have evaporated, as it were, into past history, into

---

*Everyday Faith, 184–90.

what is dead and gone. And although we do not deny their permanent existence, they have been swallowed up, as it were, and have disappeared under the one word which still expresses our present-day religious feelings, God.

Now this is not Catholic at all. And the old-fashioned, traditional Catholic practice of venerating the saints is something which still stands ahead of us almost like the distant goal of our own religious development, as a higher future. It means real, genuine, living realization of the fact that they exist, that they are living and powerful, that they are nearer to us than ever, that they are not absorbed by God but are confirmed by him, that he is truly the God of the living and not of the dead, that far from being destroyed if we approach him, it is only then that we attain our own plenitude and independence, for the real God does not need to reduce us to nothing.

Veneration of the saints is not a sort of veiled polytheism nor a puerile kind of piety which has not yet properly realized the overwhelming power and awe-inspiring mystery of God. It is the maturity of the Christian relation to God. For that maturity is aware that the creature does not disappear in the abyss of God when it abandons itself to him, but only then becomes truly living and established. It can find the creature in God because that creature has entered into him but has not been swallowed up in him.

And to find the creature in God, in its perfection, in God's definitive self-communication to this creature, is a genuine religious act which belongs to the maturity of one's relation to God. And the feature of that creature which is found in this way in God, the feature which is honored and acknowledged as eternally valid, and lovingly embraced, is not an imaginary continued existence and activity interposing this perfected creature as a daimonion and intermediary entity between God and us. It is precisely the eternity of that creature's earthly time, the irrevocable validity of the life which it lived here.

In regard to Jesus, the anamnesis by which we turn back to his history as it was and the invocation of the exalted Lord are two elements of one and the same action. For if he had not been raised on high, his history would have disappeared into the oblivion of the past, and if he were not the historical figure who precisely as such has become definitive and possesses his unique life as his eternity, he could only be invoked on high as an idea or an empty name or as an incalculable, unknown power. So it is with the saints. Those whom we know from their history we invoke as transfigured, because their history is their fulfillment.

We shall mention a few facets of St. Thomas's rich spiritual personality which we know can be a blessed presence for us even now if we open ourselves to them by honoring them. We are well aware that the selection is arbitrary. Everyone is free to interpret the picture of the saint from another angle. But this being understood, we will say in the first place that Thomas is sober and objective. Anyone who has dipped into the Summa realizes this at once. His tone is quiet, reserved, almost dull; he is at no pains to find impressive words. He does not think it necessary to amplify the great topic he is writing about with high-sounding language, for that is quite impossible. He shows almost no preference for certain themes of theology rather than others. The whole is important to him and therefore every detail.

As a further consequence, he is not dazzled by detail; he always thinks on the basis of the whole and in relation to the whole. And because he does not seek to impress but is himself impressed by the reality he is talking about, because he himself is still meditating and assimilating that reality when he is attempting to convey it in words to others, it is almost as though he were speaking to himself, quietly, economically, patient with himself and the reality, courteous to his opponents, as far as he has any or could have, because of the inner breadth and capaciousness of his mind.

He is a systematic thinker who always considers the individual in the light of clearly grasped first principles. But because he is objective, the individual never becomes a mere occasion for declaiming about principles. It is really and lovingly taken into consideration, even if at first sight it does not seem to fit into the great guiding themes of his thought. This objective sobriety reveals or hides awe, reverence, a deeply moving virile modesty, longing for that eternal light which is still directly shining even now, and the awareness that even in theology knowledge is only really theological to the extent that it remains fully and permanently conscious of its own provisional and inadequate character. Thomas is objective and sober in his thought.

Thomas's theology is his spiritual life and his spiritual life is his theology. With him we do not yet find the horrible difference which is often to be observed in later theology, between theology and spiritual life. He thinks theology because he needs it in his spiritual life as its most essential condition, and he thinks theology in such a way that it can become really important for life in the concrete.

In his spiritual life (we may recall his eucharistic hymns) he never reverts to the elementary, as though he had never engaged in theology. He does not believe that the spiritual life necessarily best develops on the basis of simplicity in the sense of mental laziness and spiritual mediocrity. It would be unthinkable for him, the theological scholar, to nourish his spiritual life like some worthy monk, for example, on the third-rate fare of the pious fantasies of some nun or other who, no doubt in good faith, presented these vagaries as divine revelations.

And though we unfortunately for the most part only study his Summa, we should not forget that he himself regarded himself primarily as an interpreter of holy scripture and that that function was simultaneously a learned and a spiritual office for himself and others. He speaks and composes hymns which combine depth, seriousness, and simplicity and they are at once his theology and his spiritual life.

Because textbooks nowadays are very often too unspiritual and spiritual books too untheological, there is always too great a danger of theology becoming a disagreeable hurdle which has to be overcome on the way to the priesthood, and that later our spiritual life and preaching draw on the small derivative rivulets of second-hand pious literature and not from scripture and the lofty theology of the fathers and the great theologians. In Thomas, however, theology and spiritual life are still one.

Thomas is the mystic who adores the mystery which is beyond all possibility of expression. Thomas is not of the opinion that because theology deals with the infinite mystery of God it may talk imprecisely and vaguely. But he is not of the opinion either that the precise language of theology should give the impression that we have discovered the secret and caught the mystery of God in the subtle nets of theological concepts. Thomas knows that the highest precision and sober objectivity of true theology ultimately serve only one purpose: to force the individual out of the lucid clarity of his existence into the mystery of God, where he no longer grasps but is moved, where he no longer reasons but adores, where he does not master but is overpowered. Only where the theology of concepts and comprehension raises itself and is transformed into the theology of overwhelming incomprehensibility is it really theology. Otherwise it is at bottom merely human chatter, however correct it may be.

The *Adoro te devote, latens Deitas, quae sub his figuris vere latitas* [I adore you reverently, *deeply hidden* Godhead. This sign truly discloses your presence] must not always be recited lyrically; it must be the central principle of all theological thought and knowledge. This is so not only now but in eternity. Even there, where we know as we are known and see face to face, what is seen, loved, and praised will be the eternal mystery. It gives itself to the heart as mystery and does not become smaller thereby but even more incomprehensible and more consuming than when it only manifests itself in signs and likenesses.

It cannot therefore be otherwise in the *theologia viatorum* [theology of those on the way]. This must become instruction in the experience of mystery as such, a mystery which has, of course, become closely present. The idle, the mindless and heartless, the lovers of comfort must not say that all that theology has to say is but straw, as Thomas said it was. But if a person of mind and heart, industry and energy has not, like Thomas, become aware, even in theology, of the deadly yet vivifying sadness, that all theology has to say is but straw, then he hasn't done theology after the model of Thomas; it has been clever but not pneumatic, not a genuine Thomism.

Thomas is alive. He is living *his* life with God. In God it has become wholly pure and established in its utter purity. It has remained his own and yet open into God's infinity and into the incalculable range of other vocations. And therefore each can say with genuine faith: St. Thomas, pray for me.

101 • The Sword of Faith*

2 February, Presentation of the Lord, Lk 2:22–40

Now we celebrate the memorial of the death of Jesus, our Lord, as his homecoming into the mystery that is God, and as the event that signifies for our lives and our deaths the promise that our lives and our deaths are always wrapped in the love of God. We celebrate this memory of Christ on the day we recall the journey to the temple of his mother, who placed her son in unconditional faith at the beginning of his life under God's disposal. We celebrate this remembrance of the death of Jesus when this university [the Catholic University at Louvain] in the course of each year calls to mind its origins and its future, and tries to take to heart the law according to which it was inaugurated.

Especially because, as a Marian feast chosen for the day of the anniversary celebration of this university, this day directs our gaze to the figure of the holy Virgin as depicted in today's pericope. Here, too, just as earlier in Luke, it is the pattern for believers. But today's pericope states one thing about the destiny of faith in a twofold way: that this final event of the history of faith, which her child is, is a sign of contradiction

---

*Redevoeringen, uitgesproken ter gelegenheid van Onze-Lieve-Vroux-Lichtmis, patroon-feest van de Katholieke Universiteit te Leuven. Louvain, 1972, 3–6. Trans. Frederick G. Lawrence, Boston College.

that can bring about both downfall and rise; and that such a happening undeniably penetrates like a double-edged sword the center of her existence, of her heart, and therewith that of every believer.

Let it be said to us again in such a festive hour: this is the way faith is. It is like a sword that pierces and divides. In Matthew 10:34, Jesus himself says that he is come to bring not peace but the sword. Faith is the enduring of this sword, and so the refusal to think precipitously of being reconciled, the readiness to live on hope in the depths with the conflict which reaches down into the fragmentariness and unintegratability of our existence, to the point (that is to say) at which the human being can only do one thing: to despair or to entrust itself unconditionally to that mysterious unity and reconciliation we call God. Faith is many things: peace, liberty, trust, joy, and much more.

But it is also this: the enduring of the sword in the midst of our existence. This sword that splits the whole of life touches everyone. Whether they will it or not. But faith in the word revealing us to ourselves does not allow us to overlook this insurmountable split, and calls us to accept it, to endure it, to bear it throughout our lives in hope. Such persevering acceptance, of course, is only given where people are always working on reconciling these incompatibilities, on integrating the irreducibly plural; for otherwise they would be in truth the ones who would deny the sword or render it harmless in our existence.

Thus it would be a lack of faith were we precipitously to wish either eudaimonistically or stoically in our private existence for the forcible bringing about of the reconciled integration of our lives, instead of suffering, patiently and in confidence, change, the incalculable, the contradictory, and the unmanageable dimensions of our lives, without waiting with some self-projected recipe to be the masters of our history. It would be a lack of faith were we to suppose we could live in the social dimension out of some ready-made ideology of whatever stripe, that could make us into absolutely dominant planners of our future, instead of ever painstakingly, but in renewed hope, being pilgrims, who are always seeking the way to the absolute future afresh, in order then one day to receive it unearned and from grace.

It would be a lack of faith were we to suppose that in the dimension of scholarship and the sciences, we possessed a system into which, in a self-glorifying fashion, we could integrate by ourselves our precisely nonintegrated bits of partial knowledge into partnerly harmony. It would be a lack of faith to fancy in this domain to heal affliction with a bit of philosophical or theological talk or with some single, monomaniacal science that will rule over all, since every progress in knowledge in all regions increasingly always confronts the individual persons precisely with what they do not know and do not control, about which they once did not know that they do not know; while true theology is precisely the reflection upon the fact that there is only one who integrates the truths, reconciled in his one truth: God who has promised us that his truth will one day be our happiness, when we do not act as if we already possessed it through a future of our sciences conquerable by ourselves. It would be a lack of faith in this area were we not to want in prayer and praise to talk about what we cannot render submissive to ourselves through our scientific systems; and if we only wanted to speak about what is clear, in the sense that it confirms our thinking in its power instead of overwhelming it.

It is faith when we accept the blow of the sword in our existence: the sword of the question, that finds no answer anymore; the sword that all life in its pain ends in death; the sword that not even love dissolves all contradictions in this life; the sword of the leave takings, disappointments, aging, foolishness we undergo ourselves: innocently naive and guilty at the same time; the sword of bitternesses that foretell the coming of death like prophets. All these sevenfold swords pierce through our existence. And if we let this hold good for us with abandonment and hope, we believe. For then our pierced heart is open for the promise that is the unnamed God himself.

According to Revelation 1:16, the double-sided sharp sword goes forth from the Son of God, who was himself pierced as the one crucified by human beings (Jn 19:34; cf. Rv 1:7). If he is the pierced one, then our faith can be nowhere except in enduring of the sword that penetrates our existence. When we say faith, we also say precisely (not only) the hope in capitulation and capitulation in hope. Whoever hears this as an elegant play of dialectic would not have understood. That person would be sent to the place where, earlier or in the future, situations with no way out are encountered in his or her lives that of themselves strike one dumb and make one desperate. There he or she could learn what is meant here.

Wherever the struggle for justice on earth again gives rise to injustice; wherever love is betrayed and little children, the innocent ones, die; where the higher kind of spirit becomes idiotic, people behave worse to each other than wolves; and on and on. Shouldn't one perhaps say something in this hour? It is indeed the hour when we celebrate the death of the Lord, the death! And if anyone thinks more cheerfully about life, accepts life more joyfully, this is surely not forbidden him or her, if we presuppose that they acknowledge this high courage and this joy as grace, which promises faith that true eternal reconciliation is indeed on the way, and so we proclaim the death of the Lord until he comes.

If the dead live, if the downcast are not the ones whose lives have collapsed into emptiness, but rather the ones whose history has discovered its definitive character in God, then we have the right and the blessed duty to acknowledge ever anew their validity to all who come toward us in the sign of faith. And therewith to her whose soul the sword of pain pierced, according to today's pericope; who was blessed, according to the saying of the same Luke, because she believed (Lk 1:45). If we acknowledge the law of her life, the law of faith, then we call upon her. Then we cherish her as the patroness of this university.

We celebrate the memory of the death of the Lord. We hereby confess that we do not wish to avoid the sword of our existence wherever it encounters us, however it meets us, as if we had no hope. We celebrate the death of the Lord in a cultic solemnity, in the blessed bitterness of life within us, around us, and also in our science, the mortally uncompletable task. Rise, let us proclaim the death of the Lord, until he comes.

102 • For Us No Angel from Heaven*

Feast of St. Joseph, 19 March, Mt 1:18–21

We are going to consider the text of scripture which the church sets before us on this feast day. It consists of four verses from the first chapter of St. Matthew. We know it well, we have often read it and heard it read. The story is one which we remember from our Bible history class in school. And yet, though it is so familiar to us all, it poses us quite a problem, not in its deeper theological meaning but simply in what it tells about the outward events in the lives of St. Joseph and the Blessed Virgin. We shall not be able to solve the problem fully. The text will remain obscure. Yet it may be that this very obscurity, when we study it more closely, may suggest thoughts that will deepen the text for us and be of significance for our own lives.

Usually we take this story to mean that Joseph had some inkling of the fact that Mary was with child but was quite at a loss for an explanation, that Mary remained silent about what the angel had told her and about what had happened to her through the power of the Most High, and that Joseph in his perplexity could think of no other course than to send her away, though she was betrothed to him.

---

*Biblical Homilies, 9–12.

All this may well be correct, but we cannot say that it is the only possible interpretation of the text. For it begins by saying that Mary "was found to be with child of the Holy Spirit." This implies that Joseph knew that she had conceived by the Holy Spirit. How could he have come to know this? We must conclude that he can only have learned it from Mary and we ask why in that case she did not tell him also about the heavenly apparition and about God's gracious action in her regard. Why should she, the calm and devout servant of God, fail to tell him, her betrothed, about these things?

Did she think, could she have thought, that Joseph could have learned them from some other source? Why should she assume without any evidence that Joseph too had received a message from heaven, when it would be so much simpler for her to tell him? And if Joseph knew of the miraculous favor bestowed on his bride, how could he ever have thought of putting her away privately?

Conversely we can ask: If Joseph did not know that her child had been conceived miraculously, how could he, described here as a "just man," that is to say, a law-abiding man, have contemplated putting her away privately? He was bound in accordance with the law as set down in the twenty-second chapter of Deuteronomy to proceed against her as against an adulteress. And if we answer: no, he must have known, it says here in the text too that he knew, why then should he have wanted to put her away at all?

Could it have been perhaps for this reason that he felt himself, was bound to feel himself, somehow shut out from this mystery which had come to pass between Mary and heaven? Since she had now been claimed by someone higher, indeed by God himself, we may well suppose that Joseph felt he could have no further claim of any kind upon her and resolved, therefore, to put her away privately.

If we interpret the text in this way — and it is at least a possible interpretation of an obscure and difficult text — then the message that Joseph received from heaven, the angel that appeared to him in a dream, takes on a new and different light. The angel does not merely tell Joseph that Mary has conceived her child through the power of God — though this fact, which Joseph already knew from Mary, is confirmed by the apparition — but has as his principal message: "Do not fear to take Mary your wife." Be a father to this child, heaven is saying, fulfill the duties of a father toward this child which heaven has sent to your bride. Protect, watch over, love, shield, take care of this child. This duty is laid on Joseph by God himself.

We can say, therefore, that he is the foster-father and guardian of the child, not just because his wedded bride has conceived a child from heaven, but because God himself wished him to take the place of a father to the Son of God who has come to save the world. This is why Joseph is told to give a name to the child, this is why Joseph is addressed as Son of David, since Jesus himself will be known and acknowledged as the son of David precisely because his earthly father is a son of David stemming from that royal lineage.

Thus from our reading of this text we can see heaven entrusting to the care of Joseph the savior of the world. Through this message from above Joseph is drawn into the great, public, official story of salvation. He acts no longer in the purely private capacity of bridegroom and later husband of Mary, but plays an official role in the salvation story. He is the guardian and protector of the Son of God, directly appointed to that office, and not just drifting into this relationship with the divine child through the accident of his betrothal to Mary.

We too are often called to be guardians of the holy one in ourselves, in our lives, in our work. At first sight, our everyday affairs may seem to have nothing to do with the history of the kingdom of God and the salvation of the world. We may seem to be concerned with nothing more than the tissue of relationships that makes up our lives, our friendships, our work. But even here we are being called upon to be the guardians of something holy, something great, God's grace in us and about us. Is there anyone who has not some of God's children entrusted to his or her care: in the home, in the school, in the neighborhood?

For us no angel from heaven appears, no dream apparition bids us: Take the child to yourself. And yet it seems as though through purely earthly incidents we are made responsible for what is heavenly and divine, for God's grace in our own hearts and in our earthly surroundings. In all these the Son of God who became man continues his life, and we are all asked whether the task of guarding this Son of God whom we meet in others will find us as true as Joseph, of whom it is said: he was faithful, he took the child and his mother to himself, he spent his whole life guarding the child so that he might become in truth the savior and the life of the world.

103 • The Feast of St. Joseph*

19 March

The Catholic church today celebrates the feast of her patron, her heavenly protector. We can understand such a feast only if we believe

---

*The Eternal Year, 73–78.

in the communion of saints, if we know by faith that God is not a God of the dead, but a God of the living, if we confess that whoever has died in God's grace lives with God and precisely for that reason is close to us, and if we are convinced that these citizens of heaven intercede for their brothers and sisters on earth in the eternal liturgy of heaven.

The meaning of such a feast can be grasped only if we believe that after death all the events of this earthly life are not simply gone and past, over and done with forever, but that they are preparatory steps that belong to us for eternity, that belong to us as our living future. For our mortality does not change to eternity in an instant; rather, it is slowly transformed into life.

The blessed men and women with whom we have fellowship in the communion of saints are not pale shadows. Rather, they have brought over into the eternal life of God the fruits of their earthly life, and thus have brought with them their own personal uniqueness.

Their God even calls them by name in the one today of eternity. They are ever the same as they were in the unique history of their own lives. We single out one individual from among them to honor him as our heavenly protector and intercessor, because his own individuality means something unique and irreplaceable to us. We mean that between him and us there exists a specific rapport that makes him a special blessing for us and assigns a special duty to us, if we are to be worthy of his protection.

From this point of view, is it possible to think that Joseph, the spouse of the Blessed Virgin and foster father of our Lord, is particularly suited to be a patron of a twentieth-century person? Is it possible to think that anyone living today will be able to see himself reflected in Joseph? Are there not people today who, if they are true to their character as willed by God, are a people of small means, of hard work, of only a few words, of loyalty of heart and simple sincerity?

Certainly every Christian and every Christian nation are charged with the entire fullness of Christian perfection as a duty that is never completed. But every nation and every human being have, so to speak, their own door, their own approach, through which they alone can come nearer to the fullness of Christianity. Not all of us will find access to the boundless vistas of God's world through the great gate of surging rapture and burning ardor. Some must go through the small gate of quiet loyalty and the ordinary, exact performance of duty. And it is this fact, I am inclined to think, that can help us to discover a rapport between earth and heaven, between Christians today and their heavenly intercessor.

The pages of the Bible tell us little about Joseph. But they tell us enough to know something of our heavenly patron. Not a single word of his has been recorded for us. He pondered, yes; that is expressly attested to. But he spoke little, so little that these words did not have to be transmitted to posterity. We know that he was a descendant of the noble lineage of David, the greatest in his nation's history. But that was the past that the present, in its sober poverty, had yet to make perceptible. This present, however, was the hard life of one insignificant carpenter in a tiny village in one corner of the world. For the poor this present meant paying taxes and standing in line.

It was the destiny of the "displaced person," who had to seek scanty shelter among strangers, until the political situation again permitted a return to his homeland, the homeland that he must have loved, since he renounced living in the neighborhood of the capital city and stayed in the "province" country of Galilee. He lived very inconspicuously in his Nazareth, so that the life of his family furnished no spectacular background for the public appearance of Jesus (Lk 4:22). However, this humble routine of the life of an insignificant man concealed something else: the silent performance of duty.

Three times the scripture says of Joseph: "He rose up." He rose up to carry out God's will as he perceived it in his conscience, a conscience that was so alert that it perceived the message of the angel even in sleep, although that message called him to a path of duty that he himself neither devised nor expected.

According to the witness of the Bible, this insignificant man's humble routine concealed a further object of value: righteousness. Joseph was a just man, the Bible says, a man who regulated his life according to the word and law of God. Not only when this law suited his desires, but always and at all times, even when it was hard, and when the law judged to his disadvantage that his neighbor was right. He was righteous in that he was impartial, tactful, and respectful of Mary's individuality and even of that which he could not understand in her.

This loyalty to duty and impartial righteousness, which is a manly form of love, also lived in him with respect to God his Father. He was a devout man and he was manly in his devotion. For him the service of God was not a matter of pious feelings that come and go, but a matter of humble loyalty that really served God and not his own pious ego. As Luke says: "Every year he went to Jerusalem for the Passover feast, according to the custom." Now we can tell what was the most important element in the life of this man whose everyday life was a life of duty, of righteousness, and of manly devotion: this life was given the charge of protecting in a fatherly way the savior of the world.

He received into his family the one who came to redeem his nation from their sin, one to whom he himself gave the name of Jesus, a name which means "Yahweh is salvation." Silent and loyal, he served the eternal Word of the Father, the Word who had become a child of this world. And people called their redeemer the son of a carpenter. When the eternal Word was audible in the world in the message of the Gospels, Joseph, having quietly done his duty, went away without any notice on the part of this world.

But the life of this insignificant man did have significance; it had one meaning that, in the long run, counts in each person's life: God and his incarnate grace. To him it could be said: "Good and faithful servant, enter into the joy of your Lord." Who can doubt that this man is a good patron for us? This man of humble, everyday routine, this man of silent performance of duty, of honest righteousness and of manly piety, this man who was charged with protecting the grace of God in its embodied life?

Contemporary Christians might find their way back to what is best in them if the individuality of this man, their patron, were again producing more stature in them. Granted, a nation must have greatness of spirit and pioneers who will lead it toward new goals. Just as much, if not more so, however, a nation needs men and women of lifelong performance of duty, of clearheaded loyalty, of discipline of heart and body. A nation needs men and women who know that true greatness is achieved only in selfless service to the greater and holy duty that is imposed upon each life; human beings of genuine reverence, conquerors of themselves, who hear the word of God and carry out the inflexible decrees of conscience. It needs men and women who through their lives bear the childlike, defenseless grace of God past all those who, like Herod, attempt to kill this grace. A nation needs men and women who do not lose confidence in God's grace, even when they have to seek it as lost, as Joseph once sought the divine child. Such individuals are urgently needed in every situation and in every class.

We have a good patron, who is suitable for everyone. For he is a patron of the poor, a patron of workers, a patron of exiles, a model for worshipers, an exemplar of the pure discipline of the heart, a prototype of fathers who protect in their children the Son of the Father. Joseph, who himself experienced death, is also the patron of the dying, standing at our bedside. We have inherited from our Father a good patron. But the question put to us is whether we remain worthy of this inheritance, whether we preserve and increase the mysterious rapport between us and our heavenly intercessor.

Joseph lives. He may seem far away from us, but he is not. For the communion of saints is near and the seeming distance is only appearance. The saints may seem eclipsed by the dazzling brightness of the eternal God, into which they have entered, like those who have vanished into the distance of lost centuries. God, however, is not a God of the dead, but of the living. He is the God of those who live forever in heaven, where they reap the fruits of their life on earth, the life that only seems to be past, over and done with forever. Their earthly life bore *eternal* fruit, and they have planted that fruit in the true soil of life, out of which all generations live.

And so Joseph lives. He is our patron. We, however, will experience the blessing of his protection if we, with God's grace, open our heart and our life to his spirit and the quiet power of his intercession.

104 • A Man Is Born*

24 June, Feast of the Nativity of St. John the Baptist, Lk 1:57–68

What story is told in today's Gospel? A man is born. A mother rejoices. And the people around, parents, relations, friends, notice what happens in the case of every person and every birth because this birth is surrounded by strange circumstances which force them to notice more clearly what takes place every time someone is born.

In the first place we are told that these friends and relations rejoiced because God had shown his favor to this mother and hence also to this child. It is a favor when God calls a human person into being, it is an act of grace, of love, of kindness, of unspeakable mercy. But is this all that obvious? Is our experience of ourselves, of our life, of our fortunes, of our reputation, so clearly such that we can praise and thank God for conferring a favor upon us? And yet it is so.

He has called us into existence, an existence that is everlasting. He has called us into his grace and this grace is he himself and his own eternal life. This existence, when we might never have existed, this eternity, behind which lies empty nothingness, this life with God and in his sight, which is given to the soul in grace and in glory, all this is a favor because it is the blessedness of God himself; and everything else in our lives, anything that may threaten this existence of ours, is transient and temporary, a test and a trial. What is given to us through human birth is a favor from God. Can we look on this life, with all its mystery, in this way and accept it day by day from the hands of God? Let us summon all the strength and all the courage at our command and say with joy: It is a favor!

Biblical Homilies, 35–37.

The second thing which strikes us in this Gospel is the fact mentioned in the text that all around were seized with fear and anxiety on the occasion of this birth. But this fear is not a phobia, not a panicky and servile anxiety from which the Christian should be free since she is in the state of love and need not, as St. John says, be afraid; the fear here spoken of is the fear of reverence in face of the fact of human existence. And all these people, who had witnessed the expectation of this child and had lived through the strange occurrences, thought: there is a mystery about this life.

He who conferred this favor is the infinite God with all his unfathomable decrees and ordinances. He calls this man into being and no one can tell at the outset all that may be bound up with this call. Behind these lesser events they see the infinite mystery of God himself beginning to work through this incipient life, mysterious and inscrutable — and they are afraid. And still this fear is the fear of reverence, without which all human life and experience is a flat and empty commonplace. We are forever frantically trying to run away from this fear and find somewhere calmer, quieter, and more comfortable, where this fear of God can no longer touch our lives. But whenever the course of our lives and divine decrees and ordinances teach us fear, then that fear is the fear of God and we are assured that it is blessed and that God loves and is faithful to those who fear him.

The third thing that strikes us in this Gospel comes at the end. The father thanks God and praises him, saying: Blessed be the Lord God of Israel, for he has visited and redeemed his people. He utters a universal praise of all God's salvation history and includes the life of this child in his Benedictus canticle, this panoramic view of all that God has done for the salvation of humankind through his people and for all peoples.

He gives thanks because this child, whom he has earlier addressed directly in the Benedictus, will be the precursor of the Lord who will prepare his way and make ready a perfect people for his God. This is something that can be said of everyone in his own way, of every one of us. A canticle could be sung for our lives, a hymn of thanksgiving, for we too belong to this chosen people whom God has called to follow his redeemer and to prepare a way before him into that future time which is always his. This is what the holy eucharist, the holy prayer of thanksgiving of Christians, should say about our lives each Sunday.

There is a God, he has called us into existence without asking our leave, because he wished to confer this favor upon us. Ever since then the fearful and yet blessed mystery of God has ruled over the soul whom he has so called and thereby made himself to be the mystery of our lives. But over and over again and at all times we can say: Praised be God who has called us into fellowship with his Son, who has loved us and saved us and called us into his unspeakable light, who has made us to be among his followers, who himself as God has walked the pathways of our life, so that we could follow him and go before him to prepare his way, until the favor of God reveals itself as the ultimate meaning of the mystery of our life, until we can sing that eternal hymn of thanksgiving that shall not cease forever.

105 • Ignatius of Loyola*

31 July

The theme of these reflections is related to the eve of the feast of St. Ignatius of Loyola, and in passing to this saint, whom — at least earlier — we called our holy father Ignatius, especially since it cannot indeed be claimed that we talk about him too much, or that his figure stands forth with particular clarity in the consciousness of us Jesuits today. Granted that the narrower theme might be selected somewhat arbitrarily, and that there would be many more important things to say about Ignatius than I can do. I also take it for granted that if I am to avoid saying only the obvious today, then I can only present somewhat subjective opinions and leave the final judgment to the audience. What eventually stands out as the outcome from these reflections for the interior religious attitudes of individuals, for their spirituality, also must be for the most part left to the meditation of each individual.

Before I come to the more focused objective of my reflections, for which I know no name, and, to be sure, for reasons that still have to be made clear, let me preface my meditation with a preparatory consideration whose significance here and now will also come out later on. I mean that it must actually be obvious in any Christian theology and interpretation of life that every human and Christian life totally shatters. Moreover, the acceptance of this shattering is a salvific dying with the crucified Christ and takes place in God's incomprehensibility. If Jesus is the authentic and final norm of our lives, there can actually be no doubt about this statement.

If life itself is a *prolixitas mortis* (a permanent dying), then indeed this shattering is, however, not just an event at the moment of medical exitus, but something that spreads diffusely over an entire life and

---

*Delivered to the Jesuits at Innsbruck on 31 July 1978. Previously unpublished. From the Karl-Rahner-Arkiv, Innsbruck. Trans. Frederick G. Lawrence, Boston College.

leaves its imprint upon it; it is something that, in the unity of its vital moments and their reciprocal circumincession, cannot occur alone just in a private sector of pure interiority; but it mortally affects also the lifework and public mission of a person, just as was true for Jesus. This shattering will not be abolished from the life and the existential consciousness of a person by the fact that this person does not talk about it, or reflect on it, but accepts it with an almost cheerful nonchalance, so that it can look as if this life is simply successful and only limited to a certain extent externally by a biological death.

If this is the case, however, then, in terms of a really Christian interpretation, one would actually have to inquire, for example, about the life of an order's founder — where and how his life and the founding of the order itself let it be noticed that they are also a shattering/dying along with Jesus. Where is that done in the lives of the founders of orders? Perhaps with Francis of Assisi a little bit. But otherwise? But in regard to Ignatius? I wouldn't know where. Just as there was and there still is today a triumphalistic ecclesiology, there is also a triumphalistic hagiography. Both are profoundly unchristian, because we have to proclaim Jesus crucified who, for the gentiles and the Jews (who are always ourselves), is and remains foolishness and a scandal.

I will break off this consideration now and recount a couple of facts from the life of Ignatius that are so seldom regarded and appreciated from a common perspective that I cannot offer a common term intelligible to everyone that embraces the facts I am focusing on, only thus making them actually understandable. Were I to say that these facts and living axioms of Ignatius come together united in the concept of the *discipleship* of the poor and humble Jesus, then this would surely be right, and would stay within the explicit Ignatian terminology; but this concept would still be so vague, pious, and trite, and would illumine too little what is most characteristic about Ignatian spirituality, since all the various Christian spiritualities intend to be discipleship of Christ.

If I say *marginality*, then I employ a concept of our day from a secularized mentality, which disregards the properly religious dimension of what I am talking about, and so it is really improperly appropriated for this job. But let us pay no attention to this terminological difficulty and apply the term to the facts and life axioms of Ignatius as we mean them here, and seek to understand them in their inner, scarcely reflected-upon unity.

It is known, first, that from his conversion until at least the period of the founding and leading of the order, Ignatius wanted and actually did live as radically poor, with the radicality and uncompromisingness of a Francis of Assisi. To see this, one has only to read his quasi-autobiography, *A Pilgrim's Journey,* and to take seriously the inner tendency of his *Spiritual Exercises.*

It is of course known as well that he wanted to carry over this radical poverty into his order, and honestly troubled himself in writing the *Constitutions* to bring this radical poverty into his order and to anchor it legally, and to protect it to the extent that, according to his judgment, it was compatible with the rest of the tasks and goals of his order. That he failed in legally and practically institutionalizing *that* radical poverty in his order which he practiced in a radical way for twenty years, seems to be an historical fact, however one may even justify it rationally, or declare it inevitable; and however much, against his own intentions, he unreflectively let the first, yet decisive step be taken that crossed over the boundary between his own Franciscan enthusiasm for poverty and the accommodatingly rational "poverty" familiar to us.

All this may remain open; the fact that Ignatius himself practiced a completely different, really sociological and economic poverty, and tried to see that it be realized in his order; the fact that the latter remained unrealized should be seen and not disputed. And why should not a portion of that shattering be seen in this second fact, which indeed has to be reckoned with in a really Christian and not triumphalistic hagiography?

But I think there is something else in Ignatius that has a rare and unnoticed affinity with this will to poverty. He does not want members of his order to take on tasks or have any posts that amount to power positions in the church. He does not want any religious habits which, even in the case of the Franciscans, became a status symbol for an entirely distinct, privileged place in church and society. Members of his order were supposed to move about (of course "honestly") like any number of clerics of that time, which did not bestow on them precisely that social status that quite recently the dignified pastor in his cassock had.

Street preaching to neglected youth was so important to him that he let it be praised in his formula of profession; in contrast to ecclesiastical practice simply taken for granted at that time, he did not at all hurry to the solemn vows of profession which alone constituted one a member of an order for the mentality of his time and for canon law, too. Simple, easy, juridically removable vows, which, from the point of view of canon law at the time, were indistinguishable from private vows, satisfied him for reception into his company, so that it only became clear with Pope Gregory XIII that also simple vows were sufficient for the constitution of life in an order, although no one can say very exactly and with sober objectivity by what the three kinds of vows thus given are supposed to be distinguished outside the purely canonical realm.

I do not know if one should not tell and consider still other dimensions that are actually pertinent here. Even in this context, one could perhaps think about Ignatius's rejection of common prayer together in choir and of other typical institutions of religious orders at that time. This was a rejection that presented itself to him and his community for the sensibility of the church at that time the way the more recent worker-priests were perceived by the official church of Pope Pius XII. One could dwell on Ignatius's love of Jews, which was as shocking for the Spain of that day as in our day would be the effect in clerical Bavaria of one who does not vote for the Christian Socialists' (CSU) party.

At any rate all these Ignatian facts and axioms, as utterly disparate as they might at first appear, point for me in a common direction. How should one name this? For lack of a better term, I would like to call the common element running through all these characteristics "a will to marginality," even though the ultimate motivation for this basic Ignatian orientation, which of course consists in the will of the unconditional discipleship of Jesus, is not made explicit in this expression. To show in terms of biblical theology that such a marginality in relation to society, both profane and ecclesiastical, is really *one* legitimate element of the discipleship of Jesus, if not always and everywhere binding everyone, would be in itself both needed and rewarding. Indeed it cannot be denied that Jesus achieved the world's redemption in a life and a death which brought him beyond all marginalization into a mortal conflict with bourgeois and religious authority. One will not want to affirm that this aspect of his life could not also be a theme of his discipleship. From this perspective surely, marginality as a possible moment of the discipleship of Jesus could be grounded in terms of biblical theology.

But what does this marginality in itself denote more exactly, if it should be a part of a possible discipleship of Jesus? If we say it ought to imitate the poor and humble Jesus, then we have certainly found a correct answer; but it is not very clear and suggestive, because we do not know so well what poverty and humility as marks of the discipleship of Jesus seriously can mean in our time.

In an economic and social context, poverty is certainly a word that is intelligible. It refers to determinate levels of the society as a whole, whose marginality grounds and explains, makes intelligible, why such "have-nots" otherwise share either in a limited measure or not at all in the rest of the cultural possibilities of a society. But then this gives rise to the question whether the "poverty" that we practice as members of an order has anything to do with this real poverty in the profane sense. Or whether the rule of a common treasury in the order, called poverty, has anything to do with poverty in the normal sense of the term.

The thirty-second General Congregation tried to maintain a real

connection between the two conceptions of poverty, as has the leg-
islation of every century since the founding of our order. It contended
that the poverty of the order was at least in some part poverty in the
profane sense. But in this respect not much is gained, and it is even
unclear what such a real poverty in an order would look like, if this
order is supposed to accomplish the tasks it rightly sets for itself. The
problem of the poor Franciscans who should study, and for this need
a warm room, quiet, and books, is still not solved.

At any rate, one would have to say that the really practical poverty
in bourgeois society does not exactly marginalize us Jesuits of today
and turn us into poor beggars, as Ignatius practiced it for at least twenty
years. His disciples of today have in this respect precious little similarity
to the Grayrobes of Alcalá.

What then is meant by humility also stays quite obscure, if one does
not make of it just an interior attitude which finally both profane and
ecclesiastical prelates also must possess, if they want to go to heaven.
So it cannot be rejected simply out of hand that poverty and humility, if
they are not supposed to be postulates of an abstract ethics of conviction, may be elucidated better precisely in terms of a social marginality,
than to seek to reverse the procedure and do the opposite.

But to keep from getting lost in the morass of problems from which
we cannot find our way out anymore, in what follows, we try to reflect
only upon marginality in ecclesiastical and not in profane society. The
phenomena from which we took our departure in the case of Ignatius
clearly indicate a marginality in the church. But limiting ourselves in
this way, we can avoid the difficult, but still practically important question whether in general there can be voluntary marginality in profane
society; or whether it pertains to the essence of this marginality to be
fatefully imposed and to be the object of a fight against it instead of a
loving choice.

What can marginality mean in a sociology of the church, and in an
ecclesiological-theological sense? Ignatius plainly strove for something
like an answer to this. This is seen from the fact that a Melchior Cano —
a great theologian, if not the greatest in Ignatius's time — explained that
what Ignatius was making and organizing was not an ecclesiastical religious order. Speculatively, and for his age, perhaps Cano was right,
and only did not argue correctly because our order, consciously or
unreflectively, and relatively quickly, also had been transformed into
a religious order in the traditional sense. Indeed, already in 1540, Ignatius experienced the fulfillment of his glowing wish to see the pope
approve his community.

But when one presupposes from the outset, without thinking, that
the categories of orders and approbation customary today suffice for

a precisely correct description, in terms of a sociology of the church and of an ecclesiology, of the procedures of 1540, then one can be asked: Is this approbation the recognition of a group of men formed from below by the free inspiration of the Spirit, which consciously and reflectively desires to form a marginal group in the church — for the sake of the freedom of the Spirit — along with every other apostolic goal, and which the church does not reject? Or does such an approbation necessarily and intentionally constitute an order, which assumes a completely defined position in the center of the church, in the structure of the official church as such, in its official clergy, and not on its margins, even if the subject of this founding of the order was the original, enthusiastic, marginal group?

How Ignatius actually perceived it is hard to say with certainty. Surely he did not intend that in any authentic sense his community be changed in its inner nature by papal approval. His brothers were supposed to issue forth from the lone encounter with God of the most immediate kind from the *Exercises*. He thought they could be truly poor and remain such. But perhaps such poverty cannot be lived in a strictly and juridically organized Order, even if it sought to bring about this artificial effect in a desperately clever synthesis? He forbade his brothers higher functions in the official church as such. He reduced the group spirituality of his community by dismantling many then taken-for-granted monastic elements to a minimum, namely, to what is more or less genuinely indispensable for all Christians even if they are not members of an order. *That* is what Ignatius wanted to know was approved as possible, meaningful, and allowed in the church. Is an order in the old sense thereby actually founded?

When I say "in the old sense," then I naturally do not deny to Franciscans the belief that already at the founding of their order the problem was already there. I also have nothing against anyone's being of the opinion that the problem was there in all the great orders that emerged from a charismatic movement from below; that the factually enacted massive institutionalization is also a bit of a contradiction, indeed, the shattering of this charismatic freedom and undefinability that was originally given with what we have called the marginality of such a group.

However that may be, the final result of this approbation which Ignatius, as we said, desired and implemented, is the becoming of an order which, as a matter of fact, at least for the most part had given up the very marginality about which we have been speaking. We have a completely established position in the hierarchical structure of the church; we belong to the officeholders of the church; taken exactly and treated realistically, this was far beyond the simple fact that we are and are supposed to be an order of priests, of which Paul VI has quite recently reminded us, even though this does not actually follow simply and obviously from our charismatic origins as demonstrated by the charismatically apostolic activity of Ignatius from his conversion down to his late ordination to the priesthood, which surely excited the mistrust of the official church, and brought him several times into the prison of the Inquisition.

We have an extraordinarily differentiated rule for the order. We are supervised and regulated today more than ever since our beginnings by ecclesiastical authority; more dependent on bishops and their authority, as is shown by the canon law outline of the new universal law concerning orders; threatened with becoming even more amalgamated. Obviously and undeniably, we carry the burden of our own history and of tasks taken on earlier, by which a perhaps not always problem-free past is a law of our future.

We are not the poor ones as Ignatius envisioned them, but rather the largely economically secure ones that in an ultimately problematic bourgeois style of life move about as ones who take it for granted; we are those who only too easily are tempted to think we are already poor if we deliver each month to our patient and considerate bureaucracy in the order our tabulated accounts about our assignments, and don't complain too loudly about the fact that too often of an evening there is only bland sausage to eat.

Normally we do not become bishops and cardinals. But we instinctively feel ourselves on the side of the official church, and of the clergy as inevitably also a sociological group and caste as well. The relative freedom of the spiritual life of the order, without too much collective activity, for us is all too easily in danger of being the temptation to lead *no* spiritual life at all because, in contradiction to the meaning of our free marginality, we are also of the opinion with the "nonmarginalized" that whatever is not organized and legally institutionalized also cannot be a sacred obligation of the free Spirit.

I think there still prevails among us — if perhaps more so in the former years during the pian era of the papacy — the mentality according to which the first and last mark of the Jesuit spirit is the unconditional identification with the concreteness of the official church and its mind-sets and tendencies, without further recourse to the Spirit of Jesus and the freedom of the Christian person, who also has to serve both office and institution.

I think there still lives among us too much the concealed but effective assumption that the order is only vital and historically viable if it possesses *the* position of power in the church and in the world beyond it; or again wins back the position it possessed in the seventeenth and eighteenth centuries or also, somewhat attenuated, in the pian epoch of the last century.

One could also narrate many other indications that make manifest how out of a free charismatic group from below with a positively intended marginality in the church, and with a minimum of institutionalization (which minimum — paradoxically — Ignatius wanted defended through *its* institutionalization and approved by the church, in order to be marginal) an order has largely come into being whose institutions in great part reduce the intended originality and implement somehow the law of their own gravity. But let this suffice. Only for the older members I might refer to the fact that in regard to times for prayer and our clothes, and so forth, the leadership of the order itself over twenty years ago sought with exasperated energy to impose norms that were not only against Ignatius's spirit, but also against his letter.

I have the impression that even now I have still spoken too unclearly about marginality, as I mean it here; I have also not made it clear how it is connected with the ultimately moving spirit of Ignatius, with its immediacy-to-God and its characteristic discipleship of Jesus; it is also not exactly clear what this manifold-encompassing marginality is and whence it comes. Perhaps one could say about this in addition: Whoever experiences the immediacy of the unique absoluteness of God, and whoever, on this account, lives or wants to live an ultimate indifference in relation to all the various realities distinct from God, of which no one except Jesus and his death into the absoluteness of God has an irrevocable synthesis of an unconditional kind with God, such a person actually has no absolutely binding place in this world or also in the church to which he or she should be appointed unconditionally and irrevocably as the only possible locus of encounter with God. Such a person is marginal and would like for this last religious homelessness (except in the death of Jesus) in his or her existence in the church, which naturally remains, to be lived out as clearly as possible and be manifest. But, as already mentioned, I cannot talk further now about this existential and ecclesiological kind of marginality.

At the start of our reflections we said that the founding of an order, if it is really supposed to be a primordially Christian event in discipleship and in union with Jesus, must also be a sharing in his cross and death and in the shattering that goes with it. We said that being crucified, which pertains to the nature of an order, cannot consist just in external persecution, but has to be an indispensable element of its *innermost* essence.

Incidentally, when at La Storta Ignatius was present before Jesus bearing his cross, he could well have thought that this could signify his entirely real crucifixion in papal Rome.

In accord with God's will in this world, the founding of an order is undeniably and necessarily also a putting on of the Spirit of freedom and of dislocated, blessed lostness in God himself as regards the cross of institutions that on the one hand let this Spirit be preserved and become effective, incarnating it in the flesh of history and of real society; and on the other they narrow it and continually threaten it mortally; and they promote the Spirit, but cannot of themselves bestow the Spirit; and they ever evoke the killing misunderstanding that the Spirit blows in infinite freedom, when the letter is already fulfilled. In this world the Spirit is attached to the cross; it becomes vital upon it; it always shatters and dies upon it, too. Though this is actually obvious, all too often we don't want to perceive it, either by absolutizing an order in a triumphalistic way, or by walking away from an order, assuming that the freedom of the Spirit is already won if we avoid the cross of institutions.

If a concrete order with its legal placement is always a cross bringing about a shattering of its own essence as the liberation into the homelessness of God, which can come to light in an ecclesiastical marginality, even if it need not do so, then this does not only mean simply that a Jesuit just ought to soberly and patiently accept this situation of the cross between Spirit and institution, between freedom and churchmanship. His life has as its task to heighten this situation in its crucifying unity of Spirit and institution.

Indeed one can so organize one's life that churchmanship, the right of the church and of the order, and so on, is from the outset at the greatest possible distance from oneself so that the Spirit does not give one pain. One can also be so identified with the factual church and its institutions that the ever overchallenging Spirit does not cause one pain, does not burden one anymore. In both manners one cheapens oneself and conducts oneself counter to Jesus and his Spirit.

In this reflection our attention should be directed to the fact that there is also a danger that we become too ecclesiastically institutionalized; although obviously the opposite danger arises just as much; and even though in this area no clear prescriptions can be given for how this crucifying antagonism can be lived and endured in concrete instances. But in any case there is always still the task to live out that marginality in the individual lives of Jesuits and in the order as such ever afresh, and maybe differently tomorrow than earlier on. This is the marginality Ignatius strove for, and which of course always has to be brought to life in a renewed way with every never escapable shattering that occurs in his order.

Surely we must today reflect newly in this regard about what this marginality can and should more exactly *mean* overall in all its different, supervening realizations. Much indeed is already unclear from the theoretical standpoint. What could it mean, today in contrast to earlier on, as regards the secret discipleship of Jesus when a professed person promises not to become a bishop and to take special care for the instruction of the young? Taken at its word, such things have lost their importance.

It is not thereby stated that there are no positions of power in the church today which we do not recognize at all, and which we unbiasedly assume as if it were self-evident, that — because they are held for the noblest of motives — they must also be in conformity with Ignatius's spirit. Must we not pose again this question of not striving for positions of power which we would have to regard as praiseworthy and useful in the church, and yet which still have to be avoided? Wouldn't we, for example, have perhaps to defend against the plan for a new law governing orders, with its domination by bishops, not because we desire to have a more independent position and power, but because otherwise, sooner or later, we ourselves would take on too many positions of ecclesiastical office in some form or other which today we perceive to be a threat?

It has already been stated that a lot of monastic ballast cast off only in the most recent times was not supposed to give us more room for comfort and bourgeois religiosity; but this freeing was supposed to create more room for a spirituality supported by the Holy Spirit of liberty and of love. If the thirty-second General Congregation's proclamation of the struggle for justice as an intrinsic and fundamental element of our task is supposed to mean something for the future of the order, then there is thereby established a solidarity with the poor and underprivileged in secular society, and hence actually also a marginalization in the church as well, which, at least for us in Central Europe, is indeed (and appears to want to remain) a bourgeois church, apparently with hardly any serious regard for the poor and underprivileged. So it seems to me that we certainly ought not simply to leave this struggle for justice merely to the Jesuits in Latin America and the Third World; we ought not to suppose unimaginatively that for us there is basically no such task.

But what does it look like concretely? Do our confreres who have sought to probe in this direction at least have our sympathy and our genuine understanding? Or do we treat them as burdensome outsiders who unjustifiably try to give us a bad conscience? As individuals none of us can accomplish very much in this direction, and the uneliminability of a human and social situation can once again also be a Christian task of a Jesuit. But if the marching orders of the thirty-second General Congregation at least become *noticed* and remain vital in the awareness of the order in our regions, a lot would already be accomplished.

A space of freedom and mobility in which something new can happen wherever the external circumstances favor it would be preserved and basically become acknowledged. But it seems to me that among us there has arisen a deathly silence about this General Congregation.

We are *Jesuits and* we pursue philosophy and theology. Do these things both have something to do with each other, or is this study merely the acquisition of a tool that we have to employ later on as something extrinsic? Is there a Jesuit philosophy and theology in anything more than a historically retrospective sense of the terms? If there is, if there should be such, does this philosophy and theology have then anything to do with that marginality we have ascribed to Ignatian spirituality in both a profane and an ecclesiastical sense? Does there then not pertain to it the courage to pursue philosophy and theology in ways not too classical or too much under the aegis of the church's reception, in a love also for what is being looked down upon in the great marketplace of the mind and for traders driven onto the margin? Even if this *also* might today mean looking precisely into Thomas Aquinas! But surely such a marginality in the sciences as concerns us especially would mean that we ought to be suspicious of tendencies toward mere restoration in which it is supposed that one has already salvaged one's own and what cannot be discarded, when actually one has seen and experienced as little as possible of what is strange.

In conclusion, and at last, that marginality about which we have spoken enough, if still unclearly, is a task for the *spirituality* of the individual in his own solitary responsibility. Whoever possesses an ultimately Ignatian indifference even toward all those realities in the church and in the world that, although good, are still distinct from God; and whoever in this indifference of love encounters God himself in the immediacy of his gracious self-communication — such a person becomes homeless in the true sense. Nothing is entirely important anymore; nowhere can one ultimately gain a foothold except in the trackless God and in the death of Jesus, in which Jesus finally entered into the unfathomability of God and became blessed in this way and not otherwise. Indeed, there is always a loving and resolute turning toward the single person, realities, tasks, out of the homeless lostness in God, because God enacts this turning and loving inclination toward his creature ever anew.

And it is obvious that this our homelessness in God's unfathomability into which we keep on falling is always only partial and incomplete, because we are always in the world already and remain so when we start to seek God and to lose ourselves in his silent desert. But this self-losing should indeed always happen in us and through us, and always be started afresh. As paradoxical as it may sound, the institutionalization of this losing ourselves in God is what we have called the will to marginality in the spirituality of Ignatius. This will has shattered repeatedly in his order. In weakness and compromises it will also shatter repeatedly in our own lives; it has to shatter, and precisely this suffering through this shattering again pertains to our task, which is finally the sharing in the death of Jesus. But only one who accepts the supererogation by God and yet receives this shattering as the gift of God in which he gives himself can stand to shatter. This is why one can be and stay a Jesuit. We should always try to be better ones.

106 • The Transfiguration of the Lord*

6 August

The life of Jesus should be an example and a warning to us. But to understand what the mysteries of Christ's life want to say to us, we must know what they mean for Jesus himself. And so we inquire what place the transfiguration assumes in the life of the savior.

To understand this we need to consider that Jesus also had a human heart susceptible to joy and sorrow, pain and consolation; a heart that in a completely sinless, holy manner, but still really, experienced the changes wrought by all these storms of the soul as we do. The Son of God assumed indeed a true human nature with body and soul; he became like to us in all things except sin. And so he could also be like us in that there was a place in his soul for the stirring of the mind, for the changes of joy and sadness, jubilation and lamentation.

As St. Augustine says: "In him who had a true human body and a true human soul, also the human emotions were not untrue." And really, if we page through the Gospels, then we discover how Jesus wept, then became happy again; how he looked upon one full of love, and upon others scornfully and with deep sadness; how he wondered at and enjoyed the one, sighed over others; how he was filled with joy, with zeal, stirred by compassion, shaken unto death, and deceived.

If we want to get a sense of what was going on in the heart of Jesus as he climbed the mount of transfiguration, then we have to take

*Sermon delivered on 6 August 1933. *Kirchen-Anzeiger St. Michael* (Munich) 6 (4–11 August 1935), no. 32, 130–31. Trans. Frederick G. Lawrence, Boston College.

into account in what period in Jesus' life the transfiguration was. The savior had already preached a good deal in Judea and Galilee; he had proclaimed that the kingdom of God had come, had taught how people were supposed to receive it, had stated clearly enough that he is the promised messiah and the true Son of God. He came unto his own and his own received him not.

To be sure, he had a troop of loyal, if also imperfect, disciples and apostles, but the people as a whole had not believed. In Judea, where the Pharisees prevailed, there was a mishap right at the start. In Galilee, to be sure, the enthusiasm was great at the start, but it soon dissipated. The people sought miracles and bread more than faith. After the eucharistic discourse, even some of the disciples became disloyal. Pharisees and Sadducees worked against him now in Galilee as well, and always asked unbelievingly for new signs. And when Jesus asked, "Whom do the people say that I am?" the best appraisal made of him was that of a prophet. So Jesus' invitation to faith in him fell on deaf ears; the people had actually rejected its messiah already. There still remains only one thing: suffering and the cross. And so six days before the transfiguration, Jesus had predicted for the first time to the apostles his passion and death.

Now we can get some sense of the sort of thoughts and feelings that might surely have filled the heart of the savior as, with his three chosen apostles, in the quiet of the evening he climbed a lone high mountain far from all people and their busy noise. It will surely have been the feeling of pain over the ingratitude, hardheartedness, and unbelief of his people, thoughts of his coming passion, readiness and resolve for the cross, but also the anxiety and sadness of the Mount of Olives.

What does Jesus, in this mood of the holiest of hearts, then do? He prays. He goes away from human beings, he climbs a high mountain in order to hold converse, there in the quiet solitude of the mountain, in the restfulness of the long nights, with his Father in heaven, with his God, in whom that fate is meaningful, in whom even a defeat becomes a victory. Jesus loved these nights of prayer that bring human beings, their decisions and their fate before the face of the eternal one. We read of these nights of prayer before the selection of the apostles, after the many miracles of healing in Capernaum, after the first multiplication of loaves of bread. So Jesus prayed also in this mood at this period in his life. There he will have prayed to the Father for his unbelieving people, for his apostles and disciples for faith and strength in the coming days of suffering. He will have said to his Father: See, I come to do your will. I am ready to drink the cup, to be baptized with the baptism of suffering. Yes, it presses down upon me, until it is accomplished.

No one goes unheard before the face of God. The Father hears the

pleas of his much beloved Son. Union with God, which Jesus otherwise holds hidden in the ultimate depths of his soul, now fills up all
the chambers of his soul, it embraces his body, drawing it, too, into
the blessedness of God's light and God's unity. "His face was like the
sun, and his clothes were as radiant as light." And still more: there appeared to him Moses and Elijah, the great proclaimer of the law and
the prophets. And Jesus in between them as a sign that the law and the
prophets have their goal and their fulfillment; as a sign that he gives the
power of fulfilling the law from within; that he is the wellspring and the
plenitude of every Spirit at work in the prophets and presently to be
poured forth upon all who believe in him. And because all redemption
and all Holy Spirit takes its departure from the cross, they talk with Jesus
about the leave taking he is supposed to set forth upon in Jerusalem.
And just as at the baptism, the voice of the Father confirms here, too,
that this poor, praying Jesus, consecrated for suffering, and heroically
prepared for the cross, is God's very beloved Son.

This then is the meaning of the transfiguration for Jesus himself: in
the dark night of earthly hopelessness the light of God shines, a human
heart finds in God the power which turns a dying into a victory and
into the redemption of the world.

107 • The Assumption of Mary into Heaven*

15 August

Today we celebrate the feast of Mary's Assumption. After her quiet
death, the Blessed Virgin and mother of God entered, body and soul,
into eternal life, the life of God himself. In Mary's case, too, the fruit of
death was life, and so this feast is also the anniversary day of a death.
It is a question of that mysterious moment when time and eternity,
transitoriness and immortality touch one another in the existence of
one human being, the moment when a mortal person enters the house
of her eternity. From this point of view we shall attempt to come a little
closer to the mystery of this feast.

If we examine the life of a human being as it appears to us externally
and immediately, we find in that life — as in all things — that common

*The Eternal Year, 129–36.

trait of being bound up with and limited by time. Everything breathes the breath of evanescence, every earthly thing lives only a moment, laboriously joining one tiny interval to the next, just as one breath follows the other, so that life may continue. And each period of time, each breath, can be the last. Each is born only for a little while, first one, and only then the next. As we seize the next, the first escapes from us, and no power calls it back to life again.

So, everything that we do — whether in the inner life of the soul or in the external work of the body — takes place in this temporal order. Everything is endlessly a coming and a going. People come into existence and pass away; they are born and they die. Everything that has its beginning here on earth must someday come to an end. The shout of joy will someday fade away; all misery will one day be wept out; someday all power will vanish like smoke. Vanity of vanities, moaned Qoheleth.

How strangely vain and puny, in a certain sense, must all our activity be: no matter how great it may have been, it cannot endure, but passes away. It hastens away as soon as possible to hide its insignificance in the empty darkness of the past. This is probably why human beings, whose hands tremble with greed and with secret horror in the face of death, snatch up in this short interval, in this short dream that we call life, as much pleasure and honor, power and knowledge as they can. But the vessel is narrow, and everything that we pour into it is finite. Both the wine of joy and the bitter water of suffering are always coming to nothing. Everything ends in death.

The immortal soul seems to be only the ground over which marches the ghastly procession of things and actions destined for death. The soul seems to exist only for this purpose, that the eternal succession of all thoughts, actions, and feelings that flutter past may be eternally accompanied by the painful knowledge of their transitory nature. The soul seems to exist only for the purpose of whispering to each moment of success the bitter truth that it shall pass away like the success that was previously experienced and seen to pass away. All living is dying.

Still there is something in these things that does not pass away. Every wave of time that seems to rise only to sink back as if it had never existed lifts something up that it does not take back again into the frightening emptiness of the past. In the indifference of all coming and going there mysteriously lives something full of meaning, something eternal: good and evil. It is as if every wave of time in its restless rise and fall is continually beating against the shore of eternity, and each wave, each moment of time, each human deed leaves there what is eternal in it: the good and the evil. Good and evil are things of eternity; they are eternity in the things of time.

It is at once a comforting and a frightful mystery: our deeds sink into nothingness, but before they die they give birth to an eternal property that does not disappear with them. The eternal goodness and badness of our perishable works sink down into the eternal "ground" of our imperishable soul, and shape this hidden ground. Even if new transitory waters keep rushing over this deep ground of the soul, neither time nor forgetting obliterates what goodness and badness have brought about in those depths. Only new goodness and repentance can make good what evil has done there for eternity; and only new evil can still destroy the hidden beauty of the goodness there. Only evil, not time; not what is transitory.

In this way the eternal countenance of our soul — and in it our eternal destiny — slowly develops while we exist in this transitory state. And then the moment comes when a person passes out of the temporal order into eternity. When this happens, a stream of transitoriness vanishes forever. The restless fluctuation of time ceases to surge over a soul in endless rise and fall, and it sets free the ground of the soul that until now was seen by God alone. The eternal countenance of the soul is now revealed — the countenance that was hidden in the depths, veiled by the haze of this life on earth. What exists now, what has endured, is eternal; and we are eternal because of what we have thus become in time. This means that an individual travels the path of his or her life through time into an eternity that is no longer time.

Mary has traveled this path. Today we celebrate the day when for her time became eternity. She too led this life of transitoriness. With her as with all the children of this earth, life was a restless coming to be and passing away. Her life began quietly and obscurely, somewhere in a corner of Palestine, and soon it was snuffed out, gently, and the world knew it not. In between these two points, her life was filled with the same restless change that constitutes our life, and it was filled with the cares common to all Eve's children: anxiety for bread, suffering and tears, and a few small joys.

So too were her hours measured out to her: a few hours of the utmost happiness in God her savior joined with many routine, ordinary hours of grief, one after another, lusterless, feeble, and seemingly so empty and dull. But finally all the hours, the sublime as well as the ordinary, had passed away; and they could all now appear as one insignificant whole, precisely because they could thus fade away into the past.

Mary's life was a life of transitoriness, just like our own. And yet, in one respect it was entirely different. How enigmatic and incomprehensible our life is, not because of the darkness of fate — Mary, too, had her share in this common loss — but because of guilt. This is what makes our life so paradoxical and so confused. In our life, the eternal that makes up a part of our moments is sometimes good, sometimes evil.

And when through God's grace a moment of repentance blots out what the evil hours would have made eternal in the depths of our being, even then there is one effect still left: these evil hours are gone forever; they are forever empty. Never again will a bright eternity issue from their womb, for they have sunk back fruitless into the nothingness of hours that "have been." No one can fetch them back again to relive them in the present, to make them good. Never again will the radiant light of the goodness that shall shine like an everlasting dawn rest upon them.

We know of only one person besides Jesus who can enter into eternity without repentance. This is Mary, the ever-pure Virgin, the immaculate one. What our heart in its bitter experience can hardly believe has become true for one human being — Mary. She need not disclaim one moment of her life; no part of it has remained empty and dead. She can stand by each deed of her life: not one was dark; not one passed away without enkindling an eternal light, without shining with the luminosity that entirely consumes the moral possibilities of each moment.

Such a life did not come to an end with Mary's death; when she died, only the transitory died, so that what was eternal in her life might be revealed — that eternal light from the many thousand candles enkindled by each moment of her life. Thus her whole life entered eternity — each day, each hour, each breaking of the waves of the life of her soul, every joy and every pain, the great and the small hours. Nothing was abandoned; everything lives on in the eternal goodness of the soul that has gone home.

Is not such a day, a day of joy for us? We know, indeed, from our own experience, that our constantly changing human life hurries on toward its eternity, to its everlasting destiny. But when the last moment of time that is meted out to an individual has come, then his mouth is closed in death, and his eyes no longer transmit a glimpse of his soul; only an enigmatic death mask looks at us — and he is silent. It is as if the passageway of death had two gates, and when the person steps into this passageway, she closes the first gate behind her before she opens the second, so that no light shines through to us from that land that lies beyond the passageway.

Is it not wonderfully consoling, then, that our faith tells us of that world into which the dead have gone and of their eternal destiny? What can move us most deeply in all this is that this witness of faith does not

merely give us information about the objective, impersonal possibilities that can begin after death. It is rather as if God's revelation, which
speaks to us of the life of God hidden in inaccessible light, reveals to
us more than that life's blessedness.

The very same word of God speaks also of the holy lives of those
who rest eternally in the merciful heart of God. God affectionately calls
each one by name: Peter, with his repentance and threefold love, is
with me; Paul, the great warrior and long-sufferer is with me; Francis,
the happy beggar, is with me; Benedict Labre is with me, and he spent
his life begging on the highway; Stanislaus is with me, and he was
simply a pious, brave child.

And so God still has many names for us: he has called us by countless names. He has thereby willed to entrust to us a sweet mystery of
his heart; he has, as it were, placed us in intimate contact with those
whom he has sheltered forever in his heart as his child, his friend, his
betrothed. And thus we know that a blessed soul's quite fixed life —
a life which cannot be repeated once it is lived, which we can call by
name, which we can narrate, in the paths of which we follow, which
we love and honor and which calls us to imitation — this life has not
disappeared, but still lives.

With meaning and profit let each moment of such a life pass before us once again and we can say again and again: the goodness
that inspired that fixed deed still shines unimpaired and bright in the
soul; the heroic spirit that sacrificed its life at that instant has outlived
death.

That is why the church celebrates feast upon feast of her saints,
fresh again every day, birthdays of an eternity, victory feasts of imperishable goodness, feasts of delight because love never ceases. They
rouse us anew every day from tired resignation to transitoriness: it is
not true that everything passes away, for the good is immortal. Wherever in this world only a tiny light of purity, of kindness, of humility, of
fortitude, of patience shines, it burns on before God's eternal light as
the reflection of his own eternally blessed light.

And just as the mysterious God is quite close to us in faith because
his own reality brings the shining rays of his beauty to the eye of our
faith, so too, in the same faith, these holy men and women of eternity
are close to us; the beauty of their goodness completes our love. It is as
if each one gently touches our soul, and we can say to each in words
of love: I am joyful over your eternal goodness, you are very close to
me, and your goodness is an eternal victory.

Thus it is with the Virgin Mary. In faith we know that the charming splendor of grace that already filled her soul when the word of her
maker called her into being is still an indestructible reality. The tender

humility, the brightness of her grand spirit, the boundless submission to God — everything that filled her soul when she said, "I am the hand-maid of the Lord" — all this is always present and new. The simple greatness of her life, the sacrifice of her Son under the cross: all this goodness and holiness that once brightened this dark world is eternal life that now, at this very hour, mixes its roar with the waves of divine life in the eternal today.

As eternal life slowly came into being during her earthly exis-tence, all that was once broken up and then vanished into the past has streamed together into a superabundance of bliss in the one now of eternity. This now of eternity, always the same and always new, beyond all time, sees how, in the uttermost depths, time makes its way.

And only the thin veil of this earthly life lies between us and this per-petual rejoicing — a veil through which the light of faith and the voice of God, who is a God of the living, penetrate. And these give witness of the eternal life of the most pure Virgin. For him who in yearning and longing reaches out for it, isn't her gracious heart close to us through the nearness of faith and of love, through the still, holy nearness of eternity?

When we, from the depths of our dying day, greet this eternal today, we will be greeted with the same endlessness of eternal life that has been roaring for two thousand years (in human measurement) and that shall never vanish. And then we reflect that this eternity rises up out of the dark valleys of our transitoriness, and we look up full of blessed hope, because in Mary's bliss we see prefigured the blessed destiny that our soul shall one day find.

If it is true that we merit more love the purer and holier we are, then whose love are we indebted to, if not that of the most Blessed Virgin and mother of Jesus? When we love goodness, we should be excited by the thought that Mary's incomprehensible goodness is now blessed and preserved in eternity.

Thus we are blessed in the pure, unselfish joy that the goodness, purity, and all the virtues that we love have achieved an eternal vic-tory through the most Blessed Virgin. We sense that her victory is our own. We know, too, that the goodness that today has become eternity was not on that account taken away from us, but works among us in blessing and grace.

That is why we should fold our hands and pray: Holy Mary, Mother of God, pray for us sinners now in this transitoriness, which was also yours, and in the hour of our death, so that we may enter into the eternity that today is yours.

108 • Mary's Assumption:
The Feast Day of Our Hope*

If we read attentively the definitions of the church's magisterium on the immaculate conception and on the assumption of the Blessed Virgin into heaven — that is, on the content of the two Marian feasts — we are struck, among other things, by the fact that the immaculate conception is taught as a "special privilege" of Mary; in the teaching on Mary's assumption there is at least no explicit emphasis on anything unusual about this assumption. It is in fact quite conceivable that this emphasis is lacking because the assumption does not need to be understood as a "special privilege."

Let us examine a little more closely the question raised by this feast. This sort of reflection is not a subtle exercise of theological ingenuity, but an aid to the appreciation of this feast as one of hope for our own life.

The fact that our beginning and Mary's are different is not very surprising. The beginning of a life is always the beginning appointed by God to a quite particular life with a definite character, with a mission that is each time unique and with its own nonrecurring history. There is necessarily a hidden correspondence between the beginning of a history and this history itself. If the history of the Blessed Virgin is that of her free conception in mind and body of the Word of God for all of us, then her beginning, which is proper to her alone, corresponds to this. But the consummation is the same for all. Certainly we bring the finality of our history into what we call in the Christian creed eternal life, and this eternal life is not a continuation of time, but the pure finality of our history in responsibility and love. But this finality comes about because God makes this existence his own. He gives himself in radical immediacy, face to face. So for Mary and for us the consummation is the same: God himself.

We cannot confess anything in regard to her assumption more glorious than what we confess as our hope for ourselves: eternal life, which God himself wants to be for us. For the hope we have for our whole person in the unity of our existence — that single existence which we explain to ourselves as a unity of body and soul — is the resurrection of the body and eternal life. In our liturgical praise of the assumption of the Blessed Virgin we seek only of the one act of God in regard to that one person, but it is something that we likewise expect for our-

---

*Opportunities for Faith, 46–50.

selves. *Ultimately,* nothing more is said of her than what God one day, we hope, will say to us. And thus all is said.

But, someone might object, is not this consummation of her whole life known to be accomplished for her "already now," while for us who are still imperfect and even for others who have died in Christ this consummation of bodily life is still to come? There is no doubt that we usually add instinctively to the content of this feast the thought: for Mary already, for the rest of those who died in Christ not yet, not until the last day. But how do things really stand? We have to admit that we don't know for certain. It is salutary, however, to reflect on this very uncertainty. Because this is perhaps a better way of entering into the mystery of the feast of Mary's assumption than by simply celebrating it point by point in pious rhymes.

First, the definition of the assumption of the Blessed Virgin does not forbid reflection also on the consummated beatitude of all who are finally saved, as already achieved in "body and soul" and not merely in the soul. Nor can we say for certain that the presence of someone's corpse in the grave is a clear proof of the fact that this person has not yet found that consummation which we call bodily resurrection.

Theologians are agreed, or are coming more and more to agree, that the heavenly consummation of the one whole person — that is, "body and soul" — can be conceived as independent of the fate of his earthly-physical materiality. The body as understood in the "resurrection of the body" which we believe is the final consummation of all who are saved, the "spiritual body" which we receive according to Paul, is our own, even though it is not materially identical with the continually changing matter which we discard at death.

From this standpoint, then, there is no compelling reason to distinguish between the "points of time" at which our bodily consummation and that of Mary take place. If today more than formerly we rightly stress the unity of the corporal-personal human being in the variety of his or her dimensions, then it is more difficult than it used to be to assign the consummation "in regard to the soul" and that "in regard to the body" to different points of time, with an interval of time between them.

In addition, we know that the eternity of redeemed life with God, for which we hope cannot be conceived as continuing time added on as a linear continuation to our earthly life but is the dissolution of that time; it may be impossible to "imagine" eternity as timeless consummation, but it is just that and not ever-continuing time.

Modern physics too confirms this attitude as it becomes more and more clear how *cautiously* we have to apply our conceptual models of successive time to reality as such. In the light of this it is again difficult to say of someone who has reached perfection in her personal life that she is "still waiting" for her bodily consummation, for in a certain sense at least it is inconceivable that the completed life of those who are finally saved and are now in the supratemporal eternity of God can be kept apart by further stretches of time from the event of consummation in death.

On the other hand we shall also be careful to avoid premature conclusions by claiming that we know positively and certainly that what we venture to say of Mary and what we expect for all holds "already now" for all who are fallen asleep in Christ. There are also good reasons, despite all skepticism in regard to a time factor beyond the line of death, for maintaining a difference between Mary and the rest of the redeemed. In its most basic utterance Christian faith knows of one bodily consummation which cannot be postponed to a still unreal future: the resurrection of Jesus. And in the light of this it is clear to faith that a consummation already accomplished "in body and soul" cannot be a contradiction in itself.

And the same faith takes absolutely seriously the history which still continues, embracing *all*, including Jesus Christ: that is, a story whose end remains significant also for those who themselves have already reached their consummation. And in this light a "not yet" for those who have "already" reached their personal consummation cannot without more ado be declared meaningless. We simply don't succeed (it is evidently impossible also in the lower dimensions of reality) in uniting in a higher synthesis and thus balancing off against each other the concepts and models of time and the concepts of eternal finality.

The pointed question we have just raised finally remains unanswered. But the very fact of raising it has revealed how close the mystery of this feast is to our hope for ourselves. We profess our faith through this feast in the unity of humankind, which is one whole. We profess our faith in the permanent validity of history as flesh and blood; we profess our hope and love for the earth, which is not merely the parade ground or theater for our spiritual life, to be abandoned as soon as finality supervenes, and which perhaps itself, even though radically transformed, enters equally with the person's spirit into the glory of the eternal God.

We acknowledge the dignity of the body, which is not merely a tool to be used and thrown away, but the historical, concrete reality and revelation of the free person who is realized in it and works within it for the finality of its freedom. And this profession of faith is not expressed in ideological propositions and principles. It is a profession of faith in the historically concrete reality of a particular human being and thus can always contain more, and in more concrete form, than can be discovered by reflection on what is stated in it.

This feast tells us that those whom God loves are redeemed, are saved, are finally themselves; they are so with their concrete history, with their whole bodily nature in which alone a person is truly himself. He is not a "ghost," not a "soul" but a human being completely saved. Everything remains. We can't imagine it. Of course not. All talk about the soul in bliss, the glorified body, the glory of heaven amounts to the unvarnished, blind statement of faith: this person is not lost. *He* is what he has become, raised up in the implacable obviousness and absoluteness of the living God, raised up in the transcendent, ineffable mystery we call God.

We can't say more than this. We don't try to paint a picture, we don't imagine anything. Everything has gone through the harsh transformation which we call death. What else could we say except that death is not the last word — or rather that it is our last word, but not God's.

The church ventures to say the word about the eternal, timeless validity of Mary. Why should she not say this of her, the mother of the Lord, if, according to scripture Mary must be called blessed by all generations? How could the church let the living history of this virgin and mother, the achievement of her faith, fall into the abyss of death where nothing any longer matters? The faith that we profess in regard to her, we profess as hope for ourselves in that blessed indifference of the believer for which time, Chronos, who devours his own children, belongs as Paul says to the powers which still rule and yet are already dethroned by him who died and rose again. And thus, even if there is the difference we mentioned between a "now already" of the Blessed Virgin and the "not yet" of the others, faith and hope have already leaped across it as a part of that "little while" of which Jesus speaks in his farewell discourses in John.

What we say then about this Marian feast is really the faith we always profess for ourselves: I believe in the resurrection of the body and eternal life for myself and for all. If we seize and grasp this profession of faith, confidently letting it fall into the mystery which is God, which God is for us, then in our hope we have also understood the meaning of the assumption of Mary into heaven.

109 • Friends of God*

24 August, Jn 15:12–16

Our Lord's words from the farewell discourse in John tell us, in accord with the church's intention today on the vigil of the apostle Bartholomew, what apostles of Jesus are. They are elected out of free grace, doers of the Lord's commands, lovers unto death, people who work works and bear fruit, and, finally, friends of Christ and of God. And that is what is most beautiful and the ultimate thing; that is what our Lord says in general here about apostles and Christian persons: *Non jam dico vos servos, sed amicos* [I do not call you servants any longer, but friends]. This statement has a sweet ring for us priests, redolent of our ordination days. But it also holds true of everyone who by baptism have become friends of God.

The Lord also tells why we are his and God's friends: The servant does not know what his master does. I have made known to all of you what I have heard from the Father. The Word of God, Jesus our Lord, has heard everything from the Father. Because he is the Word in whom the Father expresses himself utterly, who was with God from the beginning. And because this Word is Spirit, it knows itself and knows itself as the Word of the Father, it hears the self-utterance of the Father which is itself.

And this Word, which has heard everything from the Father, has spoken into our hearts. Because from the day we became sharers of the divine nature, it is spoken from the Father through our essence or nature, it resonates in the depths of our graced soul. And so Jesus has already revealed to us always whatever he has heard from the Father. Because he has given his own very self to us, himself, the one definitive Word of the Father.

Still this Word spoken by God himself into our hearts surely needs interpretation by the external preaching of the faith; this revelation is still opaque for us; this divine Word spoken into the ultimate depths of our nature still sounds only softly and like a distant echo in the foreground of our conscious living. Yet it is already gracious reality right now: we are friends of God, because the Word of God himself dwells in us and has already told us all he receives from the Father.

What is brought together for us in these weeks: faithful inquiry and the Christian shaping of life in its various areas of pursuit are all basi-

---

*Katholische Kirchenzeitung (Salzburg) 77 (8 August 1937): 274. Trans. Frederick G. Lawrence, Boston College.

cally nothing else than the concern to become ever more friends of God, and to receive ever more clearly the Word that has been spoken in us. And that is the warning for the sake of seriousness and consolation. A warning for seriousness: for what we do and speak here is not just a collection of thoughts and opinions or rules and systems, but rather should be a clearer reception of the one Word that is God. And so behind all our questions and answers, there has to stand the seriousness of the insight that it is a matter in all this of an ever better hearing of the Word through which the infinite God desired to open up and entrust to us the ultimate mystery of his very own life.

But precisely this is also our God. Our ideas and insights may come and go, illumine us in the enthusiasm of a conference and tend to become trivial again in the grayness of every day that returns afterward; nevertheless, we bear within us that Word of which it was said: but the Word of the Lord lasts unto eternity. And so we know that the joyful message of today's Gospel has been fulfilled: I no longer call you servants but friends, for I have made known to you what I have heard from my Father.

110 • Feast of St. Augustine*

28 August

On 28 August holy church celebrates the feast of St. Augustine. It reminds us of a man whose spiritual influence cannot be thought away from the intellectual history of the West. It refers us especially to the example of a saint that should spur us ever anew to imitation.

Restless — that is the first word this life tells us — our hearts are restless until they rest in you, O God. "Unceasingly I hesitated and turned away from you, the one and only; I lost myself in multiplicity." Thus did Augustine himself display the balance of his first thirty-three years of life, the balance of his youth and first years of manhood, the years of sin and error, at home in Tagaste in Numidia, at school in Madaura and in the capital city of Carthage, as professor of rhetoric in Tagaste and Carthage, in Rome and Milan. Everywhere he sought rest for his restless heart. He sought it in the enjoyment of life, in "modern" religions,

---

*Kirchen-Anzeiger St. Michael (Munich) 6 (25 August–1 September 1935): 142–43. Trans. Frederick G. Lawrence, Boston College.

the fashionable philosophical teachings of the day, and the ambitious striving of the learned.

At thirty-three, via detours and through many bitter experiences: restless is our heart until it rests in God. Only in him does our heart come to rest. He, truth, goodness, and beauty itself, must be the center-point of our hearts; he, the light of the Spirit; he, the power of our ethical knowledge; he, the consolation of our heart. Only one who knows himself in the service of God, and knows his fate in the hand of the eternal one; only one who gives his life unreservedly over in love to the holy God; only one who knows that all the streets of our life have to lead us before his face; only one who believes in him, hopes in him, loves him; this is the one who alone will have rest, and has in his or her soul the eternal ground and final security.

"Put on the Lord Jesus Christ." That is the second word Augustine wants to speak to us. That indeed is the saying that furnished the last push toward his conversion. We only discover God in Christ, for no one comes to the Father except through him. Only he knows the way, the truth, and the life, because he is these things himself. His teaching is way and truth, his grace is life and strength, his cross the true wisdom. We approach God, the rest of our restless hearts, only through God become man. Only if we believe him and in him, love him with our whole heart, are joined to him by grace, are made living members of his mysterious body, the church, healed and divinized by the life of the Head that streams down upon us, his body, in the sacraments, only then are we in the truth and in God. So Augustine lived and taught: Draw near to the Lord Jesus Christ.

"The love of Christ urges us on." This is the third word he wants to say to us. How different his life became than he himself had expected as one newly baptized. As a monk within his trusted circle of friends, he wanted his soul and his God to live in silent contemplation. As newly converted, he had wanted to make "God and the soul, nothing else," his motto. But providence had added the phrase: "And the brothers in Christ." The love of Christ urged him on.

And so his life was utterly consumed for his fellow human beings. In the love of Christ he overcame all the obstacles of his talent, his pretentious ambitions, his feelingful softness, his delicate sensibility. In the service of the neighbor he could even renounce what was dearest to him: the quiet research of a thinker and the undisturbed inwardness to God of the mystic. So as a bishop he tirelessly held his catechism classes and his sermons; so did he pillage the vineyards and olive groves of the church's property to have something for the poor; so did he smooth over in patience the disputes of his peasants, tradesmen, and fishermen; so did he write his countless letters; so did he look after the rules in cloisters and among the clergy. His writing too was a service of love, when he wrote on the nature and origin of evil and of sin; on the divinity of Christ; on the church and its sacraments that are effective by the power of Christ; on the holy Trinity; on grace without which we can do nothing; on issues of moral teaching; on the meaning of the events in the world and of history. He who sought rest for his heart in God, who was illuminated for him in the face of Christ, found him inasmuch as he selflessly served the neighbor according to Christ's example. The love of Christ urges us on.

And yet a third statement may be written about the life and dying of the bishop of Hippo, the words of Psalm 23: "Even though I walk through the valley of the shadow of death, I fear no evil, for thou art with me." When God turned on this light in the lamps of the church, the night became ever more dark outside in the world, and the shadows of death fell over the path. His homeland was torn by strife between religious, political, and social parties; Rome, the heart of the world, was vanquished and plundered by Alaric; the empire was in incessant decline.

When Augustine, a tired old man of seventy-five, lay down to die in 430, he had to await death in his city under siege. And when he looked back upon his life's work, from his human viewpoint at that time, he could really speak his words: *nihil sum nisi quod expecto misericordiam Dei* [I am nothing but what I expect of the mercy of God]. I am no longer anything; yet only one thing am I: a clinging to the mercy of God.

His African church at the beginning of the end, the parties of the Arians and the Donatists, whom he might have believed to have eliminated by his spirit, again in ascendancy; the world of an ancient culture waning, everywhere dark night and terrestrial hopelessness. And his embattled heart often put itself the question whether the last judgment stood before the door: "Even though I walk through the valley of the shadow of death, I fear no evil; for you are with me." Augustine did not doubt that he would not stray when it came to his God. The light of eternity lit up for him the darkness of his times, and faith's hope in the eternal sabbath helped him endure courageously the heavy darkness of the six terrestrial days of unhappiness and need. For him the God of unfathomable ways and judgment was still also the God of love and mercy.

111 • The Angels*

2 October

It is a truth of faith that God's infinite power of creation has created besides us other persons of a spiritual nature. This is a startling idea: here, this earth of the unending cosmos with all its stars, their uncountable courses; here this earth with natural evolution and natural catastrophes, with its humankind and its history replete with greatness and averageness, victories and defeats, laughter and crying, pleasure and suffering — and in the midst of all this, faith speaks: all this, the stars, the earth, and humankind in its entirety is only a small part of that creation which God's almighty word has called into existence, so that it might reveal his eternal power and wisdom.

Besides this there is an unsurveyable world of spirits with a life, in comparison with which, all earthly events are like a shadow; spirits with a life filled with thunderous victories and unlimited happiness, but also with a life leading into the destroying judgment of the wrath of the infinitely holy one. And from all these luminous worlds of roaring life and blinding light not a glimmer penetrates down into the depths of our material poverty; only faith informs us, only God's word impinges on our ears so that we know that the spirit, the moral deed, our relationship with God, is the ultimate and most important reality; that every care for body and life, for bread and earthly welfare, is finally only provisional, so much so that God could create his entire world of spirits where all these things are lacking that so easily seem to make up life for us, and where only one issue is at stake: God and his honor.

We are related to these remote spirits by reason of our spiritual, personal souls that are immediate to God; we are related in this essential and decisive factor: just as they, so we are also created to know God, to serve him, and so to bring about our salvation. And their affinity to us has increased by the fact that God's wisdom has willed that the content of their life also extends into our earthly days in prayer and help, that they are our guardian angels and so are, as it were, caught into the everydayness of our pilgrimage in the dust of this earth. And for this reason, they are also a model for us, given to us for imitation. Two passages in the scriptures tell us how they are supposed to be examples for us.

The first passage is the statement of Jesus: "Their angels always behold the face of my Father who is in heaven." Certainly, this is a

---

Kirchen-Anzeiger St. Michael (Munich) 6 (1 August–1 September 1935): 146–47. Trans. Frederick G. Lawrence, Boston College.

statement that announces the victory after the battle or the reward for persevering, and not the battle itself. The good angels are with God; they have entered into the land of the eternal peace, of eternal rest and security. Their life is exultant now with the eternal surge of the divine life in an eternal today. Their spirits are immersed in the infinity of God, their hearts are filled with the unspeakable jubilation of those who have discovered their eternal goal.

But we are still distant, pilgrims still on the way of the cross of this earth, far from the Lord. However, this still means that for us our journey is in heaven, and if we are commanded to be perfect as the heavenly Father is perfect, then the command to be as perfect as his angels is not an exaggeration anymore. And so it is also true of us that we are supposed always to look upon the face of the Father. We do this when our journey is before his face, when we, joined with him by grace, temples of the triune God, are his children in whose hearts the Spirit of God dwells and prays. We look upon his face when we accomplish all things for his honor, if we eat or drink or do anything else, if we live or die, if all we do is done in grace as an expression of our love for him; if we take upon ourselves our entire daily labor with its pettinesses and cares and sufferings as the will of God, as his disposing, and as proof that we seek only him in all things.

When a person makes his way through life in this way, then two are always moving along the same street: the guardian angel and the human person, and both look on their own toward God, toward the one who is the content of eternal life for both. And soon enough, there comes then for human beings too the hour when their looking toward the face of the Father is no longer struggle and perseverance, but victory and eternal reward.

Yet another statement do we read in the scriptures about the angels: "They are ministering spirits, sent forth to serve, for the sake of those who are to obtain salvation." They are servants for human beings, messengers of whom it is said that they bear the prayers of the just as in golden vessels before the throne of God, join their prayer to ours, and protect us on our way. In this way every person should be a guardian angel for the other. We are all one mysterious body of Christ, members of one another, who have joys and sorrows to share. If one member becomes better, it is a blessing for all, and each evil deed is also an injustice to each member.

How much more then every person has the office of guardian angel to those whom God has specially entrusted to them, to those who go together with us along the path of life. Their service, to which we are sent forth, is a service unto eternal salvation. Because we are not just supposed to help others in regard to earthly welfare, but for the inheritance of eternal salvation, then everything we do for our neighbor has a special responsibility and a particular consecratedness and dignity.

And this can be anything direct or indirect done in a good attitude and genuine love of neighbor, whether it be only a drink of water or a friendly word. Everything like this can become guardian angel service. But if it is guardian angel service, then it is service of God; then, when seen and done from a this-worldly viewpoint, even the most external activity becomes divine service or worship. The more even our external activity is penetrated by these thoughts, the more the often painfully perceived tension between the multiplicity and the fragmented character of external obligations and the quest for God alone is overcome. The more we become like the angels who are always in the service of those for whose sake they should inherit salvation, and who, even so, never stop looking upon the face of the Father in heaven.

112 • A Happy Death: The Witness of Thérèse of Lisieux*

3 October

It is not very original, I know, when I say that many things about Thérèse of Lisieux and her writings only charmed me or simply bored me. And when one started to explain, to interpret, to translate what at first runs counter to my expectations, so that it becomes accessible, then one still does not gain insight into why one actually is taking such pains. Surely there is so much in the world with which one can occupy oneself without tedious interpretation.

Yet for one thing: here is a person who died in the mortal temptation to empty unbelief right down to the roots of her being, and who *in* that condition believed. She believed as she was smothering with consumption, and all the pious fussing of her fellow sisters must have appeared to her as a nameless and empty pain. Here one died who *accepted* as annihilating reality what previously was discussed, what beforehand must have stood very much under the suspicion of being a dreamworld into which a young life escaped because it had real anxiety in the face of reality and truth, which hitherto looked as if it also

---

Christliche Innerlichkeit (Vienna) 8 (1977): 34–36. Trans. Frederick G. Lawrence, Boston College.

belonged in its way to the plush furniture with which the parents of the Little Flower (how touching) had crammed their living room.

And for another thing, one could indeed say: presumably many people finally die this way. Whether in one of today's antiseptic clinics, removed from their dear relatives, pressing upon them in their helplessness; whether under napalm bombs in Vietnam; oh — I don't know how, people die everywhere. But, hoping against hope, why should I not desperately believe that if you scrape away everything narrow-minded, pitiful, and pretentious in these various deaths, you will still find a person who died courageously in faith, hope, and love? And this person allows himself or herself to fall into incomprehensibility — which we call God — in such a way that what is actually happening here is worthwhile, genuine, and remains eternally valid? Whether this — one hopes so — happens in general, I do not know. I hope it is so, although only what is miserable and disappointing about human life is tangible in death.

Consequently, what is it, actually, that especially interests me about the death of Thérèse when we prescind from the pious buzz (against which I have nothing, but which I cannot take seriously) which her surroundings and even her own petty-bourgeois-Christian training produced in the context of this death? I respond to this question in a way that might be shocking to anyone not clearly domesticated beforehand in the church. Because I trust in relation to this death that it was happy (in the sense just suggested). This is something I do not know securely otherwise, but I trust it *because* the church experienced and endorsed it.

Pious *and* impious goings on at a death are of course very ambiguous, and of questionable importance. One can die worthily with the declaration one is an atheist and politely refuse the ministrations of the priest for one's sake. Or one can die with all the Christian church ceremonies, and also desire these, and be happy and consoled about it. (I mention for the sake of the watchdogs of orthodoxy that I do *not* equate the two.) And yet from catechism we know certainly that as far as the concrete case of death goes, what *ought* to be the outcome is still in itself not necessarily what the result *is* in both cases. If we are to be exactly and completely serious, there is also no necessary result in cases where such genuinely edifying things can be told about a death (even if we set aside the embellishments), as in that of Thérèse.

Simply, and essentially not because one does not know how anyone falls into the unfathomable reality, whether in voluntary self-surrender (which makes one blessed) or in a final protest, about which I have to believe, for the sake of the dignity of freedom, is also possible. But with respect to St. Thérèse the church tells me: here is a death that succeeded as an act of faith. When I say "church," I do not mean merely or primarily Rome's official declaration at the canonization. This indeed is ultimately only an echo of the conviction of the church of those who pray, make petitions, trust, praise.

It also does not disturb me very much that this conviction of the church meant here was manifested under a landslide of kitsch and infantile doings. That is always the way it is when many must and do accomplish something in common. But I trust these innumerable Christians also to have a genuine nose for cases in which something authentic and eternal happens. And I accept this consolingly as a discernment of spirits (as regards death) which occurs in God's Holy Spirit. Once this kind of death is acknowledged as one which was really and almost incomprehensible, then even though the statues of the little saint with their roses in the corners of so many churches may turn to dust again, and the rains of roses fall less thickly, I can still say: for any person, his or her death in the darkness is blessed as the rising of a light in victory over all disbelief and hopelessness.

I understand this kind of message. It has the weight of eternity that accrues to each human life. One can also take it from other people who have died and show that we can really die with Jesus, by accepting the nameless abandonment as the sheltering hand of God. But one can also let it be said of Thérèse of Lisieux, who died just three years before Nietzsche, who held that God is dead (and with him, true humanity also died), without being able to rise again.

The response here hurries ahead of the question, the answer can make the question intelligible for Christians, but also really be an answer. There are also black roses. Such may fall in turn on the night of one's dying, black roses of a hope which fall inaudibly and almost indiscernibly on such nights. On yours and — on mine.

113 • Teresa of Avila: Doctor of the Church*

15 October

Teresa has been declared a doctor of the church. This event naturally has some significance for the position and function of women

---

*Opportunities for Faith, 123–26.

in the church. The charism of teaching — and indeed of teaching directed to the church as such — is not merely a male prerogative. The idea of women being less gifted in an intellectual or religious sense is thus repudiated. It is thus expressly recognized that women may study theology, particularly since charism and the study of theology methodically accomplished cannot be regarded as opposites.

It should not be said that Teresa is an exception. For all doctors of the church, the men too among them, are exceptions. And the proclamation declaring her a doctor of the church makes it clear that women have not previously been given this title not because none of them was worthy of it, but because of reasons rooted in the cultural status of women at the time. This proclamation clearly shows that 1 Corinthians 14:34 is a time-conditioned norm (justified at the time) imposed by the apostle Paul.

People may of course wonder whether naming Teresa a doctor of the church is merely a handsome gesture, meant in the last resort to provide an excuse for not entrusting to women living in the church today those tasks or recognizing those rights which are due to them and which they are still far from possessing fully and as something that is really obvious. We may wonder also whether women themselves in the church today are really prepared to accept the position and function which they can have if they want them.

Teacher of mysticism. Teresa is proclaimed as a teacher of mysticism. This means first of all that a person who teaches something about mysticism is doing theology, is speaking in the light of revelation, saying something to the church as such for the edification of the faithful. This is itself of supreme importance. For it is by no means so obvious at first sight that the "mysticism" which Teresa and John of the Cross put forward has to do with revelation and theological teaching in the church as such. The fact that Christ or grace is mentioned in this teaching on mysticism is not itself a proof that this unique relatedness of consciousness to the things of which faith speaks — which is described by both as mystical — really belongs as such to the sphere of revealed theology.

Why is mystical experience not the opposite of faith? How far is mysticism in Teresa's sense more than a natural transformation of consciousness (produced perhaps parapsychologically or psychotechnically), which as such has nothing to do with the workings of grace or at most — like other "natural" factors of consciousness — merely provides the natural basis which grace, according to the theologians, always presupposes? Is mysticism simply a stage (albeit a high one) on the way of Christian life, or is it an almost miraculous phenomenon which God alone produces outside the normal course of Christian life? If the first alternative is correct, does this "normality" consist in the fact that mysticism in the Christian sense is the Christian achievement in the light of faith and under the influence of grace of a stage in a natural psychological development accessible in principle to every human being? Or is it simply the "normality" of a specifically supernatural development of the life of grace as such?

These and similar questions arise with fresh urgency if we take seriously the declaration that Teresa is a doctor of the church and do not try to see in it merely a timely gesture in regard to women in the church today. Such questions are still far from being answered sufficiently clearly and unanimously. The reason is not that a modern history of religion, a history of piety and a modern psychology of religion, at a time when the church is turning in a wholly new way and more impartially than formerly to the non-Christian religions, can discover much more "mysticism" outside the church than the Christian theologians could do in the past. But the question then arises as to whether mysticism outside Christianity (which certainly exists) is an "anonymously" Christian and therefore grace-inspired mysticism. Or, on the other hand, is Christian mysticism a "natural" mysticism just like non-Christian, although obviously under the influence of grace like all other free, moral actions of a human being, purified and free from baser elements like all that is naturally moral? Or are these two questions aimed after all at the same thing?

Mysticism within the present horizon of understanding. The declaration of St. Teresa as doctor of the church comes at a time when a "death of God" theology is being developed, in which God is said to count only as a mythological cipher for the radicalness of interpersonal human relations, in which we have the impression that God can no longer be discovered in a radically secularized, self-sufficient world. But even today it is still possible, indeed it is more urgent than ever, to have a theology and, even beyond this, an initiation into the human being's personal experience of God. And the classical authorities on Spanish mysticism are thoroughly good and almost irreplaceable teachers of this sort of theology and initiation, particularly adept at making this personal experience of God intelligible.

If these older mystics are to be able to help us in this task, we must of course assume for our part that in every human being (as a result of the nature of spirit and of the grace of the divine self-communication always offered to everyone) there is something like an anonymous, unthematic, perhaps repressed, basic experience of being oriented to God, which is constitutive of the human person in his concrete makeup (of nature and grace), which can be repressed but not destroyed, which is "mystical" or (if you prefer a more cautious terminology) has its climax in what the older teachers called infused contemplation.

Of course we ought to read these classical writers with other eyes than those of a devout contemplative of former times, for whom the temptation from atheism scarcely existed. Of course we ought to translate the psychology of these masters with their terminology, their perspectives, their assumptions of what they regarded as obvious, and so on, into a modern existential ontology and modern theological anthropology. For, however "descriptive" the mystical theology of these classical writers may be as compared with that of their predecessors, it still is not and cannot be a pure description, since the very experience they are describing is itself shaped up to a point by a time-conditioned element of interpretation. But the carrying over of this description of mystical experience into modern horizons of understanding is possible in principle, even though it has scarcely been attempted, since teachers of mystical theology even up to recent decades simply continued to speak the language of the classical masters. And such a translation could be fruitful, since the depth and radicality of the experience of God which these classical writers describe are not so familiar that we could discover in ourselves its starting points and traces just as easily without their help as with it.

With reference to these themes, the question may then perhaps arise as to whether the work of the great Teresa or that of John of the Cross could be more helpful to a modern theology and initiation into the experience of God. We might at first perhaps think that the radical "absence of images" in the experience of God as described by John of the Cross would make him a better interpreter of our modern experience of God than Teresa with her more frankly visionary mysticism. But if we consider that the loss of imagery today is to be counted precisely *as* a loss and not as a gain, if we see that our relationship to God today must either be mediated perhaps more explicitly than ever through our relationship to the concrete Jesus of Nazareth, to his life and death and his relationship to his fellow men and women, or it will not exist at all, then it is perhaps not so obvious that for us today Teresa of Avila must rank behind John of the Cross. The fact that her desire for penance did not lessen her appreciation of good roast partridge and that she was also an incomparably worldly-wise organizer and diplomat (which John of the Cross certainly was not): these are also things which make her mysticism particularly sympathetic to us today.

114 • Sealed with the Seal of Everlasting Love*

1 and 2 November, All Saints and All Souls Day, Rv 7:2–12

It is common knowledge how difficult and mysterious the Revelation of St. John seems to be. But much of the obscurity is only apparent. If we realize the kind of language that is used here, we can much more easily distinguish between the imagery and what the image means. The seer is looking into his own time and into his Christian life; and enlightened by the Spirit of God and his own Christian experience, he looks into the future and sees as far as the end. He sees his present and the future of Christianity in a single perspective, as it were. He is not a reporter, relating one event after another in chronological order; we cannot apply the particular things he says to any definite historical events in the future.

Rather, he keeps seeing one and the same thing in massive imagery — the crucial struggle that goes on throughout the history of the world and ends in eternal victory for God, when the eternal kingdom has been established and God has triumphed in his Christ, gathering together all that was scattered in time into his eternal glory.

This one thing is said over and over again. When the seer has admonished, warned, and corrected seven Christian communities of Asia Minor in the first few chapters of this book, he presents the first great image: he sees the eternal God and he sees that God is holding a book in his hand, a book sealed with seven seals. It is the book of universal history, the book of creation and time. What this book contains is really the history of the world, the history of salvation and damnation.

Nobody can break the seals of this book or scroll, except the lamb that was slain, the crucified, the Son of God, who is the meaning of history, who came into history and experienced and suffered all that has ever happened, as the crucified and risen Lord. And when a voice asks: Who is worthy to open the scroll and break its seals? and when nobody is found and the seer weeps because no one knows the meaning of all that we experience, then he hears a voice saying: Weep not; for the lamb that was slain, the victor, can break the seven seals of the universal history which God alone can write; he opens this history.

---

*Biblical Homilies, 188–91.

Now, continuing the same imagery, the seven seals are broken, one after another, and the same universal history is revealed from beginning to end each time, only in a different perspective; with its plagues, its disasters, and that great silence that falls when the end comes. In the same terms the seer sees the designation of God's chosen ones. He sees it in two ways: under the figure of the twelve tribes — which simply means all humankind; for we are dealing with the spiritual Israel, the whole human race which is called to God's eternal glory.

And he sees an immense multitude that no one could count, of every race and nation and language. He sees them as having already made their way through history and as beginning their eternal praise of the holy God. He sees those who are sealed, and sees them as sealed before the history of the world with its plagues really begins. They are those who are called and chosen by God's decree. This decree is the primal thing, and all the rest — universal history — is only its consequence, fitted into the decree and destined to glorify God.

The seer sees God's angel sealing the elect: from every tribe and people and tongue, from everywhere in universal history, God gathers those whom he loves. There is no question of his leaving anybody out. We are simply told that he calls and chooses his elect from everywhere to sign and seal them as his own, the possession that he perfects, saves, and keeps through all this history.

And since we are told that there are many, a great multitude which no one could number, we may hope that we too are among them and that what seems to be said here in such general terms is said of us, of you and me. We hope that we are among them, bearing God's seal invisible on our forehead, that we, each of us are already sealed as we make our way through our own whole history; and that if we were seers and could see all that is to be unto the end, we should catch sight of ourselves there before the throne of God and the lamb, hear ourselves singing praises there as we shall do one day.

This is how we must interpret today's text. We must apply it to ourselves, to each one of ourselves, to those we love, to the dead who are alive and to the living, to those who are with us in Christ and those on whom God can and does have mercy in other ways: for by God's grace all of these can be sealed. Often as we must fear for our own salvation, we have no right to exclude anyone from the hope of eternal life. So we can — we who are commanded to hope — we can and must apply today's text to everyone, to ourselves and to all the rest of humankind.

Then we remember those who have gone before us in the sign of faith and who sleep the sleep of peace, and we believe that they too are sealed; and we think of our fellow pilgrims, at our side, or a little ahead of us, or a little behind us. Soon all these differences will be no more: we are all on pilgrimage to eternity. God calls us all, and we hope that all too are sealed.

That is the seer's vision of human history and of our own lives. As we listen to this reading from God's word, we should apply St. John's vision to the personal experience of history we have had, the experience of death and pain, the experience of the pitiful poverty of human life, and the experience of its grandeur. We should hear the weeping and the laughter, the deep things people say and the superficial things that seem to be ceaselessly gabbled millennium after millennium. We should apply anything that strikes us in this universal history written today, on All Saints day, for us and for everyone, written as it were before God rings up the curtains, as it were before he lets loose the angels of history to do their work which seems so baffling and senseless.

Before we look into the book of universal history with its seven seals, we should be told that God has sealed those he calls into history, with the mark of his love. Then that history can be endured. It is obscure, and one might almost say that God should rather give us an account of our life than call us to account for it; for he is God and must therefore answer for our existence. But he has told us — and what other answer could there be for us in time, in this imperfect life, upon our shadowed journey — he has told us that he has sealed us with the seal of his eternal love and that he sends us down no road that will not lead to him, puts us into no history that will not end in his beatitude, calls no one into existence who is not chosen and sealed with God's eternal love.

On All Saints day and All Souls day we remember those who have learnt that they are sealed and called and we raise our eyes in faith and hope to our own blessed end.

115 • All Saints and All Souls Day*

All Saints day and All Souls day are the feasts of *every* saint and of *every* soul who has died and gone home into the eternal love of God. *All* of them and therefore not only those already celebrated by name in the church's feasts throughout the year but also the silent, unknown ones who have departed as if they had never even existed. There are no legends about them; their lives are recorded neither in poetry nor in history, secular or ecclesiastical. Only one person knows anything

---

*The Eternal Year, 137–44.

about these saints, and that is God. He has inscribed their names in the book of life, which is the heart of his eternal love.

But we are supposed to celebrate these saints who are not known to us by name. How can we do this — really do it, with life and zest — if not by lovingly remembering our dead? They may already be forgotten by the world; perhaps their name is not even inscribed on a gravestone. Yet they not only live on with God, but also with us, in our hearts.

Let us then prepare our hearts for these feasts of the dead who live with God. May our hearts be mindful of the dead. Be still, O heart, and let all whom you have loved rise from the grave of your breast. Is there no one among All Saints and All Souls for you to celebrate? Have you ever come in contact with love and meekness, goodness and purity and fidelity in a person? Not even in your mother, so quiet and forgetful of herself? Nor in your patient father? Should you say no, I think you would be contradicting your heart, which has its own experiences. It is not the heart's experience to have met throughout life only darkness and no light, only selfishness and no selfless kindness.

But if you have met faith, hope, and love, kindness and pardon, great courage and fidelity in persons who now are dead — a grain of virtue such as these is worth a mountain of selfishness and vice — then you have met men and women whom your heart may seek with God. Up, then, and celebrate the heart-feast of All Saints, of All Souls — *your* saints, *your* beloved souls! Sorrow and joy, grief and happiness are strangely blended into this feast. Just as they are with the things of eternity. Celebrate an All Saints of peace and loyalty. Of yearning and of faith. Celebrate your dead who are still living.

Today, then, we want to remember before God our dead, all those who once belonged to us and who have departed from us. There are so many of them that we can by no means take them all in at one glance. If our celebration is to greet them all, we must go back in memory over our path through life. When we go about it in this way, from our point of view it is like a procession of persons marching down the street of life.

At each moment, without bidding farewell, someone or other silently withdraws from the procession and, turning aside from the road, is lost in the darkness of the night. This procession becomes smaller and smaller for each one of us, for the new person constantly stepping onto our path through life only seems to be marching along with us. To be sure, many are walking the same street, but only a few walk *together with* each one of us. Strictly speaking, only those who set out together with each one of us are really journeying together with us. Only those who were with us at the very beginning of our journey to God — only those who were and still are really close to our heart.

The others are traveling companions on the same road; they are many, and they are constantly coming and going. We greet each other, and give each other a helping hand, and then, no more. But the real procession of each of our lives is made up of those whom we really love. This procession is always becoming smaller and quieter, until each one of us becomes silent once and for all, turns aside from the road, and passes away without a farewell, never to return.

That is why our heart today is with those who have already departed in just such a way. There are no replacements for them; no other human being could really fill the vacancy left by a loved one when she suddenly and unexpectedly departs and is at our side no longer. In true love no one can replace the beloved, for true love loves the beloved in those depths where each individual is uniquely and irreplaceably herself. That is why each one of those who have passed away has taken a part of our heart with him: they may be said even to have taken the heart with them, if death has trodden through our lives from beginning to end.

If someone has really loved and continues to love, then even before his own death his life is changed into a life with the dead. Could the lover forget her dead? If one has really loved, then her forgetting and the fact that she has ceased weeping are not signs that nothing has really changed, that she is just the same as before. They are, rather, signs that a part of her own heart has really died with the loved one, and is now living with the dead. That is why she can no longer mourn. We live, then, with the dead, with those who have gone before us into the dark night of death, where no one can work any more.

But how are we supposed to be able to live with the dead in the one reality of our mutual love; how are we to celebrate a feast of all the holy dead? Is this possible simply because God is the God of the living and not of the dead, because his word and even the wisdom of this world tells us that these dead still live? Because we loved the dead and still love them, we must be with them always. But are they also with us? Do they belong to this love and to the celebration of this love?

They have departed, they are silent. No word from them reaches our ears; the gentle kindness of their love no longer fills our heart. How quiet the dead are, how *dead* they are! Do they want us to forget them, as we forget a casual acquaintance on a trip, with whom we exchanged a few insignificant words? If life is not taken away from those who depart this life in God's love, but changed into eternal, measureless, superabundant life, why then should it seem to us that they no longer exist? Is the inaccessible light of God into which they have entered so faint that it cannot penetrate to us down here? Does even their love (and not only their bodies) have to abandon us in order to live with

God in his light? Does their silence imitate the silence of their God, to whose home they have gone?

That is the way it is. For God is silent just like the dead. For us to celebrate his feasts in our hearts this silent God must certainly be with us, even though he seems so distant and so silent. We certainly must love him, too, as we love our dead, the distant and silent dead, who have entered into the night. Does he not give to our love an intelligible answer when we call him to the feast of the heart, and ask him for a sign that his love exists for us and is present to us? And that is why we cannot lament the silence of the dead, for their silence is only an echo of his silence.

But if we keep silent and meek, if we listen to this silence of God's, then we begin to grasp with a comprehension that exceeds our own power to evoke or even to understand why both God and the dead are so silent. Then it dawns on us that they are near us precisely in our feast of the holy souls. God's silence is the boundless sphere where alone our love can produce its act of faith in his love.

If in our earthly life his love had become so manifest to us that we would know beyond a shadow of a doubt what we really are, namely, God's own beloved, then how could we prove to him the daring courage and fidelity of our love? How could such a fidelity exist at all? How could our love, in the ecstasy of faith, reach out beyond this world into his world and into his heart? He has veiled his love in the stillness of his silence so that our love might reveal itself in faith. He has apparently forsaken us so that we can find him.

For if his presence in our midst were obvious, in our search for him we would find only ourselves. We must, however, go out from ourselves, if we are to find him where he is really himself. Because his love is infinite, it can dwell openly and radiantly only in his own infinity; and because he wants to show us his infinite love, he has hidden it from us in our finiteness, whence he calls out to us. Our faith in him is nothing but the dark road in the night between the deserted house of our life with its puny, dimly lit rooms, and the blinding light of his eternal life. His silence in this world is nothing but the earthly appearance of the eternal word of his love.

Our dead imitate this silence. Thus, through silence, they speak to us clearly. They are nearer to us than through all the audible words of love and closeness. Because they have entered into God's life, they remain hidden from us. Their words of love do not reach our ears because they have blended into one with the joyous word of his boundless love. They live with the boundlessness of God's life and with his love, and that is why their love and their life no longer enter the narrow room of our present life. We live a dying life. That is why we experience nothing of the eternal life of the holy dead, the life that knows no death. But just in this very way they also live for us and with us. For their silence is their loudest cry, because it is the echo of God's silence. It is in unison with God's word that it speaks to us.

Over against the loud cries of our drives, and over against the anxious, hasty protestations with which we mortals assure ourselves of our mutual love, God's word enwraps us and all our noisy words in his silence. This is the way his word invites us into his life. This is the way he commands us to relinquish all things in the daring act of loving faith, in order to find our eternal homeland in his life.

And it is precisely in this way that the silence of our dead also calls out to us. They live in his life, and that is why they speak his words to us. They speak the word of the God of the true life, the word that is far removed from our dying. The dead are silent because they live, just as our noisy chatter is supposed to make us forget that we are dying. Their silence is the word of their love for us, the real message that they have for us. By this word they are really near to us, provided only that we listen to this soundless word and understand it, and do not drown it out through the noise of everyday life.

It is in this way that they are close to us whose feast we celebrate today in the silent composure of the heart. They are near us together with the silent God, the God of the silent dead, the living God of the living. He calls out to us through his silence, and they, by their silence, summon us into God's life.

Let us therefore be mindful of our dead, our living. Our love for them, our loyalty to them is the proof of our faith in him, the God of everlasting life. Let us not ignore the silence of the dead, the silence that is the most ardent word of their love. This, their most ardent word, accompanies us today and every day, for they have gone away from us in order that their love, having gone into God, may be all the closer to us.

Be mindful of the dead, O heart. They live. Your own life, the life still hidden even to you, they live unveiled in eternal light. Our living who are with the God of life cannot forget us dead. God has granted our living everything, for he has given them himself. But he goes further and also grants them this favor: that their silence will become the most eloquent word of their love for us, the word that will accompany our love home to them, into their life and their light.

If we really celebrate All Saints and All Souls as the feast of faith, of love, of quiet remembering; if our life is and is always becoming more and more a life of the dead who have gone before us in the sign of faith into the dark night of death, where no one can work; then through God's grace our life becomes, more and more, a life of faith in his light during the night of this earthly life. Then we who are dying live with the living who have gone before us into the bright, shining day of life, where no one has to work, because God himself is this day, the fullness of all reality, the God of the living.

Today or tomorrow, when we stand by the graves, or when our heart must seek distant graves, where perhaps not even a cross stands over them any longer; when we pray, "Lord, grant them eternal rest, and may perpetual light shine upon them"; when we quietly look up toward the eternal homeland of all the saints and — from afar and yet so near — greet God's light and his love, our eternal homeland; then all our memories and all our prayers are only the echo of the words of love that the holy living, in the silence of their eternity, softly and gently speak into our heart.

Hidden in the peace of the eternal God, filled with his own bliss, redeemed for eternity, permeated with love for us that can never cease, they, on their feast, utter the prayer of their love for us: "Lord, grant eternal rest to them whom we love — as never before — in your love. Grant it to them who still walk the hard road of pilgrimage, which is nonetheless the road that leads to us and to your eternal light. We, although silent, are now closer to them than ever before, closer than when we were sojourning and struggling along with them on earth. Grant to them, too, Lord, eternal rest, and may your perpetual light shine on them as on us. May it shine upon them now as the light of faith, and then in eternity, as the light of blessed life."

Be mindful of the dead, O heart. Call them into your heart today, listen to their silence, learn from them the one thing necessary: celebrate the feast of your saints. For then the God of all the living will be mindful of us who are dead, and he will one day be our life, too. And there will be one, single, eternal feast of all the saints

116 • The Feast Day of a Holy Beginning*

8 December, The Immaculate Conception

In the kingdom of God, the kingdom of love, all is bestowed on each in his own particular way, the whole pervades and prevails in each, and

---

*Everyday Faith, 163–68.

each of the mysteries of the kingdom is inexhaustible. It has only been grasped perfectly when all has been understood. The whole, however, is the inexhaustibility of the infinite mystery of God. Consequently, the mystery of the feast of the immaculate conception can be regarded under innumerable aspects. No one is forbidden to seek the particular aspect which leads her best and most fully into this mystery of God, so that she comes to God himself.

We wish to consider this as the feast of beginnings. We shall reflect on the beginning as such, on the beginning of the Blessed Virgin, and on our own.

The beginning as such. A beginning is not empty nothingness, something inconsiderable, hollow indeterminacy, what is inferior and general. That is the sort of way people mostly think today, and regard everything lofty and perfect (if they are still capable of conceiving and loving such things) as a complicated amalgam of the least precious, uniformly unremarkable, "basic elements." But the true beginning of what comes to high perfection is not empty vacuity. It is the closed bud, the rich ground of a process of becoming, which possesses what it can give rise to. It is not the first and smallest portion at the beginning of a process of becoming, but the whole of the history which is beginning, in its radical ground.

For the beginning as such is God, the plenitude of all reality. And when it is said of us that we are created from "nothing," that does indeed mean that we are not God, but it does not mean that our origin was the void, an indeterminacy indifferent to everything, it means it was God. And God posits the created beginning which is not the first moment of our time but the original ground of the whole history of our freedom in time.

For that reason the beginning is posited solely by God; it is his mystery which inaccessibly rules over us. Consequently, it only reveals itself slowly in the course of our history. That is why it has to be accepted by us in its darkness and obscurity, with trust, hope, and courage. It has to be preserved by holy anamnesis in its inaccessible mystery and in what it discloses of itself in our history.

For if that beginning is the permanent ground of human existence, and supports all, and is not something which we leave behind us as past and done with, then that beginning is the purpose of life, the content of the anamnesis which in a sacred rite renders the origin present. That is why we celebrate the birthday, the baptism, and the Pasch of the Lord. These are all festivals of the beginning which is allotted to us as human beings and as Christians.

And when we look forward with hope into the future, it is the manifestation of the beginning we are watching for. It is the beginning which is approaching us in the end, in the future the origin which has been acquired through history. If we fail to attain the fulfillment it will be because we have lost the beginning. And if the end is pure fulfillment, then the beginning must have been a pure origin from infinite love.

In the Gospel of Thomas we read, "The disciples said to Jesus, 'Tell us what our end will be like.' Jesus said, 'Have you already discovered the beginning and yet you ask about the end? Blessed is he who will stand at the beginning and will know the end and not taste death.' "

The historical Jesus certainly did not make this statement. Yet if correctly read it is true nevertheless. Yet Jesus in reality did judge the present as a falling away from the pure beginning as this was posited by God and as it was to be reestablished by himself, when he said, "In the beginning it was not so." And when Heidegger observes that origin always remains future, he expresses the same relation between beginning and fulfillment that the historical and the gnostic Jesus affirm. We must first recall this general character of a beginning when we are celebrating the feast day of a pure beginning.

The Blessed Virgin's beginning. If we have understood what a beginning really means, we will understand that what the church professes in regard to the Blessed Virgin's beginning is only the correct transposition into the beginning of what the church always knew about the Blessed Virgin from her later life and from her significance in sacred history for the church. This is so, however long it may have taken the church to accomplish this regress from the consequence to the origin, from what was brought about to what was projected, from future to source, until the church finally reached the definition of 1854.

God as beginning and the beginning posited by God may not be separated in Mary through the difference established by the guilt of humankind. For this difference was not permitted prior to Christ and as superior to his redemptive work, but in subordination to it. He, as the absolute and unconditional will of God for his world even prior to the world and its sin, was the pure and primordial beginning of God's will for the finite. Guilt was only admitted because it remained enveloped within this hidden beginning which from the start was the overflowing spring of grace, even if its previously hidden plenitude was only manifested in the actual course of its flow.

Mary, however, belongs to the will of the eternal God, the absolute will of God for the incarnation of his Logos which had already taken sin into account. Mary belongs to the beginning which contains, not to the beginning which is contained. She belongs to it of course as a posited, not as the positing beginning, as posited in God's will for the world, for the incarnation of the Logos and through this for redemption; therefore she belongs to it as a beginning redeemed in advance. And so she belongs to God's action within which he redemptively comprises sin, because in the concrete order this action of God in the incarnation of the Logos is inseparable from her in her flesh and her obedience.

As a consequence there cannot be that difference in herself between the divinely established beginning of each human being as such and the beginning of the individual inasmuch as he or she remains conjoined to the guilty beginning of humanity as a whole, the deed of Adam. Her beginning is a pure, innocent, and simple one, sheer grace, an element in the object of the redemption itself. God with absolute love always willed Mary as she who would say yes to his own word addressed to the world. For this absolutely unconditionally willed word of grace is only spoken absolutely if it is heard obediently and in the flesh, precisely by Mary in fact.

Because she was so willed, and because she was willed unconditionally, she was willed from and in the beginning as accepting. She cannot in the beginning be posited in her beginning as capable of saying no. She is endowed with grace in her beginning. Purely for the sake of Christ who is the redeemer, and therefore as an element in what is prior to the redemption, and for the sake of which God merely permitted guilt.

This beginning is the disposition of God alone, the moment when God's love bestowing itself on human beings is still collected, concentrated in itself, or rather, is originally immanent in itself as a love which has already forestalled guilt and which, because of this power, permits the weakness of guilt. Where this love posits such a created historical beginning, there is the beginning of the Blessed Virgin.

Nevertheless, or, rather, precisely in this way, this glory of a pure beginning originating in God was a beginning which had to be experienced with sorrow. The origin meant a future of everyday life, customary things, silence, the seven sorrows and the death of her Son and her own death. Only then was the beginning attained by the future retrieving the beginning. Only then was it disclosed as pure grace.

Our beginning. It is hidden in God. It is decided. Only when we have arrived will we full know what our origin is. For God is mystery as such, and what he posited when he established us in our beginning is still the mystery of his free will hidden in his revealed word. But without evacuating the mystery, we can say that there belongs to our beginning the earth which God has created, the ancestors whose history God ruled with wisdom and mercy, Jesus Christ, the church and baptism, earth and eternity.

All is there, everything whatsoever which exists is silently concentrated in the wellspring of our own existence and all the beginning posited by God uniquely and unrepeatedly is. With what is hard and what is easy, delicate and harsh, with what belongs to the abyss and what is heavenly. All is encompassed by God, his knowledge and his love. All has to be accepted. And we advance toward it all; we experience everything, one thing after another, until future and origin coincide.

One thing about this beginning, however, has already been said to us by the word of God. The possibility of acceptance itself belongs to the might of the divinely posited beginning. And if we accept, we have accepted sheer love and happiness. For even if in our beginning the difference between God's will and human will is interposed, even if in the beginning our lot is decided both by God *and* by the history of guilt, nevertheless precisely in our case even this contradiction is always merely permitted and is already encompassed by pure love and forgiveness.

And the more that love and forgiveness which encompasses and belongs to our beginning is accepted in the pain of life and in the death which gives life, and the more this original element emerges and is allowed to manifest itself and pervade our history, the more the difference, the contradiction in the beginning is resolved and redeemed. And all the more will it be revealed that we ourselves were also implied in that pure beginning whose feast day we are celebrating.

When the beginning has found itself in the fulfillment and has been fulfilled in the freedom of accepting love, *God* will be all in all. Because then all will belong to all, the differences will of course still be there but they will have been transformed and will belong to the blessedness of unifying love, and no longer to separation. And for that reason this feast is *our* feast. For it is the feast of the freely bestowed love in which all of us are comprised, each in his or her place and rank.

117 • God's Coming into a Closed World*

26 December, The Feast of St. Stephen

Today on the second day of Christmas the church's liturgy celebrates the feast of St. Stephen the deacon and first martyr of the original church of Jerusalem, who was stoned to death soon after A.D. 35, that

*Everyday Faith, 43–46.

is, shortly after Jesus' death and resurrection. We read of him in the sixth and seventh chapters of the Acts of the Apostles. The reason why his feast is celebrated on this day is that the liturgical celebration of his death in the East was already fixed on 26 December at a time in the fourth century when the Western Christmas of 25 December was not yet established in the East. So Stephen did not come to the crib, the crib came to him. The feast of Stephen came from the East into Western Europe in the sixth century when it was already linked with Christmas.

It is only by historical accident that St. Stephen's feast falls at Christmas time. There was no "ideological" intention behind it. But of course contingent historical facts often have a profound meaning, and even make better sense than things rationally worked out and devised. And so the young hero with his palm can continue to stand by the crib of the child on the straw. He fits in very well. For if we reflect what, according to scripture, Stephen's character and death have to tell us, we can see that it is definitely a Christmas message, providing we do not misunderstand Christmas itself.

He is a man of faith and of the Holy Spirit (Acts 6:5), of grace and strength (6:8). For that reason he is a man with freedom, or we might say with courage to move, to step out from merely inherited things and the secure fence of the mere letter of the law. And so, scripture tells us he foretells the destruction of the temple, and in a completely Pauline way, even before Paul, he is aware of the supersession of the legal institutional aspect of the Old Testament by Jesus (6:14).

Accordingly, in his speech in chapter 7 of Acts he sees the whole history of the redemption and ruin of his nation as a single journey, a continual setting out, a move abroad, a repeated call and summons, a mission. The call comes from infinite mystery and summons to it. It is not a tangible idol which human beings themselves have made and carry ahead as a deceptive goal guiding their movement.

Because he is perceptive in this way, Stephen himself is open to faith in that future of his people which he experiences in his own time, the coming of the messiah, and so for the message of Christmas. Because of this perception he must summarize and interpret the history of perdition, which runs parallel to the redemptive history of open movement, as resistance to the prophets "who announced beforehand the coming of the righteous one," as a resistance culminating in the treacherous death of him who is the goal of this movement (7:52f.).

And when Stephen dies, he dies into what is opening out into the infinite limitlessness of his grace-given spiritual existence. Precisely at this limitless end he sees the one who came close in order to bring infinite distance close, who came to make the world itself in its totality God's place, who puts an end to idolatry of the world and its powers because he himself is the presence of God made man among us: "I see the heavens opened, and the Son of man standing at the right hand of God" (7:56).

And so the youth with the palm of victory by the crib of the child is surely a good interpreter of Christmas. Christmas is God's coming into the closed world so that it may become open to God and heaven open for the world. Christmas means the world's journey has reached its goal because the destination of this perpetually renewed searching movement of history has been attained; but this end is the opening out of the world into God's own life which only now is brought about.

We, alas, set before us the idols of our utopias and think we can move toward them as a goal. But we once again find in them our own aimlessness, futility, and finitude which pass away and disintegrate. As Stephen preached, we make gods for ourselves which go before us (7:40). They move before us because we hold them out in front of us, for once again we project our problematic selves on the wall of the gloomy void toward which we are moving.

Of course we could not accept a goal if we were not to attain ourselves in it. Yet how could we regard a goal as valid if we were only to find ourselves in it? What is to be done then? We wish to find ourselves and yet we cannot be satisfied with ourselves. We must have both ourselves and infinity, both together. If we call ourselves human and infinity God, then we can say what our goal would have to be, if it exists: the Godman.

Christmas, however, actually says that the goal has come from God, and it is seeker and what is endlessly sought in one person: the Son of man, the Godman, the glory of God of which a glimpse can now be caught, but only if Jesus is seen standing at the right hand of God. The goal itself has approached the seeker and brought the seeker himself into what is sought so that he does not lose himself when he seeks what is wholly other.

One finds purely and simply by seeking, if one seeks with willingness to be found by God and does not merely indulge oneself in the rambling aimlessness of a movement which is not really a search. Those who see pure openness and do not confuse it with any concrete form, who are ready to take the here-and-now and the everywhere-and-always as identical, and to do so not merely as an abstract postulate which commits one to nothing but in the concrete details of life; those who in this way and for this reason find the only person in the history of humanity whom it is possible to take to be this unity of God and man: Jesus Christ — these in their search succeed in finding, in their unending movement arrive, not because the two are identical from the human person's side, but because God himself has found the seeker.

If we accept ourselves totally as we really are, as we are through the fact that the Word of God himself has become flesh and out of our darkness made Christmas, then we find what we seek. Then the heavens are open for us in a Christmas way as they were for Stephen, and in faith we see the glory of God, because we see the one Son of man in triumph, the infinite man. Truly, since Christmas came into existence the heavens are open, because the heavens have come onto the earth. The believer sees God who gazes at him in a human face and loves her with a human heart. Since then the infinite is close and the finite opens out onto infinite expanses.

118 • If You Can Put Up with Him, So Can I*

1 Pt 3:8

The phrase that we wish to ponder is: "Have unity of spirit." Now it is an odd thing. Nowhere in scripture, neither in the Greek manuscripts nor in the Latin, is there more than the words: "Have unity of spirit." And yet the text used in the liturgy [before Vatican II] says: "Have unity of spirit in prayer." This harmony and concord, then, is interpreted to mean that we must be united in prayer. No doubt the letter of St. Peter refers to a general disposition to get on with people. But we may follow the suggestion of the liturgy and take it that this concord should be expressed and embodied in prayer.

This idea is obvious enough. We know only too well what a trial we are to each other. We are so different from one another: we have had different experiences, we are of different temperaments, of different origins, we come from different families, we have different talents and different jobs to do — small wonder if it is difficult for us all to be of *one* mind. We have different views and we understand each other imperfectly. And being so very different from other people we may well grate on them, unconsciously weary them with what we are, what we think, what we do, what we feel.

---

*Biblical Homilies, 176–78.

Mutual harmony and comprehension, being of one mind, is difficult for us. Now we can only live together and bear with each other, bear one another's burdens, if we do our best to be of one mind, if we are self-effacing and self-possessed, if we can hold our tongue even when we are right, if we can let others be themselves and give them their due, if we refrain from rash judgment and are patient. Then it becomes possible, at least in a rough and ready way, to be of one mind. We may not achieve empathy together but we can be of one mind in Christian forbearance, each bearing the other's burden. This means that I bear the burden the other is to me simply by being himself or herself, because I know I am a burden to him or her simply by being myself.

Now the liturgy says that we must be of one mind in prayer, must absorb the bitterness of discord and incomprehension into prayer: "Forgive us our trespasses, as we forgive them that trespass against us." That in itself is a kind of prayer for harmony, a kind of being of one mind in prayer, for here a person is reconciled with his or her brother or sister — as today's Gospel enjoins — before bringing his or her gift to the altar, even if the gift is only a prayer. But we must not only pray for concord and bring a peaceable, forbearing heart to our prayer; we must also take our brother or sister into our prayer and so make the prayer come true. Often we are not of one mind simply because we are so different from each other.

How then can we achieve unity of spirit? Only in God, who is the one goal of the most diverse things and the most diverse human beings; only in God, in whom we live and move and have our being, is that unity possible. And we are in God only when we are praying. Could we not sometimes try taking our neighbor with us to God — the person who gets on our nerves so, who annoys us with everything he or she is and does, who seems to be so unfair to us, so unsympathetic, so heartless? Could we not say to God: Here is someone with whom I cannot get on. She belongs to you. You made her. If you do not will her to be the way she is, at least you allow her to be that way. Dear God, I want to put up with her the way you put up with me. Would we not find our heart a little lighter, more at ease, more patient?

And then if we knew that somebody else was really praying for us, if we knew that she was not just talking, mouthing pious platitudes, but taking her heart to the feet of God, daring to speak to that sacred majesty that never dies, to say with all her heart, with the audacity one can only have in Christ Jesus: "Our Father, who art in heaven"; to say to him: "My God, my Lord, my redeemer, my compassion, my eternity, my love," and then if she should take me into such a prayer and commend me to her God, would not something ineffable happen?

Could I go on feeling bitter toward her if in that sanctuary, with patience and tenderness, she had spoken lovingly to her God about me?

I think being at one in prayer does have a meaning. Only if we become more and more at one in prayer, shall we be worthy of God's eternal kingdom, for that kingdom is the kingdom of those who are eternally diverse and eternally at one in the love of one God.

119 • One Tiny Light in Endless Darkness*

Sunday Before Ash Wednesday, Lk 18:31–43

Today's Gospel is at once stern and consoling. It has two parts, with no direct connection between them. The first part contains the third prophecy of the Lord's passion, and the second part the miracle worked for the blind man outside Jericho.

This third prophecy of the passion, which occurs here in the eighteenth chapter of St. Luke, is also found in Matthew, chapter 20, and Mark, chapter 10. But if we compare the Lukan text with Matthew and Mark, one thing strikes us. Though the three accounts agree almost word for word, Luke stresses the fact that the disciples do not understand the prophecy. Now I think we might meditate a little on this point.

Those who we are plainly told did not understand the words of Christ — which we find so easy to understand — are none other than the twelve, his apostles, the foundation stones of his church, Peter and the other eleven, whom he chose, whom he called, who saw his miracles, whom he gathered about him so as to make them the beginning of the new people of God. They do not understand what he is saying. They cannot grasp the fact that he must suffer. They are not even willing to make head or tail of his declaration that in three days he will rise again.

The evangelist uses three expressions to tell us that they understand nothing. If we translate quite literally, then we may render them as follows: the disciples cannot take in any of what is said, and the saying is hidden from them. They can make nothing, they are unwilling to make head or tail, of what they are told. In the first place we are simply

---

*Biblical Homilies, 62–64.

given the fact: they cannot take in what is said, they cannot fit it into what they already know, they cannot draw this darkness into the light that illumines their lives. Then in the second place the matter is obscure in objective reality; it is said in extenuation that this saying is something hidden, wrapped in the darkness of mystery, so that it is not accessible to the disciples. But however that may be, we are told in the third place that they make no real effort to penetrate the mystery which confronts them, no real effort to understand it.

This is said of apostles, and it is said of them three times. Yet we must add that the apostles remain with Jesus. Even when they see that they do not understand what is going on, they remain steadfast. They are faithful. They are patient. They make Jesus, as it were, an advance payment of confidence and time, giving him a chance to grow in their hearts. And we must add that God bears with them. Though their hearts are darkened, though they do not understand, though in their inertia they hardly want to understand, they remain undergirded by God's mercy, his faithfulness, his providence, and his love.

Mystery uncomprehended stands between them and the Lord, yet does not separate them. Neither abandons the other. Each cleaves to the other, because God loves and is faithful, because a person realizes that though he may not understand the mystery, God and God's loyal grace are only to be found where that mystery is.

Is there a lesson here for our own life? If we compare all that we can grasp and understand, all that is clear and straightforward in our lives with the obscure and the baffling, the hidden and uncomprehended, the mysterious and unspeakable, then we seem to see a tiny light burning in the midst of endless darkness. How can it be otherwise so long as we are here making our way among parabolic shadows, still on pilgrimage toward the everlasting light, the unapproachable light that only God can be?

Would it not be folly to expect everything to be intelligible, or to accept no more than we can understand? The incomprehensible must lay hold on us, for only then shall we be open to God the infinite, and only if we are that, have we the hope and the promise that we shall find everything.

Let us be patient and faithful. Let us wait, and accept the incomprehensible from God's hand. Let us believe, even when God tells us truths through his gospel and through his providential dispensation — that is, when he tells us what he wishes to through what we do not understand.

The same word, the same Greek word, used here in Luke, chapter 18, is used of Mary in chapter 2. She did not understand the saying which he spoke to her, and it is written of her that she kept all these things in her heart. Let us faithfully keep what we do not understand in our own heart. One day the infinite light of beatitude will burst forth from it.

120 • God Cheerfully Puts Up with Us*

Sunday after the Transfiguration, Rom 12:16–21

Verses 16 to 21 of chapter 12 form a kind of paragraph in the letter to the Romans which we could simply entitle: Loving our neighbor or loving our enemies.

At first glance this passage may seem to be nothing out of the ordinary. Good heavens, why not advise Christians to be peaceable so far as they can, even with bad neighbors? Why not recommend living a quiet life, stretching a point, giving in on occasion? After all, everybody knows it is the wiser person who gives in, though nobody wants to be the one to do it.

If we interpret the text in this way, its lesson seems obvious enough. Not repaying evil for evil, being intent on good, refraining from strife, leaving vengeance to God, even doing good to an enemy on occasion — all fair enough. This last admonition might be thought to involve rather more than do the maxims of everyday prudence; yet Paul seems to base it too on perfectly sober practical considerations, when he says: "For by so doing you will heap burning coals upon your enemy's head" — you will make him feel ashamed, and, Paul obviously thinks, as often as not make him realize that you wish him well and that therefore there is no point in his continuing to be your enemy. "Overcome evil with good," says St. Paul. Simple enough: good horse sense.

And yet, have we often tried it out? Can we say without more ado that we have overcome evil with good? In this world evil of whatever kind you will has an uncanny power; and part of its power is this, that when it attacks a person, even an innocent one, it involves him, the victim, in evil too. It really seems to be true that one must fight fire with fire, evil with evil, that to allow oneself to be put upon is to play the fool. Not that St. Paul is an absolute pacifist, preaching unqualified nonresistance as a rule of life.

*Biblical Homilies, 99–102.

This is not his attitude. In chapter 13, close upon these verses, he speaks of authority that bears a sword, that can use force, that must punish, that we must be subject to for conscience' sake, that can exact respect. Accordingly when Paul says here that we are to overcome evil with good, he does not mean that we must practice absolute nonviolence at every juncture in practical life.

But he does mean that someone proves himself a Christian by overcoming evil with his own goodness; by not answering a harsh word with harshness, one unloving word with another; by holding his peace when he has been grieved, not even complaining to another about what has happened; by patiently bearing with his neighbor, though the neighbor does not even realize he is a trial to anyone; that by this ampler, purer, selfless, silent goodness a person, as it were, causes evil to sink back into its own nothingness; he snuffs out evil, he turns it into good.

Now this is a proper attribute of God. It is God who holds his peace and waits, is patient and forgiving; who draws good out of evil; whose goodness, forbearance, and magnanimity let a human being follow evil, as it were, to the point of absurdity, where he realizes that he cannot go on that way any longer, turns about, and strikes out in a new direction. When we are going astray, God does not always choose to be stern, placing some insuperable obstacle in our path. Crushing evil is not the only way he has of dealing with it: he is a more gracious goodness, a holier justice, that can turn even evil into good.

Though Paul also speaks of the day of wrath, he says in this passage: And so we ought to imitate the goodness of God, which does away with the evil of this world. That is no small task. I think we shall all have to admit that we have never done it yet. Many a time in our daily lives we have an opportunity to be patient with others, to be kind though they are not, to refrain from giving tit for tat, to be considerate and helpful to people who are unlikely to do the same for us.

And perhaps those closest to us, even our best friends, are the people most difficult for us to put up with; perhaps we only manage it by holding our tongue. Well, if so, then we may hope that God will put up with us too. If we are so often a burden even to ourselves, must we not often be a fearful burden to God? (Humanly speaking, of course; but we may speak *humanly* of God.) He endures us patiently and cheerfully, rather like a loving mother who understands her child and his ways, even if he is obstinate, foolish, and capricious. We can count on God's being patient with us in that way, count on it joyfully, even — we could almost say — with a holy shamelessness; for God is truly long-suffering and forbearing.

But tell me, must not those near to us — and far from us — be able then to count on such a frame of mind in ourselves? We expect it of others as a matter of course; and if others treat us so, then they say nothing about the fact; it seems to us the most natural thing in the world and we take no notice. Now if we once start sternly demanding this attitude of ourselves, then it may dawn on us that many a good soul treats us with longanimity and forbearance, and never a word about it. Then we shall be more grateful, and find the burden that others lay on our shoulders a little lighter and less irksome, even find that is the yoke of Jesus Christ, a burden of grace which instructs us, enables us to keep our balance, makes us more mature and more humble, makes us love God more. If we act on it in the plainest, most ordinary way, the simple little lesson of today's Gospel will bring us very close to God's heart.

APPENDIX

On the Selecting and Editing
of the Texts

Karl Rahner's texts for the church year are found dispersed through-out his works. They are largely occasional pieces that in part have been published more often as meditations for the corresponding feasts of the church year in journals and periodicals. In his published books they were variously gathered into selections. The present collection attempts a systematic assembly of the entire complex. This edition raises no critical claims and furnishes no analysis of revisions or even a reader's guide. It proceeds from the fact that many small changes have been undertaken on account of technical constraints, but some could also arise because of stylistic improvements and material re-touching. The regathered pieces therefore in general follow the latest publications in book form.

A great portion of the text was composed before the reform of the order of liturgical readings or the liturgical year in the wake of the Second Vatican Council. Since this collection intends to make the texts accessible for the practice of spiritual life, the job was set to adapt the meditations and sermons to the new order. Mostly this was possible without great difficulties (see Foreword). In many cases the divisions of the pericopes have nevertheless been changed — especially as the new order of readings in part also permits shorter and longer alternative versions. Hence attention must be paid to whether only sections of the official liturgical texts for any given day provide the basis of the meditations.

The texts from scripture were not printed, even though in the original publications this was partially already the case, since this would have increased the scope of the volume too much.

The American translation editor decided to eliminate the extensive German Source Reference section and to indicate in the footnotes the major source for the sermon or homily. The (A), (B), or (C) in the scriptural header indicates the liturgical cycle.

Not included were texts already published in volumes 3, 7, 8, 16 of Rahner's *Theological Investigations,* which are relevant here and include his spiritual writings. This sort of writing is also scattered in the rest of the volumes from volume 16 on. Two independent, some-what more comprehensive publications for Christmas (*Gott ist Mensch geworden,* 1975, and *Die Gabe der Weihnacht,* 1980, both from Herder: Freiburg im Breisgau) were not included again. Meditations on the feast days of our Lord are also contained in Karl Rahner's *Spiritual Exercises*[1] and *The Priesthood.*[2]

The redaction of the texts is limited to the necessary simplifications (e.g., the spelling of biblical names, the abbreviations of biblical books, etc.), translations of Latin citations, corrections of unequivocal mistakes, some omissions conditioned by the liturgical changes.

Additional Rahnerian Texts for the Church Year

For *Christmas:* Karl Rahner, "Prayer at Christmas," *Prayers for a Lifetime* (New York: Crossroad Publishing Company, 1984), 46; "The Birth of Our Lord," *Spiritual Exercises,* trans. Kenneth Baker, S.J. (New York: Herder and Herder, 1965), 146–50; "Thoughts on the Theology of Christmas," *Theological Investigations III,* trans. Karl-H and Boniface Kruger (Baltimore: Helicon Press, 1967), 24–34; "Christmas, the Festival of Eternal Youth," "Holy Night," and "Peace on Earth," *Theological Investigations VII,* trans. David Bourke (New York: Herder and Herder, 1971), 121–26, 127–31, 132–35; "Christmas in the Light of the Ignatian Exercises," *Theological Investigations XVII,* trans. Margaret Kohl (New York: Crossroad Publishing Company, 1981), 3–7.

For *New Year:* "The Comfort of Time," *Theological Investigations III,* 141–57.

For *Holy Week:* "See, What a Man!" "The Scandal of Death," "He Descended into Hell," "Hidden Victory," *Theological Investigations VII,* 136–39, 140–44, 145–50, 151–58; "The Holy Eucharist," "The Agony in the Garden," "From the Garden to the Cross," "Our Lord's Death on the Cross," *Spiritual Exercises,* 210–16, 217–26, 227–33, 234–43; "The Doctor and Good Friday," *Opportunities for Faith,* 139–44.

---

1. Trans. Kenneth Baker, S.J. (New York: Herder and Herder, 1965).
2. Trans. Edward Quinn (New York: Seabury Press, 1973).

For *Easter:* "Experiencing Easter," "Encounters with the Risen Christ," *Theological Investigations VII,* 159–68, 169–76; "On the Spirituality of the Easter Faith," "Jesus' Resurrection," *Theological Investigations XVII,* 8–15, 16–23; "The Resurrection and Ascension of Our Lord," *Spiritual Exercises,* 244–50.

For *Ascension:* "He Will Come Again," "The Festival of the Future of the World," *Theological Investigations VII,* 177–80, 181–85.

For *Pentecost:* "Experiencing the Spirit," *The Spirit in the Church,* trans. John Griffiths (New York: Seabury Press, 1979), 3–31; "Do Not Stifle the Spirit," "The Church as the Subject of the Sending of the Spirit," "The Spirit That Is over All Life," *Theological Investigations VII,* 72–87, 186–92, 193–201; "Experience of the Holy Spirit," *Theological Investigations XVIII,* trans. Edward Quinn (New York: Crossroad Publishing Company, 1983), 189–210; "The Spirit as the Fruit of Our Redemption," *Spiritual Exercises,* 251–61.

For the *Sacred Heart:* " 'Behold this Heart!': Preliminaries to a Theology of Devotion to the Sacred Heart," "Some Theses for a Theology of Devotion to the Sacred Heart," *Theological Investigations III,* 321–30, 331–52; "Ignatian Spirituality and Devotion to the Sacred Heart," *Christian in the Market Place,* trans. Cecily Hastings (New York: Sheed and Ward, 1966), 119–46; "The Man with the Pierced Heart," *Servants of the Lord,* trans. Richard Strachan (New York: Herder and Herder, 1968), 107–19; "The Theological Meaning of the Veneration of the Sacred Heart," "Unity — Love — Mystery," *Theological Investigations VIII,* trans. David Bourke (New York: Herder and Herder, 1971), 217–28, 229–47.

For *Venerating the Saints:* "The Church of the Saints," *Theological Investigations III,* 91–104; "Why and How We Can Venerate the Saints," "All Saints," *Theological Investigations VIII,* 3–23, 24–29; "Prayer to the Saints," *The Courage to Pray,* trans. Sarah O'Brien Twohig (New York: Crossroad Publishing Company, 1981), 31–87.

For *Venerating Mary: Mary Mother of the Lord,* trans. W. J. O'Hara (Wheathampstead, Hertfordshire: Anthony Clarke, 1963); "The Immaculate Conception," "The Interpretation of the Dogma of the Assumption," *Theological Investigations I,* trans. Cornelius Ernst, O.P. (Baltimore: Helicon Press, 1961), 201–13, 215–27; "The Dogma of the Immaculate Conception in Our Time," *Theological Investigations III,* 129–40; "Mary and the Church," *Spiritual Exercises,* 262–69.

For *Venerating St. Ignatius:* Karl Rahner, "Ignatius of Loyola Speaks to Modern Jesuit," *Ignatius of Loyola,* historical introduction by Paul Imhof, S.J., color photographs by Helmuth Nils Loose, trans. Rosaleen Ockenden (Cleveland: Collins, 1979), 9–38.

INDEX OF
BIBLICAL
PASSAGES

OLD TESTAMENT

NEW TESTAMENT